Commercial Contract Law

This book offers a critical and comparative analysis of exemption, frustration, and *force majeure* within the framework of three pivotal legal instruments: the United Nations Convention on Contracts for the International Sale of Goods (CISG), the UNIDROIT Principles of International Commercial Contracts (UPICC), and English contract law.

Rooted in principles of fairness and legal predictability, the book argues that the CISG, UPICC, and English law provide mechanisms through which contractual obligations may be excused when unforeseen events render performance impossible. While conceptually related, the book reveals substantive and procedural divergences in how each legal system interprets and applies the principles of exemption, frustration, and *force majeure*. Systematically examining the similarities, differences, and evolving intersections of each legal framework, particularly in relation to mistake, termination, avoidance, risk, and hardship, the book employs a historical and jurisprudential context, highlighting both theoretical and practical applications. It suggests a Draft Model Frustration Clause (DMFC), aimed at addressing deficiencies in existing legal frameworks and providing a harmonized clause better suited for contemporary international commercial practice.

The book will be of interest to researchers in the field of commercial law, contract law, and business law.

Ndubuisi Augustine Nwafor is a Lecturer and active member of the Research in Public International Law (RIPIL) Group at Bristol Law School, University of the West of England (UWE), Bristol, UK. He was formerly an Associate Professor at the University of Nigeria, Nsukka. His teaching and research interests include international commercial law and plastic pollution governance. He has received several prestigious fellowships, including the International Ocean Institute (IOI) Canada Fellowship in 2018 and the Association of Commonwealth Universities (ACU) Blue Charter Fellowship in 2020 and 2021.

Routledge Research in International Commercial Law

Available titles in this series include:

Progressive Commercialization of Airline Governance Culture
Jan Walulik

Economic and Environmental Regulation of International Aviation
From Inter-National to Global Governance
Steven Truxal

Combining Mediation and Arbitration in International Commercial Dispute Resolution
Dilyara Nigmatullina

Non-State Rules in International Commercial Law
Contracts, Legal Authority and Application
Johanna Hoekstra

Commercial Law in the South Pacific
Mohammed L Ahmadu and Bridget Fa'amatuainu

Digital Finance Law
Common and Civil Law
Robert Walters

Good Faith in International Commercial Arbitration
Georgios Martsekis

Artificial Intelligence and International Arbitration Law
Revolution or Evolution
Magdalena Łągiewska

Commercial Contract Law
Exemption, Frustration, and *Force Majeure*
Ndubuisi Augustine Nwafor

Commercial Contract Law

Exemption, Frustration and *Force Majeure*

Ndubuisi Augustine Nwafor

Routledge
Taylor & Francis Group
LONDON AND NEW YORK

First published 2027
by Routledge
4 Park Square, Milton Park, Abingdon, Oxon OX14 4RN

and by Routledge
605 Third Avenue, New York, NY 10158

Routledge is an imprint of the Taylor & Francis Group, an informa business

British Library Cataloguing-in-Publication Data
A catalogue record for this book is available from the British Library

ISBN: 978-1-041-12729-1 (hbk)
ISBN: 978-1-041-13049-9 (pbk)
ISBN: 978-1-003-66784-1 (ebk)

DOI: 10.4324/9781003667841

Typeset in Times New Roman
by Deanta Global Publishing Services, Chennai, India

Contents

Foreword

In an era marked by unprecedented international instability, the legal frameworks governing global trade are under significant scrutiny. The COVID-19 pandemic and the ongoing geopolitical tensions stemming from the Russia-Ukraine conflict have exposed vulnerabilities in the mechanisms that underpin international commerce. It is during such tumultuous times that the principles of contract law, particularly the doctrines of pacta sunt servanda (the sanctity of contracts) and clausula rebus sic stantibus (the necessity of exceptions due to changed circumstances), are put to the test.

In this context, Ndubuisi Augustine Nwafor's monograph, Commercial Contract Law: Exemption, Frustration, and *Force Majeure*, emerges as a timely and essential contribution to the field. This work is not merely a reiteration of existing legal doctrines; rather, it represents a rigorous comparative inquiry into three pivotal systems of international trade law: the United Nations Convention on Contracts for the International Sale of Goods (CISG), the UNIDROIT Principles of International Commercial Contracts, and English common law, specifically the Sale of Goods Act 1979.

Nwafor's analysis is particularly noteworthy for its refusal to accept the prevailing ambiguities that often cloud the interpretation of these doctrines in international sales. He meticulously unpacks the terminologies of "impediment" under the CISG, "*force majeure*" under UNIDROIT, and "frustration" under English law, revealing the conceptual differences that can lead to conflicting outcomes in international dispute resolution. This clarity is crucial, as it addresses a fundamental challenge faced by practitioners and scholars alike: the need for a coherent understanding of these doctrines in the context of global trade.

One of the most commendable aspects of Nwafor's work is his nuanced treatment of the frequently conflated concepts of hardship and frustration. In a legal landscape where economic onerousness is increasingly invoked as a justification for non-performance, Nwafor takes a principled stance. He argues for a clear demarcation between hardship, aimed at balancing the apportionment of commercial losses through renegotiation, and frustration, which seeks to excuse liability in damages when performance becomes objectively impossible. This distinction is not merely academic; it has profound implications for the stability and predictability of international contracts.

Central to Nwafor's thesis is the introduction of a Draft Model Frustration Clause (DMFC), which stands as a significant innovation in the field. By explicitly excluding commercial hardship and bad bargains from the definition of impediments that excuse performance, the DMFC imposes a more stringent test of impossibility. This approach not only enhances legal certainty but also provides a practical roadmap for harmonising international commercial law. The DMFC addresses long-standing weaknesses associated with imprecise terminology and inconsistent judicial outcomes, offering a framework that is both clear and equitable.

Therefore, Nwafor's monograph is a vital resource for practitioners and scholars navigating the complexities of international trade law. It provides a comprehensive analysis of the doctrines of exemption, frustration, and *force majeure*, while also proposing innovative solutions to the challenges posed by these legal principles. As global trade continues to evolve in response to unprecedented disruptions, this work will undoubtedly serve as a cornerstone for future discussions on the stability and resilience of international commercial law.

I look forward to seeing how your manuscript develops further and am excited about the potential impact of your work on the field.

Professor Chrispas Nyombi
Professor of International Commercial Law
Member of the World Bank ICSID Panels of Arbitrators
Member of the Permanent Court of Arbitration, The Hague
University of Derby
College of Business, Law and Social Sciences
One Friar Gate Square
Derby DE1 1DZ

Preface

The doctrine of exemption, frustration, or *force majeure* is a vital area of commercial law. It allows a party to a contract to be relieved from their obligations if an event beyond their control makes performance of the contract impossible. This aims to promote fairness in such unforeseen circumstances. However, the doctrine remains complex to apply and often uncertain. This challenge has become even more apparent with the COVID-19 pandemic. While many scholars believe that the pandemic should generally be considered within the doctrine, discharging parties from their contractual obligations without fault, recent judicial rulings following the pandemic tend to support the mainstream view. Courts, in most instances, have been cautious to excuse performance, favouring a strict interpretation of contractual provisions and *force majeure* clauses. This disagreement between academic expectations and judicial practice raises new concerns about the proper scope and application of the doctrine.

This book undertakes a comparative analysis of the doctrine of exemption, frustration, and *force majeure* under the CISG, the UNIDROIT Principles, and English law, illustrating their theoretical foundations and practical implementations. It observes that the separate elements of exemption, frustration, and *force majeure* are not identical – differences and similarities in how these doctrines are interpreted and applied are examined in detail, both separately and together. For example, the broad and adaptable wording used in the definitions of these doctrines under the CISG and the UNIDROIT Principles leaves much to be desired. Therefore, one key argument of the book is that describing these impossibility doctrines in vague terms within international law could hinder uniform application, as differing national legal interpretations would lead to inconsistent outcomes. This issue, among others, has impeded the development of the doctrines of exemption, frustration, and *force majeure*. Additionally, the English law perspective on the doctrine of frustration, as derived from the Sale of Goods Act 1979 and common law, is insufficient and in need of modernisation.

This book, therefore, aims to thoroughly examine the applications, interpretations, and future developments of the doctrines of exemption, frustration, and *force majeure* within the legal instruments central to this study. It also includes a comparative analysis of how this doctrine relates to other closely connected concepts, such as mistake, termination, avoidance, risk, and hardship. The work concludes with the presentation of a Draft Model Frustration Clause (DMFC), which seeks to go beyond the limitations of current doctrines and provide a more coherent and effective practical approach to address the long-standing flaws in this area of law.

Acknowledgements

I would like to acknowledge my PhD supervisory team, Professor Hong-Lin Yu and Emeritus Professor Fraser Davidson, for laying the groundwork for this monograph during my doctoral studies. I am grateful to Professor Simone Lamont-Black for examining my thesis and identifying areas for further research that have informed this monograph. I thank Professor Chrispas Nyombi for reviewing this monograph and for writing the foreword. Likewise, I am grateful to my parents, Edwin and Mary-Gladys (Late), and my brother, Kanayo, for their generous financial support throughout my educational and research pursuits. Finally, I dedicate this work to my lovely wife, Morningglory, and my daughters, Mediatrix and Ave, for providing the stability I needed while writing this book.

List of Abbreviations

ABV	Full Meaning
AJCL	*American Journal of Comparative Law*
BLR	*Belgrade Law Review*
BGB	Bürgerliches Gesetzbuch (Germany)
BGBI	Bundesgesetzblatt (Germany)
DLR	*Duquesne Law Review*
EdinLR	*Edinburgh Law Review*
CIETAC	China International Economic and Trade Arbitration Commission
CISG	United Nations Convention on the Contract for International Sale of Goods 1980
CISGonline	Internet database, University of Basel
CISG Pace	CISG W3 Database, Internet database, Pace University School of Law
CLOUT	Case Law on UNCITRAL texts.
CLWR	*Common Law World Review*
Dickinson J. Int ‘ l l l l l l l Law	*Dickinson Journal of International Law*
DJCIL	*Duke Journal of Comparative & International Law*
EJCL	*European Journal of Contract Law*
EJLR	*European Journal of Law Reform*
ERCL	*European Review of Contract Law*
ERPL	*European Review of Private Law*
FJIL	*Florida Journal of International Law*
IBJL	*International Business Law Journal*
ICC	International Court of Arbitration
ICCLR	*International Company and Commercial Law Review*
ILR	*International Law Journal*
IRLE	*International Review of Law and Economics*
INCOTERMS	International Commercial Terms of the ICC, revised 2000
JBL	*Journal of Business Law*
LQR	*Law Quarterly Review*

JCL	*Journal of Comparative Law*
JIA	*Journal of International Arbitration*
JITLP	*Journal of International Trade Law and Politics*
JLA	*Journal of Legal Analysis*
JLC	Journal of Law and Commerce
JLS	Journal of Legal Studies
J. Priv. Int. L	*Journal of Private International Law*
K B	Law Reports, King's Bench Division (Great Britain)
LRFC	Law Reform (Frustrated Contracts) Act 1943
NILR	*New York International Law Review*
NJCL	*Nordic Journal of Commercial Law*
NJILB	*Northwestern Journal of International Law and Business*
OLG	Oberlandesgericht (German/Austrian Regional Court of Appeals)
OICCUNIDROIT	Principles of International Commercial Contracts
PILR	*Pace International Law Review*
Q B	Law of the Queen's Bench Division (Great Britain)
SSRN	Social Science Research Network
SOGA	Sale of Goods Act 1979
TLR	*Tulane Law Review*
ULIS	Uniform Law on the International Sale of Goods
ULR	*Uniform Law Review*
UNICITRAL	United Nations Commission on International Trade Law
UNIDROIT	The International Institute for the Unification of Private Law
UNILEX	International Case Law, UNIDROIT
UCC	The Uniform Commercial Code (UCC or the Code) 2007 Edition
ULIS	Convention relating to a Uniform Law on the International Sale of Goods 1964
ULF	The Uniform Law on the Formation of Contracts for the International Sale of Goods 1964
VJICLA	*Vindobona Journal of International Commercial Law and Arbitration*

Table of Cases

Nigerian Cases

British Cases

Canada

New Zealand

Switzerland

United States of America

Arbitration/ CISG/UNIDROIT Principles Cases Argentina

Austria

Belarus

Belguim

Bulgaria

Canada

China

Denmark

France

Germany

Greece

Hungary

Italy

Mexico

Netherlands

Russia

Serbia

Slovenia

Spain

Switzerland

Furniture case (III), Handelsgericht des Kantons Zürich (Commercial Court Canton Zurich) Switzerland, 09 September 1993 – HG 930 138.U/HG 93, CISG-online 79 <https://cisg-online.org/search-for-cases?caseId=6059> 40n60, 63n9

Grinding machines case, Bundesgericht/Tribunal fédéral (Swiss Federal Supreme Court) Switzerland, 20 December 2006 – 4C.314/2006, CISG-online 1426 <https://cisg-online.org/search-for-cases?caseId=7348> 92n12

Ukraine

Equipment case, Ukraine [21 June 2002] (Tribunal of International Commercial Arbitration, Ukrainian Chamber of Commerce & Trade) <http://cisgw3.law.pace.edu/cases/020621u5.html>. 170n25

United States of America

Hilaturas Miel, S.L. v Republic of Iraq, US District Court for the Southern District of New York, USA, 20 August 2008 – 06 Civ 12, CISG-online 1777 <https://cisg-online.org/search-for-cases?caseId=7695>. 31, 31n22

Magellan Int'l Corporation v Salzgitter Handel GmbH, US District Court for the Northern District of Illinois, USA, 07 December 1999 – 99 C 5153, CISG-online 439 <https://cisg-online.org/search-for-cases?caseId=6409>. 185n70

1 General Introduction

1.1 Background

When parties enter into a contract, they do so on the presumption that each would perform their obligations. No party enters a contract with the expectation of a breach. Even a fraudulent party does not ordinarily contract with the intention of suffering a failure in performance. At least, he expects the other party to come through. Thus, once agreed, the role of the law is to hold parties to the terms of their agreements. Through the available remedial process, the law may compel a defaulting party to perform what they contracted to do or restrain them from acting in a particular way that will undermine the purpose for which the parties entered into a contract. So sacred is the agreement between the parties that in most, if not all, jurisdictions, it is the rule that a court of law has no jurisdiction to rewrite a contract for parties.[1] Nonetheless, the law recognises circumstances in which a party may genuinely be prevented, by factors beyond their control, from fulfilling contractual obligations.[2] Hence, the development of the doctrine of frustration/*force majeure*/exemption in contracts.

1 See for instance in Nigeria, the Supreme Court held, "It is not the function of the court to re-write a contract for the parties, but where the intention is expressed in a transaction, a legal interpretation of the nature of the agreement between the parties under the law will be pronounced by the court." *Ajagbe v Idowu* [2011] 17 NWLR (Pt. 1276) 422 at 444, paras A-B; See also: *Olanrewaju Comm. Services Ltd. v Sogaolu* (2015) 12 NWLR (Pt. 1473) 311 at 325, para G; *Edilcon Nig. Ltd. v UBA Plc* (2017) 18 NWLR (Pt. 1596) 74 at 99, paras D-F.

2 It is worthy of note that this phrase may speak to two related doctrines, namely the rule in *Hick v Raymond & Reid* [1893] AC 22 (HL) and the doctrine under review, the doctrine of frustration of contract. Under the former, the doctrine operates to absolve a promisor from damages for delay in performing a contract when the circumstances preventing the timely performance of the contract are beyond his making. The doctrine is not as simple as it is stated. For instance, as John E Stannard noted, "When the obligation is to perform on a certain day, such events do not provide any defence unless they are severe enough to frustrate the contract, but where the obligation is merely to perform within a reasonable time, a wider latitude is allowed. J.E. Stannard, *Delay in the Performance of Contractual Obligations* (Oxford University Press 2007) 19. However, under the doctrine of frustration, the supervening circumstance is said to discharge the contract altogether. See Hirji Muliji v Cheong Yue SS Co [1962] AC 497 (HL). Stipulating the test for frustration, the second proposition of Bingham L.J. five propositions in Lauritzen A. S. v Wijsmuller B.V. (The Super Servant Two) [1990] 1 Lloyd's Rep. 1., is that frustration operates "to kill the contract and discharge the parties from fur-

DOI: 10.4324/9781003667841-1

Although the doctrine of frustration/*force majeure*/exemption has long existed,[3] the outbreak of the coronavirus pandemic, which has so far been the most impactful disruptive event of the 21st century on global commerce,[4] has made the doctrine more popular than it used to be. One of the countermeasures against the spread of the virus was the imposition of lockdowns, including travel bans and sit-at-home regulations amongst others by the governments of nations. These measures have been reported to have ignited curiosity, both in practice and theory, with regards to the principles of frustration, *force majeure*, and hardship, especially as to whether these principles, as currently espoused, are adequate to resolve emerging conflicts which will result from unforeseen disruptions.[5]

Relatedly, the ongoing Russia-Ukraine war has had a significant negative impact on international trade, global supply chains, and business operations worldwide,[6] with consequential effects on the performance of contractual obligations.[7] This is

---

ther liability under it" and that therefore it cannot be "lightly invoked" but must be kept within "very narrow limits" and ought not to be extended. Of utmost importance, the doctrine of frustration only applies where the supervening event renders performance something "radically different" from what was contemplated by the contract.

3 As the editors of Chitty on Contract suggested, although the doctrine of frustration dates back to the landmark case of Taylor v Caldwell [1863] 3 B&S 826, it remains confined to a narrow scope in modern legal application. This limitation stems primarily from two reasons. First, courts are generally reluctant to allow parties to invoke frustration simply to escape from an unfavourable or unwise commercial bargain. As has been emphasised in case law, frustration "is not lightly to be invoked to relieve contracting parties of the normal consequences of imprudent commercial bargains." Second, commercial contracts frequently include provisions that address potential disruptive events. Clauses such as *force majeure*, hardship, or intervening event clauses are often inserted to preemptively allocate the risk of such occurrences. When a contract contains express provisions dealing with the supervening event, the doctrine of frustration does not apply. Therefore, the broader the contractual provisions for unexpected events, the less room there is for the application of the doctrine of frustration. Before the pivotal decision in Taylor v Caldwell [supra], the common law did not recognise supervening events as a valid excuse for non-performance. The principle was that parties were expected to anticipate such risks and allocate them in the contract. A classic example is Paradine v Jane [1646] Aleyn 26, where a tenant was sued for rent arrears despite claiming he had been forcibly evicted by an enemy force, an event beyond his control. The court held him liable, as he had assumed a contractual obligation and was expected to fulfil it regardless of unforeseen events. Chitty on Contracts, 28th edn, vol 1 (HG Beale ed., Sweet & Maxwell 1999) para [24–003 – 24–004].

4 Ajayi Lp, *Disruptions and the Law* (LexisNexis, 2022) 93; Andrew Schwartz, "Frustration, the MAC Clause, and COVID-19" (2021) 55 *UC Davis L. Rev*. 1771.

5 Ajayi Lp, (n 4) at 94.

6 According to Zafar Najafov, Azar Hasanov, and Piotr Gawliczek, this is the first war in the history of mankind in which nuclear facilities became the object of aggression. From the first day, Russia directed its troops towards the nuclear facilities of Ukraine – the exclusion zone in Chernobyl, the nuclear fuel storage in Pripyat. Russia has seized Zaporozhye Nuclear Power Plant, the largest in Europe, and is trying to seize Southern Ukraine Nuclear Power Plant. Russia also focuses on the Rovno NPP, located near the Belarusian border, and regularly makes statements about the possibility of using nuclear weapons. See Zafar Najafov, Azar Hasanov and Piotr Gawliczek, "*The Effect of the Russian-Ukrainian War on International Politics and Global Security*" *ROCZNIK BEZPIECZEŃSTWA MORSKIEGO ROK XVIII – 2024.*

7 Ibid.

unsurprising, given the strategic roles both countries play in global commerce. Russia and Ukraine are major exporters of key agricultural commodities, supplying approximately 30% of the world's wheat and barley, 20% of its maize, and over 50% of its sunflower oil.[8] Additionally, Russia and its neighbour Belarus account for nearly 20% of the world's fertiliser exports.[9] Russia is also a major global supplier of natural gas and ranks as the second-largest exporter of crude oil. The war has disrupted production and key supply routes in both countries. Moreover, Russia's trade flows have been further constrained by a series of sanctions imposed by the United States, the European Union, and their allies since the outbreak of the conflict.[10]

Countries such as Germany and Japan, which had long pursued a partially "pacifist" foreign policy orientation and recorded remarkable economic growth after the Second World War, have now shifted course towards *Realpolitik*.[11] Germany, for instance, has allocated nearly US$109 billion for military modernisation following significant constitutional amendments in the Bundestag establishing a special military fund, and it plans to devote more than 2% of its GDP to defence spending in line with NATO's 2014 targets.[12] Similarly, Japan has announced a US$320 billion defence programme to be implemented over five years beginning in 2023, notwithstanding the restrictions of Article 9 of its Constitution – the "war renunciation" clause. It has also entered into several defence pacts, including Reciprocal Access Agreements (RAAs), with Australia, the United Kingdom, Italy, and the United States.

This trend of increased military expenditure has resonated globally. Historically neutral states such as Sweden and Finland have abandoned their previous stance of non-alignment and applied for NATO membership. A review of recent policy instruments, such as NATO's 2022 Strategic Concept, the United States National Security Strategy, and Japan's National Security Strategy, confirms a clear shift away from isolationist or purely defensive policies in the conventional sense.[13]

As stated earlier, the ongoing crisis has also disrupted globalisation. Shortages of grain and fertiliser resulting from the conflict, together with trade disruptions triggered by sanctions, have shaken the global economy. The energy crisis, in particular, has been weaponised with the same strategic impact as missiles or bombs, as hydrocarbons have become central tools of geopolitical contestation. The most affected are states heavily reliant on energy imports. Collectively, these

8 Ibid. See also United Nations, Brief No 1: Global Impact of War in Ukraine on Food, Energy and Finance Systems 3 <https://unsdg.un.org/resources/global-impact-war-ukraine-food-energy-and-finance-systems-brief-no1> accessed 11 October 2025

9 Ibid.

10 Ibid.

11 Zafar Najafov, Azar Hasanov and Piotr Gawliczek, (Supra) n.6.

12 Ibid.

13 D.K. Nivedita and K. Taimur, "Российско-украинский конфликт: будущее глобальной безопасности" (Valdai International Discussion Club, Russia, 23 February 2023) <https://ru.valdaiclub.com/a/highlights/budushchee-globalnoy-bezopasnosti/> accessed 11 October 2025

developments underscore the global magnitude of the crisis. It is believed that such events may create circumstances that necessitate the application of the doctrine under review.

On COVID-19, legal scholars have argued that the outbreak of the pandemic with its attendant lockdowns should operate to discharge parties from their contractual obligation without fault under one or more default excuse doctrines – impossibility, impracticability and frustration.[14] As Givati, Kaplan, and Listokin note, the COVID-19 crisis "rendered many contracts obsolete," with state-mandated closures transforming agreements—ranging from commercial leases to wedding event contracts – into "one-sided albatrosses."[15] In any case, the impact of COVID-19 highlights the relevance of the doctrines under review.[16]

In the same vein, there have been views that the COVID-19 pandemic may be characterised as an Act of God so extraordinary and unforeseen when compared with the routine difficulties inherent in service contracts that it justifies recourse to the doctrine of impossibility, thereby excusing the service provider from performance. An illustrative example often cited is that of a babysitter whose obligations became impossible to discharge under pandemic conditions.[17] In fact, the perspective has been advanced that the performance of a contract may be excused where the performance of same would lead to the spread of communicable diseases. This view, it has been argued, is supported by caselaw. The view is canvassed under a general principle that courts should refuse to enforce and rewrite (under the remedy of reformation) contracts whose performance would generate a negative externality.[18] According to Johnston, these scholarly proposals stood in stark contrast to judicial practice. With few exceptions, courts declined to excuse performance and instead upheld contractual obligations despite the imposition of COVID-19 lockdowns and business restrictions. In the rare cases where relief was granted, it was because the court construed a *force majeure* clause to encompass pandemic-related lockdown orders and identified the specific obligation as one falling within the scope of the clause. By contrast, courts almost never accepted default excuses such as 'impossibility,' 'impracticability,' or 'frustration' to relieve commercial tenants

14 Jason Scott Johnston, "An Economic Perspective on Contractual Excuse: Lessons from COVID-19" (2025) 30(1) *Stanford Journal of Law, Economics & Business* 72–132; A.A. Schwartz, "Contracts and COVID-19" (2020) 73 *Stan. L. Rev. Online* 48.

15 Yehonatan Givati, Yotam Kaplan and Yair Listokin, "Excuse 2.0" (2024) 109 *Cornell L. Rev.* 629, 630.

16 Examining art 79 of the United Nations Convention on Contracts for the International Sale of Goods (CISG), Jevremovic opines that the impact of COVID-19 will bring further challenges in the uniform application of the Convention; and it will do so through one of its most controversial provisions: art 79. See Jevremovic, Nevena, Article 79 CISG: Testing the Effectiveness of the CISG in International Trade Through the Lens of the COVID-19 Outbreak (1 October 2021). Poomintr Sooksripaisarnkit and Dharmita Prasad (eds), *Blurry Boundaries of Public and Private International Law* (Singapore: Springer Nature 2022) https://ssrn.com/abstract=4069247 accessed 10 October 2025.

17 Andrew A. Schwartz, "Contracts and COVID-19" (2020) 73 *Stan. L. Rev. Online* 48, 52.

18 David A. Hoffman & Cathy Hwang, "The Social Cost of Contract" (2021) 121 *Colum. L. Rev.* 979, 984. See also Jason Scott Johnston, (supra) n. 14.

from rent obligations. Far from treating COVID-19 lockdowns as rendering contracts "obsolete," judges resolved the disputes by closely interpreting and applying the contractual language governing the parties' rights and duties.

In recent times, a handful of cases have been litigated on the economic effect of the foregoing on contracts across the globe in which parties invited the courts and various tribunals to hold that as a result of these events, their contracts have been frustrated, and thus be discharged from performing their obligations under the contract.[19] For the most part, tribunals have yet to be convinced that the COVID-19 pandemic should excuse obligations, damages or even warrant renegotiation as a result of hardship. For instance, in *Attianese S.p.A. v P. S. Import ApS*,[20] the parties entered into a contract for the sale of tomato-derived products. Following delivery, a dispute arose regarding the applicable purchase price. The Seller contended that it was entitled to a price adjustment, relying on provisions of Italian domestic law concerning hardship, rather than invoking art 79 of the United Nations Convention on Contracts for the International Sale of Goods (CISG). The Seller argued that the economic consequences of the COVID-19 pandemic and the armed conflict in Ukraine constituted events of hardship justifying the price increase. It was further submitted that the Buyer's failure to expressly reject the revised pricing amounted to tacit acceptance. The Court dismissed the Seller's claims. It held that the conditions for hardship under Italian law had not been established and further concluded, by reference to art 8(3) CISG, that the Buyer's conduct could not be interpreted as acceptance of the increased price.

It is therefore against this backdrop that this book sets out to undertake a comparative law analysis of this exemption to the doctrine of absolute obligation of contract. The doctrine of frustration/*force majeure*/exemption[21] is fluid and complicated; it has over the years served as an avenue through which a party who has committed no breach of contract can be excused from the performance of the obligations of the contract and/or exempted from liability in damages if there is an unforeseen impediment or event which occurs to render the performance of contractual obligations impossible.

The issues arising from this book are the interplay of the doctrine of exemption/*force majeure*/frustration under the CISG, UNIDROIT Principles, and English law. This doctrine does not exactly mean the same thing under these legal instruments; there are some obvious points of convergence and divergence that

19 See for instance Attianese S.p.A. v P. S. Import ApS, Sø- og Handelsretten (Maritime and Commercial Court), Denmark, 11 October 2024 – BS-40411/2023-SHR, CISG-online 7177 <https://cisg-online.org/search-for-cases?caseId=15094> accessed 12 October 2025 and Dyco Hotels Pty Ltd & Ors v Laundy Hotels (Quarry) Pty Ltd [2021] NSWCA 332 [2021].

20 Attianese S.p.A. v P. S. Import ApS, Sø- og Handelsretten (Maritime and Commercial Court), Denmark, 11 October 2024 – BS-40411/2023-SHR, CISG-online 7177 <https://cisg-online.org/search-for-cases?caseId=15094> accessed 12 October 2025.

21 Exemption and *force majeure* for the purpose of this book shall be used interchangeably; they refer to a situation where a non-fault, unforeseen, uncontrollable impediment or inhibition occurs to make further performance of a subsisting contract impossible.

need to be carefully examined. It will be worthwhile attempting a critical comparison of the subject matter of this book.[22] This book also investigates relationships between the doctrines of exemption/frustration/*force majeure* and other principles such as risk, avoidance, mistake, hardship, and the application of remedies under the subject matter of this research.

In light of recent developments, the efforts here are geared towards developing new perspectives on the interpretation of the aforementioned relationship, proposing recommendations for legal reform in areas where gaps have been identified in the relevant legal instruments, and ultimately presenting a "Draft Model Frustration Clause" that encapsulates and reflects the reforms advocated in this book.[23]

The aims of this book are to streamline the positions of the CISG, the UNIDROIT Principles and the English law as regards their relationship with the doctrine of frustration/exemption/*force majeure* of contracts and to proffer a better understanding of the working relationship among the three major legal instruments of focus in this research. The efforts here are demonstrated through a methodological comparative and critical analysis of the laws, doctrines, principles and jurisdictions that are the focus of this study. The pattern will also feature a historical framework of various issues this research is set out to incisively evaluate.

1.2 From *Pact Sunt Servanda* to *Clausula Rebus Sic Stantibus* – Legal Basis of the Doctrines of Exemption/ Frustration/ *Force Majeure*

1.2.1 Pact Sunt Servanda

One of the main principles of national and international business law is the general principle of pacta *sunt servanda* which is deeply rooted in the canon law *Codex Iuris Canonici*, the law code of the Catholic Church. *Pacta sunt servanda* is a Latin maxim which simply means that agreements must be respected.[24] This moral code of conduct became the foundation of the law of the merchants.

22 A. H. Puelinckx, "Frustration, Hardship, *Force Majeure, Imprévision, Wegfall der Geschäftsgrundlage*, Unmöglichkeit, Changed Circumstances: A Comparative study in English, French, German and Japanese Law" (1986) 3 *J.Int'l Arb,* No. 2, at 47; The writer opines that:

> "Frustration is not the equivalent of *force majeure* or Unmöglichkeit, nor is *force majeure* Unmöglichkeit; even *force majeure* under Belgian law is not *force majeure* under French law. Although all these concepts belong to the same family, the distinction between them is extremely important in drafting choice of law clauses in international contracts."

23 This book is a comparative law analysis with the sole significance of critically narrating the position of the CISG, UNIDROIT Principles, and the English common law as regards the doctrine of frustration/exemption/*force majeure*. This doctrine is very important in the field of contract and commercial law; it is a gateway doctrine through which numerous other doctrines and principles can be appraised. The Draft model Frustration Clause proposed in this book operates to create a more restrictive and definable frustration/exemption/*force majeure* doctrine that will help cushion the uncertainty effect of English common and statutory law, mercurial stance of the CISG, and the bland position of the UNIDROIT Principles.

24 Michael G. Rapsomanikas, "Frustration of Contract in International Trade Law and Comparative Law" (1979–1980) 18 *Duquesne Law Review* 551–605; the writer opines that:

This maxim is one of the most important heritages of the *lex mercatoria*; it is equally the backbone of international law. This maxim is the meeting point of law and morality,[25] and it is very much at the heart of commercial and international relations.[26] The universal nature of the maxim was captured succinctly by Mahmassahi in *LIAMCO v Libya*[27] when he stated that:

> The principle of the sanctity of contracts ... has always constituted an integral part of most legal systems. These include those systems that are based on Roman law, the Napoleonic Code (e.g. art 1134) and other European civil codes, as well as Anglo-Saxon Common Law and Islamic Jurisprudence 'Sharia.'

Contract of sale of goods relationships come with various challenges and risks; prices may suddenly increase, inflation may rise, and performance may become more onerous, but in all these, parties are still expected to perform the agreement they entered into. A sales contract, for instance, guarantees the buyer that the purchased goods will be at their disposal at a given date (or at least that they will obtain compensation if the supplier fails to deliver them at that date); it guarantees the supplier payment of the specified amount at the agreed date.

It has also been held that the principle of *pacta sunt servanda* implies that the contract is the law of the parties,[28] agreed to by them for the regulation of their legal relationship, and generates not only the obligation of each party to a contract to fulfil its promises but also the obligation to perform them in good faith, to compensate for the damage caused to the other party by their non-fulfilment and to not terminate the contract unilaterally except as provided for in the contract.[29]

Roman law, at least, as *jus strictum*, did not recognise the problem of frustration, always abiding by the express terms of the agreement, irrespective of how onerous for the debtor the contract could become.

25 Dietrich Maskow, "Hardship and *Force Majeure*" (1992) Am. J. Comp. L. 657, 658. The principle of *pacta sunt servanda* reflects natural justice and economic requirements because it binds a person to their promises and protects the interests of the other party. Since effective economic activity is not possible without reliable promises, the importance of this principle has to be emphasised.

26 In the *Sapphire v National Iranian Oil Company* Arbitral Award 15 March 1963, I.L.R., 1967, 136 181; the arbitrators expressly stated, "It is a fundamental principle of law, which is constantly being proclaimed by international courts, that contractual undertakings must be respected. The rule *pacta sunt servanda* is the basis of every contractual relationship."

27 [April 12 1977] Y B. Comm. Arb [1981] 89 at 101

28 Wouter Den Haerynck in "Drafting Hardship Clauses in International Contracts," Structuring International Contracts, Dennis Campbell ed. (Kluwer Law International, 1996) 231–232; the writer was of the view that : "for instance, in France, the principle *pacta sunt servanda* (as incorporated in Art 1134 of the French Civil Code) prevails over the principle *rebus sic stantibus*. If the contract does not contain any provision regarding events of changing circumstances, then the performance of the contract will be enforced without any changes to the contract."

29 ICC Award No 5485 [1987] Y B. Comm. Arb [1989] 156 at 168.

1.2.2 Clausula Rebus Sic Stantibus

There are exceptions or limits to the principle of *pacta sunt servanda* in the forms of the peremptory norms of general international law, called *jus cogens* (compelling law), and the *rebus sic stantibus* principle. The legal principle *clausula rebus sic stantibus*, as part of customary international law, also allows for treaty obligations to be unfulfilled due to a compelling change in circumstances. This explains the principle that unexpected events can affect the performance of the contract. A contract will only guarantee performances when it does not yield to the pressure of unforeseen developments.[30]

The exempting principle of *rebus sic santibus* was already recognised by ancient Roman law.[31] According to the Code of the Roman Emperor Justinian, a party to a contract is not liable for impossible performances. Thomas Aquinas used Aristotle's theory of human responsibility to explain the conclusions of the Canonists. He writes that choice was an act of will, and one could only choose what was possible. A promise to do the impossible was not binding.[32] All promises were subject to a condition[33] and impossibility can be an exempting condition by which a promise could be broken. This principle (*rebus sic santibus*) tries to find a balance between the obligation to perform a signed contract and the discharge of a party from performance in cases of unexpected and impossible events.

While the various national law systems deal with the principle of *rebus sic stantibus*, this principle can also be found in the international law domain.[34] Unexpected or unforeseen events are much more frequent in international business than in national contracts. It is part of the nature of international contracts that they are concluded and executed in less stable political, economic, and juridical surroundings than national contracts. Joseph Perillo writes while analysing the doctrine of *pacta sunt servanda* that:

> [T]raditional doctrines in both the systems of common law and civil law have solidly supported the doctrine of *pacta sunt servanda* – agreements must be kept though the heavens fall. The major exceptions in civil and common

30 van Houtte Hans, "Changed Circumstances and *Pacta Sunt Servanda*" in: Gaillard (ed.), *Transnational Rules in International Commercial Arbitration* (1993) ICC Publ. Nr. 480,4, at 105.

31 James Gordley, "Impossibility and Changed and Unforeseen Circumstances" 52 (Summer 2004) *American Journal of Comparative Law* 513–530; the author quoted a famous Roman text which contained the maxim, "there is no obligation to the impossible;" Corpus Iuris Civilis Dig. 50.17.185 (533) (*Celsus libro octavo digestorum*).

32 Thomas Aquinas, *Summa Theologiae* I-II q. 13 a. 5 ad 1.

33 Baldus de Ubaldis, *Commentaria Corpus iuris civilis* to Dig. (1597) 12.4.8.

34 The 1969 Vienna Convention on the Law of Treaties, art 62, states:

> A fundamental change of circumstances which has occurred with regard to those existing at the time of the conclusion of a treaty and which was not foreseen by the parties may not be invoked as a ground for terminating or withdrawing from the treaty unless (a) the existence of those circumstances constituted an essential basis of the consent of the parties to be bound by the treaty and (b) the effect of the change is radically to transform the extent of the obligations still to be performed under the treaty.

> law systems are the doctrines of impossibility of performance, sometimes denominated "*force majeure*," and frustration of the venture. In many legal systems the traditional doctrine continues to receive solid support and relief for hardship is limited to these two doctrines, either performance is made impossible by *force majeure* and the contract disappears[35]

The above legal analysis points to the fact that the doctrine of exemption/*force majeure*/frustration is an exception to the doctrine of absolute contract. An obligation to perform can be exempted when an unforeseen event happens after or before the conclusion of the contract to effectively discharge the contract, but the privilege accorded by this doctrine should not be applied loosely in order to defeat the positive binding nature of contractual promises.[36]

1.3 Discrepancies in the Terminologies Used in the Legal Instruments

1.3.1 The CISG

The United Nations Convention on Contract for the International Sale of Goods (CISG) garners the most attention of this book; this is a treaty law enacted in 1980 under the auspices of UNCITRAL,[37] and saddled with the sole function of governing the international sale of goods.[38] Since the inception of the CISG, it has generated a lot of excitement; a plethora of cases had been conclusively decided based on its applications, different hierarchies of courts and tribunals have had something to say about the provisions of this convention, and it has created a field day for the academics and practitioners who never ceased to critically and analytically develop the jurisprudence of the convention. All these have contributed immensely to making the CISG one of the most tested and applied conventions of the 21st century. However, there are some pitfalls that have taken the shine out of this illustrious convention. The incongruous draftsmanship exhibited under art

35 Joseph Perillo, "*Force Majeure* and Hardship under the UNIDROIT Principles of International Commercial Contract" (1998) Universidad Panamericana, 111–113https://ir.lawnet.fordham.edu/cgi/viewcontent.cgi?article=1782&context=faculty_scholarship accessed 11 October 2025.

36 I.C.C. award No. 1512 (1971),YB. Comm. Arb., 1976, 128, 129; the Arbitrator held while declining to apply the *rebus sicstantibus* principle to the above matter thus:

"The principle '*Rebus sic stantibus*' is universally considered to be of strict and narrow interpretation, as a dangerous exception to the principle of sanctity of contracts. Whatever opinion or interpretation lawyers of different countries may have about the 'concept' of changed circumstances as an excuse for non-performance, they will doubtless agree on the necessity to limit the application of the so-called 'doctrine *rebus sic stantibus*' (sometimes referred to as 'frustration,' '*force majeure*,' 'Imprévision,' and the like) to cases where compelling reasons justify it, having regard not only to the fundamental character of the changes but also to the particular type of the contract involved, to the requirements of fairness and equity and to all circumstances of the case."

37 United Nations Commission on International Trade Law (UNCITRAL) has been recognised as the core legal body of the United Nations system in the field of international trade law; its aim is to modernise and harmonise the rules on international business.

38 Michael J. Dennis, "Modernizing and Harmonizing International Contract Law: The CISG and the UNIDROIT Principles Continue to Provide the Best Way Forward" (2014) 19(1) *Unif. L. Rev* 114.

79 of this Convention has ultimately succeeded in creating more disaffection than any other article of this convention.[39]

Art 79 of the CISG provides that:

(1) A party is not liable for a failure to perform any of his obligations if he proves that the failure was due to an impediment beyond his control and that he could not reasonably be expected to have taken the impediment into account at the time of the conclusion of the contract or to have avoided or overcome it or its consequences.

(2) If the party's failure is due to the failure by a third person whom he has engaged to perform the whole or a part of the contract, that party is exempt from liability only if:
   (a) he is exempt under the preceding paragraph; and
   (b) the person whom he has so engaged would be so exempt if the provisions of that paragraph were applied to him.

(3) The exemption provided by this article has effect for the period during which the impediment exists.

(4) The party who fails to perform must give notice to the other party of the impediment and its effect on his ability to perform. If the notice is not received by the other party within a reasonable time after the party who fails to perform knew or ought to have known of the impediment, he is liable for damages resulting from such non-receipt.

(5) Nothing in this article prevents either party from exercising any right other than to claim damages under this Convention.

"Exemption," as used under art 79 CISG, has its own peculiar meaning different from the traditional *force majeure* or frustration doctrines;[40] this is in order to avoid pitching the tent of this provision under any legal system.[41] Basically, exemption

39 John Honnold stated that "in spite of strenuous efforts of legislators and scholars we face the likelihood that Art 79 may be the Convention's least successful part of the half-century of work towards international uniformity;" John O. Honnold, *Uniform Law for International Sales under the 1980 United Nations Convention* (Kluwer Law International, 3rd edn, 1999) 472–495.

40 Jelena Vilus, "Provisions Common to the Obligations of the Seller and the Buyer" in Petar Sarcevic & Paul Volken eds., *International Sale of Goods: Dubrovnik Lectures* (Oceana, 1986) ch. 7, 239–264, he writes that: "in this field, as in many others, the notions of common law and civil law differ. As a result, the international drafters wanted to create a new concept by amalgamating different ideas which, of course, have their positive and negative aspects."

41 Denis Tallon, "Art 79" in *Bianca-Bonell Commentary on the International Sales Law* (1987) Giuffrè: Milan, 572–595; the author argues that:

"Thus Art 79 was elaborated on a variegated background. Significantly, however, the Convention avoided reference to the domestic theories recapitulated above. It developed a system of its own, which in fact results from a slow maturation process that started with ULIS. This autonomy, illustrated by the lack of reference to accepted wording and concepts of domestic laws (*force majeure*, frustration, impracticability), renders the interpretation of Art 79 extremely difficult because one cannot resort to these laws as a guide." See also Yesim M Atamer, "Art 79" in Stefan Kröll and othas used under the CISG is a rule of damages which shields a party from paying damages if non-performance was caused by an impediment which was beyond the control and foreseeability of the party and whose consequences the party cannot overcome or take into account at the time of the conclusion of the contract.[42] Generally, art 79 deals with what is often known in the national sales law under the label of *force majeure*, impossibility, frustration, impracticability, or hardship.[43]

Under the doctrine of exemption, the contract is not automatically discharged, as sundry remedies except liability in damages can conveniently apply,[44] this is unlike the doctrine of frustration in English law, where the automatic discharge of the contract applies, and this has been a major difference between the two doctrines.[45] In fact, Treitel argues that "the effect of an impediment under art 79 of the CISG resembles those of an excuse for non-performance in English law rather than those for frustration."[46] The fact that art 79 of the CISG also permits the situation of temporary frustration further sets it apart from the doctrine of frustration under English law.[47]

Arts. 79 and 80 of the CISG are listed under the "exemption" category, and they all work in tandem, though art 80 is wider in its applications. It provides that "A party may not rely on a failure of the other party to perform, to the extent that such failure was caused by the first party's act or omission." This provision (art 80) is provided under section IV, (Exemptions) part of the Convention (CISG). It has been argued that art 80 has the seductive charm of a self-evident statement[48] thus any party whose actions or omissions prevented the other party from performing the contract shall not be allowed to rely on the latter party's failure to perform.[49]

Although art 79 CISG is one of the most challenging and important CISG provisions, the CISG tried to strike a balance between the demands of both civil and

---

ers (eds), *UN Convention on Contracts for the International Sale of Goods (CISG)* (Hart Publishing, 2011) 1056.

42 Ibid.

43 Ingeborg Schwenzer and others, *International Sales Law* (Hart Publishing, 2nd edn, 2012) 583.

44 Rodrigo Uribe, "Change of Circumstances in International Instruments of Contract Law: The Approach of The CISG, The PICC, The PECL, And The DCFR" (2011) 15(2) *VJ* 233–266.

45 Fengming Liu, "The Doctrine of Frustration: An Overview of English Law" (1988) 19 *J. Mar. L. & Com.* 261.

46 Geunter Treitel, *Frustration and Force Majeure* (Sweet & Maxwell, 1994) para 15–039, 536.

47 Ibid; see also Matthew Parker and Ewan McKendrick, "Drafting *Force Majeure* Clause" I.C.C.L.R

48 Honnold (n 39) para 436, p496.

49 This is regarded as a rule of exemption under the international contract on the sale of goods. It is a rule that tries to strike a balance between the breaches of the parties which resulted in a two-way cause of failure of obligations to perform a contract. Honnold made the rhetorical remark that art 80 not only governs problems of exemption from liability but may have unwittingly modified all the remedial provisions of the CISG. see Honnold (n 39) 496–500; see also *Medicine's Case*, Russia [26 January 2006] Arbitration proceeding 53/2005 Cited as: <http://cisgw3.law.pace.edu/cases/060126r1.html> accessed on 30 September 2025; it was held that "a delay by a buyer in sending a request for the procurement of some vital documents which would have aided completion of the contractual obligations is enough to bring Art 80 of the CISG into play when apportioning damages from the breach that follows."

common law systems. The result is therefore a Convention whose uniform mantra, as enshrined in art 7 of the Convention, has been seriously undermined by the sheer multiplicity of interpretations different national jurisdictions can give to the provision of art 79. It has been noticed by Schlechtriem, while analysing uniform law provisions like art 79, that:

> Such laws provide at first only verbal uniformity, and there is always a great danger of, in the application and/or interpretation of a uniform law, practitioners and legal writers paying only lip service to the uniform law, reading and applying it in a manner in keeping with their domestic law.[50]

A common law jurisdiction will always strictly interpret art 79 towards common law strict frustration rules, where any impediment short of impossibility will rarely be entertained; on the other hand, a civil law country like Germany under its wider *Wegfall der Geschäftsgrundlage* doctrine[51] will be tempted to lump together the doctrine of hardship and frustration under art 79, thereby relaxing the rules to accommodate impracticable circumstances. This is because the doctrine of hardship is well developed under the civil law and its absence under the CISG will leave a civil law practitioner with no choice but to interpret art 79 accordingly.[52]

It can be argued that art 79 of the CISG is more suited to be categorised as one of the items under art 4 of the CISG (provision ousting from the jurisdiction of the CISG questions of validity of a contract).[53] It should be an exclusive matter under which the national laws would exercise jurisdiction.[54] This argument is based on

50 Peter Schlechtriem, "Basic Structures and General Concepts of the CISG as Models for a Harmonisation of the Law of Obligations" [2005] <http://www.cisg.law.pace.edu/cisg/biblio/schlechtriem12.html> accessed 15/9/2025, also cited as Peter Schlechtriem "Basic Structures and General Concepts of the CISG as Models for a Harmonisation of the Law of Obligations" (2005) 10 *Juridica International* 27–34.

51 German concept of impossibility is entirely different. It only excludes the general claim for specific performance notwithstanding fault and foreseeability on the part of the debtor. The question whether the debtor has to pay damages is a matter of fault. See Richard Backhaus, "The Limits of the Duty to Perform in the Principles of European Contract Law" (2004) 8.1 *Electronic Journal of Comparative Law* <http://www.ejcl.org/81/art81-2.html> accessed 15/9/2025.

52 Apparently, under the common law, just like the CISG, there is no developed distinction between frustration and hardship; hardship can be grouped under impracticability of performance. Normally, a contract under the common law and even the CISG cannot be held to have been frustrated for a mere impracticality of performance unless it is such that goes to the root of the contract and radically changes it as opposed to what was contracted earlier.

53 This is because "When defining 'impediment,' most jurisdictions started by determining if and how their national doctrines for exemption fit within the CISG's concept of 'impediment.'" See Brandon Nagy "Unreliable Excuses: How do Differing Persuasive Interpretations of CISG Art 79 Affect its Goal of Harmony?" (March 2013) 26(2) *New York International Law Review*.

54 This suggestion may not be true, Todd Weitzmann writes that "validity defence can generally be distinguished from an excuse defence on the basis that validity is concerned with the balance between the parties in the formation process, while excuse is concerned with the problems arising when an unforeseen development subsequent to the date of the contract renders performance either impos-

the fact that art 79 is susceptible to homeward interpretations[55] and any doctrine that has the capacity to extinguish obligations between parties in a contract should be better left under the national law sphere.[56] This is because the yardstick through which obligations can be excused and the severity of elements that can ground this form of discharge vary from jurisdiction to jurisdiction. There are always the temptations to adapt the law to reflect a particular national law's purpose in such circumstances.

However, it can also be argued that since exemption takes effect after or before the conclusion of a contract, it has no place on the validity items; the contract is not vitiated *ab initio* but only exempted liability in damages due to an uncontrollable impediment for which the parties are not liable.

Another major problem bedevilling the doctrine of exemption, under the CISG, according to Jacob S. Ziegel, is "the conceptual differences in approach to exemption among the major legal systems, because of lack of unanimity about the solutions to the policy issues, and also of the unsettled state of the law even within a given system."[57] For instance, art 79 of the CISG and art 7.1.7 of the UNIDROIT Principles do not ostensibly provide for the doctrine of frustration of purpose, whereas this is an integral and equitable facet of the doctrine of frustration under the common law.[58]

1.3.2 The UNIDROIT Principles

The International Institute for the Unification of Private Law (UNIDROIT) principles use the term *"force majeure,"* and this does not exactly resemble the French traditional *force majeure* doctrine, though it bears striking similarities; UNIDROIT Principles *force majeure* can also be differentiated from the popular *force majeure* clauses seen under commercial contracts which have gained popularity in the international commercial law practice.[59] The UNIDROIT Principles of International

sible or difficult." See Todd Weitzmann, "Validity and Excuse in the U.N. Sales Convention" (1997) 16 *Journal of Law and Commerce Process* 265–290.

55 Harry Flechtner, "Art 79 of the United Nations Convention on Contracts for the International Sale of Goods (CISG) as Rorschach Test: The Homeward Trend and Exemption for Delivering Non-Conforming Goods" (2007) 19 *Pace International Law Review* 29–51.

56 Anja Carlsen "Can the Rules of Hardship Be Applied as a Validity Defence?" <http://www.jus.uio.no/pace/can_upicc_hardship_provisions_be_applied_when_cisg_is_governing_law.anja_carlsen/_4.en.html> accessed 03/09/2025; the author writes that: "The purpose of Art 4(a) is mainly to protect domestic public policy concerns and this purpose can generally be achieved by the decisive-test approach because of the number of instances in which the CISG does not purport to provide solutions to subjects with important domestic policy concerns."

57 Jacob S. Ziegel, "Report to the Uniform Law Conference of Canada on Convention on Contracts for the International Sale of Goods" (1981) <http://www.cisg.law.pace.edu/cisg/text/ziegel79.html> accessed 10 September 2025.

58 JD Feltham, "The U.N. Convention on Contracts for the International Sale of Goods" [1981] *J. Bus. L.* 346, 359.

59 Aditi Patanjali, "A comparative study and analysis of the doctrine of frustration under the CISG, UNIDROIT Principles and UCC" (2012) 23(5) *I.C.C.L.R* 174.

Commercial Contracts (2016 Edition) is a legal document drawn up by UNIDROIT first in 1994[60] which aims at the harmonisation of the international commercial contract.[61] This legal instrument comprises tested and well-documented *lex mercatoria*,[62] it is not a positive enactment but enjoys the flexibility of its adoption or application being subject to the choice of the contractual parties. Art 7.1.7 of the UNIDROIT Principles provides that:

(1) Non-performance by a party is excused if that party proves that the non-performance was due to an impediment beyond its control and that it could not reasonably be expected to have taken the impediment into account at the time of the conclusion of the contract or to have avoided or overcome it or its consequences.
(2) When the impediment is only temporary, the excuse shall have effect for such period as is reasonable having regard to the effect of the impediment on the performance of the contract.
(3) The party who fails to perform must give notice to the other party of the impediment and its effect on its ability to perform. If the notice is not received by the other party within a reasonable time after the party who fails to perform knew or ought to have known of the impediment, it is liable for damages resulting from such non-receipt.
(4) Nothing in this article prevents a party from exercising a right to terminate the contract or to withhold performance or request interest on money due.

The provision of the UNIDROIT Principle on *force majeure* is similar to the CISG, though there are some noticeable differences. It has been debatable whether or not it can be a gap-filling instrument intended to help in the interpretation of the provisions of the CISG. This research will expose the shortfalls of this legal instrument and will posit that it is a bad imitation of the CISG which failed to add something new to the solutions of frustrated contracts.[63]

The French civil code provisions, especially art 1148, are very similar to the *force majeure* under art 7.1.7 of the UNIDROIT Principles. Under both provisions, liability for damages is excluded in a circumstance where an impediment makes

60 There have been three (3) Editions since the first (1994) edition. The current edition is the 2016 edition. The 2016 edition of the UNIDROIT Principles is not intended as a revision of the previous editions. The main objective of the fourth edition of the UNIDROIT Principles is to take better account of the special needs of long-term contracts. As a result, the 2016 edition of the UNIDROIT Principles, like the 2010 edition, consists of 211 articles (as opposed to the 120 articles of the 1994 edition and the 185 articles of the 2004 edition).

61 Aldo Mascareño and Elina Mereminskaya, "The Making of World Society Through Private Commercial Law: The Case of the UNIDROIT Principles" (2013) 18(4) *Unif. L. Rev.* 447.

62 Michael Joachim Bonell, "The UNIDROIT Principles of International Commercial Contracts: Towards a New *lex mercatoria*?" (1997) 2 *I.B.L.J* 145–187.

63 Alejandro M. Garro, "Comparison between Provisions of the CISG Regarding Exemption of Liability for Damages (Art. 79) and the Counterpart Provisions of the UNIDROIT Principles (Art. 7.1.7)" (2005) <http://cisgw3.law.pace.edu/cisg/principles/uni79.html> accessed 24/9/2025.

the performance of the contract impossible. *Force majeure* in the French civil law context plays a central role in both contractual and delictual liability; it sets a limit to strict liability, and it is characterised by irresistibility, unforeseeability, externality and impossibility.[64]

According to French jurisprudence, which stemmed from Arts. 1147[65] and 1148[66] of the Civil Code, termination of contracts is possible in cases of *force majeure* (terms cas fortuit and "cause étrangère" are used interchangeably). It will be safe to say that Arts. 79 of the CISG, 7.1.7 of the UNIDROIT Principles and 1148 of the French civil code are similar in their exclusion of damages over matters concerning contractual impossibility. It has been held in the *Électricité de France* case[67] that though the company has pleaded *force majeure* as justifying particular interruptions of electric supply by violent storms, such a plea only brought exemption from damages and did not affect the continuity of the contract, as the French concept of *force majeure* recognises partial frustration.[68] In like manner, it has been held, relying on art 7.1.7 of the UNIDROIT Principles, that *force majeure* exempts only from liability for non-performance but does not extinguish the obligation itself.[69]

Another distinguishing aspect of the UNIDROIT Principles is that it deals with *force majeure* in the chapter on non-performance, whereas commercial hardship is dealt with in the chapter on performance. The logic of this division is that if

64 Barry Nicholas, "*Force Majeure* in French Law" in *Force Majeure and Frustration of Contract,* ed. Ewan McKendrick (Lloyd's of London Press Ltd, 2nd Edition, 1995) c 2, 21.

65 Art 1147 of French Civil Code provides thus:

> The debtor is condemned, where appropriate, to the payment of damages, whether for non-performance of the obligation or for delay in its performance, whenever he does not show that the failure to perform derives from an extraneous cause which cannot be imputed to him, even though there is no bad faith on his part.

66 Art 1148 of the French Civil Code provides that:

> There is no place for any damages when, as a result of a *force majeure* or an accident, the debtor has been prevented from conveying or doing that to which he was obliged or has done what was forbidden to him.

67 Barry Nicholas, "*Force Majeure* in French Law" in *Force Majeure and Frustration of Contract,* ed. Ewan McKendrick (Lloyd's of London Press Ltd, 2nd Edition, 1995) c 2, 26.

68 Mestre (1991) Rev. trim, de droit civ.659. 34.

69 Kaptransstroy v TechnoSpecStroy, Eighth Arbitrazh Appellate Court, Russian Federation, A70-17666/2017, 12 September 2018, UNILEX <https://www.unilex.info/principles/case/2499> accessed 12 October 2025. In this case, the Court considered both the Russian Civil Code and art 7.1.7 of the UNIDROIT Principles of International Commercial Contracts, which defines *force majeure* as an impediment beyond a party's reasonable control, unforeseeable at the time of the contract, and unavoidable in its effects. The Court underscored that while *force majeure* may exempt a party from liability for non-performance, it does not extinguish the underlying contractual obligation. By invoking art 7.1.7 of the UNIDROIT Principles, the Court aligned Russian jurisprudence with international standards governing contractual performance and *force majeure*. It reaffirmed that only events that are truly beyond a party's control, unforeseeable, and unavoidable may qualify as *force majeure*. Ordinary and foreseeable risks, such as natural market fluctuations, particularly those that a reasonable and experienced commercial operator should anticipate, do not meet the required threshold.

performance is impossible, it will not be performed; whether the non-performance is excused or will be the basis for a money judgement for damages or restitution is a question dealt with under non-performance.[70] If performance is burdensome, the consequences of the burden are dealt with as an aspect of performance.[71] *Force majeure* under Arts. 7.1.7 UNIDROIT Principles refers only to impediments which make performance impossible and not those only making it onerous,[72] as the UNIDROIT Principles have a separate provision for hardship[73] which will be discussed in detail in Chapter 5 of this book.

It is also the case that *force majeure* under the UNIDROIT Principles does not affect the validity of the contract. This is a major point of departure from the French law doctrine of *force majeure*, which provides that if the performance of the obligation in a contract is wholly and permanently impossible, then the contract is void and it is only the court that can order its restitution or rescission of the contract, but in practice the court has wider powers to deal with the consequences of a *force majeure* situation.[74]

While it has been debated hotly whether or not the remedy of specific performance can apply under arts. 79 CISG, no such question is raised under arts. 7.1.7 UNIDROIT Principles, because it clearly enumerates that the applicable remedies include termination of the contract or withholding performance or requesting interest on money due. The omission of specific performance under this list sends a signal that the UNIDROIT Principles do not consider it an applicable remedy under the *force majeure* provision.[75] Article 79 of the CISG provides that a third person's failure to perform can constitute grounds for exemption in some instances, but this is absent under art 7.1.7 of the UNIDROIT Principles.[76]

Furthermore, *force majeure* clauses do not represent the doctrine of *force majeure* as provided under art 7.1.7. The *force majeure* clauses are boilerplate or standard form provisions, which cover natural disasters or other "Acts of God," war or the failure of third parties (such as suppliers and sub-contractors) and a lot to

70 The UNIDROIT Principles clearly tilt toward French doctrine of *force majeure*, and it does appear art 7.1.7 will only apply in a situation of absolute impossibility of performance. This explains why there is a provision for hardship that deals with a situation where performance of the contract is merely onerous.

71 Charlie Webb, "Performance and Compensation: An Analysis of Contract Damages and Contractual Obligation" (2006) 26(1) *Oxford Journal of Legal Studies* 41–71.

72 Nicholas (n 64) 25.

73 Michaël J. Bonell, "Unification of Law by Non-Legislative Means: The UNIDROIT Draft Principles for International Commercial Contracts" (1992) 40 *Am. J. Comp. L.* 617, 618–619.

74 Nicholas (n 64); he writes that "French law shares with other civil law systems the principle which the common law doesn't accept that an obligation to do the impossible is void."

75 Maskow (n 25); see also art 106 (4) of the Common European Sales Law excluded specific performance. It provides that: "If the seller's non-performance is excused, the buyer may resort to any of the remedies referred to in paragraph 1 except requiring performance and damages."

76 Scott D. Slater, "Overcome by Hardship: The Inapplicability of the UNIDROIT Principles' Hardship Provisions to CISG" (1998) 12 *Florida Journal of International Law*, 231–262.

perform their obligations to the contracting party.[77] It is important to remember that *force majeure* clauses are intended to excuse a party only if the failure to perform could not be avoided by the exercise of due care by that party.[78]

The question as to whether or not a *force majeure* clause will excuse damages is subject to the parties' drafting choice. For instance, under English common law, there is no readily recognised concept of *force majeure,* but such clauses dealing with *force majeure* may differ substantially, and everything will turn on the precise words adopted in the contract.[79]

However, art 7.1.7 of the UNIDROIT Principles crafted provisions that are wider in scope than the CISG, English common law, and even the civil law aspect of the provisions and practice of frustration or *force majeure.* It has been observed that art 7.1.7 of the UNIDROIT Principles includes the ground covered in common law systems by doctrines of frustration and impossibility of performance and in civil law systems by doctrines such as *force majeure*, but it is identical with none of them.[80]

Critical and comparative analysis of art 79 of the CISG and its counterpart art 7.1 of the UNIDROIT Principles will show that aside from minor differences in syntax, the noticeable difference is the absence of a counterpart to art 79(2) of the CISG in the UNIDROIT Principles.[81] The above omission reflects the gap between the assumed function that this paragraph was to take in the mind of its drafters and the misunderstandings inherent in the distinction of excuses based on the failure of a third person to perform.

One can also notice the difference in phraseology between the last paragraphs included in both instruments. Article 79(5) of the CISG is moulded in terms of limiting the exemption to liability for damages, though leaving open the application of termination and other similar remedies, whereas arts 7.1.7(4) of the UNIDROIT Principles approve the application of the remedy of termination, withholding

77 Jennifer M. Bund, "*Force majeure* Clauses: Drafting Advice for the CISG Practitioner" (1998) 17 *Journal of Law and Commerce* 381–413; the writer opines that: "By including a *force majeure* clause, parties can delineate the types of 'extraordinary circumstances' that will excuse performance, thereby increasing predictability."

78 Jay Kelley, "So What's Your Excuse—An Analysis of Force Majeure Claims" (2007) 2 *Tex. J. Oil Gas & Energy L.* 91.

79 Aubrey Diamond in Ewan McKendrick (ed.), *Force majeure and Frustration* (Lloyd's of London Press Ltd, 2nd edn, 1995) 262; Ewan McKendrick added at page 34, "while stressing the relationship between frustration and *force majeure* that 'Frustration can apply when there is an existing *force majeure* clause because a *force majeure* clause is simply evidence that the parties have made express provision for the alleged frustrating event and thus reasonably contemplate the occurrence of those events, but under English law, frustration is purely a supervening, unforeseeable event and not like the event of *force majeure* that has been contemplated and provided for'."

80 UNIDROIT Principles of International Commercial Law (2004) P 206.

81 Nagy (n 53) writes that "The main message of art 79(2) is that the 'seller bears the risk that third-party suppliers or subcontractors on which the seller depends may breach their own contract with the seller, so that the seller will not be excused when failure to perform was caused by its supplier's default'."

performance or requesting interest on money due and leaving open the application of other remedies.

Both arts 79(4) of the CISG and 7.1.7(3) of the UNIDROIT Principles refer to the availability of damages in a situation where a party who fails to perform any of his obligations in a contract due to an impediment fails to give the victim party notice of the impediment at a reasonable time after the party who fails to perform knew or ought to have known of the impediment; this is totally unavailable under the common law doctrine of frustration.[82]

1.3.3 The English Law

The English common law doctrine of frustration has strong ties with the doctrine of exemption and *force majeure* discussed above, but unfortunately they are not exactly the same, both in principles and in consequences. It has been held that the common law system does not know the concept of impediment or hardship, but rather adopts the general approach of classifying "frustration" as circumstances, be they specific events or general events which have affected the contract in such a way as to make it radically different from that which was originally concluded. Bugden and Lamont-Black are of the opinion that for there to be frustration, there must be a supervening and subsequent event, where the event is of an original nature; it may in appropriate cases serve to vitiate the contract ab initio under the doctrine of mutual mistake.[83]

Under the common law, a contract may be discharged on the ground of frustration when something occurs after the formation of the contract which renders it physically or commercially impossible to fulfil the contract or transforms the obligation to perform into a radically different obligation from that undertaken at the moment of entry into the contract.[84] It has been held by Lord Ratcliffe that:

> [F]rustration occurs whenever the law recognizes that without default of either party a contractual obligation has become incapable of being performed because the circumstances in which performance is called for would

82 Although adjudication can be anchored based on the doctrine of good faith if similar circumstances occurred under common law frustration. It also appears that art 7.4.1 of the UNIDROIT Principles, which excludes damages when non-performance is excused under the UNIDROIT Principles, is in support of the similar provision of art 79(5) of the CISG, but there is no similar provision under the Sales of Goods Act of 1979 other than the provision under Section 7 which will render any sale that falls within the provision avoided.

83 Paul M. Bugden and Simone Lamont-Black, Goods in Transit (Sweet & Maxwell, 2013) para 25–027, 648; see also Ingeborg Schwenzer and others, *Global Sales and Contract Law* (Oxford University Press, 2012) para 45.13, 652.

84 Chitty on Contracts, 27th edn (London: Sweet and Maxwell, 1994) 1633; See also Nigel Baker, "Frustration of Contract" (1999) 4(11) *Employment Law Newsletter (ELN)* 86; the writer held that "A contract can be frustrated where unforeseen events, beyond the control of the parties to the contract, render its performance impossible or radically different from that which was first envisaged when the contract was concluded."

> render it a thing radically different from that which was undertaken by the contract. *Non haec in foedera veni*. It was not this I was promised to do.[85]

Common law doctrine of frustration is different from the doctrine of exemption under art. 79 CISG and *force majeure* under art 7.1.7 UNIDROIT Principles, because frustration leads to automatic discharge of the contract,[86] even though sundry remedies provided under Law Reform (Frustrated Contracts) Act 1943 can apply, but arts 79 and 7.1.7 respectively only excuse liabilities from damages.

Under the CISG, non-performance due to an exempting impediment is nevertheless seen as a breach, though such a breach doesn't attract damages, but this is not seen as such under the common law doctrine of frustration, and this explains why damages are not applicable under the common law frustration, as damages entail breach.[87] It will be worthwhile to make the observation that there is an important difference between the common law's approach to frustration and the conceptual basis of art 79. At common law, the contract is only frustrated if the intervening event has destroyed its substratum or so radically interfered with performance that the whole complexion of the contract has been altered: hence a temporary impediment is not sufficient unless it has this effect, though in certain occasions it can be allowed.[88] Both under arts 79 of the CISG and 7.1.7 of the UNIDROIT Principles, a temporary impediment of substantial gravity clearly is a sufficient excuse, especially when it is such that temporarily renders the performance of the contract impossible.[89]

The English statutory law is one of the tripods upon which this research rests. It is a body of laws that comprises statutory laws like the Sale of Goods Act of 1979. The statutory laws are those positive enactments of the Act of Parliament; they are the product of draughtsmen and always reflect common law and judicial activism. Furthermore, the Sale of Goods Act 1979 is the ultimate legislation that governs contracts of sale of goods in the United Kingdom; it is applicable in England, Scotland, Northern Ireland, and Wales.

It is the amended and consolidated version of the defunct Sale of Goods Act of 1893.[90] Section 7 of the Sale of Goods Act 1979 provides that:

85 Davis Contractors Ltd v Fareham Urban District Council [1956] AC 696.

86 Treitel, *Frustration and Force Majeure* (n 46) 52.

87 Ingeborg Schwenzer and others (n 43) para 45.60, 663.

88 Tamplin Steamship Co. Ltd. v. Anglo-Mexican Petroleum Products Co. Ltd. [1916] 2 A.C. (397); see also Bugden and Lamont-Black (n 83) para 25–027, 648 where the writers argue that: "the application of the overall test of frustration in any particular case may often require a multi-factorial approach taking into account both matters in existence at the time of the contract and subsequent matters."

89 Nimrat Kaur, "Impediment: A Concept under CISG, UNIDROIT and Indian Contract Law-A Comparative Analysis" (2011) 15 *VJ* 91.

90 Fidelma White, "Sale of Goods Law Reform: An Irish Perspective Sale of Goods Law Reform" (2013) *CLWR* 42 two (172); the author writes that "The cornerstone of sale of goods law in the common law world is the English Sale of Goods Act 1893. The 1893 Act was not a reforming stat-

> Where there is an agreement to sale specific goods and subsequently without any fault on the part of the seller or buyer the goods perish before the risk passes to the buyer, the contract is avoided.

The scope of the application of this section (Section 7 of Sales of Goods Act 1979) is that it only applies to specific goods that have perished; it must be an agreement to sell, and the risk has not been passed to the buyer. It will be germane to note as an aside that there are other statutory enactments like the Trading with the Enemy Act of 1939, which operations can act to frustrate a contract under English Law.[91]

On further analysis of Section 7 of the 1979 Act, it will be important to point out that English statutory law, as shown under Section 7 of the Act, favours concrete solutions to specific problems as opposed to general principles and a vague, open-minded style of drafting of arts. 79 of the CISG[92] and 7.1.7 of the UNIDROIT Principles.[93]

It has been argued further that the extensive use of indefinite legal concepts and the abstract nature of many norms in the CISG do not augur well with the expectations of the English legal community, where it has been argued that ambiguity in legislation leads to uncertainty in law, and this is undesirable in the tradition of commercial law.[94] To buttress the above point, a phrase like "due to an impediment" used in arts. 79 of the CISG and 7.1.7 is elastic and bogus; it provides no guidance for interpretation or adjudication of what can be the typical impediment.[95] There is an attempt at a solution by the introduction of interpretative sections or a glossary in the proposed Draft Model Frustration Clause provision recommended in Chapter 8 of this book.

Section 7 of the Sale of Goods Act 1979 is in sharp contrast with the provisions of both arts. 79 of the CISG and 7.1.7 of the UNIDROIT principles. The former

---

ute; instead, it sought to make sales law more accessible via a statutory codification of the existing common law."

91 According to Section 1(2) of this Act Emergency Laws (Miscellaneous Provisions) Act 1953 Section 2: it is a criminal offence to supply any goods to or for the benefit of an enemy or to obtain any goods from an enemy in time of war. Indeed, both at common law and under this statute, all commercial intercourse between a British subject and an enemy becomes illegal upon the outbreak of war. As a result, any existing contract of sale which involves such intercourse by reason of the performance or further performance of the contract is frustrated by the outbreak of war, or upon one of the parties acquiring the status of an enemy.

92 Review of the Convention on Contracts for the International Sale of Goods, 2000–2001, Edited by Pace International Law Review (Kluwer Law Intl, 2002) 34.

93 Barry Nicholas, *International Sales: The United Nations Convention on Contracts for the International Sale of Goods,* (Matthew Bender, 1984) ch. 5, pages 5-1–5-24; he was of the opinion that :

"Elastic words are obviously more undesirable in an international enactment than in a national one. A national enactment is drafted against a background of one system of law and the draftsman can fairly confidently predict how his text will be understood by the courts, particularly if he uses words which have already acquired a patina of legal meaning. An international enactment, on the other hand, has no such background or context."

94 Ibid.

95 Ibid.

provides for narrow elements through which the question of frustration can be answered, unlike the latter's wider and more encompassing elements.[96] The elements that must be present and operative before Section 7 of the 1979 Sale of Goods Act can apply are, to wit: the goods to which the agreement relates must be specific goods, there must be an agreement to sell and not the actual sale, the goods must have perished, the risk must not have passed to the buyer, and the goods must have perished without any fault of the parties.[97] It is a fact that the above listed elements are not in tandem with both the CISG and the UNIDROIT principles. A quick overview of the provision of the CISG will show that art 79 of the CISG is radically different from the provision of Section 7 of the Sale of Goods Act 1979.[98]

1.4 Impossibility Perspective in Terminologies

By and large, the doctrine of *force majeure*, exemption and frustration will avail a party seeking to be excused from the consequences of damages (for arts. 79, 7.1.7) if they can show that the inhibiting event was unforeseeable, insurmountable, external and impossible to perform or be overcome.[99] Aditi Patanjali and a host of other writers use these doctrines interchangeably,[100] though making sure to draw the line whenever there is an obvious discrepancy among these impossibility doctrines.

Interestingly, these three concepts are all a product of the *clausula rebus sic stantibus* principle; this principle is an exception to the rule of mandatory performance of contractual obligations or what is widely referred to as the theory of sanctity of contract (*pacta sunt servanda*). The effect of the *clausula rebus sic stantibus* is to discharge contractual obligations because circumstances have changed since the conclusion of the contract so as to destroy a basic assumption which the parties

96 The Sale of Goods Act 1979 is considered to be a classic example of a codifying statute; that is, it draws on established judge-made common law principles and converts them into a more accessible statutory form. It is an improvement on the original but repealed Sale of Goods Act of 1893 as drafted by Sir Mackenzie Chalmers. Technicalities thrived during Chalmers' era, and this can be seen by the technically narrow way Section 7 is drafted.

97 A.G. Guest (ed.), *Benjamin's Sale of Goods* (Sweet & Maxwell, 6th edn, 2002) para 6–029, 285.

98 Paragraph (1) of art 79 of the CISG describes the circumstances when a party "is not liable" for a failure to perform any of his obligations. Paragraph (2) is an extension of the first paragraph and is concerned with the effect of non-performance by a third party whom the contracting party has engaged to perform some of his duties. Paragraph (3) regulates the period of the exemption, and paragraph (4) imposes a duty of notification on the party failing to perform. Paragraph (5) deals with the consequences of non-performance and the remedies available to the parties.

99 Babatunde Osadare, "*Force Majeure* and the Performance Excuse: A Review of the English Doctrine of Frustration and Art 2–615 of the Uniform Commercial Code" <https://iiste.org/Journals/index.php/JLPG/article/download/35571/36598> accessed 13 September 2025.

100 Sarah Howard Jenkins "Exemption for Non-performance: UCC, CISG, UNIDROIT Principles – A Comparative Assessment" (1998) 72 *Tulane Law Review* 2015–2030; She agreed that: "*Force majeure* under the Principles is a restatement of exemption under the Convention with some clarification of the remedial rights reserved."

had made when they entered into the contract.[101] Rapsomanikas[102] supporting the close links among impossibility doctrines concurred with the opinion that:

> Whether one's preference is directed toward the term 'frustration,' 'impossibility,' or 'changed circumstances,' the situation expressed by all these words is basically the same; in all legal traditions, it arises when unforeseen occurrences, subsequent to the date of the contract, render performance either legally or physically impossible, or excessively difficult, impracticable or expensive, or destroy the known utility which the stipulated performance had to either party.[103]

1.5 Structure of the Book

This book will not stop at only critically and comparatively evaluating the doctrine of exemption/*force majeure*/*frustration* under the CISG, UNIDROIT Principles, and English law respectively; but other similar provisions like arts 8.108 of the Principles of European Contract Law (PECL), art 3:104 of the Draft Common Frame of Reference (DCFR) and art 88 of the Common European Sales Law (CESL)[104] will also be alluded to as they are in consonance with the subject matter of this book. Franco Ferrari, while tracing the relationship between art 79 of the CISG and art 3:104 of the DCFR, writes that:

> Both the CISG and the DCFR exempt the debtor or the buyer from liability when some impediments occur. Thus there can be no doubt that art 111–3:104 DCFR (Excuse due to impediment) which governs the consequences

101 Treitel (n 46) para 2–045, 57–58.

102 Rapsomanikas (n 24) 551–605.

103 Hans Smit, "Frustration of Contract: A Comparative Attempt at Consolidation" (1958) 58 *Colum. L. Rev*, 287, 287.

104 Art 88 of the CESL 2011 provides thus:

1 A party's non-performance of an obligation is excused if it is due to an impediment beyond that party's control and if that party could not be expected to have taken the impediment into account at the time of the conclusion of the contract, or to have avoided or overcome the impediment or its consequences.
2 Where the impediment is only temporary the non-performance is excused for the period during which the impediment exists. However, if the delay amounts to a fundamental non-performance, the other party may treat it as such.
3 The party who is unable to perform has a duty to ensure that notice of the impediment and of its effect on the ability to perform reaches the other party without undue delay after the first party becomes, or could be expected to have become, aware of these circumstances. The other party is entitled to damages for any loss resulting from the breach of this duty.

when an event which is not the fault or responsibility of the debtor from performing the obligation is largely modelled on art 79 of the CISG.[105]

The basic principle of impossibility is a common factor among these laws; there are diverse approaches and perspectives in the different laws of how this doctrine operates, and it is within the scope of this book to explore those areas of discrepancies. All three of these doctrines are exceptions to the principle of strict contractual liability, according to which the obligor is responsible for any failure to bring about the promised result even after observance of due diligence.[106]

Against the foregoing background, the pattern of discussions in this research is analytically linked to one another; the table of contents will provide an organic run of ideas that are fashioned to bring to the fore the historical, critical, and comparative relevance of the title of this book. Chapter 1 lays the foundation for setting into motion the discourse of this book. It introduces the major concepts and doctrine which are the focus of this research and goes on to lay down the scope of the applications and interpretations of the doctrine of exemption/ *force majeure*/ frustration under the CISG, UNIDROIT Principles, and the English law. This chapter also connects the doctrine of frustration with the doctrine of *pacta sunt servanda* under the three laws of focus in this research.

Chapter 2 provides elaborate discussions of the elements or ingredients that constitute exemption/ *force majeure*/ frustration under the CISG, UNIDROIT Principles and the English law. This chapter sets the tune and tenor for further penetrating analysis of the book topic.

Chapter 3 follows suit with a detailed, comparative analysis of the relationship between *exemption/force majeure/frustration* and risk under the laws discussed in this research. What a court is doing when it applies a provision such as art 79 is determining which party ought to bear the risk of the occurrence that has given rise to the dispute.[107] The chapter further presents a critical evaluation of the importance of risk in a frustrated contract. It follows that whenever it can be shown that risk has passed to a party, or where the parties apparently contracted to undertake certain risks in a contract, then an impediment that falls within the contracted risk cannot be said to have frustrated the contract.

Chapter 4 goes on to draw similarities and differences between the doctrine of exemption/*force majeure*/frustration and the termination (avoidance) of contract.[108] Though these two concepts are methods of discharge of obligations in a contract,

105 Franco Ferrari (ed.), *The CISG and its Impact on National Legal Systems* (European Law Publishers, 2008) 402.

106 Jan Kleinheisterkamp, "Art 7.1.7" in *Commentary on the UNIDROIT Principles of International Commercial Contracts (PICC)*, ed. Stefan Vogenauer (Oxford, 2009) para 1, 766.

107 Edwin Patterson, "The Apportionment of Business Risks Through Legal Devices" (1924) 24 *Colum. L. Rev*, 335.

108 Barry Nicholas argues that the right to avoid the contract is useful, as we have seen, in enabling the buyer to bring the contract to an end where the non-performance by the seller is so extensive as to amount to fundamental breach. See Nicholas (n 64).

they lead to different legal implications. However, termination/avoidance is needed in managing the fallout of exemption/frustration/*force majeure*.

Chapter 5 explores the relationship between the doctrines of hardship and frustration/exemption/*force majeure* under the CISG, UNIDROIT Principles, and the English law. This is definitely a very important part of this book as these two doctrines have always confused the courts, practitioners and academics. They have been used interchangeably in denoting a situation where there is a radical change of the onus to perform a contract due to an unforeseen impediment. While CISG and English law fail to provide a detailed guideline or enactment for the doctrine of hardship, the UNIDROIT Principles do provide for hardship and can be used (national law can also serve this purpose by the rules of private international law) to the effect of filling the gap created by the absence of this doctrine in the former laws (English law and CISG).[109]

Chapter 6 oversees the incisive comparative appraisal of the relationship between the doctrine of frustration/exemption/*force majeure* and the doctrine of mistake. Chapter 7 explores the applicability of various contractual remedies to the doctrines of exemption/*force majeure* and frustration under the CISG, UNIDROIT Principles and English law.[110] For instance, the unexplained liberty given under art 28 CISG in respect of countries to have the option to refuse one of the remedies (specific performance) made available under art 79(5) is a great pointer that the doctrine of exemption will not be a success story at the global stage. National laws' sphere of interests will always compromise the uniformity mantra of the CISG. The chapter starts with a detailed evaluation of the link between the art 80 principle of shared liability and the doctrine of exemption. The chapter also provides vivid discussions on the interpretations of the remedy of damages, specific performance, price reduction, termination, restitution and the applications of the Law Reform (Frustrated Contracts) Act of 1943.

Chapter 8 concludes this research by recommending a model clause with the intention of making contributions to knowledge and literature in this area. This chapter will host the synchronised manifestations in the "Draft Model Frustration Clause" of all the recommendations for amendments of the doctrine of exemption/*force majeure*/frustration in the three legal instruments of discussion in this book.

109 This gap-filling proposal is very contentious and has divided both the opinions of scholars and courts, as can be seen in the subsequent chapters of this book.

110 Nicholas (n 67) held that "the system of remedies is ill-adapted to the situation dealt with in art 79. The remedies, of course, are simply the general remedies for the kind of non-performance which a common lawyer calls breach of contract, whereas in art 79 we are not dealing with breach. We are concerned with adjusting the rights of two innocent parties." See also G.E. Palmer, *The Law of Restitution* (Boston, 1978) vol. 1, 77–79.

1.6 Summary

This chapter, apart from giving the general synopsis of the expectations and outcome of this book, also goes a long way to lay the foundation for insightful discussions on the different issues that define the aims and objectives of this book. It also provokes discussions on the two important Latin maxims of "*pacta sunt servanda*" and "*rebus sic stantibus*" and how they lay the foundation for the doctrine of strict liability of contractual obligation and that of exemption due to impossibility. This is followed by a thorough analysis of the terminologies and doctrines used in this book thereby setting in motion the veritable mission of this research, which is to critically and comparatively analyse the doctrine of exemption/ *force majeure*/ frustration under the CISG, UNIDROIT Principles, and English law.[111] This chapter provides the introduction of the relationship between the doctrine of exemption/*force majeure*/frustration and other legal concepts like hardship, termination, risk, and legal remedies. The aim of this brief introduction is to prepare for more discerning discussions that feature these legal concepts in the subsequent chapters of this book. Finally, the chapter is wrapped up with a brief introduction of all other chapters featured in this book.

111 The analysis of the terminologies is very important in order to fine-tune the obvious and latent overlap in the use of the doctrines of *frustration/exemption/force majeure* as the main subject matter of focus in this book. These doctrines are not on all fours, but they have the common elements of unforeseeability and impossibility while interpreting their effect on the fortuitous turn out of impended events.

2 Elements of Exemption/*Force Majeure*/ Frustration

2.1 Elements of Exemption under the CISG

2.1.1 Due to an Impediment beyond His Control

Throughout the gamut of art 79 of the CISG, the word "impediment" is not defined, nor is any clue given as to the circumstances upon which an inference of what can be described as "impediment" or what is meant by "beyond his control" is given. It is disturbing that the interpretations of what the draughtsmen must have considered to be the meaning of this phrase cannot be found in any rule of law, but are chiefly found within the blurred ambit of rule of thumb, and this rule of thumb no doubt is very loyal and amenable to different national law backgrounds – thereby making a mockery of the uniformity efforts of the CISG.[1]

There is an effort, however, in chapter eight (Draft Model Frustration Clause) of this book to put a definite perspective into the interpretations of this and other phrases prevalent in the definition of frustration. This will be achieved by annexing a glossary or an interpretative section that could define these exemption elements. While criticising the loophole in the use of elastic words in art 79, Barry Nicholas was of the opinion that:

> Elastic words are obviously more undesirable in an international enactment than in a national one. A national enactment is drafted against a background of one system of law and the draftsman can fairly confidently predict how his text will be understood by the courts, particularly if he uses words which have already acquired a patina of legal meaning. An international enactment, on the other hand, has no such background or context. Or rather it has as many backgrounds as there are legal systems within which it may be applied. The objection to elastic words like 'due to an impediment' is therefore that

1 Nagy (n 53) ch. 1; the author writes thus, "Whatever 'impediment' was originally intended to mean, since the CISG entered into force, its ultimate meaning is the product of its application and interpretation by courts and arbitration tribunals. When defining 'impediment,' most jurisdictions started by determining if and how their national doctrines for exemption fit within the CISG's concept of impediment.'"

DOI: 10.4324/9781003667841-2

> they will be read in the context of each system's view of the limits within which an excuse of this kind should be admitted.[2]

In order for a party to succeed under art 79, they must satisfactorily prove that the failure to perform any of their obligations under the contract is; (i) "due to an impediment" otherwise known as the "impediment" test, (ii) the impediment is beyond his control, better known as the "control test."[3] According to Schwenzer and Fountoulakis, art 79(1) provides that whenever one of the contractual duties cannot be performed and that failure is "due to an impediment" which is beyond the defaulting party's control, that party is exempted from liability if the impediment is neither foreseeable nor could have been avoided or overcome.[4] However, if the parties are aware of the impediment at the time of the conclusion of the contract, the promisor's unqualified promise that they will be able to perform must, as a rule, be understood to be a guarantee.[5]

In trying to elucidate on the impediment test, a German court, while interpreting what impediment meant in the *Chinese Goods Case,* was of the opinion that "an impediment must be an unmanageable risk or a totally exceptional event, such as *force majeure*, economic impossibility or excessive onerousness."[6] It is also important to adumbrate on the point that over the years, the courts faced with the interpretations of the provision of art 79 of the CISG have tried to fashion out what may constitute excessive onerousness in order to justify an exemption under art 79. This effort has seen the controversial proposition that defective goods may constitute excessive onerousness in order to warrant the application of art 79 of the CISG; however, starting off with discussions on defective goods does not make other traditionally known exemption impediments less important. Stoll and Gruber were of the view and asserted that:

> A seller who does not itself manufacture the generic goods (i.e., the seller acts as "only a dealer or a commission agent" who procures the goods from a supplier for resale to its customer) should be exempted if he received the goods from a reliable supplier and the defect could not have been discovered

2 Barry Nicholas, "Impracticability and Impossibility in the U.N. Convention on Contracts for the International Sale of Goods" in Galston and Smit (eds) *International Sales: The United Nations Convention on Contracts for the International Sale of Goods* (Matthew Bender 1984) ch. 5, pages 5-1–5-24.

3 Larry A. DiMatteo and others, "The Interpretive Turn in International Sales Law: An Analysis of Fifteen Years of CISG Jurisprudence" (Winter 2004) 34 *North-Western Journal of International Law and Business* 299–440.

4 *International Sales Law* (Routledge-Cavendish 2007) 566.

5 Peter Schlechtriem and Ingeborg Schwenzer, *Commentary on the UN Convention on the International Sale of Goods* (2nd edn, Oxford University Press 2005) 813.

6 Chinese goods case, Schiedsgericht der Handelskammer Hamburg (Court of Arbitration of the Hamburg Chamber of Commerce), Partial Award (on the merits), 21 March 1996, CISG-online 187 <https://cisg-online.org/search-for-cases?caseId=6162> accessed 12 October 2025.

> using methods which could reasonably be expected of a reasonable person in the seller's position and was therefore unavoidable.[7]

The rationale for Stoll and Gruber's assertion is that in international trade, it is not always practicable for the seller to oversee the production or procurement of the goods which are the subject matter of the contract of sale. This is because most international trades depend on the use of suppliers who are neither the sellers nor the buyers' agents but mere independent contractors over whom the seller has little or no control and whose business relations are sometimes only built upon good faith. This proposition, however, has not received the imprimaturs of some leading American legal writers in the field of international sale of goods law. Barry Nicholas states that:

> I have just said that the word "impediment" is unavoidably vague, and yet paradoxically its choice was the result of much discussion in the Working Group, arising out of a widely shared desire to ensure that art 79 could not be used by a seller to escape his liability for defective performance and, in particular, defects of quality, by pleading that they were beyond his control and that he could not have been expected to take them into account. This possibility might arise if, for example, in the state of technical knowledge as it was when the contract was made, the defect could not have been detected.[8]

The above view echoed the earlier stance of Honnold, who was convinced that art 79 does not "reverse the rule" that the seller is responsible for the loss that occurred in the scenario where defective goods which he (the seller) has not been reasonably foreseen to be so (defective) are sold to the buyer. Honnold went on to say that "loss to the buyer is placed on the seller even when the seller is not at fault, as when a seller resells defective goods, obtained from a responsible supplier in sealed containers, which the seller has no reasonable opportunity to inspect."[9]

7 Harry Flechtner citing Stoll and Gruber in "Art 79 of the United Nations Convention on Contracts for the International Sale of Goods (CISG) as Rorschach Test": "The Homeward Trend and Exemption for Delivering Non-Conforming Goods" cited as [2007] <http://cisgw3.law.pace.edu/cisg/biblio/flechtner7.html>.

8 Nicholas (n 2).

9 Honnold (n 39) ch. 1, 472–495. The position of the critics that defective goods can come under art 79 of the CISG was pored over and avoided during the legislative history of the 1980 Vienna Conference which gave birth to art 79 and other articles of the CISG. At the 33rd meeting of the First committee, the summary of the records of the meeting as provided in paragraph 11 (eleven) reads that:

> It was necessary to appreciate the importance of the concept of "impediment" in paragraph 1 in order to appreciate the significance of the wording of paragraph 2. In ULIS (1964) exemption could be based on a "condition" over which the party had no control. In UNCITRAL it was felt that the language was open to too broad an interpretation and might apply where a seller supplied defective goods but could not be proved to have been at fault. To avoid that construction, it had been decided to replace "circumstance" by the concept of "impediment." That concept implied that the seller was not to be held free of responsibility for defects in the goods he supplied, even if he had not been at fault in regard to his own manufacturing processes. It was also understood that, even under Art 65(1)

Conversely, some civil law jurisdictions are ready to reconsider this strict and insensitive interpretation of art 79 of the CISG and are prepared to adapt the law to the reasons and peculiar circumstances of any given case. The German court was prepared to change its position and consider "defective goods" as an excessively onerous impediment demanding the benefit of the exemption under art 79 in the "Vine wax" case.[10]

Even so, the court in the case of *Christian Flippe v Douet Sport Collections S.a.r.l.*[11] applies the view that defective goods can constitute an impediment. The buyer, a promoter of a Judo club in Switzerland, bought some sweatsuits from the seller; there were later a dozen letters of complaint from the purchasers, relating to a significant shrinkage, in the range of 6 to 8 centimetres, of the goods after washing. It was held that:

> Seller finding itself in the position of a seller of a product whose manufacture and notably whose elaboration of the fabrics are beyond [seller]'s control, it is proper, in the absence of a showing of bad faith on seller's part, to allow seller the benefit of art 79 CISG.[12]

This case has summed up the basic conditions which must be present before a seller of non-conforming goods which they did not produce should be held to enjoy the exemption cover of art 79. If, contrary to the case above, the seller had a form of control in the production of the sweatsuit or had foreseen that the shrinkage would occur or had fallen short of the standards of good faith, then the benefit of the exemption in art 79 would not have been extended to him (seller).[13]

[became CISG Art 79(1)], there would be no "impediment" if a seller instead of doing the manufacturing himself, bought goods from a supplier and those goods proved defective.

See Legislative History of the United Nations Convention on Contracts for the International Sale of Goods (1980) Vienna Diplomatic Conference <https://cisg-online.org/Travaux-preparatoires> accessed 12 October 2025.

10 The above point was canvassed but denied application due to the peculiar facts of the matter in the Vine wax case, Oberlandesgericht Zweibrücken (Court of Appeal Zweibrücken), Germany, 31 March 1998 – 8 U 46/97, CISG-online 48 <https://cisg-online.org/search-for-cases?caseId=6449> accessed 24 September 2025.

The court held in the above case that: "In the given circumstances, the defect had not been beyond the seller's control; despite the ongoing business relationship, it was not reasonable for the seller simply to have relied on its supplier's product without tests, because it was a newly developed product."

This case is very important in the development of the notion of "impediment," the seller can be held to have reasonably foreseen the alleged impediment. He has the duty of care to act in good faith in seeing that his suppliers conform to the production demands of the contract of sale of goods.

11 Christian Flippe v Douet Sport Collections S.a.r.l., Commercial Court Besançon, France, 19 January 1998 – 97/009265, CISG-online 557 <https://cisg-online.org/search-for-cases?caseId=6521> accessed 12 September 2025.

12 Ibid.

13 Similarly, the Supreme Court panel of the Federal Republic of Germany has laid down the rule that art 79 CISG also applies to the delivery of goods that do not meet the requirements of the contract. In the Milk Powder case, the buyer alleged that the rancid taste, noticed by the ultimate buyers,

More so, there are other categories of "impediments" that can fall within the purview of art 79. It has been held that a government order, directives, legislation banning the importation or exportation of goods, act of war or natural disasters, and industrial actions like strikes can well be considered as an "impediment" that can bring about exemptions under art 79 of the CISG. On the other hand, insolvency may not be regarded as an impediment under art 79(1) CISG; this is because the buyer will always guarantee his payment obligation, and this risk hardly shifts.[14] Similarly, the Serbian Supreme Court, in interpreting the scope of "impediment" under art 79 of the CISG, rejected a buyer's claim for exemption from liability where the buyer failed to exercise the level of care required in international commercial transactions.[15] In that case, the buyer and seller had an established practice of communicating via email. After delivery of the goods, the buyer was to pay the purchase price in three instalments. The first two payments were successfully made to the seller's designated account. However, before the third payment, the buyer received an email, purportedly from the seller, directing payment to a different account. The buyer complied, but it was later discovered that the seller's email account had been hacked, and the new account was fraudulent. The buyer argued that the hacking incident constituted an impediment beyond its control, especially since email had been their usual mode of communication and it could not have reasonably foreseen such a cyber attack. The Supreme Court rejected this argument, holding that the buyer failed to exercise the level of care required in international commercial transactions, particularly when dealing with electronically transmitted instructions. The Court noted that the fraudulent email deviated from the parties' established business practice in at least two respects: it was sent outside of regular business hours (at 20:11), and it introduced payment instructions that had never been used before, namely, payment to a new foreign account.[16] Thus, it appears that where an impediment could have been avoided

---

was caused by an infestation of the powdered milk by an organic enzyme called lipase that already existed at the time of the transfer of the risk as a result of the faulty processing of the milk. After some dogged fighting throughout the hierarchy of German courts, the Supreme Court held that:

> Seller can only be freed from its obligation to pay damages for its failure to comply with the contract if it can prove that any lipase infestation of the delivered milk would not have been detectable, even upon the careful use of the necessary methods of analysis before any further processing, and that a possible infestation in the manufacture of the powdered milk was based on grounds that were outside of its sphere of influence … As long as the cause of the lipase infestation before the transfer of the risk cannot be determined, the factual testimony of [seller 1] as taken into account by the appeal to this Court, lacks the necessary cumulative exonerative proof. See, the Milk Powder case Bundesgerichtshof (German Supreme Court), Germany, 9 January 2002 – VIII ZR 304/00, CISG-online 651 <https://cisg-online.org/search-for-cases?caseId=6594> accessed 28 September 2025.

14 Joseph M. Lookofsky, *Understanding the CISG* (Kluwer Law International, 3rd edn, 2008) para 6.32, 154

15 [...] v Luka Food d.o.o, Vrhovni kasacioni sud (Serbian Supreme Court), Serbia, 22 April 2021 – 135/2021, CISG-online 6859 <https://cisg-online.org/search-for-cases?caseId=14773> accessed 10 October 2025.

16 Ibid.

through reasonable scrutiny and diligence, failure to exercise such caution would disqualify a party from claiming exemption under art 79 CISG.

It is also important to note that an impediment under art 79 CISG includes that which existed before the conclusion of the contract[17] which is unforeseeable and unknown to the parties and whose consequences they cannot control or overcome.[18]

In the Ukrainian *Coal Case 1*,[19] the Court held that the debtor who is not able to fulfil his obligation because of *force majeure* is obliged to notify immediately the other party in accordance with clause 8 of the contract. The Governmental prohibition for coal export and the Decrees of the Ukraine Government for export restrictions of coal on which the [buyer] relies in his letter of 22 February 1996 do not correspond either with the requirements of the CISG for the existence of *force majeure* nor with the clauses of the contract. They occurred before the conclusion of the contract.[20] From the ratio of the above decision, it can be deduced that if the impediment which was Ukraine Government restriction of exportation of coal had happened after the conclusion of the contract, and other conditions for the application of art 79 had been present, then the exemption under art 79 would have prevailed.

Act of war can also constitute an impediment that can frustrate the contract.[21] In *Hilaturas Miel S.L. v Republic of Iraq*[22] because hostilities prevented inspection and acceptance of the goods per the terms of the contract while the letter of credit was in effect, performance under the contract was impossible. Iraq, as the buyer, does not bear a legal duty to compensate Hilaturas for goods that were never delivered due to unforeseen events outside the control of the parties. Because the war precluded the performance of the contract prior to its expiration by the termination of the letter of credit, summary judgment dismissing the contract claim as frustrated is appropriate.

17 Christopher Brunner, *Force Majeure and Hardship under General Contract Principles: Exemption for Non-Performance in International Arbitration* (Wolters Kluwer 2009) 232.

18 Fritz Enderlein & Dietrich Maskow, “International Sales Law,” *Oceana* (1992), p. 323; See also Peter Schlechtriem, *Uniform Sales Law* (Manz: Vienna 1986) 33. He was of the view that “if it was reasonable not to have expected such an impediment to performance, art 79 applies -- even in the face of a domestic validity law which terms such contracts invalid on the grounds of mistake.” Though Tallon and Lee Wanki disagreed with the view that an impediment that occurred before the conclusion of the contract can be categorised under art 79, this is because they believe that domestic validity laws on such matters override the Convention. See Denis Tallon, Bianca-Bonell Commentary, pp. 577–578 and Wanki W. Lee, “Exemptions of Liability Under the 1980 United Nations Convention” (1990) 8 *Dickinson J. Int’l L.* 386–387.

19 Ukrainian Coal Case 1, Arbitration Court at the Bulgarian Chamber of Commerce and Industry, Bulgaria, 24 April 1996 – Arbitration Case 56/1995, CISG-online 435 <https://cisg-online.org/search-for-cases?caseId=6405> accessed 28 September 2025.

20 Ibid.

21 Robin Burnett and Vivienne Bath, *Law of International Business in Australasia* (The Federation Press, 2009) 44.

22 Hilaturas Miel, S.L. v Republic of Iraq, US District Court for the Southern District of New York, USA, 20 August 2008 – 06 Civ 12, CISG-online 1777 <https://cisg-online.org/search-for-cases?caseId=7695> accessed 28 September 2025.

As can be seen in the cases cited above, it does not just take an impediment to make an exempting factor; the impediment must be correlative to the control test.[23] This means that the party must go the extra mile to show that they has no control over the so-called impediment, either by showing a lack of foreseeability of the impediment or by proving that the impediment is one that is absolutely and demonstrably independent of their wish.[24] It will be politic to add at this juncture that ignorance or indolence, no matter how well cached, will be fatal to the control test, so is also evidence of bad faith.

One of the important examples of the control test was enunciated in the *Art Books case*.[25] The main issue that arose for determination is whether or not the seller can be exempted under art 79 (2) for the delay caused by the first carrier they engaged to deliver the goods to the buyer. The court held that by applying art 31 of the CISG that once the seller handed the goods over to the first carrier for delivery to the buyer; he had fulfilled their obligation and could be exempted under art 79(2) of the CISG. This is because the control test will not require the seller to influence the mode or efficiency of delivery of the goods by the first carrier; if only it can be shown that the goods get to the first carrier in time, then whatever impediment that keeps the goods from getting to the buyer is beyond the control of the seller.[26] In a nutshell, Schlechtriem and Schwenzer interpreted the phrase "beyond control" to imply:

> Sphere of control within which it is objectively possible for, and can be expected of the promisor to secure the trouble-free passage of the measures necessary to prepare and perform the contract by adopting measures of organization and appropriate control.[27]

Thus, the promisor is not exempted by even unforeseen illness, death, or arrest of himself or any of his key employees; this is because, in accordance with the normal trade understanding, the risks of such personal impediments to performance are borne by the promisor (defaulting party).[28] Correlative to this seller's risk is the buyer's utility risk; it has been pontificated that the seller's procurement risk mirrors the buyer's utility risk once the seller can render performance, and then the buyer will be foreclosed from rejecting performance on the grounds of an unexpected ruinous economic situation. The buyer cannot refuse the goods on the

23 Iryna Dikovska, "War, Sanctions and Exemption from Liability under Contracts Falling within the Scope of the CISG" (2024) 105 *Studia Iuridica* 7.

24 Ann Morales Olazábal and others, "Global Sales Law: An Analysis of Recent CISG Precedents in US Courts 2004-2012" (2011) 67 *Bus. Law.* 1351.

25 Art books case, Handelsgericht des Kantons Zürich (Commercial Court Canton Zurich), Switzerland, 10 February 1999 – HG 970238.1, CISG-online 488 <https://cisg-online.org/search-for-cases?caseId=6456> accessed 28 September 2025.

26 Manish Choudhary, "Transfer of Risk and Liability of Carrier in International Sales: A Comparative Analysis" (2023) 5(1) *Indian JL & Legal Rsch.* 1.

27 Schlechtriem and Ingeborg (n 5) 814.

28 Ibid.

ground that the purpose for which the goods were intended has ceased to exist or because they has alternative products available in the market.[29]

Industrial actions like strikes can also constitute an impediment under art 79(1) CISG. It has been held that strikes that are within the internal confrontational circles of a factory cannot be regarded as an impediment since they can be foreseeable or controlled, but when a strike falls within the external powers of the labour union or is based on causes often found in the enterprise[30] then it can be regarded as an impediment.

2.1.2 Could Not Reasonably Be Expected to Take the Impediment into Account

This is one of the elements that must be present before the exempting prerogatives of art 79 can be invoked. It revolves around the notion of "foreseeability." Expectations and foresight are very essential in any commercial relationships; parties must have their reasonable expectations, the non-realisation of which can possibly lead to the affected party seeking a cause of action under the fundamental breach provision of art 25. Schwenzer and Fountoulakis, while discussing this element, posit that "the contract terms, applicable practices and trade usages, as well as all relevant circumstances, must be considered in order to determine whether the defaulting party should have contemplated the existence or occurrence of the impediment."[31]

In the *Euro Diesel case*,[32] the tribunal noted that the seller's loss, comprising penalties paid to its supplier (for the purposes of fulfilling the buyer's order) was a loss foreseeable to the buyer since, according to the tribunal, agreeing to penalties in such a transaction was a common practice in the type of transactions which the buyer, as a professional trader, could have foreseen at the time of conclusion of the contract.

The fact remains that parties to a contract of sale of goods are expected to take all the necessary measures in the evaluation of possible risks and impediments that may stand in their way of the performance of the contract. Failure to take all the possible impediments into account may result in non-application of art 79. For example, goods which were unique and which were the subject of the contract may have already perished at the time of the conclusion of the contract. However, the seller would not be exempted from liability under this article if they reasonably could have been expected to take the destruction of the goods into account at the time of the conclusion of the contract. Therefore, in order to be exempted from

29 Ibid., 816.

30 Enderlein and Maskow (n 18).

31 Ingerborg Schwenzer and Christiana Fountoulakis, *International Sales Law* (Routledge–Cavendish 2007) 567.

32 Euro Diesel case [Serbia 15 June 2010] (Foreign Trade Court attached to the Serbian Chamber of Commerce) <http://cisgw3.law.pace.edu/cases/100615sb.html> accessed 15 September 2025.

liability, the seller must not have known of their prior destruction and must have been reasonable in not expecting their destruction.

Furthermore, it is also important to note that there are some impediments which are beyond the parties' reasonable evaluation or even intuition. These are fortuitous events that catch parties unaware and reverse the direction of the contract of sale of goods. Such happenings can comfortably be associated with art 79, and the exemption remedy provided therein can be invoked. A veritable application of this element can be seen in the *Metallic Sodium case.*[33] It was held that a buyer's claim of exemption based on regulations suspending payment of foreign debts would be denied because, in this case, the regulations were in existence (and thus should have been taken into account) at the time of the conclusion of the contract.[34] Finally, on this element, the examination of the *Steel Bars case I*[35] will be very instructive. Here, the seller refused to deliver additional goods on the contract price due to an increase in the price. The tribunal held that the seller could be relieved of the obligation to deliver the goods at the contract price only if the contract contained a price adjustment clause or in case of frustration of the contract, which was not the case here, since the increase in the market price was, in fact, not sudden, substantial or unforeseeable.

It follows from the plethora of cases cited above that a party who wants to rely on the element that they "could not reasonably be expected to take the impediment into account" must demonstrate how impossible it would have been for a reasonable person in the circumstances to have anticipated the impediment that torpedoed the contract of sale of goods and thus renders performance impossible and not just cumbersome.[36] The courts, on their part, are very careful not to relax the strict rule of foreseeability and be willing to preserve the business efficacy of the contract of

33 Metallic sodium case, Международный коммерческий арбитражный суд при Торгово–промышленной палате Российской Федерации (Tribunal of International Commercial Arbitration at the Russian Federation Chamber of Commerce and Industry (MKAC), Arbitration, 16 March 1995 – 155/1994), CISG-online 205 <https://cisg-online.org/search-for-cases?caseId=6179> accessed 12 October 2025.

34 Failure to open letter of credit and penalty clause case, ICC International Court of Arbitration, 1992 – 7197, CISG-online 36 <https://cisg-online.org/search-for-cases?caseId=6017> accessed 29 September 2025.

35 Steel Bars case 1 ICC International Court of Arbitration, 26 August 1989 – 6281 (Final Award), CISG-online 8 <https://cisg-online.org/search-for-cases?caseId=5990> accessed 29 September 2025.

36 Tomato Concentrate Case, Oberlandesgericht Hamburg (Court of Appeal Hamburg), Germany, 4 July 1997 – 1 U 143/95, CISG-online 1299 <https://cisg-online.org/search-for-cases?caseId=7222> accessed 19 September 2025. In this case, the seller was not exempted from liability under art 79, even though heavy rainfall had reduced the production of tomatoes. The French seller claimed "*force majeure*;" the crop of tomatoes was not entirely destroyed, and the supply was not exhausted; thus, performance was still possible, and heavy rainfall is always foreseeable among farmers.

sale of goods by not granting exemptions based on flimsy proof of this element; the unforeseen event must also be exceptional.[37]

The reason for this stringent position of the court, according to Perillo, is that:

> It is difficult to believe that judges in reviewing the "factual" question of foreseeability can refrain from taking into account the larger consequences of a finding of foreseeability. If, in one case, American entry into the Second World War had been declared to be unforeseeable, how many thousands, or tens of thousands of contracts would have to be dissolved because of impossibility or frustration? How many shipping and sales contracts would have been thwarted by the Suez closings? How broadly would international trade be disrupted and how much uncertainty would be injected into domestic and international trade?[38]

Thus, where there is a doubt about whether a party has done enough to take into account the impediment that affects the performance of the contract, the court will decide in favour of preserving the subsistence of the contract.[39]

2.1.3 Could Not Reasonably Be Expected to Have Avoided or Overcome It or Its Consequences

This is akin to the element discussed directly above; the only difference is that while the element of "could not reasonably be expected to take the impediment into account" is pre-"impediment" the latter is post-"impediment." This simply means that the party in the former is expected to take into account all the areas of risk and possible impediments before the conclusion of the contract of sale of goods, while in the latter, the impediment might have happened, and what is being considered here is how diligent the party is in trying to avoid or overcome the consequences of the impediment.

This element places emphasis on the consequences of the impediment rather than the impediment itself,[40] the unforeseeable impediment exempts the non-performing

37 Peter Mazzacano, "The Treatment of CISG art 79 in German Courts: Halting the Homeward Trend" (2013) Comparative Research in Law & Political Economy, Research Paper No. 7.

38 Perillo (n 35) ch. 1.

39 Chengwei Liu, *Perspectives from the CISG, UNIDROIT Principles, PECL and Case Law* (2nd edn, Case annotated update April 2005) <https://www.academia.edu/37883872/Remedies_for_Non_performance_Perspectives_from_CISG_UNIDROIT_Principles_and_PECL> accessed 22 September 2025; the writer argues that:

"It is consistent with the basic idea that if the event were foreseeable, the defaulting party should, in the absence of any contrary provision in the contract, be considered as having assumed the risk of its realisation. For instance, if the refusal of a licence were foreseeable at the time of the conclusion of the contract, it may thus be expected that the party in charge of obtaining the licence should have arranged the insertion of a clause relating to the consequences of refusal. Otherwise, in such cases, one may say that it was at fault in not having foreseen it."

40 Schwenzer and others (n 43) ch. 1, para 45.39, 658.

party only if they can prove that they could neither avoid the impediment[41] nor, by taking reasonable steps, overcome its consequences.[42] Tallon was of the opinion that:

> To avoid means taking all the necessary steps to prevent the occurrence of the impediment while to overcome means to take the necessary steps to preclude the consequences of the impediment. It is closely associated with the condition of the external character of the impeding event. The attention should be focused on the behaviour of the defaulting party.[43]

Tallon's view echoes the Secretariat Comment on this element, which provides that:

> Even if the non-performing party can prove that he could not reasonably have been expected to take the impediment into account at the time of the conclusion of the contract, he must also prove that he could neither have avoided the impediment nor overcome it nor avoided or overcome the consequences of the impediment. This rule reflects the policy that a party who is under an obligation to act must do all in his power to carry out his obligation and may not await events which might later justify his non-performance. This rule also indicates that a party may be required to perform by providing what is in all the circumstances of the transaction, a commercially reasonable substitute for the performance which was required under the contract.[44]

41 Niklas Lindström "Changed Circumstances and Hardship in the International Sale of Goods" (2006/1) *Nordic Journal of Commercial Law*; the author writes that: "Even if all elements discussed above are fulfilled, an exemption under Art 79 still requires that the breaching party could not have avoided or overcome the impediment or its consequences. Hence, a party is required to take active appropriate measures in order to avoid the impediment or the consequences of the impediment."

42 Dionysios P. Flambouras in "The Doctrines of Impossibility of Performance and clausula rebus sic stantibus in the 1980 Vienna Convention on Contracts for the International Sale of Goods and the Principles of European Contract Law: A Comparative Analysis" (Autumn 2001) 13 *Pace International Law Review* 267. More so, Schlechtriem and Ingeborg (n 5) argue that: "Even an impediment, which the promisor could not have taken into account when concluding the contract does not exempt him, if overcoming the impediment is both possible and reasonable to him. A party who stands aloof and watches a preventable impediment destroy the subject matter of a contract of sale of goods or makes performance of the contract impossible cannot be heard to plead that the situation is such that they cannot be expected to reasonably avoid even though the impediment is as a result of no fault of his."

43 Denis Tallon, in Bianca-Bonell Commentary on the International Sales Law, Giuffrè: Milan (1987) 572–595; it has also been held that "With respect to the possibility of avoiding or overcoming an impediment, case law applies a strict standard, also a party encountering the impediment could incur considerable extra costs or accept a bargaining loss in order to overcome it" see Ingeborg Schwenzer and others (n 43) 584.

44 Secretariat Commentary, CISG-online <https://cisg-online.org/Travaux-preparatoires/1979-secretariat-commentary> accessed 2 September 2025.

It is not always easy to decipher what is expected of a party in order to prevent an impediment or overcome its consequences. However, Schlechtriem,[45] gave a clue on this when he wrote that:

> [T]he terms of the contract will often describe the extent to which the obligor is expected to prevent impediments to performance which lie outside his own area of control. In the absence of express terms, the parties' promises to perform are to be interpreted on the basis of art 8. The standard, as in art 74(1) of ULIS, is based on the expectations and intentions of reasonable parties.[46]

From the opinion expressed above, the writer is trying to place the task of understanding the requirement imposed upon the parties in preventing or overcoming the impediment on the terms of the contract. A perusal of the contractual terms can help in ascertaining if, actually, a party has done what they is supposed to do to prevent an impediment and would also reasonably determine the question of whether or not the impediment is beyond his control.

Art 79 is one of the *sui generis* provisions, and its applicability can be compartmentalised into the no-fault rule. Parties become covered or uncovered by the provisions of art 79 not because of their fault, but because, on pure rational analysis, the impediment that frustrated the contract cannot be said to have been foreseen or its consequences reasonably overcome or avoided. This is similar to strict liability; in fact, it has been suggested that "with respect to the possibility to avoid or overcome an impediment, case law applies a strict standard." [47] This strict posture is evident in the scenario discussed above and goes a long way to drive home the message that a party must strictly satisfy this element before it can be construed in his favour. It has been argued that a party is still liable if a breach of contract is a concurrent cause of the failure to perform.[48]

45 Schlechtriem (n 18).

46 Ibid.; Peter Schlechtriem goes on to opine that:

> "For example, whether a party supplying goods has assumed the risk of fluctuating markets or the risk of war must, in the end, be decided with reference to the actual case and the particular contract. Though the circumstances permitting exemption cannot generally be equated simply with '*force majeure*,' efforts were made to define them narrowly. On the other hand, it is irrelevant whether the impediment existed before the conclusion of the contract – the 'pre-existing impossibility' or 'pre-existing inability' of German law – or whether it did not arise until later."

47 Schwenzer and Fountoulakis, (n 31) 567.

48 Ibid.; this can be explained further by the doctrine of proximate cause. If the action of the party is the proximate cause of the loss, then mere acting upon the proximate cause by any other unforeseen exigencies will not operate to shift responsibility. The doctrine of proximate cause was laid down in the case of Leyland Shipping v Norwich Union [1918] AC 350; in this case, the insured ship was torpedoed. She was taken by tugs to the outer harbour to be docked. She then sprang a leak after knocking against the quay. Fearing a gale, she was then ordered to a berth where she moored. Her bulkheads gave way and sank. The House of Lords held the ship was in imminent risk of sinking from the moment she was injured by the torpedo attack.

2.1.4 Notice under Art 79 of the CISG

The requirement of giving notice under the CISG is taken very seriously whenever the question of liability for a breach or other sundry matters comes up for determination. Art 79(4) provides that:

> The party who fails to perform must give notice to the other party of the impediment and its effect on his ability to perform. If the notice is not received by the other party within a reasonable time after the party who fails to perform knew or ought to have known of the impediment, he is liable for damages resulting from such non-receipt.

Tallon described this rule of notice as probably implied in the principle of good faith. It is in any event in harmony with international practice and is often the subject of a particular clause in the parties' agreement. The duty to notify exists only when the occurrence of the impediment is certain, not when it may still be avoided (although it may be difficult to determine what is and what is not avoidable). The defaulting party must notify the other party of the impediment and its probable consequences, i.e., they must indicate whether the non-performance is partial or total, temporary or definitive.[49] It is evident from the whole provision of the CISG that parties should not be taken by surprise and should always be informed of the situation that may have the tendency to affect their honest expectations in the contract. Therefore, the requirement that the notice be received (to take effect) represents a reversal of the general CISG transmission-risk rule.[50]

The above also underscores the role communication plays in the relationship of parties in the contract of sale; information must be passed on without delay so as to alert the affected party to the possibility of knowing how best to protect his contractual interest. However, there is confusion over whether or not art 79(4) creates a rule of damages, or whether it is an exception to the provision that forecloses damages in art 79(5) CISG.

It has been argued that if the notice has not been given or received within a reasonable time, the defaulting party is liable for damages. It should be noted that the damages for which the latter is liable are only those which result from the failure to give notice as opposed to those which follow from the non-performance of the contract.[51] The former will, in effect, often constitute an additional charge for the defaulting party, as the other party will have been unable to take the steps necessary

49 Tallon (n 41) ch. 1.

50 Joseph Lookofsky, Art 79 Liability Exemptions for Failure to Perform in "The 1980 United Nations Convention on Contracts for the International Sale of Goods" Published in J. Herbots editor / R. Blanpain general editor, International Encyclopaedia of Laws – Contracts, Suppl. 29 (December 2000) 1–192.

51 Joern Rimke "*Force majeure* and hardship: Application in international trade practice with specific regard to the CISG and the UNIDROIT Principles of International Commercial Contracts" (1999–2000) Pace Review of the Convention on Contracts for the International Sale of Goods, Kluwer 197–243.

to alleviate the consequences of non-performance.[52] This argument found basis in the provision of the article itself, which ends with the sentence, "he is liable for damages resulting from such non-receipt." This sentence suggests that there is a dichotomy between the damages suffered as a result of just non-receipt of the notice by a party and the damages suffered as a whole for non-performance of the contract due to an impediment, and the party who fails to give the notice should only be liable for the former. The present author is of the view that art 79(4) is a likely exception to the provision of art 79(5) which permits every other remedy except the remedy of damages.

It does appear that the rule espoused in this art 79(4) is to the effect that if a party who is unable to render performance is basing his inability on the exempting provision of art 79, then they need to notify the other party of the existence of the impediment within a reasonable time and of their inability to render performance as expected in the contract. Failure to do so will not only give the other party the right to invoke their other rights under the contract as envisaged under art 79(5) but will equally lift the ban on the parties" right to claim damages for the non-receipt of notice.[53] In any case, failure to give notice in a timely and reasonable manner be seen as being inconsistent with principles of reasonableness and good faith. Thus, where a lessee failed to give notice within a month after the alleged impediment arose, their claim of the extraordinary and unforeseeable nature of the event was discountenanced and he was held liable for noncompliance with contractual notification duties.[54]

2.1.5 Exemption and Burden of Proof under Art 79 of the CISG

It has been argued that since the CISG does not provide for procedural laws[55] thus the consideration of the burden of proof should be left in the province of the national laws.[56] For instance, the case of *Maaden v Thyssen*,[57] was decided in

52 Ibid.

53 It can possibly be argued on the other hand that the view expressed by Tallon (n 18) that "damages for which the latter is liable are only those which result from the failure to give notice as opposed to those which follow from the non-performance of the contract will be muddling up the issue of damages since it is not possible always to differentiate between damages arising from failure to give notice and damages arising from impossibility of performance."

54 See generally, China International Economic and Trade Arbitration Commission [CIETAC], 4 February 2002 (CISG/2002/17) (ruling that a buyer's failure to provide timely notice of an impediment under Article 79(4) precluded their exemption from liability and rendered them liable for resulting damages).

55 Kaptransstroy v TechnoSpecStroy, Eighth Arbitrazh Appellate Court, Russian Federation, A70-17666/2017, 12 September 2018, UNILEX <https://www.unilex.info/principles/case/2499> accessed 12 October 2025.

56 Warren Khoo, "Art 2" [1987] <http://www.cisg.law.pace.edu/cisg/biblio/khoo-bb2.html>.

57 Maaden General Foreign Trade Organisation for Metal & Building Materials v Thyssen Stahlunion GmbH, ICC International Court of Arbitration, 26 March 1993 – 6653/ES/FMS, CISG-online 71 <https://cisg-online.org/search-for-cases?caseId=6051> accessed 3 September 2025.

favour of national law having the final say on who bears the burden of proof since the answer to such a question cannot be found within the provisions of the CISG. This decision, with due respect, is reached *per incuriam* without the benefit of holistic consideration of the principles upon which the CISG foundation is built.

The borderline between substantive law and the procedure of proving it cannot be properly partitioned. It is in line with common sense and practice that the rules of procedure are sometimes embedded in substantive law, thereby providing the necessary guidance required in pursuing a particular cause of action. This view was buttressed by Franco Ferrari when he argues in his "commentary on burden of proof under the CISG"[58] that:

> [T]he prevailing view appears to be that the issue of buden of proof is a matter governed, at least implicitly, by the CISG. This view has been justified on the grounds that the CISG itself provides at least one rule on the burden of proof, namely the one to be found in art 79, which is why it cannot be asserted that the CISG does not govern the issue at hand. Further, the issue of burden of proof is so closely linked to the substantive law that a rule on its allocation has to necessarily be derived from the CISG. Considering this view, the issue of burden of proof is a matter governed, albeit not expressly, by the CISG.

The general principle of law popular among both civil and common law jurisdictions is that "anyone who asserts must prove." The party who invokes *force majeure* in order to be released from its obligations under a contract must prove the occurrence of the *force majeure* event of the kind specified in the clause and that it has had the effect stated in the clause on his ability to perform the contract.[59] This trite principle of law translates to the effect that any person who seeks to derive a benefit or exemption from a particular provision of the substantive law must prove that his cause is such that it is on all fours with the elements or the requirements of such provision. This is why the first sentence of art 79 uses the phrase "if he proves." This phrase leaves no doubt of who owes the duty to prove the existence of an exemption in the contract of sale of goods.

The Furniture case III[60] is apt when explaining the finer points of this well-received principle of procedural law in the instant case. The court held that it was implicit in the Convention that the buyer had to prove the existence of defects and that it gave notice of lack of conformity within a reasonable time. It will be proper to point out that in certain situations, the court, while applying the CISG, will allocate the cost of the trial to the party who owes the burden of proof. This

58 Franco Ferrari "Burden of Proof under the CISG" [2000–2001] Pace Review of the Convention on Contracts for the International Sale of Goods (CISG), Kluwer Law International (2000–2001) 1–8.

59 Ibid.

60 Furniture case (III), Handelsgericht des Kantons Zürich (Commercial Court Canton Zurich) Switzerland, 09 September 1993 – HG 930 138.U/HG 93, CISG-online 79 <"https://cisg-online.org/search-for-cases?caseId=6059" https://cisg-online.org/search-for-cases?caseId=6059>.

scenario came up for consideration in *Agristo N.V. v Macces Agri B.V.*[61] where the court held that the monetary instalment should be paid to the expert requested by the parties in order to help in the determination of their matter has to be paid by the seller, since it bears the burden of proof for the facts and circumstances which could constitute an impediment beyond control for the seller.

Under art 79, the apportionment of the burden of proof is explicitly stated in the gamut of the provision.[62] It is the party who seeks exemption from the performance of his obligations under the contract of sale of goods that would be required to prove his position and support his case with all the compulsory elements that must be present and operative before the remedy of exemption can be set into motion. This view is plausible because those facts that are exclusively in a party's sphere of responsibility and which therefore are, at least theoretically, better known to that party have to be proven by that party, since it is that party who exercises control over that sphere.[63]

2.1.6 Third Person and Exemption under the CISG

The above has been mentioned briefly during the discussion of the *Art Book* case,[64] it follows from the provision of art 79 of the CISG that the delegating party remains liable for the performance of the contract even though it has been delegated to a third party. This is different from a novation contract, as it does impose the duty of invoking the protection provided under art 79(1) of the CISG, and also that the third party could also have enjoyed the same protection if they had been the contracting party.[65]

The delegating party from the provision of art 79(2) is not allowed succour by mere reason of his delegation, and they are expected to find an alternative mode of performance in case the third party fails.[66] A party cannot be excused under art 79 by the fact that they have been diligent in choosing, instructing and controlling a third

61 District Court Maastricht Netherlands, 09 July 2008 – 120428 / HA ZA 07–550, CISG-online 1748 <"https://cisg-online.org/search-for-cases?caseId=7666" https://cisg-online.org/search-for-cases?caseId=7666> accessed 3 September 2025.

62 Rheinland Versicherungen v Atlarex s.r.l. Tribunale di Vigevano (District Court Vigevano) Italy, 12 July 2000 – 405, CISG-online 493 <https://cisg-online.org/search-for-cases?caseId=6461> accessed 20 September 2025. It was held in this case that the plaintiff failed to produce the actual letter by which it claimed to have given timely notice to the seller of the non-conformity of the goods to the defendant under art 39(1) CISG; the court held that the plaintiff buyer failed to meet its burden of proof under the procedural law of Italy as well as under the CISG.

63 Ferrari (n 58).

64 Art Book Case, Handelsgericht des Kantons Zürich (Commercial Court Canton Zurich), Switzerland, 10 February 1999 – HG 970238.1, CISG-online 488 <https://cisg-online.org/search-for-cases?caseId=6456> accessed 12 October 2025.

65 Michael Bridge, *The International Sale of Goods* (Oxford, 3rd edn) para 12.70, p. 617–618.

66 Ibid.

party to perform a contract which accords him (the delegating party) some benefit. This is because liability under the CISG is not based on fault or lack of diligence.[67]

2.2 Elements of Frustration under the UNIDROIT Principles

Under art 7.1.7 of the UNIDROIT Principles, there are similar provisions and interpretations to what is obtainable under art 79 of the CISG.[68] This is not a surprise, since it merely cemented the view that the UNIDROIT Principles are not a rival of the CISG but rather an ally, apart from art 79(2) of the CISG, which provides for the liability or otherwise of a third person under the exemption doctrine, which has no counterpart under the UNIDROIT Principles; then all other provisions are similar in both instruments, except that the UNIDROIT Principles specifically exclude specific performance in applying as a remedy under the art 7.1.7 provision. Joern Rimke, while pontificating on the relationship between the two legal instruments, writes that:

> The UNIDROIT Principles may further serve as instruments for the interpretation and filling the gap of international uniform law. The main idea is to preclude an easy resort to the domestic law indicated by the conflict of laws rule by the forum. The principles provide guidelines for an "autonomous" interpretation – an interpretation based upon the uniform law's international character. The judge or arbitrator is offered a rule that is likely to be more suitable to an international commercial contract than a domestic rule of contract law. Supplementing an international instrument with the UNIDROIT Principles has the additional advantage of enhancing consistency and fairness in the adjudication of international commercial disputes.[69]

It follows then that the elements that must be operative in order to make the exemption of *force majeure* applicable are the same in both laws. The party who claims *force majeure* under art 7.1.7 must go on to prove that there is an impediment beyond his control, that they could not reasonably be expected to have taken the impediment into account at the time of the conclusion of the contract, and that they are not reasonably able to have avoided or overcome it or its consequences; all these are in *pari materia* with the elements discussed under art 79 of the *CISG*.

67 Atamer in Stefan Kroll and others (eds) (n 41) ch. 1, para 60, 1079.

68 Both under the CISG and the UNIDROIT principles, the doctrine of *force majeure*/exemption shares a similar outlook and serves the same purpose. There is almost verbatim repetition of the provision of art 79 of the CISG save for some syntactic arrangement and the total absence of a corresponding art 79(2) counterpart under art 7.1.7 of the UNIDROIT Principles.

69 Rimke (n 51).

2.3 Elements of Frustration under English Common Law

The doctrine of frustration under the common law has had a trajectory progression. What started as the doctrine of absolute obligations of contractual duties[70] has now been ameliorated to incorporate the doctrine that exonerates a party whose performance of the contract is hindered by uncontrollable, supervening circumstances and which makes performance impossible. Obviously, the doctrine of absolute liability is unconscionable and fraught with injustices in some cases if it would permit a party to tender performance where it is practically impossible. The growth of the doctrine of frustration emanated from the weaknesses, limitations and many criticisms suffered by absolute liability.[71]

Absolute liability "never applied where a contract called for personal performance by a party who died or was permanently incapacitated or in the situation of supervening illegality."[72] This exception paved the way for the judicial activism that brought about the birth of the doctrine of frustration in the common law. The doctrine of frustration under the English common law is predicated on the fact that a contract is discharged because, by implication, the parties have agreed that it will no longer be binding if the frustration event occurs. This approach was adopted by Blackburn J in *Taylor v Caldwell*[73] and is called the implied term doctrine.[74] It is therefore important to note that unlike the CISG and the UNIDROIT Principles or even the Sale of Goods Act of 1979, there are no clearly compartmentalised elements of frustration under the common law; however, what exists is a gamut of judicial reasoning and analysis which is entrenched in the common sense of what equity and fairness ought to be should a situation of frustration arise.

The whole idea and discussion are convoluted and revolve around such questions as: if the frustrating event is a supervening impossibility, if the parties have control or anticipated it or are at fault, and if it cannot be said that the loss, destruction or the fortuitous event is substantial and significant enough to sever further obligations to perform by the parties, thereby not falling within the normal commercial risks associated with trades and commerce. These questions are organically related and act in unison in defining the spheres and application of frustration under the common law.

70 Paul Richards, *Law of Contract* (Longman, 2002) 306.

71 Ewan Mckendrick, *Contract Law* (Palgrave Macmillan, 5th edn, 2003) 315.

72 Edwin Peel, *Law of Contract* (Sweet & Maxwell, 2007) 866.

73 [1863] 3 B&S, 826 at 836.

74 However, there is still the view that far from the terms of the contract being implied parties' disposition not to be bound by a frustrating event, the court is to do justice in a situation where neither party contemplated, nor was at fault for any frustrating event, and the English common law courts see it as incumbent on them to mitigate the possible harshness of such events; this is known as imposed term theory.

2.3.1 Supervening Impossibility

This is one of the foundations of frustration under English common law; it also marks the parting point between the doctrine of frustration and that of mistake.[75] It is also where the line is drawn between what is the reasonable expectation of the contract and what falls beyond those reasonable expectations. It "supervening impossibility" relates to the element of the doctrine of frustration under the common law where the inhibition to performance of the contract occurs after the conclusion of the contract.

The finest illustration of this element was in the case of *Taylor v Caldwell*.[76] In this case Caldwell (D) contracted to permit Taylor (P) the use of the Musical Hall at Newington. Caldwell was to retain possession of the hall, and Taylor merely had the use of it for four days to present four concerts in exchange for 100 pounds per day. The contract stated that the hall must be fit for a concert, but there was no express stipulation regarding disasters. The hall was destroyed by fire before the first concert was to be held, and neither party was at fault. The concerts could not be performed at any other location, and Taylor sued for breach and sought reimbursement for costs in preparing for the concerts. The issue that came up for determination was whether or not contract performance is excused for impossibility of performance if performance depends on the continued existence of a person or thing, and that person or thing ceases to exist. Lord Blackburn answered this question in the affirmative.[77]

The rule propounded by Lord Blackburn is only applicable when the contract is positive and absolute and not subject to any condition either expressed or implied. It can be gleaned from the case above that where there is a positive contract, the performance of which is incapacitated by a supervening event not anticipated in the contract, then it is a proper case for the frustration doctrine to apply. The decision

75 P. S. Atiyah, *Introduction to the Law of Contract* (Claredon Law series, 5th edn, 1995) 229–230; the author however writes that " In principle there is no essential distinction between cases of frustration and other cases involving the allocation of risks of subsequent events. The only real justification for separating off cases of impossibility is that there is an established body of case law here which enables one to say with some confidence that a promisor does not normally assume the risk of total subsequent impossibility simply by making a promise as part of a contract."

76 [1863] EWHC QB J1.

77 Lord Blackburn held that:

"If contract performance depends on the continued existence of a person or thing, and that person or thing ceases to exist, performance may be excused for impossibility of performance. If the nature of the contract is such that the parties must have known at the time of contracting that it could not be fulfilled unless some specified thing continued to exist, it is not a positive contract, and there is an implied condition that the parties will be excused from performance if that thing ceases to exist without fault of the parties. However, if a party gives an express or implied warranty that that thing will continue to exist, that party is liable for breach if it ceases to exist. When there is a positive contract to do a thing the contractor must perform it or pay damages, although in consequence of unforeseen accidents, the performance of his contract has become unexpectedly burdensome or even impossible."

above has also moulded the modern trend of the doctrine of frustration and was succinctly captured in the famous dictum of Lord Radcliffe.[78]

Similarly, in *BP Exploration Co (Libya) Ltd. v Hunt (No 2),*[79] Mr Hunt owned an oil concession in Libya. He contracted with BP to exploit the oil. The court held that the contract had been frustrated by the act of the Muammar Gaddafi-led government expropriating Hunt's licence and share. The supervening impossibility must be such that it will not merely provide a defence for a party against a claim or cause of action brought by the other party; it must strike at the root of the contract and effectively relieve the parties of further obligations in the contract.

Another case that explores the importance of the element of "supervening impossibility" is *Joseph Constantine Steamship Line Ltd. v Imperial Smelting Corp Ltd*[80] where Viscount Simon L.C. stated that:

> The question here is where the onus of proof lies; i.e. whether, when a supervening event has been proved which would, apart from the defendant's "default" put an end to the contract, and when at the end of the case no inference of "default" exists and the evidence is equally consistent with either view, the defence fails because the defendant has not established affirmatively that the supervening event was not due to his default. ... In this connection it is well to emphasize that when "frustration" in the legal sense occurs, it does not merely provide one party with a defence in an action brought by the other. It kills the contract itself and discharges both parties automatically.

The above quotation goes on to establish there must be a supervening impossibility which will be unconnected with any fault by the parties before the doctrine of frustration could apply. This element of fortuitousness distinguishes frustration from other similar doctrines.

78 Davis Contractors Ltd. v Fareham UDC [1956] AC 696, [729]. It was held in this case that:
"Frustration occurs whenever the law recognises that without default of either party a contractual obligation has become incapable of being performed because the circumstances in which performance is called for would render it a thing radically different from that which was undertaken by the contract. *Non haec in foedera veni.* It was not this that I promised to do."
The circumstances mentioned in the above dictum must be un-contemplated, supervening circumstances; otherwise, the doctrine of frustration will not be applied. Certain acts of governments have contributed to the development of the doctrine of frustration. It is commonplace in developing countries for violent changes of government to usher in radical changes in government policies; this, to a great extent, affects existing contracts which might have been entered into based on the status quo existing when the contract was made. In this type of case, parties can be discharged from their obligations in the contract by invoking the doctrine of frustration.

79 [1983] 2 AC 352.

80 [1942] AC 154.

2.3.2 *Without Fault of the Parties*

This element is very important when determining whether or not a contract of sale or any other form of contract could be said to be frustrated. The parties must neither be at fault nor foresee the events that act to frustrate the contract.[81] This element can manifest in various situations associated with the frustration of contract.[82] This book will therefore discuss the fragments arising from this element.

2.3.2.1 Non-Fault or Knowledge of the Parties

Incapacity to perform envisages the situation where the direct performance cannot, positively and conclusively, be tendered due to personal events of a supervening nature that make performance impossible without the fault of the parties. The development of this reasoning started in the contracts that involved stewardship, apprenticeship or other personal contractual obligations that would not be performed due to supervening misfortune like death, permanent incapacity or permanent loss of ability.

The hallmark of the above line of thought was effectively laid down in the case of *Cutter v Powell.*[83] In this case, the claimant's husband (Mr Cutter) agreed by contract to act as a second mate on the ship the "Governor Parry" on a return voyage to Jamaica. The claimant sought to claim a sum to represent the six weeks' work undertaken when Mr Cutter suddenly died. The claimant's action failed. Payment was on condition that he worked on the ship to Liverpool; since he did not fulfil this condition, the widow was entitled to nothing. The court reasoned that

81 In *Re Shipton, Anderson and Harrison Brothers* [1915] 3KB 676, a contract was concluded for the sale of wheat lying in a warehouse. The Government requisitioned the wheat, in pursuance of wartime emergency regulations for the control of food supplies, before it had been delivered, and also before ownership in the goods had passed to the buyer under the terms of the contract. It was held that the seller was excused from further performance of the contract as it was now impossible to deliver the goods due to the Government's lawful requisition. The decision taken above is imperative since the subsequent actions of the Government to requisition the wheat were not foreseen by the parties during the formation of the contract of sale, and as long as the decision is in force, performance of the contract will be impossible and illegal.

82 The first situation is where the event occurs without the fault or knowledge of the parties, and then if other elements are present, it makes an easy decision for the court to hold that the contract has been frustrated.

The second situation is where the parties or one of the parties are aware of the event that renders the performance of the contractual obligations impossible.

In such instances the court can hold that the contract is not frustrated since prior knowledge of the event will defeat the applicability of the doctrine of frustration.

The third situation is the situation where the event that brings about the frustration is an act of a third party which may be foreseen or unforeseen. If foreseen, the conclusion is that there will be no frustration, but if unforeseen, then depending on the circumstances of the case, the court may hold in favour or not of frustration. Then there is a situation of self-inflicted frustration, which the courts are always reluctant to uphold as falling into the category of events that can frustrate a contract and also the important principle of law that a foreseen event will not frustrate a contract.

83 [1795] EWHC KB J13.

since the "death" of the claimant's husband was as a result of no fault of the parties and since it wasn't anticipated that such an event would occur during the contracting of the agreement, then the case could be properly regarded as frustrated.[84]

2.3.2.2 *With Prior Knowledge or Self-Inflicted Frustration by the Parties*

It will be worthwhile to note that the prior knowledge of a possible state of incapacity or death or an event would not frustrate or discharge a contract if the parties are aware of a particular state of affairs like ill health or a previous mental condition or existence of a potential state of affairs that can frustrate a contract.[85] This reasoning formed part of the ratio of the case of *Condor v Baron Knights*,[86] a 16-year-old agreed by contract to play the drums for the perpetrator's band for seven nights per week for five years. The claimant suffered a mental breakdown and was told by his doctor that he should not perform more than four nights per week. The band dismissed him as they did not have prior knowledge of his mental health, and he brought a claim for wrongful dismissal.[87] The claimant's action was unsuccessful, as his medical condition made it impossible for him to perform his contractual obligations, and the contract was thus frustrated. The case above has shown the situation where harm or incapacity to perform frustrated a contract; there are other examples that can be associated with the principle above.

In the case of *Edwinton v Tsavliris Russ*[88] the Court of Appeal's judgement was to the effect that a twenty-day charterparty of a vessel for salvage services was not frustrated where, three days before it was due to end, the vessel was unreasonably detained for a further three months, as part of an attempt by the port authority to extract port dues in respect of the casualty which the vessel was causing. The Court of Appeal found that the contractual risk of such delay was firmly on the charterer

84 The incapacity of the subject matter of the contract or where a performance is based on the working condition of a machine, vessel or plant, must be such that conclusively points at the impossibility of the machine to perform or deliver the contractual obligations, which in turn would work to frustrate the contract if the disrupting event has the capacity of fundamentally rendering the contract of no commercial value.

85 Blackburn Bobbin Co Ltd. v T W Allen & Sons Ltd. [1918] 2 KB 467.

86 [1966] 1 WLR 87.

87 If a contract has been so frustrated, then a complaint of unfair dismissal is not available because the contract has been discharged; thus, the automatic discharge consequences of the frustration prevent a claim for unfair dismissal.

88 [2007] EWCA Civ 547: 12 June 2007. More so, a similar decision to the Herne Bay Steam Boat case was reached in the recent case of *CTI Group v Transclear SA* [1964] 2 OB 226, where the Court of Appeal held per Lord Justice Moore-Bick that :

"In my view, it is impossible to hold that the contract in this case was frustrated. As the decided cases show, the fact that a supplier chooses not to make goods available for shipment, thus rendering performance by the seller impossible, is not of itself sufficient to frustrate a contract of this kind. In order to rely on the doctrine of frustration, it is necessary for there to have been a supervening event which renders the performance of the seller's obligations impossible or fundamentally different in nature from that which was envisaged when the contract was made."

and the risk of detention by littoral authorities in a salvage situation where there was a concern about pollution was foreseeable.

However, it is a matter of common knowledge that a self-induced frustration cannot be allowed to discharge a contract.[89] This assertion was given judicial approval in *Ocean Tramp Tankers Corporation v V/O Sovfracht*. Lord Denning M.R. held that there was no frustration of the contract in this case. He reasoned that the charterers could not rely on any self-induced frustration (sailing into the canal) as a ground for arguing that the contract was frustrated. If they had not tried the Suez Canal, they would have had to sail round the Cape, but this would not have rendered the contract radically different. The rationale behind the decision above is based on the fact that self-induced frustration is itself a breach of contract, and it has been a trite principle of law that a party should not be allowed to rely on a breach in order to reap benefit from a cause of action.

This fair position of the law was juristically captured by Lord Brandon of Oakbrook in the case of *Paal Wilson & Co. A/S v Partenreederei Hannah Blumenthal*[90] where he held that inaction to act debars parties from relying on the doctrine of frustration. This decision was reached while adjudicating on whether or not a delay to arbitrate a dispute concerning non-merchantability of a vessel has frustrated and discharged the arbitration agreement.[91]

It is also the opinion of the law that self-induced unavailability of a subject matter cannot be a ground for frustrating the contract and can be regarded

89 It is a settled opinion of the common law that even if the party's breach is only one of the factors leading to the frustrating event, they cannot plead frustration. The above-established view of the law was crafted in the case of Eugenia [1964] 2 QB 226, where a charterer who, in breach of contract, sent a ship into a war zone so that the ship was detained, had his plea of frustration rejected since the frustrating event was by his (the charterer's) self-induced action. It has also been held not to have fallen within the common law scope of frustration when a ship's unseaworthiness that amounted to a breach of contract caused a delay which resulted in the vessel being caught up by war thereby preventing the completion of the voyage. The court held in *Monarch & Co. v A/B Karlshamns Oljefabriker* [1949] AC 196 that failure to make the ship seaworthy can sometimes be regarded as a self-induced frustration. It is equally the law that where the frustrating event is as a result of a deliberate act of a party, that party is foreclosed from pleading frustration; it is irrelevant if his deliberate act is not necessarily a breach of contract. But the innocent party can rely on the event as a frustrating event; the above view was laid down in the case of *Denmark Production Ltd. v Boscobe Production* Ltd. [1969] 1 QB [699]. Finally, there can be no frustration if a party has been negligent in incurring the frustrating event.

90 [1983]1 All ER 34.

91 Ibid., Lord Brandon held that:

"In the instant case the continuing deterioration, during the period of delay, in the amount and quality of evidence which could be made available to the arbitral tribunal when the hearing eventually takes place constitutes the events of which the cumulative effect by August 1980 is relied on as amounting to frustration of the arbitration agreement. The delay, so far as it was not justified to enable proper preparation for the hearing to be made by both parties, could have been put to an end by the sellers by taking steps available to them in the arbitration proceedings. That they elected not to do so would, in my view, be sufficient in itself to debar them from relying on frustration; a fortiori when their election not to do so was a breach of a primary obligation on their part under the arbitrating agreement."

as a self-induced frustration. In *Maritime National Fish Ltd. v Ocean Trawlers Ltd*,[92] Maritime National Fish contracted to hire St. Cuthbert, a steam trawler fitted with an otter trawl, from Ocean Trawlers Ltd. The hire was to last for twelve months. Both parties knew that the use of such a vessel without a licence from the Minister was illegal under the Fisheries Act (c. 73 Revised Statutes of Canada) 1927. Subsequently, Maritime National Fish applied for five licences from the Canadian government for the five trawlers they were using. However, only three were granted. Maritime National Fish did not name the St. Cuthbert from Ocean Trawlers as one of the licensed vessels and refused to go through with the hire on the grounds the contract was frustrated. At first instance, Maritime National Fish prevailed, the trial judge holding that it was not unreasonable to imply a condition to the effect that if the law prohibits the operation of this boat as a trawler, the obligation to pay hire will cease. The Privy Council, while reversing the decision, held that Maritime National Fish had not been bound not to select the hired trawler; they had merely chosen not to in lieu of only receiving three of the five licences they had expected. It was held that "[T]he essence of 'frustration' is that it should not be due to the act or election of the party. Thus, the contract was not frustrated." However, this decision would have been different if the unavailability of the trawlers was a decision independent of the fault of the Maritime National Fish Ltd.

2.3.2.3 Impossibility Caused by Fault of a Third Party

Where the incapacity or impossibility revolved around the incapacity or fault of a third party, then the contract will be frustrated if the incapacity of the third party completely rendered the performance of the contract impossible. But if there can be other benefits to which the contract can be put or give rise, then the contract under common law will not be frustrated since the aim has not been completely defeated.[93] In the case of *Herne Bay Steam Boat v Hutton*,[94] the defendant hired out the claimant's steamship; the purpose of the contract was to take paying passengers to view the Naval Review, which was part of King Edward VII's coronation celebrations. The defendants were also offering a day's cruise for the passengers. The Naval Review was cancelled as the King was ill. The defendant did not use the steamship, and the claimant brought an action for the agreed contract price. The defendant argued the contract had become frustrated due to the cancellation of the Naval Review. The court held that it was not frustrated. The contract had not been deprived of its sole commercial purpose, as it was still possible to perform

92 [1964] 2 QB 226.

93 Richard Stone, *The Modern Law of Contract* (Routledge Cavendish, 8th edn, 2009) 537; the author writes that "the effect on such contract must be sufficiently fundamental to lead to it being regarded as frustrated."

94 [1903] 2 KB 683.

the day's cruise. The Naval Review was not the only commercial purpose of the contract.[95]

2.3.2.4 *Foreseeability of the Event*

The parties must not foresee the frustrating event, nor must it come within their reasonable knowledge or contemplation; otherwise, the contract of sale will not be accepted to have been frustrated. However, Bugden & Lamont-Black argue that a contract may still be frustrated even though the supervening event was generally foreseeable or actually contemplated, especially where there is no undertaking to be bound in any such event.[96] This view falls within the context of *force majeure* clause operation.

In *Atisa S.A. v Aztec A.G*,[97] this case involved a contract dated January 1980, whereby the seller sold to the buyer 13,000–14,000 MT of sugar f.o.b. and stowed in Mombasa. The sale was subject to the rules of the Refined Sugar Association. The shipment was to be in March 1980. The contract contained a *force majeure* clause, and the obtaining of an export licence was the obligation of the seller. The seller was to buy the sugar from the Kenyan government. The Kenyan government indicated that it would cancel its contract with the seller but did not do so, merely saying it was invalid. The buyer commenced arbitration proceedings against the seller and succeeded. On appeal, the court held that the contract was not frustrated since the seller was aware and possibly foresaw the actions of the Kenyan government. Thus, it is a business risk within the foreseeable knowledge of the seller that the Kenyan government may cancel its contract with them.[98]

2.3.3 *Significant Destruction of the Subject Matter*

This is the third element that, under common law, is required in order to hold that a contract has been frustrated. It has been held that the destruction of the subject matter after the conclusion of the contract, which renders performance of the

95 However, it can be argued that though viewing the Naval review was not the only sole purpose of the contract, it was the most striking and fundamental obligation of the contract; the above judgement seemed reached *per incuriam* in the sense that the court did not consider that the cruise in the ship is only ancillary to the main contract and the main obligation of the contract was to view the review. The mere fact that the event that scuttled the contract was the illness of the king would have swayed the court to hold that the contract was frustrated, since the fundamental purpose of the contract has been rendered impossible.

96 Bugden & Lamont-Black (n 83) ch. 1; see also Edwinton Commercial Corp v Tsavliris [2007] EWCA, civ 537.

97 [1983] 2 Lloyd's Rep 579.

98 Even if it can be proved that certain strange risks can emanate from a particular trade which have become notorious with such trade, a party to a contract where such an event arises cannot be heard to say the contract has been frustrated. This is because the supervening occurrence is not a one-off event as required by the doctrine in order to relieve parties of their business obligations.

contract impossible, would lead to the contract being adjudged frustrated.[99] It has been noted that sometimes a total, absolute destruction of a subject matter may not always be necessary.[100] If the situation is such that it makes continuance of the obligations earmarked in the contract impossible, then the court will hold that the doctrine of frustration can apply.

The case of *Asfar and Co v Blundell*[101] served as a litmus test for the above caption. A vessel, on board which dates (fruit) had been shipped, was sunk during the course of the voyage and subsequently raised. On arrival at the port of discharge, it was found that, although the dates still retained the appearance of dates and although they were of some value for the purpose of distillation into spirit, they were so impregnated with sewage and in such a condition of fermentation that there had been a total loss of cargo. Lord Esher held that:

> [B]ut if the nature of the thing is altered, and it becomes for business purposes something else, so that it is not dealt with by business people as the thing which it originally was, the question for determination is whether the thing insured, the original article of commerce, has become a total loss. If it is so changed in its nature by the perils of the sea as to become an unmerchantable thing, which no buyer would buy and no honest seller would sell, then there is a total loss. That test was applied in the present case by the learned judge in the Court below, who decided as a fact that the dates had been so deteriorated that they had become something which was not merchantable as dates. If that was so, there was a total loss of the dates and the contract was frustrated.

There are also some examples of such contractual events that may work to render the contract commercially unperformable and a complete loss.[102] More so, another hybrid situation can arise in building contracts where the subject matter of the con-

99 The popular case of *Taylor v Caldwell* is a classic example of this situation. Hitherto, it is not always the case to have situations that are so simple to adjudicate; there are some complex situations where even though the subject matter of the contract has been destroyed, they are still in a state whereby commercial value can still be derived from it. In such instances, it is difficult to draw the line on how to discern or decipher the degree of destruction or the quantum of value that can make a destroyed subject matter commercially wholesome or not. The answer to this question will require the circumstances of each case to be considered on its own merit and the intentions of the parties to the contract to be examined.

100 Robert Upex and Geoffrey Bennett, *Davies on Contract* (Sweet & Maxwell, 9th edn, 2004) 257.

101 [1896] 1 QB 123 Court of Appeal .

102 The case of *Jackson v Union Marine Insurance* (1874) LR 10 CP 125 is apt in this respect. In this case, Jackson chartered a ship to Rathbone which ran aground before it completed the charter party and remained incapacitated for a considerable time. The issue before the court was whether, under these circumstances, Rathbone was released from his contract to load under the charter party. If this was the case, then there would have been a total loss of business within the meaning of the insurance policy. In respect of Rathbone's release, the jury held that the delay for repairs was so long that it brought the contract in a commercial sense to an end. The lengthy discontinuance of the services of the ship caused the bottom to drop in the contract and thereby radically rendered it a commercial misnomer.

tract (the building) is destroyed before completion. The general position of common law as decided in the case of *School Trustee of Trenton v Bennet*[103]is that "where a party, by his own contract, creates a duty or charge upon himself, he is bound to make it good if he may, notwithstanding any accident by inevitable necessity, because he might have provided against it by his contract."

However, where the other party has an obligation to perform or controls part of the building work or where a builder agrees to work on an existing building in order to install new machinery, then a distinction must be drawn.[104] In the case of *Butterfield v Bryon*,[105] it was held that where a person unconditionally contracts to build a house, they are liable for breach if it is not completed. However, if the other party owns or controls part of the house, such that the contractor could not proceed to finish their contractual obligation without the performance of the owner, there is an implied condition that the parties would release each other from performance if the house was destroyed by inevitable accident.

2.3.3.1 *Absence of the Subject Matter*

There is no doubt that the availability or obtainability of the subject matter of a contract is very essential in the performance of the contract. It has been argued that there can be frustration of contract if the subject matter or a thing or person essential for the purpose of its performance, though not ceasing to exist or suffering permanent incapacity, becomes unavailable for the purpose of the performance of the contract.[106]

By and large, as a general rule, temporal unavailability of the subject matter cannot frustrate the contract if the subject matter's absence will not fundamentally change the nature of the contract and its performance. However, where it is clear from the terms or nature of the contract that a specific time will be of essence in the contract, then unavailability of the subject matter within that said time or period would frustrate the contract. The argument that the frustrating event is only but temporal will not suffice. In *Robinson v Davison*[107] a piano player became ill prior to a concert he was contracted to play in. The contract was held to be frustrated. The rationale behind the decision of this case was that even though the pianist's illness was not of a permanent nature, it was such that it deprived him of the ability to perform on the day of the concert. It is obvious that time was purely of great essence, and failure to perform on the day would render the contract frustrated, since the ability to perform subsequently would be immaterial.

There is also contention among scholars on the scenario when time is not of the essence of a contract. Trietel argues that in such cases the contract is frustrated not

103 [1859] 27 NJL 513 13.
104 Peel (n 72) 185.
105 [1891] 153 Mass 517.
106 Peel (n 72) para 19–016, 931.
107 (1871) LR 6 Ex 269.

by the mere fact but by the length of the delay in performance.[108] This argument draws support from the case of *Jackson v Union Marine Insurance Co*,[109] where the contract of charter party was held to have been frustrated because of the length of the delay.[110]

Another type of contract under English common law that needs to be examined is the contract of employment or contract involving personal services. If an interruption or impediment, such as illness or conscription, temporarily interferes with the performance of a contract, then holding the contract to be frustrated depends on the degree and proportion of the temporal impediment on the contract. If it is such that it radically goes to the root of the contractual relationship and obligations, then the doctrine of frustration can justifiably apply.

In *Morgan v Manser*,[111] a manager who was conscripted in 1940 for military activities was held to have his contract of employment as a manager for a music hall artiste frustrated. The reason is that, since the terms of the employment were for 10 years starting from 1938, it is likely that as of 1940 the manager would remain in the military for a very long time. This case could be compared with *Nordman v Rayner & Sturgess*,[112] where an internment that lasted only for one month was held not to be enough to frustrate a long-term commission agency. Nevertheless, it is not all contracts that involve personal services which can be frustrated due to the impossibility of one of the parties to perform.

In the case of a contract involving an independent contractor, this book will suggest that the degree or proportion of the frustrating event should receive a stricter interpretation. This is due to the fact that an employer who employs an independent contractor for a particular service has no control over the manner by which an independent contractor performs the contract.[113] An independent contractor contracts with an employer to do a particular piece of work. This working relationship is a flexible one that provides benefits to both the worker and the employer. An independent contractor contracts to do work for another person according to his or

108 Ibid., 873.

109 [1874] LR 10 CP 125.

110 Similar to Jackson's case was the *Metropolitan Water Board v Dick, Kerr and Co* [1910] AC 119. In this case the defendant contracted with the plaintiff to build a reservoir within six years. After two years the Minister of Munitions required the defendant to cease work and remove and sell its plant. The plaintiff claimed the contract subsisted on the basis of a contract provision allowing a time extension in the event of any difficulties. The House of Lords held that the contract was frustrated on the basis that if it were resumed after such interruption, it would effectively be a different contract.

111 [1948] 1 KB 184.

112 [1916] 33 T.L.R. 87

113 The personal misfortune, like illness, constriction, or internment of the independent contractor, will be such that, practically from all sense of it, renders performance impossible before it can frustrate a contract. Otherwise, common sense will require an independent contractor to perform the contract as agreed; certain events that would easily avail an employee *stricto sensu* would not avail him due to the greater portion of risk that falls within the ambit of his (independent contractor) status under the law.

her own processes and methods. The contractor is not subject to another's control except for what is specified in a mutually binding agreement for a specific job.[114]

2.3.3.2 *Failure of a Source*

Where the availability of the subject matter of a contract depends on its availability from a source, then failure of the subject matter to be materialised from the source can lead to the contract being frustrated.[115] A contract that tomatoes would be produced from a particular field for sale would fail if the crop fails or the harvest is too poor to service the performance of the contract; this view was laid down by Lord Haldane in *Tamplin Steamship Co v Anglo-Mexican Petroleum Products Co*[116] where his lordship held thus:

> When people enter into a contract which is dependent for the possibility of its performance on the continued availability of a specific thing, and that availability comes to an end by reason of circumstances beyond the control of the parties, the contract is prima facie regarded as dissolved

However, where one of the parties has the sole knowledge of a particular source of a subject matter of a contract and it is proven that the availability or otherwise of that source is exclusively within his contractual risk purview, then they would not be allowed to plead frustration when that source fails.

In *Blackburn Bobbin Co Ltd. v T W Allen & Sons Ltd*,[117] by a contract made in the early part of 1914, the defendants sold timber to the plaintiffs that would be imported from Finland and delivered to the plaintiffs free on rail at Hull. The deliveries were to commence in June or July 1914 and to continue during the season which would terminate in November. The contract did not contain the exceptions of war or *force majeure*. The practice before the war was to load timber into vessels at ports in Finland for direct sea carriage to England, but this practice was not known to the plaintiffs, nor did they know, as the fact was, that timber merchants in England do not keep Finnish timber in stock. Up to the outbreak of the war in August 1914, the defendants had not delivered any of the timber, and after that date, owing to the disorganisation of transport caused by the war, it became impossible for the defendants to obtain any Finnish timber for delivery to the plaintiffs, and the defendants contended that the contract had been dissolved by the outbreak

114 Kamal Puri, "Copyright and Employment in Australia" (1996) 27(1) IIC 53.

115 An express covenant that goods will come from a particular source would be frustrated if the source fails to provide the goods. However, where the commonly intended source only partially fails, a term will be implied requiring the supplier to deliver the smaller quantity available. They are relieved only to the extent of the deficiency. See Mindy Chen-Wishart, *Contract Law* (Oxford University Press, 3rd edn, 2010) 319–320.

116 [1916] 2 AC 397.

117 [1918] 2 KB 467.

of war. The court held that the contract had not been frustrated, and that the defendants were liable in damages for the non-delivery of the timber.[118]

Arriving at the above decision is not always easy, since it throws the heavy burden of interpreting the intention of the parties to the court or tribunal, and in the absence of plausible positive evidence, the contract would not be torpedoed by frustration when the allegedly implied source of subject matter fails. It has been decided that where parties expected certain delivery of subject matter to come from a particular factory in a particular country, failure to obtain the subject matter because of war or hostility will definitely be a ground for holding the contract frustrated. Thus, where a contract to supply a chemical from Germany was made impossible due to the First World War of 1914, the parties were discharged from the contract as being frustrated since they both believed the chemical would come from Germany.[119]

There can be a situation where the supervening partial failure of the source of the subject matter of the contract can give rise to various outcomes. The most applicable outcome is that the seller may be excused to the extent of the failure or deficiency to produce the subject matter.[120] The seller can also be asked to deliver the quantity produced if it is of economic value,[121] or the buyer may be justified and discharged from his obligation to accept the delivery if the quantity delivered is of no economic value or fundamentally below the reasonable contractual expectations.[122]

2.4 Elements of Frustration under Sale of Goods Act of 1979

Under the Sale of Goods Act of 1979, the elements of frustration are limited to contracts of sale of goods involving "specific goods." The general principle guiding the statute is that a contract of sale will be frustrated after an agreement to sell has been entered into, though the property in the goods has not passed on to the buyer, and then the goods perished without the fault of any of the parties.[123] The important

118 On the other hand, where both parties are impliedly hoping to get the subject matter of the contract from a particular source, and there is no other possible source contemplated within the contract, but the implied source is not a term of the contract, neither is it mentioned, then depending on the circumstances of the case, the court may give a decision in favour of the contemplated source being an implied term of the contracts and which the parties positively and unequivocally expected it to be part of the contract.

119 Re Badische Co [1912] 2 ch. 331.

120 Peel (n 72) 877.

121 Ibid.

122 Ibid.

123 This should be contrasted with Section 6 of the 1979 Act, which provides for the doctrine of mistake. Section 6 provides for the situation where, without the knowledge of the seller, the specific goods which they have agreed to sell have "perished" at the date of contract. The section is not without doubt as to the main principles that govern its application. It has been suggested to emanate from the concept of impossibility of performance, though it looks more like the concept

elements that must be present before the doctrine of frustration can apply within the meaning of the 1979 statute are discussed below.

2.4.1 Agreement to Sell Specific Goods

Under Section 7 of the Sale of Goods Act, it is not every situation that arises where goods perished that can lead to frustration; there must be an agreement to sell and not an outright sale. The difference between the two is that, in the former, the sale is still inchoate since the risk and property have not been transferred to the buyer, but in the latter case, the property and the risk having passed to the buyer, will be presumed to have fallen under a normal commercial situation. Whatever exigencies may arise should be met by appropriate insurance cover.

Section 7 does not suggest the form of agreement that can be expected before the doctrine of frustration can apply under Section 7. While there is no doubt that good practice demands that a written agreement to sell is more convenient for the parties and the courts in a situation where there will be a need to determine whether or not such an agreement is in place, there is, however, no rule that forecloses the use of an oral agreement to sell.[124] The basic rules that govern the application of Section 7 are laid down in the Section 18 rules (2) (3) of the Sale of Goods Act of 1979. Section 18 (Rule 2) provides that:

> Where there is a contract for the sale of specific goods and the seller is bound to do something to the goods for the purpose of putting them into a deliverable state, the property does not pass until the thing is done and the buyer has notice that it has been done.

While Rule 3 provides that:

> Where there is a contract for the sale of specific goods in a deliverable state but the seller is bound to weigh, measure, test, or do some other act or thing with reference to the goods for the purpose of ascertaining the price, the property does not pass until the act or thing is done and the buyer has notice that it has been done.

---

of common mistake because it contemplates a situation where the goods have already perished or non-existing before the conclusion of the contract.

124 An oral agreement to sell, otherwise known as a parole agreement, can still be admitted under the grounds required under Section 7 if it is direct, positive, and clearly shows the mutual intentions of the parties to have such an agreement to sell specific goods.

It is a matter of inescapable conclusion from these two rules that whenever there is a conditional[125] sale of specific goods, then section 7 will apply.[126]

Another important part of this element is the phrase "specific goods." According to Section 61(1) of the Sale of Goods Act 1979 as amended by Section 2(d) of the Sale of Goods (Amendment) Act 1995, "specific good" means:

> Goods identified and agreed on at the time a contract of sale is made and includes an undivided share, specified as a fraction or percentage, of goods identified and agreed on as aforesaid.

This definition is very important and necessary in order to pigeonhole the unique aspect of the application of the doctrine of frustration under the statute. It has been held that an agreement to sell "a quarter share in a named racecourse is an agreement for the sale of a specific good."[127]

This brings this discussion to the case of *Howell v Coupland*,[128] where Coupland agreed to sell to Howell 200 tonnes of potatoes to be grown on a specified field. Due to a partial failure of the crop, Coupland was able to deliver only 80 tonnes. It was held that Coupland was relieved of liability to deliver the remaining 120 tonnes. This case has been criticised as falling outside the ambit of Section 7 of the Act; this is because the sale was not for specific goods ascertainable but for future goods, and more so, 80 tonnes of the goods were delivered by the seller, and this would have been left open for the buyer to choose to accept or reject. This case has been held not to be consistent with the provisions of Section 61(1) of the Act which defines what "specific good" means or connotes.

While it seems possible that future goods can never be equated as specific goods, it does appear that for the purposes of Section 7 of the 1979 Act, future goods may sufficiently be specific to come within its application.[129] Although it is not always easy to identify whether future goods are specific or not, it has been held in *Kursell v Timber Operators & Contractors Ltd*[130] that trees sold in the Latvian forest have

125 This could be distinguished from an unconditional or absolute contract. An unconditional sale means a sale not subject to any condition precedent or subsequent. An unconditional sale cannot be frustrated since both the risk and property must have passed to the buyer before the event of frustration. Whereas a conditional sale can still be frustrated if other elements required under Section 7 are met. See P. S. Atiyah and others, *The Sale of Goods* (Pearson Educational Ltd, 11th edn, 2005) 311.

126 Ibid., 360.

127 Trietel (n 46) ch. 1, 6–036, p 323.

128 [1876] 1 QBD 258.

129 See Atiyah & others (n 125) 313; some future goods are mathematically specified so that they can be presumed ascertained. Once a future good has been reasonably identified to the contract, then its perishing before the risk passes to the buyer and without the fault of either party will be deemed to have frustrated the contract.

130 [1927] 1 KB 298.

not been specific as not all the trees were to pass but only those conforming to the stipulated measurements.[131]

For all these, it has been argued that where there is an agreement to sell part of specific goods, and if the agreement is not severable, then any supervening impediment like the perishing of the goods before the risk is passed to the buyer which occurs without the fault of the parties, will be held to have affected the totality of the unseverable agreement and thereby frustrate the contract.[132] There is also a general rule, as can be deduced from the construction of Section 7 of the Sale of Goods Act, that an agreement to sell unascertained goods cannot be frustrated by perishing of the goods; thus, the Latin maxim *genus numquam* perit – which means that "whole species of goods cannot perish." However, it has been argued that in certain circumstances, the doctrine of frustration can apply in exceptional cases involving an agreement to sell unascertained goods.

It has been hypothetically suggested that "if a person agrees to sell a crop to be grown on a particular field, the contract may be frustrated by the failure of the crop."[133] However, even though there may be a favourable argument to the effect that unascertained goods can be subject to the doctrine of frustration under the Act, the courts are always cautious to go this extra mile in developing the law. This reluctance could be seen in the rhetorical question by Lord Justice Pickford in the case of *Blackburn Bobbin Co Ltd. v Allen & Sons* where he asks, "Why should a purchaser of goods, not specific goods, be deemed to concern himself with the way in which the seller is going to fulfil his contract by providing the goods he has agreed to sell?."[134] This question is reeking with the hesitancy by which English law treated claims for the frustration of an unascertained sales of goods where the goods perished before the transfer of risk and property.

131 But in this case the judges found that the contract has been frustrated by the Latvian Assembly law that nationalised the forest. Scrutton L.J. held that "I agree with the view of Rowlatt J that so much remained to be done under the contract that the doctrine of frustration would apply. That doctrine depends on whether in the particular contract there is an implied term that its validity shall depend on the continued existence of something, or state of facts or law. Here I think it is clear that the continued existence, apart from temporary interruptions, of a state of law in which the contract could be performed was contemplated by the parties."

132 The above principle of law was articulated from the case of *Barrow, Lane & Ballard Ltd. v Phillip Phillips & Co. Ltd.* [1929] 1 KB 574; the defendant contracted for 700 bags of nuts said to be in a warehouse. 109 bags had in fact disappeared, possibly stolen, and another 450 subsequently disappeared as well. At the time of the contract, there were only 591 bags available for delivery, and ultimately only 151 bags remained available for delivery. The contract was held to be avoided. The 700 bags were regarded as indivisible despite the fact that the buyers paid for the portion of the consignment that they actually received. The sellers sued for the outstanding sum for the part of the consignment the buyer refused to pay for. The claim failed since the contract was avoided.

Conversely, if it can be shown that the part of the contract could be severed from the others without changing the meaning and the essence of the contract of sale of goods, then the perishing of the goods will only frustrate the contract in issue without galloping to frustrate the other subsisting severable contracts.

133 Atiyah and others (n 125) 362.

134 [1918] 1 KB 540 at 550.

2.4.2 The Goods Perished Without Fault of the Parties

This second element is the defining element of the doctrine of frustration under the 1979 Act. It has been stated before that what singles out frustration under the contract of sales of goods as provided under the Act *vis-à-vis the* common law position is that the Act is narrowed down to the situation that involves the perishing of the specific goods under Section 7.[135] If other frustrating events work to fundamentally render the agreement inoperable, then the more elaborate common law doctrine of frustration will be applicable but not Section 7.

However, the word "perish" is not without controversy; it has been held in the *Horn v Minister of Food*,[136] where Morris J opined that potatoes which had rotted before delivery and thereby were unfit for human consumption had not perished because they could still be described as potatoes. However, it has been suggested that goods need not have been totally destroyed, provided that they have been so altered in nature by damage or deterioration that they have become for the business purposes something other than that which is described in the contract of sale.[137] Thus, the persuasive precedence of the New Zealand case of *Rendell v Turn-bull*[138] will be most instructive. Under the New Zealand Sale of Goods Act which is similar to their English counterpart, goods have been held to have perished where a lot of potatoes unknown to the parties at the time of the bargain had started "second growth" to such an extent as to be unfit for human food.[139]

Another operating factor under this element is that the goods must have perished without fault. This implies that either directly, remotely, constructively, or by necessary implications, the perishing of the goods shall not be the act of any of the parties. It has been held that the fault of either party delaying delivery will subject that party to the risk arising from the delay.[140] The doctrine of frustration only thrives on fortuitous happenings; it does not permit fault or blame, for either of them will vitiate the doctrine, and the contract of sale will be held not to be frustrated.

2.4.3 The Seller Has Not Passed the Risk to the Buyer

The reason for this element is that, should the risk be said to have passed to the buyer, then the sale would have been completed, and any event that caused the goods to perish will be treated as falling under the vagaries of foreseeable

135 It will be instructive to note that both the common law and the Act deal with only supervening impossibilities, unlike the CISG and the UNIDROIT Principles where the impediment can be precedent or subsequent. Moreover, under common law and the Act, the doctrine of temporary frustration is not known or developed.

136 [1948] 2 All ER 1036.

137 A.G. Guest (n 97) ch. 1, para 6–035, 322.

138 (1908) 27 NZLR 1067.

139 Samuel Williston and Clarence Martins, *The Law of Contract* (Baker Voorhis, 1920).

140 Michael Bridge, *The Sale of Goods* (Oxford University Press, 2003) 133.

commercial transaction risk cover.[141] The passing of risk is important to the doctrine of frustration under Section 7 of the 1979 Act since it is the point which will help in deciding whether or not the perishing of the goods is either of the parties' commercial responsibility. If the risk has not passed to the buyer, then the contract is avoided; this means that the buyer is not liable for the price and the seller is not liable for non-delivery.[142] It has been suggested that even if the goods are at the buyer's risk, but the property is still with the seller, the conditions for the application of Section 7 have not been fulfilled.[143]

2.5 Conclusion

This chapter gives a detailed analysis of all the elements that must be present before exemption, *force majeure* and frustration could apply under the CISG, UNIDROIT Principles, and English law. It highlighted the basic elements of impossibility, unforeseeability, uncontrollability, and no-fault as the cornerstone of the doctrine of exemption/*force majeure*/frustration. It can be added that these elements are also the basis of the Draft Model Frustration Clause (DMFC) proposed in chapter eight of this book.[144]

However, there are variations to the applications of these elements. While Section 7 of the 1979 Act provides a very narrow parameter for its applications, the common law hinges on the impossibility radically affecting the outcome of the contract. The CISG and UNIDROIT Principles are almost similar in their use of legal phraseology and familiar interpretations of elements.

While the aim of the doctrine under the CISG and the UNIDROIT Principles is to exempt liability in damages, the aim of the common law/§7 of the Sale of Goods Act is to determine the contract on the basis of automatic discharge of the parties. Common law and Section 7 of the 1979 Act operate to discharge both parties from their future obligations in the contract; for instance, the buyer is not liable for the price and the seller is not liable for non-delivery if the doctrine of frustration applies;[145] though the provisions of the Frustrated Contracts Act of 1943 have brought better means of apportioning consequences.

This is a major difference with art 79 of the CISG and the UNIDROIT Principles, where all applicable remedies are still available except damages.

141 It has been held that nothing in Section 7 precludes its application simply because the risk has not been foreseen at the contract date. Just because a risk is foreseen does not mean that the parties have implicitly agreed that the seller should bear responsibility for it. However, sometimes it appears the parties intend the risk to oust the jurisdiction of Section 7; see Michael Bridge (n 140) 134.

142 Atiyah and others (n 125) 36.

143 AG Guest and others (n 97) ch. 1, 6–035, 322.

144 The doctrine of frustration/exemption/*force majeure* and the Draft model frustration clause share the same major elements. These elements make the application of this doctrine sui generis under commercial/contract law. While legal consequences and mode of application could differ, the basic features of impossibility, unforeseeability, and non-fault are uniformly associated with the doctrine.

145 Atiya & others (n 125) 349.

3 Risk and Exemption/*Force Majeure*/ Frustration

3.1 Exemption and Risk under Art 79 of the CISG

3.1.1 Background

The doctrine of exemption under the CISG is basically predicated on how the risk of liability and exemption from damages play out when a party fails to perform any obligations owed in the contract due to unforeseen circumstances beyond their control. It must be proved that they could not reasonably be expected to have taken the impediment into account at the time of the conclusion of the contract or to have avoided or overcome it or its consequences.

Goods might suffer loss or damage at various points in time, from the formation of the contract of sale of goods till the actual handing over to the buyer.[1] This loss, if it is accidental, will fall within the concept of risk; the incidence of risk according to Bugden and Lamont-Black, is relevant in determining any right of suit and/or damages and the question of insurable interest.[2]

Risk can be defined as a situation of physical loss, deterioration or damage of the goods sold without the act or omission of any of the parties. Risk plays a great role whenever the issue of frustration of contract of sales comes up for determination.[3] This statement is applicable even in the extreme situation of exemption where the parties are absolved from liabilities in damages. However, it is always open to the

1 B.von Hoffmann, *International Sale of Goods: Dubrovnic Lectures* (P. Sarcevic and P. Volken eds, Oceana, 1986) 267.

2 Bugden & Lamont-Black (n 83) ch. 1, para 3–026, 79. See also Enderlein and Maskow (n 18) ch. 2, 261.

3 Joseph Lookofsky, published in J. Herbots editor / R. Blanpain general editor, International Encyclopaedia of Laws - Contracts, Suppl. 29 (December 2000) 1–192 , cited also as "Art 66 Passing of Risk" [2000]

<http://cisgw3.law.pace.edu/cisg/biblio/loo66.html>; He argues that

"The mere fact that the seller and/or the buyer are likely to carry insurance designed to protect against the economic consequences of the 'risks' discussed here does not dispense with the need to determine which of the two parties actually 'carries' the risk when a given loss occurs, in that one of the parties must bear the burden of asserting a claim against the insurer, suffer some depletion of current assets while waiting for settlement."

DOI: 10.4324/9781003667841-3

parties to introduce an express provision into their agreement regarding the allocation of unforeseeable risks[4] this is in line with the doctrine of party autonomy.

At this juncture, it will be apt to attempt a definition of risk from the viewpoint of the CISG. This exercise becomes imperative since the concept "risk" is very fluid and takes its meaning from its usages. Barry Nicholas in his treatise on art 66 of the CISG argues that:

> In the Convention, however, the word (risk) is used in the narrower and more traditional sense of the incidence of the loss resulting from any casualty to the goods which is not due to an act or omission of the other party. In this sense, the statement that the risk passes to the buyer at a certain moment means that from that moment the buyer must bear that loss. In terms of practical consequences this means that the buyer (a) must perform his obligations under the contract even though the object sold is lost or damaged and (b) has no rights against the seller arising out of any non-performance by the seller which is due to such loss or damage.[5]

This working definition of risk under the CISG is very important in putting the context through which risk is expressed in its proper perspective. It also avoids the lumping together of risk and property, which is the major obvious difference between the concept of risk under English common law and risk under the CISG.[6]

Once a party assumes the risk which comes with some bundle of obligations, they would not be shielded from liability under art 79 of the CISG when faced with events which fall squarely outside his control. This is because it will be contradictory for a party who legally bears the risk to also turn round and say the obligation is frustrated and thus exemption from his liabilities, though they can be exempted from paying damages if the elements of art 79 are proved.[7] Sometimes it is not difficult to decipher who owns the risk in a contract of sale of goods. For instance, if the goods are sold directly by the producer, then the chance of exonerating the producer from liability is slim since they bear the risks of design, fabrication and

4 Atamer, "Art 79" in Stefan Kröll (eds) (n 41) ch. 1, para 89 1093.

5 Barry Nicholas, in Bianca-Bonell Commentary on the International Sales Law, Giuffrè: Milan (1987) 483–486.

6 Art 4 of the CISG excludes the issues concerning the effect of which the contract of sale of goods has on the property of the goods sold. It provides thus:

"This Convention governs only the formation of the contract of sale and the rights and obligations of the seller and the buyer arising from such a contract. In particular, except as otherwise expressly provided in this Convention, it is not concerned with:

(a) the validity of the contract or of any of its provisions or of any usage;
(b) The effect which the contract may have on the property in the goods sold.

7 Atamer (n 41) ch. 1, para 12, 1060; the writer presented a hypothetical scenario thus: A seller who delivers steel to a particular destination will be excused from damages if an unforeseeable hindrance caused the ship not to enter the harbour and deliver, but the buyer can ask for replacement of the goods or reduction of price as the risk of deterioration is with the seller until delivery at the right place is completed.

instruction errors.[8] Any party who owes the risk will not be exonerated from fulfilling his own side of the bargain even if there is an insurmountable impediment.[9]

In the *German wood case*,[10] where the Swiss buyer of a consignment of wood delayed payment of the sale price due to uncertainty as to who was entitled to receive the sale price. The plaintiff and a third person stated that they were the assignees of the sum owed to the seller domiciled in Germany. The court did not view that as an impediment to the discharge of the buyer's obligation to pay interest on arrears as from the payment due date. However, the defendant was exempt from payment of damages on the basis of art 79(5) CISG. The decision reflects the reasoning that once the risk of payment has passed to the buyer in accordance with art 66, confusion as to whom to make the payment to will not be seen as an impediment that will exempt the buyer from performing his obligation to pay, but they can be exempted from paying damages if the doctrine of exemption is applicable.

Problems of allocation of risk under the contract of sale of goods can spawn into different forms. John Honnold identified the various faces of risk in international sales when he writes that:

> I believe that these norms reflect several practical considerations: Damage during carriage usually is discovered only when the goods reach the buyer. In international transactions the seller is likely to be far from the damaged goods; the buyer is in a better position to assess the damage and to make a claim against the carrier or the insurer. In many transactions, before the seller ships, the buyer will arrange for the issuance (or confirmation) of a letter of credit by a bank near the seller. The seller, in exchange for the payment, will surrender a negotiable bill of lading and an insurance policy which the bank will forward to the buyer. The buyer will have these documents in hand when he examines the goods and discovers the damage; these facts will make it particularly efficient for the buyer to deal with the damage claim. In addition, where a seller must send goods to destinations that are both near and far, the added burden and insurance costs for the remote sales would either

8 Ibid., para 75; the author writes that:

"The producer/seller will be liable for any production error as well as any development error; this is predicated on the reasons that giving the producer/seller the opportunity to exonerate himself from non-latent defects will open the door to the misuse of the fault principle."

9 In the Hungarian furniture case, Oberlandesgericht Hamm (Court of Appeal Hamm), Germany, 23 June 1998 – 19 U 127/97, CISG-online 434 <https://cisg-online.org/search-for-cases?caseId=6404> accessed 13/9/2025, the court held that: "The court found that the buyer was not obliged to pay the purchase price according to art 66 CISG, because the plaintiff did not prove that the goods were lost after the risk had passed to the buyer. In the case at hand, the passing of the risk had to be determined according to art 69(2) CISG, as under the parties' agreements, the buyer was bound to take over the goods at a place other than the seller's place of business."

10 Amtsgericht Willisau (Court of First Instance Willisau) Switzerland, 12 March 2004 – 10 01 5, CISG-online 961 <https://cisg-online.org/search-for-cases?caseId=6885> accessed 31/9/2025.

> complicate the seller's price quotations or deprive some buyers of their natural advantages of nearness to supply.[11]

The above depicts a synopsis of the manner risk and liability are allocated in the international sales transaction. This will bring a further discussion to the theories of "risk bearing."

There is a controversy over what is required in a situation of exemption that makes performance impossible and causes loss to the parties even though risk has passed.[12] Jenkins,[13] was of the view that both traditional and modernist theorists are trying to fathom what happens to risk and how it swings after an unforeseen event. The traditionalists' approach is conservative and deeply entrenched in the principle that the loss should be allowed to lie where it has fallen. This traditional view is myopic and too narrow for modern commercial engagements.

It is equally inequitable in a situation where a party is in a position to lose everything as a direct consequence of the unforeseen event. Thus, sometimes affirmative contractual justice and fair play can be done in allocating the risk of the loss. On the other hand, the modernist approach is predicated on the view that the court must act to adjudicate on the situation by gauging who is in a better economic advantage to shoulder the burden occasioned by the loss and thereby bearing the risk. Posner and Rosenfield, the major proponents of this economic theory of modernism, advocated that:

> Risk of loss resulting from an unforeseen frustrating event should be allocated to the 'superior risk bearer'. If the promisee is the superior risk bearer, the obligation of performance by the promisor is discharged. Likewise, if the promisor is allocated the risk of the unforeseen event and the loss thereof, as the superior risk bearer, performance must occur to avoid liability for breach regardless of the increased burden. Determining which of the two parties is the superior risk bearer requires an assessment of which party was (1) in a better position to prevent the risk from materializing or (2) in a better position to insure against the risk. Determining whether one is the least cost insurer requires a determination of (1) risk-appraisal costs, including both

11 John Honnold published in Galston & Smit ed., International Sales: The United Nations Convention on Contracts for the International Sale of Goods, Matthew Bender (1984) ch. 8, pages 8-1–8-15.

12 Nevertheless, it is important to note that the provision of art 79, which simply says that "the contract is avoided" in the event of frustration, left much to be desired. It does not answer the question of who bears the risk of the loss caused by the frustration of the contract of sale or how the loss is allocated; this incomplete assessment of the frustrating situation does not augur well with a streamlined, consistent commercial practice, which is the hallmark of modern commercial engagements.

13 72 Tulane Law Review (1998) 2015–2030: also cited as "Exemption for Non-performance: UCC, CISG, UNIDROIT Principles -- A Comparative Assessment" <https://cisg-online.org/files/commentFiles/Jenkins_72_TulLRev_1998_2015.pdf> accessed 26 September 2025.

> the probability that the risk will materialize and the magnitude of the loss if it does and (2) transaction costs.[14]

This modernist proposition is, however, not practicable since the yardstick for measuring who is "the superior risk bearer" is not always tenable. That a party is in a better position to insure against a risk or in a better position to prevent risk, or in a more comfortable financial position to cushion off the consequences of the loss, does not mean that he bears the obligation to be allocated the risk. Professor Kull, who is an advocate of the traditional approach, suggests that the Posner/Rosenfield approach is inconsistent with the goals of gap filling; that is, providing a result that the parties would choose themselves as a suitable generalised default rule. Kull concluded that no rational contracting party would willingly adopt the "superior risk bearing" approach as a default rule, "given the parties' inability to determine *ex ante* how the court would resolve the factual determination of risk bearing capacity *ex post* and after the unforeseeable frustrating event has materialized."[15]

3.1.2 Risk, Liability, and Exemption

Art 66 of the CISG provides that "[l]oss of or damage to the goods after the risk has passed to the buyer does not discharge him from his obligation to pay the price, unless the loss or damage is due to an act or omission of the seller." While a successful situation of exemption will operate to extinguish the liabilities of the parties from paying damages, the case of risk is different in the sense that loss or damage to the goods, after the risk has passed to the buyer, will not lift the obligation upon the buyer to pay the price and damages unless the loss or damage is as a result of the fault of the seller.[16]

Art 66 can also apply in cases where non-performance results from an unforeseeable impediment provided the risk has passed to the buyer and loss or damages are not due to the act or omission of the seller.[17] On the other hand, if the goods have been destroyed due to an impediment beyond the seller's control, before the risk passes to the buyer, then the seller is only shielded under payment of damages but not from attempting performance a second time or any other applicable remedies.[18] Additionally, when the risk has passed to the buyer, the procurement risk for money is borne by him; they are deemed to have guaranteed their financial capacity so that a specific performance claim for price is granted even if there is an

14 Richard A. Posner and Andrew M. Rosenfield, "Impossibility and Related Doctrines in Contract Law: An Economic Analysis" (1977) 6(1) *The Journal of Legal Studies* 83–118.

15 Andrew Kull, "Mistake, Frustration, and the Windfall Principle of Contract Remedies" (1991) 43(1) *Hasting L.J* 43–44.

16 This is in contradistinction with the no-fault policy that underlies the doctrine of exemption under the CISG.

17 Dennis Tallon, in Bianca-Bonell Commentary on the International Sales Law, Giuffrè: Milan (1987) 572–595.

18 Atamer (n 41) ch. 1, para 22, 1063.

impediment beyond his control.[19] A buyer is not released from payment of the price even if the money is stolen or lost, and they also bear the utility risk of not being able to put the goods to the planned use.[20]

The rationale behind art 66 is that it will be improper for a seller to be allowed to bear the loss when the risk has already passed to the buyer. It is also a commercial reality that most times the seller has more to lose when the goods are damaged after risk has passed to the buyer. Such losses can take the shape of the non-receipt of the payment price for the goods they have already procured and sold almost by law to the buyer. Physical delivery or receipt of the property will not excuse a buyer who has already taken over the risk of the goods.[21] This was clearly illustrated in *Ceramicas S.L. v Hanjin Shipping Co. Ltd*[22] where the Appeal Court held that the buyer bore the risks of transport from the time at which the goods were loaded onto the vessel. Citing art 66 CISG, it accordingly ruled that the buyer was the injured party and its claim justified. The risk of the goods had been transferred to the buyer despite the goods being handled for delivery by a carrier.

On the second part of art 66, the seller is liable for the loss if it is a result of his act or omission. This part is premised on the trite principle of law that a party should not be allowed to profit from his wrongdoing. The application of this second part of art 66 was captured in the *Piperonal Aldehyde case.*[23] A Chinese seller and an American buyer entered into a sales contract for Piperonal aldehyde. The contract stipulated delivery CIF to New York. The buyer faxed the seller repeated warnings on the sensitivity of the goods, advising him to keep them from high temperature and to arrange for non-stop shipment. The seller breached this agreement;

19 Ibid., para 23, 1064.

20 Ibid., 1084.

21 In the *Clothes case* Thessalonika 2008 Court of First Instance <http://cisgw3.law.pace.edu/cases/080002gr.html> accessed 15/9/2025, a Greek company (seller) sold to an Italian company (buyer) clothes for 41,874.70 Euro. The buyer approached the court and alleged both defect and destruction of some of the goods. The court found the buyer's objections legal but rejected them as a matter of substance and ordered the buyer to pay the balance of the purchase price that was due. The decision above was reached because the risk had already passed to the buyer, and the buyer did not, as a matter of fact, prove that the loss or damage resulted because of the act or omission of the seller. It is also instructive to note that this case did not fall within the purview of the doctrine of frustration; this is because it is not every loss that a party suffers that gives rise to frustration. Moreover, the loss must be substantial if not fundamental and will be capable of effectively discharging any arising obligation to perform the contract by the parties.

22 Italy [February 2003] [Appellate Court] Cite as http://cisgw3.law.pace.edu/cases/030215s4.html, in this case, The dispute involved not the buyer and seller under the international sales contracts, but the Spanish buyer (consignee) and the carrier. The goods were destroyed as a result of a fire on board the vessel on which they were being transported. The buyer sought damages and to be declared the owner of the goods, which was considered moot by the lower court judge, whereas the buyer's appeal was upheld as risk was deemed to have passed to him. (Abstract prepared by María Del Pilar Perales Viscasillas).

23 China International Economic & Trade Arbitration Commission (CIETAC) Arbitration award China 1999 (CISG/1999/01), CISG-online 1669 <https://cisg-online.org/search-for-cases?caseId=7588> accessed 17 September 2025.

he neither arranged for non-stop shipment nor was his phone notice to the carrier sufficient, which, besides, it did not prove. Tests revealed that the goods were damaged by high temperature during transport. After negotiations, the buyer, the seller and the insurer agreed on indemnifications for the buyer paid by both the insurance company and the seller. Subsequently, the buyer and the seller entered into a supplemental agreement in which the seller agreed to pay the buyer additional money. Consequently, the court ordered the seller to pay the buyer the promised sum. The decision above was easily reached when considering the fact that damage to the goods was because of the act and omission of the Chinese seller.

Nevertheless, the *Norwegian salmon case*[24] is very important in showing the relationship between risk, liability and exemption. In this case, a Norwegian seller, the plaintiff, sold raw salmon to a Danish company (the "Company"), which, after processing it, sold smoked salmon to a German buyer, the defendant. When the Company got into financial difficulties and, as a result of the bankruptcy of the Company, the buyer did not receive the salmon and, as such, refused to pay the purchase price. Then, the seller sued the buyer; the first-instance court allowed the claim. The buyer appealed, declaring the avoidance of the contract. The appellate court upheld the decision of the first-instance court, and the decision was based on the fact that the risk of payment of the price had been passed to the buyer.

The court held that the seller's confirmation order constituted an offer for the delivery of raw salmon and that the request for prompt confirmation clearly showed the seller's intention to conclude a purchase agreement with the buyer. The buyer accepted the offer by signing the confirmation order and as such, the parties concluded a purchase agreement. The court found that no additional interpretation of the confirmation order under art 8 CISG was necessary and that the receipt of the signed confirmation order by the seller, through the Company, was of no particular relevance. The court further held that the seller discharged its delivery obligation, although delivery occurred at a place other than the place stipulated by the contract and the Incoterm DDP. This was insignificant, as the buyer was indicated as the recipient of the raw salmon in the delivery note. The court also found that the seller was not in fundamental breach of contract under art 25 CISG. Despite the financial difficulties of the Company and the delivery of the salmon at the Company's place of business, the fulfilment of the contract was not jeopardised. The court concluded that the seller complied with its obligations and that the risk had passed to the buyer; thus, the buyer was obliged to pay the purchase price (under art 66 CISG), even if it did not receive the raw salmon[25] the contract is still subsisting and not frustrated.

24 Oberlandesgericht Oldenburg (Court of Appeal Oldenburg), Germany, 22 September 1998 – 12 U 54/98, CISG-online 508 <https://cisg-online.org/search-for-cases?caseId=6476> accessed 12 October 2025.

25 Ibid.

However, in reality, parties can actually decide on what to do in the event of loss or damage when risk has been passed to the buyer.[26] Honnold is of the view that:

> [O]f course, none of these problems can arise when the parties have the foresight to solve the problem in their contract - either by plain, blunt words or when risk passes to the buyer, or by incorporating a prefabricated solution in a standard contract or in a trade term as defined by Incoterms. And even when the contract gives no explicit solution, the matter may be settled by the practices established by the parties or by trade usage. These solutions are available under art 9 of the Convention, which corresponds to UCC 1–205. In all of these cases, the Convention (art 6) gives international force to choices made by the parties; here, as elsewhere, the Convention bows to the old-fashioned principle of liberty of contract.[27]

In consonance with Honnold, Lookofsky is of the opinion that modern commercial standard practices involving documentary credits do not follow the reasoning of art 66 to its logical conclusion. He goes on to articulate that:

> It is also important to note that, in practice, many international sales are 'documentary sales,' whereby the seller hands the goods over to a carrier and receives, in exchange, a bill of lading (or equivalent). The bill of lading, together with other relevant shipping documents, is then tendered to the buyer (or to the buyer's bank) in return for payment of the price. If the contract is a 'shipment' contract, the holder of the bill of lading normally bears the risk of loss or damage from the time the goods are placed on board; in the case of a 'destination' contract, the risk remains with the seller until the carrier arrives at the destination.[28]

This practice, though contrary to the provision of art 66, can be justified under art 9 of the CISG, which provides that the parties are bound by any usage to which they have agreed and any practices which they have established between themselves. Adding to the above, it has been held in the *Frozen Pork case (I)* that "suspicion

26 Annemieke Romein, "The Passing of Risk: A Comparison between the Passing of Risk Under the CISG and German aw," Heidelberg bookbook: English translation (1999) or 4 *Vindobona Journal* (2000) 62–79; the author writes that :

"When art. 66 CISG mentions 'loss of or damage to the goods,' it means such incidents, which are not caused by one of the parties to the contract or by persons for whom they are responsible, but incidents which are caused by independent third parties or incidents which are not caused by human persons. It must happen accidentally from the point of view of the contracting parties; in other words, it must be casual loss or damage. This comprises factual losses as well, such as theft, vandalism, accidents, unloading in emergencies and other physical impairments."

27 John Honnold (n 39) ch. 1, 394–397.

28 Lookofsky (n 3) 1–192.

of a health-threatening condition of the goods had to be regarded as a lack of conformity, even if the suspicion arose after the passing of risk."[29]

3.1.3 *Risk, First Carrier, and Exemption*

Art 67 of the CISG is a special provision which, together with art 68 of the CISG, defines the rights, positions, obligations and liabilities that arise from the passing of risk when a third party carrier is involved. Art 67 provides that:

(1) If the contract of sale involves carriage of the goods and the seller is not bound to hand them over at a particular place, the risk passes to the buyer when the goods are handed over to the first carrier for transmission to the buyer in accordance with the contract of sale. If the seller is bound to hand the goods over to a carrier at a particular place, the risk does not pass to the buyer until the goods are handed over to the carrier at that place. The fact that the seller is authorised to retain documents controlling the disposition of the goods does not affect the passage of the risk.
(2) Nevertheless, the risk does not pass to the buyer until the goods are clearly identified to the contract, whether by markings on the goods, by shipping documents, by notice given to the buyer or otherwise

The interpretation of this article has raised a lot of critical discussions among scholars; the use of "first carrier" and again "carrier" and the making of retention of document of title irrelevant to the passing of risk have no doubt created an academic buzz in the area of interpretation of art 67.[30] For instance, Schlechtriem is of the view, while offering an interpretation of art 67 that:

> [F]or sales involving carriage, art 67(1) contains the traditional solution for the passing of risk, namely, that the risk passes to the buyer when the goods have been handed over to the first carrier for transmission to the buyer (art 67(1) sentences 1 and 2); the law does not distinguish between carriage by sea, road or air or by a combination of modes, and it does not split the risk in cases of multimodal transportation. The basic case – where the goods are handed over to the first carrier (art 67(1) sentence 1) – is frequently modified by special contractual provisions, such as trade terms, whereby a carrier is to be given the goods at a particular place for (further) transmission; the transfer

29 Bundesgerichtshof (German Supreme Court), Germany, 02 March 2005 – VIII ZR 67/04, CISG-online 999 <https://cisg-online.org/search-for-cases?caseId=6923> accessed 19 September 2025.

30 Johan Erauw was of the opinion that "The question whether the contract 'involves carriage of the goods' so that art 67 applies, turns on the parties' agreement. In one case, a contract provision requiring the buyer 'to pick up' the goods and to 'take the goods to' its facilities in another country was held to mean that the contract 'involved carriage of the goods' and thus was governed by art 67 where the contract also included an 'FOB' delivery term." See Johan Erauw, "CISG Articles 66–70: The Risk of Loss and Passing It" (2005–06) 25 *Journal of Law and Commerce*, 203–217.

of the goods to this carrier – and not to the first – marks the passage of risk (art 67(1) sentence 2).[31]

An apt illustration of the application of arts 66 and 67 of the CISG was shown in the case of *Bedial, S.A. v Paul Müggenburg & Co. GmbH.*[32] An Argentine buyer and a German seller concluded a contract containing a C & F clause for the sale of dried mushrooms to be shipped to the buyer. In the course of their transport to Buenos Aires, the goods deteriorated. The buyer sued the seller, claiming lack of conformity of the goods. In accordance with art 67 CISG, the court held that the risk passed to the buyer when the goods were handed over to the first carrier for transmission to the buyer in keeping with the contract of sale.

In addition, the court held that the C & F clause obliged the seller to hand over the goods to the carrier and to pay the freight. However, a C & F clause does not affect the passing of the risk. Further, it should be noted that the buyer, pursuant to the C & F clause in the contract of sale, had taken out an insurance policy for transportation risks.

In accordance with art 66, the court held that the buyer, after passing of the risk, was not discharged from its obligation to pay the purchase price, even in the event of loss or damage to the goods, unless the loss or damage was due to an act or omission of the seller. In this case, the damage to the goods occurred after the passing of the risk to the buyer, who did not adduce that it was owing to an act or omission of the seller; accordingly, the court dismissed the action.

However, the important question to ask here is whether or not the buyer would have gone for the option of stating that the contract of sale was frustrated due to the deterioration of the mushroom. The answer to this question will depend on the facts of the case; if the deterioration of the goods has been as a result of an impediment beyond the control of the parties, which the parties did not foresee, and the consequences of which the parties cannot overcome, then the buyer will still pay the price but will be exonerated from paying damages under art 79 of the CISG.

The next delicate issue that is begging for explanation is who is the "first carrier" or the "carrier" as is provided under the Convention. It has been suggested that although the question was not discussed in Vienna, only the independent carrier was considered a carrier for the purposes of art 67. Accordingly, if the seller transports the goods with his own personnel, even though they are not obligated to do so, he maintains the risk of loss.[33] Barry Nicholas was of the opinion that "The word 'carriage' (and the associated word 'carrier') presumably excludes those

31 P. Schlechtriem, *Uniform Sales Law: The UN-Convention on Contracts for the International Sale of Goods* (Manz, Vienna 1986).

32 Argentina 31 October 1995 CISG-online number 229 (Appellate Court) <https://cisg-online.org/search-for-cases?caseId=6273> accessed 19 September 2025.

33 Barry Nicholas, "Art 67" in Bianca-Bonell Commentary on the International Sales Law, Giuffrè: Milan (1987) 487–495.

cases in which the movement of the goods is effected wholly by the parties' own means of transport. For there to be 'carriage', there must be a third party (the 'carrier') who undertakes to move the goods."

Similarly, the word "involves" cannot mean simply that a consequence of the sale will be carriage of the goods but must refer to a provision in the contract, express or implied, requiring or authorising carriage to be arranged.[34] This will nearly always mean that the seller is required or authorised to arrange for carriage, since in those cases in which the buyer is to arrange for collection of the goods, the contract will not in practice specify the means of collection.[35] Therefore, what is the status of a carrier who is under the same parent company as the seller? Would they be regarded as an independent contractor or personnel of the seller?

This book will argue that in such a situation, where the activities of the carrier are directly overseen by the seller so that there is no independent contract between the seller and the carrier, the carrier invariably will be regarded as personnel of the seller and wouldn't be regarded as a carrier as contemplated under art 67 of the CISG. On the other hand, if the carrier and the seller operate as part of a larger undertaking and need a distinct contract before the carrier gets involved, and if the seller has no control over the activities of the carrier, then the carrier can be regarded as coming under the provision of art 67.

It is a settled view of the law that a carrier who is entrusted with the obligation of door-to-door delivery of the goods cannot be heard to say that "he is a mere carrier without the obligation to oversee storage if the goods get damaged in transit." This issue was canvassed and succinctly given legal imprimatur in the *Ice cream case.*[36] In this case, the parties are not the seller and buyer, but rather the seller's insurance company, Catalana Occidente S.A., Seguros y Reaseguros (defendant), and the carrier, T.C. Campillo (plaintiff). The case arose because the contracted goods suffered significant damage when the container in which they were placed after unloading broke at the Havana port before they were delivered to the buyer. The seller's insurance company indemnified the seller and claimed against the carrier, who appealed in the present case. The court established that Campillo was not a mere carrier but a mediator, and, according to the contract, its obligations extended to transporting the merchandise "from door to door." This meant that it was liable for the damages incurred while the merchandise was in storage since the company which owned the container was a mere intermediary for whose services Campillo was liable.[37]

34 Ibid.

35 Ibid.

36 Spain 20 October 1999 Appellate Court Alicante <http://cisgw3.law.pace.edu/cases/991020s4.html>.

37 It can be argued that even when the goods have been handed over to the first carrier and risk presumably passed to the buyer, any failure to perform the obligation which is due to an impediment

Nevertheless, whether the loss or damage to the goods involves the carrier or the parties, it has been decided that injury caused by a *force majeure* event should be borne by the party who owes the risk; this is the decision in the *Yugoslav caviar case.*[38] The facts of this case are thus: a Yugoslav company sold and delivered caviar to a Hungarian company. According to their contract, the buyer must pick up the fish eggs at the seller's address and transport the goods to his facilities in Hungary. Payment was due two weeks after the delivery of the goods, at which time the UN embargo against Yugoslavia took effect in Hungary. The seller assigned the claim for the price of the goods to a company located in Cyprus. The buyer acknowledged the assignment but could not pay on the basis that the UN embargo was a *force majeure.*

The arbitral court found that the damage caused by *force majeure* had to be borne by the party to whom the risk had passed, i.e., the buyer. In this situation, the arbitral court found it necessary to point out that the risk of loss of freight had to be borne by the buyer, unless the parties' contract or applicable law provided otherwise (art. 67 CISG). The arbitral court held that the buyer was obliged to pay the price of the delivered goods with interest.[39]

This book will support the court's decision, albeit on the grounds that the buyer did not show that payment of the price was impossible, since they had the option of paying through the assignee company in Cyprus.

Also, it is sound commercial practice to ensure that the goods are identified in the contract, whether transported by the seller or carrier, by stating the buyer of the goods and any other necessary details categorically. Thus, a bill of lading which indicated that a container said to contain the specified brand name and number of goods had been delivered to a freight forwarder, but which did not indicate the name of the buyer as the recipient, was not sufficient proof of delivery (art 67(1) CISG). The above quotation formed part of the ratio of *Video Cameras and Equipment case.*[40]

There is also confusion about at what point in the transaction it can be said that the goods have been "handed over" to the carrier. The answer to this question can be found in the *Italian plants case*[41] where it was held that "the handing over of the goods in the sense of art 67(1) CISG is only completed upon conclusion of the

---

beyond the control of the seller will surely bring the contract of sale within the sphere of art 79 (2) (a) (b) of the CISG.

38 Arbitration Court attached to the Hungarian Chamber of Commerce and Industry, 10 December 1996 – VB 96074, CISG-online 774 <https://cisg-online.org/search-for-cases?caseId=6702> accessed 21 September 2025.

39 However, the above case is not antithetical to the provision of *force majeure* under art 79 of the CISG. If the court actually established that the *force majeure* event, which was the UN embargo, is effective, then this research suggests the buyer pay the price but can only be exempted from paying damages if exemption is proved.

40 Oberlandesgericht Köln (Court of Appeal Cologne), Germany, 09 July 1997 – 2 U 175/95, CISG-online 495 <https://cisg-online.org/search-for-cases?caseId=6463> accessed 21/9/2025.

41 Landgericht Bamberg (District Court Bamberg), Germany, 23 October 2006 – 2 O 51/02, CISG-online 1400 <https://cisg-online.org/search-for-cases?caseId=7322> accessed 22 September 2025.

loading." This means that whenever loading is completed in a delivery envisaging the carriage of goods, the goods have been handed over to the carrier, and, by necessary implication, the risk associated with the goods has passed to the buyer. It is interesting to observe that the international principle of law articulated under art 67 is now even permeating into domestic laws, thereby shaping decisions in accordance with the spirit and letter of the Convention.[42]

3.1.4 Risk, Goods Sold in Transit, and Exemption

Deciphering the position of the law when goods sold in transit got lost or perished is very recondite, especially when considering who bears the risk and if the doctrine of exemption will be applicable, particularly when the subject matter of the contract of sale has been destroyed, diminished or lost unknowingly to the contracting parties. Discussing the above caption will bring into consideration the provision of art 68 of the CISG which provides that:

> The risk in respect of goods sold in transit passes to the buyer from the time of the conclusion of the contract. However, if the circumstances so indicate, the risk is assumed by the buyer from the time the goods were handed over to the carrier who issued the documents embodying the contract of carriage. Nevertheless, if at the time of the conclusion of the contract of sale the seller knew or ought to have known that the goods had been lost or damaged and did not disclose this to the buyer, the loss or damage is at the risk of the seller.

The above provision is different from the provision of art 67 since it envisages the situation where the actual sale of the goods comes into play when the goods have already started their journey;[43] it is a very delicate situation which has the preponderance of risk weighing higher on the side of the seller. This is because it is a sale that requires the highest level of good faith due to the position of the buyer, who may be indulging in the sale purely based on the representations of the seller. The first part of the provision of art 68 is specially crafted in order to run the errand of the buyer. Joseph Lookofsky[44] buttressed this view when he writes that:

> First sentence of art 68, whereby the risk passes at the time of contracting was intended by its proponents to protect buyers in developing countries, but the rule has been criticized by Western experts as 'unworkable' in most cases: particularly when damage during transport results from an event difficult to pinpoint in time.

42 F.A.S. Italiana s.n.c. - Ti.Emme s.n.c. - Pres.Cons.Ministri (Avv.gen.Stato) Corte Costituzionale (Italian Constitutional Court) Italy, 19 November 1992 – 465, CISG-online 52 <https://cisg-online.org/search-for-cases?caseId=6032> accessed 22 September 2025.

43 Johan Erauw, "CISG Articles 66–70: the Risk of Loss and Passing It" (2005) 25 *JL & Com.* 203.

44 Lookofsky (n 3) 1–192.

However, Nicholas, giving a general overview of the provision, was of the belief that:

> The first sentence of the Article lays down the primary rule that the buyer bears the risk from the moment the contract is made (i.e., while the goods are in transit). When the damage clearly results from an identifiable event, such as a storm or a collision, there may be no difficulty in applying the rule, but it may often not be possible to identify a particular event as the cause (or the exclusive cause) of the damage. Moreover, if the damage is attributable in part to an event occurring after the making of the contract and in part to an event occurring before then, both the buyer and the seller will have to pursue claims arising from the events.[45]

More to this, the second part of art 68 tries to create a retroactive passage of risk to the buyer when the goods are handed in transit to a carrier who issued the documents embodying the contract of carriage.[46] This applies if the circumstances so indicated and provided for the risk to pass retroactively from the moment the goods are handed over to the carrier. This obviates any difficulties of proof and has the advantage that only the buyer must pursue claims arising from damage occurring while the goods are in transit. On the other hand, it places on the buyer the consequences of any inadequacy in the insurance, unlike what happens in the first situation where both the buyer and the seller can be fit and proper to pursue a claim arising from a situation where damage is attributable in part to an event occurring after the making of the contract and in part to an event occurring before then.[47]

The third part, which states "if the seller knew or ought to have known of the loss or damage at the time of the conclusion of the contract and did not disclose the fact to the buyer, the risk remains with the seller."[48] appeals to common sense. Of course, it shares the same fundamental principle of equity and fairness, which is a common trend in the sphere of commercial law. Knowledge of any circumstances that will be a snag to fulfilment of contractual obligations will be applied against the party with such knowledge. This provision is also similar to the provision of art 79 of the CISG; foreseeability or actual knowledge of the ruinous condition of a contract of sale defeats the application of the doctrine of exemption.

An example of the application of art 68 was most evident in the Russian case of *Diamant Ltd. v Kirov District Tax Inspectorate of the City of St. Petersburg.*[49] The court faced with the challenge to consider if, in accordance with the provision of art 68 of the CISG, risk and property in goods pass differently. The court held that,

45 Nicholas (n 2) ch. 2, 496–501.

46 Johan Erauw, "CISG Articles 66–70: The Risk of Loss and Passing It" (2005) 25 *JL & Com.* 203.

47 Ibid.

48 CISG art 68.

49 Federal Arbitrazh Court for the Northwestern Circuit, Russian Federation, 03 June 2003 – A56-37941/02, CISG-online 947 <https://cisg-online.org/search-for-cases?caseId=6871> accessed 23 September 2025.

in accordance with art 68 CISG, the risk in respect of goods sold in transit passes to the buyer from the time the goods are handed over to the carrier who issued the documents evidencing the contract of carriage. Therefore, according to the established international practice, the time of the seller's fulfilment of his obligations to the buyer is the time of the transfer of a right to (property in) goods. As a rule, this time is related to the passing of risks from the seller to the buyer. Thus, if a contract does not provide for the time of the transfer of a right to property in goods and other property, the time of the passing of risks of loss to the buyer may be considered to be the time of such transfer, i.e., the time when the goods are handed over either to the buyer himself or to a carrier.[50]

3.1.5 Risk of Goods Placed at Buyer's Disposal, Fundamental Breach, and Exemption

It will be an inchoate exercise to leave out thorough analysis of art 69 of the CISG; this is because it presents a common day-to-day experience that buyers and sellers encounter in the international contract of sale of goods. Art 69 of the CISG provides that:

(1) In cases not within articles 67 and 68, the risk passes to the buyer when he takes over the goods or, if he does not do so in due time, from the time when the goods are placed at his disposal and he commits a breach of contract by failing to take delivery.
(2) However, if the buyer is bound to take over the goods at a place other than a place of business of the seller, the risk passes when delivery is due and the buyer is aware of the fact that the goods are placed at his disposal at that place.
(3) If the contract relates to goods not then identified, the goods are considered not to be placed at the disposal of the buyer until they are clearly identified to the contract.

The above-stated provision of art 69 of the CISG can be described as a blanket provision that covers those areas not touched in the more specialised provisions of arts 67 and 68. It therefore lays down a residual rule that applies ordinarily in the absence of the peculiar circumstances of the two preceding articles. Art 69(1) provides the rule for cases not involving carriage when the buyer is not bound to take over the goods at a place other than the seller's place of business.[51]

50 Kristin Dutton, "Risky Business: The Impact of the CISG on the International Sale of Goods – A Guide for Merchants to Limit Liability and Increase Certainty Inside and Outside of the CISG" (2005) 7 *Eur. JL Reform* 239.

51 Michael Bridge, in analysing the art 69, writes that:

"The residual risk is found in Article 69 CISG and is expressed to apply where Articles 67–68 CISG do not apply. The basic rule in paragraph (1) is that the buyer is on risk from the moment he takes over the goods or when he commits a breach of contract in not taking delivery of goods that have been placed at his disposal. For the goods to be considered as placed at the buyer's disposal,

Thus, where the buyer has the responsibility to take over the goods at the seller's place, the risk generally passes when the buyer actually takes over the goods; if the buyer does not take over the goods on time, the risk passes at that point in time when the buyer commits this breach. If the contract permits the buyer to collect the goods within a given period, the risk will not pass until the period has expired, even if the goods were held available during that period.[52]

The rationale of the underlying paragraph (1) is that as long as the seller has control of the goods, they should bear the risk; he is in the better position to protect the goods and to provide for their insurance. Indeed, they are likely to be covered by the standing policies held by the seller in respect of his premises and their contents, whereas the buyer would probably need a special policy to cover the particular risk.

The buyer would also face difficulties in proving that any loss or damage was "due to an act or omission of the seller" as provided under art 66.[53] This paragraph (1) of art 69 suggests two elements that must be present before it can apply: first, arts 67 and 68 will not apply, and the buyer should be in physical control of the goods before the risk should be presumed to have passed to him; second, in the case where physical possession or control is not tenable, the buyer should have the goods at his disposal and, from his own act or omission, default in going ahead with taking delivery of the goods, thus committing a breach of contract. This second element also implies that the knowledge of the disposability of the goods is relevant in determining whether the risk has passed to the buyer or not.

The second paragraph applies when the buyer is to take delivery in a place other than the place of business of the seller, such as in a sale to destination – at the buyer's place of business; the risk will be deemed to have passed when the buyer has the earliest opportunity to take over delivery. Where delivery is to be made at a place which is not the buyer's place of business, such as in the case of warehoused goods, risk passes only when delivery is due and the buyer is in a position to pick up the goods and aware that the goods have been placed at his disposal. Where the buyer does not know, for example, from receipt of a warehouse document or a notice of release that the goods are available, the risk does not pass until the buyer has been notified and a full, uncomplicated disclosure of the itinerary of the goods provided.[54] In other words, paragraph (2) can also be associated with cases in which the contract provides for the buyer to take over the goods from a third party, most commonly from a public warehouse.

---

they must at least have been identified to the contract, as required by paragraph (3). A special rule applies under paragraph (2) where the buyer is bound to take over the goods at a place other than the seller's place of business. For risk to be transferred in such a case, delivery must be due and the buyer must be aware of the fact that the goods are at his disposal at that place." See Michael Bridge, "The Transfer of Risk under the UN Sales Convention 1980 (CISG)" in Camilla B. Andersen & Ulrich G. Schroeter (eds), *Sharing International Commercial Law across National Boundaries* (Wildy, Simmonds & Hill Publishing 2008) 77–105.

52 Lookofsky (n 3) 1–192.

53 Nicholas (n 2) ch. 2, 502–507.

54 Schlechtriem (n 50) ch. 1, 91.

Here the policy considerations are different; the seller is in no better position than the buyer to protect and insure the goods or to prosecute claims arising out of their loss. The policy of the paragraph is therefore that the risk should pass as soon as the buyer is in a position to collect the goods. The reasoning behind this paragraph is that it will be unconscionable to hold the seller liable in a situation where delivery is due and the buyer is aware of it but does not take the steps to take delivery. Commercial diligence and risk apportionment weigh heavier on the side of the buyer in such a scenario.

The Mobile grain dryer case[55] will be most instructive in bringing to the fore the general principle upon which art 69 is based. In this case, a Danish seller agreed to sell and deliver a mobile grain dryer to a buyer in Germany. The dryer fell and got damaged when the buyer's personnel were trying to tow it away. Making a general reference to art 69 CISG, the court found it reasonable to interpret the contract between the parties to mean that delivery of the dryer took place at the latest when the buyer took possession, i.e., when the dryer was unloaded from the truck by the buyer's personnel. For this reason and since the court found that the accident was not attributable to the seller or its personnel, the court held the buyer is liable to the seller for the agreed price.

The above case is not connected with the requirement of exemption under the CISG. None of the parties can base a cause of action under it since the impediment that caused loss to the contract of sale is not only foreseeable but was ignited, managed and actively aided by the activities of the parties. Hence, the proper issue for determination will be who bears the risk of loss, and that was properly done justice to in accordance with art 69(2) of the CISG.

Finally, under paragraph 3 of art 69, it is worthwhile identifying the goods to the contract; this has been briefly discussed earlier in this chapter.[56] It is also a settled view of the CISG that the passing of risk as provided for in arts 67, 68, and 69 will not diminish the remedies a buyer has where it is established that the seller has committed a fundamental breach of the contract. This is the message of art 70 of the CISG, which provides that "[i]f the seller has committed a fundamental breach of contract, arts 67, 68 and 69 do not impair the remedies available to the buyer on account of the breach." Inasmuch as this provision sounds plausible, it is filled with inconsistencies, especially when the fundamental breach is such that can prevent the risk from passing to the buyer at all. Lookofsky, while analysing art 70, is of the opinion that:

> [I]n the case of fundamental breach, although the risk has passed, the buyer may be able to insist on the delivery of substitute goods, or to avoid the

55 Randers Byret (District Court Randers) Denmark, 08 July 2004 – BS 2-2229/2002, CISG-online 2152 <https://cisg-online.org/search-for-cases?caseId=8068> accessed 24 September 2025.

56 This can be done by correctly stating in the accompanying documents the destination, buyer, nature and other relevant information that often go with the goods (subject matter of the contract) in accordance with any legislative instruments, bye-laws, trade usages and customs, or parties' established practices.

> contract, i.e. avail herself of remedies which would not ordinarily be available as regards goods lost or damaged as a result of Acts of God, etc. Nor will the fact that the buyer is unable to make restitution necessarily constitute a bar to avoidance in such a case.[57]

However, one obvious point remains important, and this point is that the buyer will not be allowed to claim damages for loss caused by an act of God, which translates to exemption, *force majeure* or frustration, but other practicable remedies can apply against the seller.

More so, Barry Nicholas added that the effect of art 70 is not confined to reversing the incidence of risk in respect of damage or loss while the goods are in transit. The seller's risk may extend to damage or loss occurring after the buyer has received the goods.[58] He went on to give a hypothetical case that:

> Suppose, for example, that Seller is bound to deliver to Buyer fifty tonnes of cocoa by 31 March; on that date he delivers only twenty tonnes, and this consignment is destroyed a few hours after its arrival by a fire in Buyer's warehouse which is not due to his act or omission.

If the delivery by the due date of only twenty tonnes constitutes a fundamental breach, the buyer may declare the contract avoided since his right to do so is preserved by art 82(2)(a). The same will be true if the seller's delivery of non-conforming goods constitutes a fundamental breach and the goods are subsequently destroyed in similar circumstances.

This hypothetical case goes a long way to support the fact that even passing of risk to the buyer would not cure a defective performance by the seller, especially if the defect constitutes a fundamental breach; then the legal rights and remedies of the buyer would not lapse. In conclusion, risk plays a very vital role under art 79 of the CISG. The doctrine of exemption does not impair the legal or contractual allocation of risk, but the importance of risk and whether it is to be borne by the sellers or buyers is in the realm of insurance.[59] It has been held that if a party has an insurable risk, they can insure that risk irrespective of whether they own the goods in law or not.[60]

3.2 Risk and *Force Majeure* under the UNIDROIT Principles

The UNIDROIT Principles do not, like the CISG and the Sale of Goods Act, provide for the passing of risk in rules; Gabriel is of the opinion that issues of risk of loss are resolved either by the express terms of the parties, by trade usages, or by

57 Lookofsky (n 3).

58 Nicholas (n 2) ch. 2, 508–512.

59 International contract for sale of goods does exclude only liability for damages under art 79 because parties to international trade are more capable of obtaining various insurance covers that will help to abate the risk of loss prevalent under the international trade sphere.

60 James Crabtree and others, *International Sale of Goods* (Croner Publications Ltd, 1991) 192.

other applicable laws.[61] Generally, where the parties have not allocated the risk, the sphere of risk is correspondingly with the sphere of control. If the Obligor could foresee and avoid or overcome the impediment, then art 7.1.7 will not apply.[62] This is because the notion of impediment under art 7.1.7 connotes that the event which causes the non-performance must be exogenous to the obligor's realm of risk.[63]

All possible risks of insurmountable inhibitions to performance should be foreseen by a future obligor. This is called the pre-contractual duty of best efforts to anticipate. Therefore, if a reasonable person of the same kind in the same circumstances at the time of conclusion of the contract had anticipated the event that leads to non–performance, the obligor who fails to accommodate the risk contractually assumes the risk of its performance being delayed or prevented.[64] Furthermore, all personal and private circumstances, illness, lawful or unlawful arrest, and any personal misfortune that befalls the obligor's wards or employees belong to the obligor's sphere of risk.[65] Similar to the personal circumstance is the obligation to deliver goods which are specified only in kind; the obligor owes the procurement risk to procure and deliver such goods. Some *force majeure* events, like strikes, can act as a *force majeure* impediment/inhibition if they affect transport.

This should be contrasted with a strike that is caused by wages or work conditions disputations. This type of strike falls within the ambit of the risk of the obligor and cannot constitute a *force majeure* impediment under art 7.1.7.[66] However, the obligee's ability to perform his financial obligations is a fundamental assumption underlying all contracts, and his failure cannot be exempted under art 7.1.7 of the UNIDROIT Principles even when the doctrine of *force majeure* becomes applicable. These obligations can only be excused by the order of a court in a bankruptcy proceeding.[67]

There are some provisions under the UNIDROIT Principles that can be used as default rules of risk. These provisions have helped in entrenching the relevance of risk in commercial contracts.[68] Art 6.1.6 provides thus:

61 Henry Gabriel, *Contracts for the Sale of Goods: A Comparison of Domestic and International Law* (Oceana Publications Inc, 2004) 187.

62 Kleinheisterkamp (n 106) ch. 1, 771.

63 Ibid.

64 Ibid., 772.

65 The rationale behind this rule is that the obligor is not expected to be exempted from the liability arising from impediment which comes up by way of personal circumstances. The foreseeability of such circumstances cannot be lightly waived. See Ibid., para 17, 772.

66 It can be summarised here that if the cause of the strike is extraneous and outside the managerial control of the obligor, then even a dispute as regards wages could be regarded as an impediment, for instance if it follows from a wider action of a national or federal trade union.

67 Perillo (n 35) ch. 1.

68 Whether the absence of provisions for risk in the UNIDROIT Principles is an oversight or intentional omission will depend on one of the traditional functions of the principles, which is to "provide a gap-filling" role to major legislative instruments or conventions that govern commercial contract transactions. Thus, the general rules of risk, in as much as they are not incompatible with the provisions of the UNIDROIT Principles, can apply.

(1) If the place of performance is neither fixed by, nor determinable from, the contract, a party is to perform:
  (a) a monetary obligation, at the obligee's place of business;
  (b) any other obligation, at its own place of business.
(2) A party must bear any increase in the expenses incidental to performance which is caused by a change in its place of business subsequent to the conclusion of the contract.

The legal implication of this provision is that damage or loss that happens after the obligor performed timeously at the right place must be borne by the obligee. It is the law that the obligee cannot urge or demand the obligor to perform a second time when the risk has passed to the obligee at the place of performance.[69] However, art 6.1.6(2) is a default rule since it can only apply in a situation where the place of performance is neither fixed by nor determinable from the contract. On the other hand, art 6.1.6(2) provides for the rule whereby the party changing its place of business, which has the effect of bringing a change in the performance, has to bear the additional expenses caused by the alteration. This burden of risk cannot be dispensed with even if the change of place of business is caused by an insurmountable impediment, though there can be an excuse in damages in accordance with the *force majeure* provision of art 7.1.7. Atamer has suggested that:

> As far as the change of place of business leads to an increase in risk (such as resulting from a more dangerous route for transport) and therefore, an increase in insurance fees, these fees must be borne by the changing party under art 6.1.6(2).[70]

It has been held that the reference to the place of business is considered to be a dynamic reference for the purposes of the place of performance. It follows that if a notice of change in the place of business is not transmitted, then the owner of the monetary obligation (obligor) could perform at the original known place of business of the obligee without incurring any breach of contract or running the risk of non-performance. Also, the obligor of the non-monetary obligation is judged to have performed late if the obligor is not able to arrive at the new place of business in time; the obligor will bear the risk of late or non-performance.[71]

Exploring further, art 6.1.7 of the UNIDROIT Principles, which provides for payment by cheque or other instruments, is very important when considering the risk of loss or theft of pull-order. This article provides that:

(1) Payment may be made in any form used in the ordinary course of business at the place for payment.

69 Art 6.16 of the UNIDROIT Principles line of reasoning is similar to art 69 of the CISG. See Atamer (n21) 645.
70 Atamer (n 41) ch. 1, 653.
71 Ibid., 653.

(2) However, an obligee who accepts, either by virtue of paragraph (1) or voluntarily, a cheque, any other order to pay or a promise to pay, is presumed to do so only on condition that it will be honoured.

When a buyer is an obligor, then there is a presumption that they carry the risk of insolvency of the paying agent. If the paying agent becomes insolvent after receiving the obligor's funds but before transferring them to the obligee, the obligor bears the risk of loss even if there is an established impediment under art 7.1.7; the obligor can be excused from damages but has the obligation to pay a second time.[72]

In conclusion, UNIDROIT Principles are non-binding *lex mercatoria* rules which do not claim to solve all the problems associated with commercial contracts but instead create flexible rules which could be used to supplement or be supplemented with other major laws. It can be suggested that based on the interpretations of art 1.6 of the UNIDROIT Principles,[73] arts 66–70 (Risk) of the CISG can apply *mutatis mutandis* to the provisions of the UNIDROIT Principles since the fundamental principles of the UNIDROIT Principles are based on the principles guiding the application and interpretation of international uniform law instruments like the United Nations Convention on the International Contract of Sale of Goods (CISG). It should be added that the standard trade terms as per the Incoterms[74] are often employed in transactions involving the UNIDROIT Principles, the CISG or the common law during the allocation of risk. The ultimate effect of whatever rules of risk that apply is to allocate liability to the parties of the obligations owed in the contract. Generally, under the Incoterms rules, the risk of loss of or damage to the goods passes from the seller to the buyer when the seller has fulfilled his obligations to deliver the goods, though the goods must have been duly appropriated to the contract.[75]

Under the C.I.F. contract, the risk passes as from shipment when the shipping document is tendered to the buyer, and this could also be accomplished retrospectively.[76] Any impediment after the risk has been passed under the C.I.F. contract will not be enough to frustrate the contract, as the buyer will be liable to pay the price. A C.I.F. contract is an agreement to sell goods at an inclusive

72 Atamer (n 41) ch. 1, 662.

73 Art 1.6 UNIDROIT Principles:

(1) In the interpretation of these Principles, regard is to be had to their international character and to their purposes, including the need to promote uniformity in their application.

(2) Issues within the scope of these Principles but not expressly settled by them are, as far as possible, to be settled in accordance with their underlying general principles.

74 In sale on FOB, CIF, CFR, risk passes to the buyer not on the passing of the property, but on shipment, and the seller is not therefore liable for any loss or damage to the goods. See Bugden & Lamont – Black (n 83) para 3–028, 79.

75 Bugden & Lamont-Black (n 83) ch. 1, para 3–029, 80; see also Mestre (1991) Rev. trim. de droit civ. 659

76 Michael Bridge, *The International Sale of Goods* (Oxford University Press, 2nd edn, 2007) para 8.53, 369

price covering the cost of the goods, insurance and freight. Even if the goods have been lost before the documents are tendered to the buyer but after shipment, the risk would have passed to the buyer, and they must pay the price. His remedies will be against the carrier or the underwriter but not against the seller on the contract of sale.[77] A C.I.F. contract could be frustrated if it provides for a method of performance which becomes impossible or where the agreed mode of performance becomes impossible.

Under the traditional FOB contract, risk will be presumed to pass when the goods have been put on board,[78] the implication of this is any inhibition that causes the goods to perish will not relieve the buyer from paying the price, and then property passes when the goods are delivered to the first carrier.[79] It has been held in the case of *Olbert Metal Sales Ltd. v Cerescorp Inc*[80] that the above rule of risk does not change, even if the seller reserves the right of disposal. This stance can be contrasted with the CISG, where the risk and property pass altogether upon when the goods are handed over to the first carrier.[81] The CISG does not make a difference between transfer of risk and transfer of property.

Also, the notice of shipment is very important in both the FOB contract transfer of risk, the CISG and the Sales of Goods Act 1979. Art 67(2) CISG provides for the rule of notice; Section 32(3) of the 1979 Act also provides that:

> Unless otherwise agreed, where goods are sent by the seller to the buyer by a route involving sea transit, under circumstances in which it is usual to insure, the seller must give such notice to the buyer as may enable him to insure them during their sea transit; and if the seller fails to do so, the goods are at his risk during such sea transit.

It has been held that the above rule of notice also applies to FOB contracts; in *Wimble v Rosenberg*[82] it was held that the rule in Section 32(3) applied to FOB contracts. Failure to stick to the rule of notice of risk in order for the buyer to insure the goods will leave the risk at the doorstep of the seller. This is similar to the rule of notice under art 79(4) and art 7.1.7(3) of the CISG and the UNIDROIT Principles, respectively. Under these provisions, the party who fails to give notice

77 Ibid., para 19–125, 1557. The author writes that:

"A C.I.F for the sale of specific goods which has perished before shipment can be frustrated under Section 7 of the Sale of Goods Act 1979 but not so if the goods are unascertained or generic goods. This principle of law may not apply though to the C.I.F contract under the UNIDROIT Principles and the CISG as these two legal instruments do not make a distinction between specific/unascertained or generic goods.'

78 Stock v Inglis (1884) 12 OBD 564.

79 Shepherd v Harrison (1871) LR 5 HL 116.

80 [1997] 1FC (Canada) 899.

81 Art 67 CISG; but the risk does not pass to the buyer until the goods are clearly identified to the contract, whether by markings on the goods, by shipping documents, by notice given to the buyer or otherwise.

82 [1913] 3 KB743.

of any impediment is to bear the burden of risk and be liable in damages for non-receipt of the notice.

3.3 Risk and Frustration under the English Common Law and the Sale of Goods Act 1979

3.3.1 Background

Under the doctrine of frustration provided in the common law and Section 7 of the 1979 Act, the contract is avoided and both parties are relieved from all their obligations under the contract.[83] However, this will not be the case if the special rules as to the passing of risk of loss provide that any of the parties bears the risk.[84] Thus, the special rules of risk in a specific type of contract will readily displace the doctrine of frustration. For instance, under the contract of sale of goods, the doctrine of discharge (frustration) can be displaced by the operation of the rules as to risk if under those rules, the risk can pass early rather than at the later stage of the contract performance.[85]

Risk implies that a party is bound to bear the accidental loss of or damage to goods,[86] while frustration implies the allocation of risk in a contract when a situation that is outwith the fault and liabilities of the parties happens to render the contractual performance impossible. Whenever a contractual party knowingly contracts to assume a risk, then the contract will not be said to have been frustrated if the impediment that renders the contract impossible of performance fell within the contracted risk.[87]

Generally, under the 1979 Act which reflects the position in the common law, if the risk falls on the buyer, they must take the risk of damage or loss, take delivery of the goods and pay for them. If the property in the goods has passed, the seller will be able to bring an action against the buyer for the price under Section 49(1) if the buyer fails to pay for the goods.

Where the goods are destroyed after the risk has passed to the buyer, the contract is not avoided, the buyer must pay the price, and the seller is under no further obligation to deliver replacement goods, but if payment has been made illegal or impossible, the contract will then be totally discharged.[88] A buyer who pays the

83 Risk and frustration are hugely relevant under the common law and the Sale of Goods Act of 1979. It seems that the principles and precedents laid down under the common law have found a way of being codified as positive statutory provisions under the 1979 Act.

84 Treitel, *Frustration and Force Majeure* (n 46) ch. 1, para 3–007, 77.

85 Ibid., para 3–010, 81.

86 Atiyah (n 75) ch. 2, 342.

87 Before the doctrine of frustration can apply, the court must be satisfied that neither party has agreed to run the risk of the event in question. The court construes the contract to see if the risk is expressly provided for (a *force majeure* clause) or if there is evidence of intention to run such risk. Indeed, *force majeure* clauses are common in modern commercial contracts so that the parties know where they stand right from the outset.

88 Treitel (n 46) ch. 1, para 3–010, 84.

price when the risk has passed and in the situation of subsequent perishing of the goods or property will be recompensed by any insurance money available to cover the risk; this is where Section 47(1) of the Law of Property Act of 1925 comes in to play.[89] This provision is to the effect that a contract is still subsisting despite the destruction of the subject matter after the date of sale or exchange of property. The buyer owes the risk and must pay the price, but the insurance money must be paid over by the vendor to the buyer on completion, as the buyer who pays the price should also be entitled to an insurance benefit. However, the buyer/purchaser must pay the proportionate part of the premium from the date of the contract and when the risk has passed.[90]

Likewise, if the risk is with the seller and they are unable to deliver the goods as ordered, he will be liable in damages for non-delivery under Section 51 of the 1979 Act unless he is able to make substitute performance. The seller is not discharged from their obligations in tendering ancillary performances like the delivery of shipping documents even though the goods have been destroyed after the risk has been passed to the buyer and the seller owes no more obligation to redeliver the goods.[91]

But in a situation where the goods have perished or where any other type of impediment causes radical disruption of performance before the risk passes, then this can be a game changer that can drastically alter the rule of allocation of risks and liabilities as the doctrine of frustration can justifiably apply to such a situation. It can be summarised thus that no impediment can discharge a contract of sale of goods after the risk has passed, though there can be discharge by impediment before the passing of the risk.[92]

3.3.2 *Passing of Risk and Frustration under Section 20 of 1979 Act*

Michael Bridge holds the opinion that "risk involves the allocation of loss due to an external event for which neither party is responsible." He goes on to add that:

> Such events will typically include loss or damage caused by the act of God and by the misbehaviour of third parties such as the carriers, it may include loss due to governmental intervention such as requisition[93]

89 Law of Property Act 1925 Section 47(1) provides that:

"Where after the date of any contract for sale or exchange of property, money becomes payable under any policy of insurance maintained by the vendor in respect of any damage to or destruction of property included in the contract, the money shall, on completion of the contract, be held or receivable by the vendor on behalf of the purchaser and paid by the vendor to the purchaser on completion of the sale or exchange, or so soon thereafter as the same shall be received by the vendor."

90 Ibid., Section 47(2)(c).

91 Manbre Saccharine Co Ltd. v Corn Products Co Ltd. [1919]1 K.B 198.

92 Treitel (n 46) ch. 1, para 3–010, 83.

93 Michael Bridge, *The Sale of Goods* (Oxford: Clarendon, 1997) pp. 112–20, 124–31.

This remark succinctly points to the fact that the passing of risk is very central to the determination of the doctrine of frustration under the Act. There is always the question of at what point risk passes in determining whether or not liability has fallen on a party. Guidance to this poser can be seen under Section 20 of the Sale of Goods Act of 1979.[94]

The Section 20 rule of passing of risk can only be relevant in a frustration under Section 7 of the Act if the contract of sale is for specific goods and the goods have perished without the fault of the parties before the risk is transferred to the buyer. But if the risk has been transferred to the buyer at the time the goods (specific) perished, then it will be assumed that the buyer will bear the risk of loss of the goods and pay the price.[95] In *Horn v Ministry of Food*[96] it was held that the contract was not avoided because deterioration of the potatoes occurred after the risk had passed to the buyer.

There is also a distinction in the passing of risk and its concomitant implications when a buyer deals as a merchant or as a consumer.[97] Section 20(4) of the 1979 Act provides that the goods remain at the seller's risk until they are delivered to the buyer if the buyer is a consumer. This means that the misfortune of perishing or any other impediment will not relieve the seller of the obligation to deliver the goods to the buyer (consumer).[98]

94 Section 20 of the Sale of Goods Act 1979 provides thus:

(1) Unless otherwise agreed, the goods remain at the seller's risk until the property in them is transferred to the buyer, but when the property in them is transferred to the buyer, the goods are at the buyer's risk whether delivery has been made or not.
(2) But where delivery has been delayed through the fault of either buyer or seller, the goods are at the risk of the party at fault as regards any loss which might not have occurred but for such fault.
(3) Nothing in this section affects the duties or liabilities of either seller or buyer as a bailee or custodian of the goods of the other party.
(4) In a case where the buyer deals as a consumer or, in Scotland, where there is a consumer contract in which the buyer is a consumer, subsections (1) to (3) above must be ignored and the goods remain at the seller's risk until they are delivered to the consumer.

95 The rationale behind this conclusion is not the most plausible; it can be argued that there are not different legal consequences between when the goods perished while still under the risk of the seller or the buyer. The contract should be avoided in both instances if the destruction of the goods can be proved to be supervening and without the fault of the parties. But again, it seems the special rule of risk will displace the doctrine of supervening impossibility in this scenario because of the commercial policy of not allowing parties to get out of an obligation which risk they have assumed.

96 [1948] ALL E.R 1036

97 Trietel, *Frustration and Force* (n 46) ch. 1, para 3–010, 83; "The rule under section 20(4) of the 1979 Act may not be varied by oral agreement and if varied, then it can come under the scrutiny of the Unfair Contract Act of 1977 and can be dealt with as an exemption clause."

98 The above rule will still apply even though property may have passed to the buyer and they have paid for the goods before delivery. See Trietel, Frustration and *Force majeure* (n 46) ch. 1, para 3–009, 80.

Generally, risk passes with the property,[99] but this is not as simple as it looks, practically and in accordance with Section 16 of the 1979 Act, property cannot pass until the goods are ascertained and become specific goods.[100] If a buyer has acquired property in the goods, it implies that the goods must have been ascertained, and risk would have well passed. It becomes then a completed sale rather than an agreement to sell, and Section 7 of the 1979 Act (doctrine of frustration) does only apply to an agreement to sell, and if the goods have perished, the person who bears the risk cannot be excused in such a scenario and has the option and risk of procuring insurance cover as well.[101]

The problem of not deciphering the exact point of passing of risk and subsequent perishing of the goods was in issue in the case of *Stern v Vickers Ltd*,[102] it was held that the contract of sale of goods cannot be avoided when the goods perished and the buyer must pay the price since the risk had passed to the buyer when he handed over the delivery order to a third party who kept the goods as a bailee for the seller.

The court further held that the buyer bears the risk, though the property is still with the seller due to the fact that the buyer has not taken delivery of 120,000 out of 200,000 gallons of spirit the third party bailee held. It can be added that delivery to a carrier for onwards transmission to the buyer means risk has passed to the buyer and the contract cannot be discharged by supervening impossibility.[103]

There is also an element of fault in the determination of who bears the risk when a contract of sale of goods has been frustrated under the common law or Section 7 of the 1979 Act, and Section 20(2) of the 1979 Act. Where the buyer's or the seller's fault causes any loss to the goods, then the goods are at the risk of such a party. In the case of *Denby Hamilton& Co. Ltd. v Barden*[104] the buyer was late in taking delivery of an apple juice and delayed in giving the seller relevant information on customer delivery details; the court held risk had been passed to the buyer though property had not, and the contract could not be avoided even under Section 7 of the 1979 Act because the perishing of the goods was due to the buyer's fault.

Controversially, Section 33 of the Sale of Goods Act 1979 provides that:

> Where the seller of goods agreed to deliver them at his own risk at a place other than that where they are when sold, the buyer must nevertheless (unless

99 It is not always that the risk passes with the property in accordance with Section 20(1) of the 1979 Act; sometimes the risk can pass before or after the property has passed. For instance, in a hire purchase and conditional sale, the risk always passes to the debtor or hirer at the beginning of the contract along with an obligation often to insure the goods.

100 However, where the sale is of a specified quantity of unascertained goods which form part of a bulk that is identified either in the contract or by subsequent agreement between the parties, property in an undivided share in the bulk can now, by virtue of Section 1(3) 1995 Sale of Goods (Amendment) Act, pass to the extent to which the buyer has paid for the goods.

101 Trietel (n 46) ch. 1, para 3–014, 87.

102 [1923] 1KB 78.

103 Section 32 (1) of the Sales of Goods Act 1979.

104 [1949] 1ALL ER 435.

otherwise agreed) take any risk of deterioration in the goods necessarily incident to the course of transit.[105]

Assuming the deterioration as mentioned under Section 33 above results in the total perishing of the entire goods so as to make the aim of performing the contract defeated, it can be held that the contract cannot be avoided because the buyer owns the risk of incidents associated with the transit of the goods. However, the use of the phrase "where the seller of goods agreed to deliver them at his own risk" shows that the seller also has some risk since it beats common sense and logic that a seller who assumed a further risk to transit the goods should not be held liable if there is an incident of impediment that deteriorates the goods during the subsistence of the further risk.[106]

3.4 Conclusion

Both under art 66 of the CISG and Section 20 of the 1979 Act, there is a consensus that whenever the buyer owns the risk, then they must pay the price or perform any other obligations that come within the territory of their performance. The buyer cannot under any of these laws (CISG, UNIDROIT Principles, and English law) be reprieved from payment obligations.[107] However, while Section 20 of the 1979 Act provides for risk passing with the property, the CISG has no such requirement as the issue of right and transfer of the property in the goods is excluded from the jurisdiction of the CISG.[108] This book will deduce that art 66 of the CISG can be interpreted in the light of any national law of the contracting states that allow risk passing with the property.

Whenever it can be proven that the risk has passed or still remained with either of the parties, the legal implication is that the doctrine of exemption under the CISG and *force majeure* under the UNIDROIT Principles will be inapplicable to exonerate a party from the consequences of his non-performance. Also, under the common law and the 1979 Act, the doctrine of frustration cannot apply to discharge and enable the buyer to avoid the consequences of his lack of performance when the risk has passed to him (the buyer), but it can avail a seller who has not delivered if the conditions are met. The doctrine of frustration is therefore more lenient under Section 7 of the 1979 Act.[109] This is because a seller who owns the risk when the

105 Sale of Goods Act 1979 Section 33.

106 Section 33 of the 1979 Act is not a very elegant piece of drafting as both the risk of further transit of the goods and that of deterioration of the goods cannot be severed. Anyone who owes/agrees to the risk of transportation of the goods should take proper care to protect the goods from perishing and should bear the risk in the event of loss.

107 Bridge (n 140) ch. 2, para 8.43, 362; more so, the author writes that under the 1979 Act, the fact of risk remaining with the seller is neutral as far as the incidence of risk is concerned. The contract may or may not be frustrated when the goods, either specific or initially unascertained, perished.

108 Art 4 of the CISG, the issue of transfer of property will be better reserved for the contracting states' national laws or any other laws the parties agreed to bind and regulate their contract.

109 Andrew Phang, "Frustration in English Law-A Reappraisal" (1992) 21 *Anglo-Am. L. Rev.* 278.

goods perish before the risk passes to the buyer and without the fault of the parties, where there is an agreement to sell specific goods, will be relieved of liability for non–delivery and the buyer is relieved of the obligation to pay the price,[110] but under the CISG and the UNIDROIT Principles, the seller is only relieved from damages for non-performance but will still be held responsible to deliver, and the buyer will be liable for the price.

It can be recapped that under the CISG, common law, the 1979 Act and even the UNIDROIT Principles, the agreement of the parties regarding who bears the risk is paramount and must be respected except when such agreement fails the good faith test.[111] Also, the incoterms discussed above like FOB, CIF, FAS, and CFR can apply separately or jointly with other extant rules of risk discussed in this chapter.

110 Atiyah (n 75) ch. 2, 349.

111 Both art 7 of the CISG and art 1.7 of the UNIDROIT Principles of International Commercial Contracts 2010 provide for the observance of good faith.

4 Relationship between Avoidance/Termination with Exemption/*Force Majeure*/Frustration

4.1 Exemption and Avoidance under the CISG

4.1.1 Background

One of the most important remedies under the CISG is termed "avoidance" of the contract. Ulrich Magnus writes that under the CISG, avoidance is the one-sided right of a party to terminate the contract by its mere declaration.[1] Such termination of a contract is the hardest sword that a party to a sales contract can draw if the other party has breached the contract.[2] The fundamental aim of the remedy of avoidance is to relieve a party from further obligations when there is a fundamental breach of contract by failure of a party to perform any of his obligations owed in the contract or, in the case of non-delivery/payment of price/accepting delivery if under the *Nachfrist* rule (additional time to perform), performance of any outstanding obligation has not been complied with.

It has been held that "the CISG is based on the principle that avoidance is generally only possible if the breach of contract is so fundamental that the party at fault at least ought to have known that the other party would not have further interest in being bound by the contract."[3] This can be contrasted with the doctrine of "exemption," which is based on the principle that the debtor or a party is not liable in damages for a breach of an obligation if the reason for the breach was neither controllable nor foreseeable.[4]

1 Ulrich Magnus, "The Remedy of Avoidance of Contract Under CISG-General Remarks and Special Cases" (2005) 25 *JL & Com.* 423.

2 Ibid.

3 Peter Schlechtriem and Petra Bulter, *UN Law on International Sales* (Springer, 2009) 143.

4 Ibid., 200. The difference between the doctrine of exemption of contract and avoidance of contract under the CISG lies at the "cause" of the reason or impediment that brings about failure of obligation. While under exemption of contract it can be said that the cause of the impediment must be without the fault of the parties, the same cannot be said of avoidance; avoidance of a contract can only be justified when a party has committed a breach by his own fault that is fundamental in nature and also tantamount to a breach of the terms or intentions of the contract. It can also be said that while avoidance of the contract is internally rooted in the controllable and foreseen actions and omissions of the parties, the factors that bring about the situation of frustration are always external and beyond the reasonable contemplation of the parties at the time of entering into or negotiating the terms of the contract of sale of goods.

DOI: 10.4324/9781003667841-4

Non-performance under art 79 can be regarded as a breach whenever it can be established, and thus the remedy of avoidance could apply.[5] Under arts 49 and 64 of the CISG, the convention gives both the buyer and the seller, respectively, the right to avoid a contract of sale of goods, but it is not every breach of contract or every fault of a party that affects performance of the contract that attracts the remedy of avoidance.[6] The hallmark of the international sale is to reserve this important but often abused remedy for a situation of serious fundamental breach which has the capability of denying the innocent party of his honest expectations from the contract. Art 49 provides thus:

(1) The buyer may declare the contract avoided:
  (a) if the failure by the seller to perform any of his obligations under the contract or this Convention amounts to a fundamental breach of contract; or
  (b) in case of non-delivery, if the seller does not deliver the goods within the additional period of time fixed by the buyer in accordance with paragraph (1) of art 47 or declares that he will not deliver within the period so fixed.
(2) However, in cases where the seller has delivered the goods, the buyer loses the right to declare the contract avoided unless he does so:
  (a) in respect of late delivery, within a reasonable time after he has become aware that delivery has been made;
  (b) in respect of any breach other than late delivery, within a reasonable time:
    (i) after he knew or ought to have known of the breach;
    (ii) after the expiration of any additional period of time fixed by the buyer in accordance with paragraph (1) of art 47, or after the seller has declared that he will not perform his obligations within such an additional period; or
    (iii) after the expiration of any additional period of time indicated by the seller in accordance with paragraph (2) of art 48, or after the buyer has declared that he will not accept performance.[7]

And art 64 provides thus:

(1) The seller may declare the contract avoided:
  (a) if the failure by the buyer to perform any of his obligations under the contract or this Convention amounts to a fundamental breach of contract; or

5 Stefan Kroll and others (eds), *UN Convention on Contracts for the International Sale of Goods* (Hart Publishing 2011) para 2, 1056; It should be noted that art 79 can be regarded as a rule of damages which gives a party the chance to fully avoid paying damages if the non-performance was caused by an impediment which was beyond control and could not reasonably have been taken into account at the time of the conclusion of the contract.

6 Ingeborg Schwenzer, "Avoidance of the Contract in Case of Non-Conforming Goods (Article 49 (1)) A) CISG" (2005) 25 *JL & Com.* 437.

7 CISG art 49.

(b) if the buyer does not, within the additional period of time fixed by the seller in accordance with paragraph (1) of article 63, perform his obligation to pay the price or take delivery of the goods, or if he declares that he will not do so within the period so fixed.

(2) However, in cases where the buyer has paid the price, the seller loses the right to declare the contract avoided unless he does so:

(a) in respect of late performance by the buyer, before the seller has become aware that performance has been rendered; or

(b) in respect of any breach other than late performance by the buyer, within a reasonable time:

(i) after the seller knew or ought to have known of the breach; or

(ii) after the expiration of any additional period of time fixed by the seller in accordance with paragraph (1) of article 63, or after the buyer has declared that he will not perform his obligations within such an additional period.[8]

When a contract of sale has been fundamentally breached or when delivery is not effected or taken or payment for goods made after an additional period of time, then it is a proper situation for the application of the remedy of avoidance by a party who is injured or likely to be injured by the breach. Avoidance must not be imaginary or misconceived; otherwise, far-reaching consequences and extensive waste may follow in the wake of contract avoidance.[9] This is probably why Larry A. DiMatteo *et al*[10] are of the view that "the limitations of the avoidance remedy to the events of arts 49(1)(a)(b) and 64(1)(a)(b) are consistent with the CISG underlying policy of contract continuance."

The general rule is that avoidance requires a showing of a particularly serious breach. Victor Knapp argued that when the conditions of arts 49 and 64 are met, the seller is authorised (but not obliged) to declare the contract avoided. The seller may even in this case require the buyer to perform their obligation and sue them for performance (art 62), or invite them to perform their obligation within an additional period of time under art 63. By doing so, they of course do not lose their right to declare the contract avoided under art 64.[11] Thus, while the mode of operations and the elements that can constitute a ground for the avoidance of a contract and exemption of a contract are different under the CISG, their outcome and legal implications are almost identical. This is as a result of the peculiar nature of the provision of arts 79, 49, and 64 of the CISG; hence, all these doctrines tend to bring succour to a party who will suffer commercial misfortune as a result of non-performance of the other party.

8 CISG art 64.

9 Bzhar Abdullah Ahmed and Hassan Mustafa Hussein, "Avoidance of Contract as a Remedy under CISG and SGA: Comparative Analysis" (2017) 61 *JL Pol'y & Globalization* 126.

10 Di Matteo (n 3) ch. 2, 135.

11 Victor Knapp, in Bianca-Bonell Commentary on the International Sales Law (Giuffrè Milan, 1987) 465–474.

A succinct example of the application of the remedy of avoidance can be seen in the *Grinding machines case*[12] where it was held that in accordance with art 49(1)(b) CISG, the buyer could declare the contract avoided if the seller made delivery of the goods subject to a consideration to which it was not entitled. The court observed that the defendant had proposed to the plaintiff that it would pay that part of the sale price which, in its opinion, was in fact due following set-off against outstanding debts under the first contract. The plaintiff did not accept that proposal and continued to demand payment of the full sale price still owed to it under the contract. If the defendant's right of set-off in fact existed and the plaintiff's claim for payment of the sale price was consequently extinguished through set-off for a corresponding amount, which implied that the plaintiff was demanding a consideration to which it was not entitled in such a form. Thus, the defendant had rightly declared the contract avoided. This case also supports the view that if a party wrongly pleads exemption/*force majeure* or frustration and thereby refuses to render performance, then the contract can be avoided by the victim party.[13]

Also, avoidance under the CISG comes with a bundle of consequences;[14] art 81 of the CISG provides that:

(1) Avoidance of the contract releases both parties from their obligations under it, subject to any damages which may be due. Avoidance does not affect any provision of the contract for the settlement of disputes or any other provision of the contract governing the rights and obligations of the parties consequent upon the avoidance of the contract.
(2) A party who has performed the contract either wholly or in part may claim restitution from the other party of whatever the first party has supplied or paid under the contract. If both parties are bound to make restitution, they must do so concurrently.

Accordingly, a seller that has supplied anything to the buyer may demand it back by way of restitution; liability for damages for any breach of contract is not eliminated.[15] Avoidance is also permitted under art 79 of the CISG; when a party is prevented from performing his obligation due to unforeseen impediment, the contract can be avoided though the non-performing party will be exempted from liability in

12 Bundesgericht/Tribunal fédéral (Swiss Federal Supreme Court) Switzerland, 20 December 2006 – 4C.314/2006, CISG-online 1426 <https://cisg-online.org/search-for-cases?caseId=7348> accessed 21/9/2025.

13 Germany 21 March 1996 der Handelskammer Hamburg (Court of Arbitration of the Hamburg Chamber of Commerce)– Partial Award (on the merits), CISG-online 187 <https://cisg-online.org/search-for-cases?caseId=6162> accessed 21/9/2025.

14 Chengwei Liu, "Effects of Avoidance: Perspectives from the CISG, UNIDROIT Principles and PECL and Case Law" (2005) 1 *NJCL* 1.

15 Gabriel (n 61) ch. 3, 223.

damages.[16] Restitution under art 81(2) can apply under art 79 of the CISG, subject to the provision of art 82 of the CISG which provides that:

(1) The buyer loses the right to declare the contract avoided or to require the seller to deliver substitute goods if it is impossible for him to make restitution of the goods substantially in the condition in which he received them.
(2) The preceding paragraph does not apply:
 (a) if the impossibility of making restitution of the goods or of making restitution of the goods substantially in the condition in which the buyer received them is not due to his act or omission;
 (b) if the goods or part of the goods have perished or deteriorated as a result of the examination provided for in article 38; or
 (c) if the goods or part of the goods have been sold in the normal course of business or have been consumed or transformed by the buyer in the course of normal use before he discovered or ought to have discovered the lack of conformity.[17]

It follows from the above that if the buyer cannot make restitution of the goods substantially in the same condition in which the buyer received them, then the buyer loses the right of avoidance under art 81 of the CISG or the right to require the seller to supply substitute goods, though there is a limitation to this proviso under art 82(2) (a- c).[18] In a situation where the buyer loses the right to avoid the contract or require delivery of substitute goods under art 82 CISG, then all other remedies under the convention according to art 83 CISG are not affected.[19]

16 Michael Bridge, "Avoidance for Fundamental Breach of Contract under the UN Convention on the International Sale of Goods" (2010) 59(4) *I.C.L.Q.* 911–940; he writes that: "Under art 81 of the CISG, the primary consequence of avoidance is that it releases both parties, and not just the party exercising the right of avoidance, from their contractual obligations. The non-performing party, however, unless exempted under art 79, remains bound to pay damages in accordance with art 74 and related provisions."

17 CISG art 82.

18 Tallon (n 43) ch. 2, 607–610, is of the opinion that:

"The buyer's loss of the right to avoid the contract when restitution has become impossible is not recognized everywhere. In countries where avoidance is ordered by the judge, the impossibility of returning the good has repercussions on the granting of that remedy. The rules exist, however, in common law and in German law (see § 351 of the Federal Republic of Germany Civil Code). It is designed to penalise the buyer by whose fault the goods deteriorated."

19 Art 83 CISG provides that;

A buyer who has lost the right to declare the contract avoided or to require the seller to deliver substitute goods in accordance with art 82 retains all other remedies under the contract and this Convention.

4.1.2 Elements of Avoidance under the CISG

4.1.2.1 Fundamental Breach

Leonardo Graffi is of the opinion that fundamental breach is a milestone concept of the United Nations Convention on Contracts for the International Sale of Goods (hereinafter CISG), since it is the necessary precondition for avoiding the contract under art 49 (1)(a) and 64(1)(a).[20] The definition of what a "fundamental breach" is given in art 25 CISG.[21] A fundamental breach of contract is at the heart of the remedy of avoidance; it also goes a long way to draw the line between circumstances under which a fundamental breach could arise and the circumstances where exemption arises.[22] The concluding part of art 25 which says "unless the party in breach did not foresee and a reasonable person of the same kind in the same circumstances would not have foreseen such a result" can be interpreted to mean that the most striking difference between "avoidance" and "exemption" lies in the fact of the cause of the breach to the contract.[23] If there is an attribute of fault to any of the parties, then it is a proper situation where avoidance or other sundry remedies can apply, but if the cause of the breach has no nexus with any acts or omissions of the parties but is totally a fortuitous happening, then it is a matter to be considered under the ambit of "exemption."

In the international contract of sale of goods, the most common breach that can go to the root of the contract is non-conformity of the goods supplied to the contract or non-payment of the price of goods supplied. The fundamental breach provision

20 Leonardo Graffi, "Case Law on the Concept of 'Fundamental Breach' in the Vienna Sales Convention" (2003) 3 *I.B.L.J.* 338–349.

21 Art 25 CISG provides:

> A breach of contract committed by one of the parties is fundamental if it results in such detriment to the other party as substantially to deprive him of what he is entitled to expect under the contract, unless the party in breach did not foresee and a reasonable person of the same kind in the same circumstances would not have foreseen such a result.

22 Michael Bridge "Avoidance for fundamental breach of contract under the UN Convention on the International Sale of Goods" (n 140) ch. 2, argues that art 25 doesn't do enough to define the comprehensive meaning of fundamental breach. He writes thus: "Art 25 may be criticized for its vagueness and the lack of guidance it gives on the meaning and scope of its internal features. It is one of the CISG's characteristics that it eschews the definition of essential expressions, such as the meaning of 'sale' and 'goods.' Even if one accepts this degree of forbearance to be somewhat extreme, there is no substantial case for defining in the CISG every term or expression that is used."

23 However, a party who wants to invoke any of the international sale law remedies based on the fact of fundamental breach by non-conformity would be required to prove that the non-conformity in fact existed and is such that it goes to the root of the contract of sale and thus defeats the beneficial and commercial aims of the contract. This is the ratio in the People Fisheries (Pvt) Ltd. v Pescados Videla SA, Audiencia Provincial de Barcelona (Court of Appeal Barcelona) Spain, 24 March 2009 – 403/2008, CISG-online 2042 <https://cisg-online.org/search-for-cases?caseId=7959> accessed 20/9/2025) where the court refused to allow the Spanish buyer to avoid the contract for lack of proof of substantial non-compliance with the requirements of the contract.

This case established the fact that avoidance is not granted for the mere asking; a party who seeks this remedy must show positively and with uncontradicted evidence how the activities of the party allegedly in breach constituted a fundamental breach of contract.

of art 25 covers the situation where non-conforming goods are delivered.[24] It has been held that it is not every defect that can lead to non-conforming goods being labelled under fundamental breach; such a defect causing the non-conformity must be objectively serious and not capable of being remedied by the seller.[25] This species of breaches was adumbrated in the complicated *Assembly and technical documentation case* [26] where a Russian buyer claimed compensation from an Austrian seller for avoidance of a contract for international sale of technical equipment and compensation for the cost of equipment, assembly, commissioning, training and materials. The court held that the seller's failure to observe the conditions relating to assembly of the equipment constituted a fundamental breach of the contract, as provided for in art 25 CISG and the terms of the contract.[27]

Michael Will[28] has a further view on the interpretation of the intentions of art 25, and he argues that "the definition purports to separate a non-fundamental and a fundamental breach of contract. The distinction is of cardinal importance for the system of remedies because it can determine the life or death of the contract."

This view found support in the case of *Mitias d.o.o. v Solidea S.r.l., Tribunale di Forlì*.[29] The buyer, a company incorporated under Slovenian law, bought from the seller, an Italian limited company, various models of shoes, paying the agreed amount of around 7,000 EUR. After delivery, the buyer discovered defects in a large part of the purchased items; thus, the goods could not be sold to third parties. The request by the buyer for partial avoidance of the contract was allowed. The CISG links specific consequences to the concept of fundamental breach, allowing

24 John Honnold, *Uniform Law for International Sales Under the 1980 United Nations Convention* (4th edn, Wolters Kluwer, 2009) para 304, 436. Honnold goes on to write that "If a buyer discovers that goods are non-conforming while they are still in the possession of the seller before being transported, it has been suggested that the buyer may reject the goods and avoid the contract."

25 Schlechtriem and Schwenzer (n 5) ch. 2, para 7, 578.

26 Supreme Arbitrazh (Commercial) Court of the Russian Federation, Russian Federation, 15 October 2009 – VAS-11307/09, CISG-online 2927 <https://cisg-online.org/search-for-cases?caseId=8841> accessed 19 September 2025.

27 Ibid. The M-A-M Ltd. v Dana Automacion, S.A., Audiencia Provincial de Navarra (Court of Appeal Navarra), Spain, 30 July 2010 – 175/2008 / 169/2010, CISG-online 2315 <https://cisg-online.org/search-for-cases?caseId=8231> accessed 17/9/2025 is also very apt in portraying the application of art 25 of the CISG. In this case, the court held that the seller is guilty of fundamental breach of the contract since the goods he contracted to supply had been unfit for their purpose, namely use in the manufacture of axle spindles for vehicles. It was clear, in view of the nature of the fault and the sector for which the goods were intended, that the breach had been committed by the seller and that that breach had deprived the buyer of what it was entitled to expect under the contract, namely non-defective steel rods suitable for producing automotive axle spindles, there being no grounds for exemption insofar as the seller could have foreseen such an outcome once the activity of the buyer was known to it. It can be added from this present case that if the cause of the impediment had been unforeseen by the seller and was such, with a grave consequence which he cannot control or overcome, then it would have been a proper case for the application of the doctrine of exemption.

28 "Art 25" [1987] <http://cisgw3.law.pace.edu/cisg/biblio/will-bb25.html> accessed 18/9/2025.

29 Mitias d.o.o. v Solidea S.r.l., Tribunale di Forlì (District Court Forlì) Italy, 09 December 2008 – 2280/2007, CISG-online 1729 <https://cisg-online.org/search-for-cases?caseId=7647> accessed 13 September 2025.

the party that acted according to the contract to declare the contract avoided in its entirety or offering the buyer substitute goods.[30]

The Convention does not differentiate between the breach of a main obligation and an ancillary obligation. Even a breach of an ancillary obligation may be considered fundamental if it is firmly connected to the trade in goods. Art 25 gives a uniform definition without distinguishing several types of breach, such as delay, non-payment, impossibility to perform or non-delivery. Thus, only where conformity cannot be remedied by the seller or can only be remedied with serious inconvenience to the buyer is there the chance to avoid the contract. If performance were still possible, the buyer would still have an interest in keeping the contract alive but not against all commercial odds. In *Mitias d.o.o. v Solidea S.r.l., Tribunale di Forlì*[31] the court concluded that the defects could not be removed. Consequently, there was no adequate alternative for making up for the lack of conformity without an unreasonable inconvenience to the buyer. It is therefore reasonable that the buyer refused the offer to remedy. The fundamental breach thus legally leads to avoidance of the contract.[32] But where from the facts of a particular case it is evident that the seller can neither remedy the breach nor show due diligence in ameliorating the loss suffered by the buyer, then it is a proper case for avoidance if the buyer deems it so.[33]

30 Art 25 provides a definition of fundamental breach. That provision is re-echoed in art 49, also stating the circumstances in which the buyer can avoid the contract. Art 25 CISG does not specify when a fundamental breach is relevant but simply contains the criteria for distinguishing between a fundamental and a non-fundamental breach.

31 District Court Forli Italy, 09 December 2008 – 2280/2007, CISG-online 1729 <https://cisg-online.org/search-for-cases?caseId=7647> accessed 17 September 2025.

32 Francesco A. Schurr, European Journal of Contract Law (3/2009) 160–161.

33 Arens Sondermaschinen GmbH v Smit Draad / Draad Nijmegen B.V., Gerechtshof Arnhem (Court of Appeal Arnhem) Netherlands, 07 October 2008 – 104.003.479, CISG-online 1749 <https://cisg-online.org/search-for-cases?caseId=7667> accessed 12 September 2025, it was held that "in determining whether a breach of contract amounts to a fundamental breach within the meaning of art 25 CISG, it is also relevant whether the breach of contract can be repaired within a reasonable time. This is because the seller may, even after the date for delivery, remedy at his own expense any failure to perform his obligations."

Also in Diversitel Communications Inc. v Glacier Bay Inc, Canada, 6 October 2003 – 03-CV-23776 SR, CISG-online 1436 <https://cisg-online.org/search-for-cases?caseId=7357> accessed 16 August 2025;

the defendant is an American company with its head office in Oakland, California. On 26 August 2002, the plaintiff entered into a contract with the defendant for the supply of vacuum panel insulation. The plaintiff required delivery of the insulation to meet the terms of a pre-existing contract with the Canadian Department of National Defence (DND). As a term of its contract with the defendant, the plaintiff set out a specific schedule of delivery of the insulation by the defendant.

The defendant admits it breached the terms of its contract by failure to deliver on time, as a result of problems it encountered with its principal supplier. The court agreed with the plaintiff that even the common law conditions for avoidance had been met in this case, on the finding that the parties had made time of the essence in the contract by their conduct and communications. The defendant's failure to perform in time was thus a fundamental breach as understood in the common law. The court granted summary judgment to the plaintiff and awarded pre- and post-judgment interest calculated according to local law.

Thus, art 25 is unlike the common law approach to the issue of fundamental breach, which is the a *priori* classification of the term breached into conditions and warranties. The most common law sales of goods law, according to Jacob Ziegel and Claude Samson, adopted an a *priori* system of classification into warranties and conditions with respect to the implied terms of title, description, merchantability, fitness, and sale by sample. The breach of a condition, as thus defined, *prima facie* entitles the aggrieved buyer to reject the goods and avoid the contract, even though the actual breach is minor in character.[34]

It is fortunate that this line of reasoning has been ameliorated by the decision in *Hong Kong Fir Shipping Co Ltd. v Kawasaki Kisen Kaisha Ltd*[35] where the court devised the "innominate term" based not on whether you call a particular contract term a "warranty" or a "condition," but on how serious the breach of the term was.

4.1.2.2 Non-Delivery / Refusing to Take Delivery or Payment of Price within Additional Period of Time

This is an omnibus ground for avoidance; it is both provided for in art 49(1)(b) and art 64(1)(b) of the CISG. Examining paragraph (1)(b) of art 49, the buyer may avoid the contract on a ground other than fundamental breach. This is not instantaneous, but only if the seller fails to deliver the goods at the time agreed by the parties in the contract of sale of goods. Delivery is very vital in the sale of goods. It is considered such a fundamental obligation that its breach opens the *Nachfrist*-avoidance-mechanism rule. If non-delivery amounts to, or during the *Nachfrist* turns into, a fundamental breach, the fundamental breach rule in sub-paragraph (a) will apply, and the seller may avoid the contract.[36]

On the other hand, the declaration by the seller of avoidance of the contract under art 64(1)(b) requires that (a) the buyer fails to perform either his obligation to pay the price or his obligation to take over the goods but none other, and (b) they fail to perform one of the said obligations within the additional period of time fixed by the seller under art 63 or they inform the seller that they will not perform their obligation within the period of time so fixed; (c) it is, however, not relevant whether the buyer's failure to pay the price or to take over the goods constitutes a fundamental breach of contract.[37]

34 Jacob Ziegel and Claude Samson, "Report to the Uniform Law Conference of Canada on Convention on Contracts for the International Sale of Goods" [1981] <https://books.google.com.ng/books/about/Report_to_the_Uniform_Law_Conference_of.html?id=BnkaHQAACAAJ&redir_esc=y> accessed 17 August 2025.

35 [1962] 1 All ER 474.

36 Michael Will, in Bianca-Bonell Commentary on the International Sales Law, Giuffrè: Milan (1987) 205–221.

37 Knapp (n 11) 465–474.

The Nachfrist rule requires either the buyer or seller to fix an additional time for the performance of the contract.[38] It can be fixing an additional time for delivery in the event of failure to deliver by the seller or fixing additional time for the payment of the price in the situation where the buyer has taken delivery and refuses to pay the price of the goods to the seller.[39] In either case, it is a rule that will empower either of the parties to go ahead and exercise the right of avoidance without necessarily proving the existence of a fundamental breach.[40]

A classic example of the application of the *Nachfrist* rule in both art 49(1)(b) and 64(1)(b) was most evident in the *Ford Escort Cabrio Case*.[41] In this case, the defendant (buyer), a German car retailer, ordered a car from the plaintiff (seller), a wholesaler having its place of business in Denmark. The order stipulated that the car be delivered by a specified date. The seller accepted, adding its standard conditions in which it reserved a change of the date of delivery. When the car was not delivered by the date specified in the buyer's offer, the buyer fixed an additional period of one week. The seller did not reply. After the additional period had lapsed

38 HT Nguyen, ANC Nguyen, and LNT Tran, "Extension for Contract Performance under the CISG 1980 and Implications for Vietnamese Businesses" (2022) 6(2) *Journal of Economics, Law and Management* 2689.

39 Ibid.

40 Hengyi Zhang, "Buyer's Remedies and Cure by Seller-A Study of the Harmonization of European Sales Law from the Perspective of Comparative Private Law" (2014) 11 *US-China L. Rev.* 1428.

41 Germany 27 April 1999 Appellate Court Naumburg 9 U 146/1998 CISG-online 512 <https://cisg-online.org/search-for-cases?caseId=6480> accessed 23 August 2025.

See also Used printing machines case (I), Oberlandesgericht Celle (Court of Appeal Celle) Germany, 24 May 1995 – 20 U 76/94, CISG-online 152 <https://cisg-online.org/search-for-cases?caseId=6130> accessed 28 September 2025.

; In this case, the buyer, an Egyptian businessman, and the seller, a German company trading in used printing machines, concluded an oral contract for the sale of nine used printing machines that were to be shipped to Egypt. The parties agreed upon two shipments, the first including six machines and the second three machines.

According to the contract, the buyer was obliged to pay a considerable part of the contract price before the first shipment, which he did. But the first shipment contained only three machines. After having demanded shipment of the missing machines several times, the buyer declared that it had no longer any use for three of the still missing machines. The seller answered: "We are sorry that we shall not deliver the machines any more which we have kept to your disposal." With respect to the last three machines, the buyer fixed a final period of two weeks for delivery. The seller did not deliver within that period but offered shortly afterwards shipment against advance payment. The buyer refused this and declared, now seven weeks after fixing the additional delivery period, the contract avoided as far as the missing machines were concerned. The buyer demanded compensation for its loss as well as repayment of the sum by which the advance payment exceeded the price of the three delivered machines.

With regard to the last three machines, the contract was avoided by the buyer's unilateral declaration (Articles 49(1) (b), 47(1) and 51(1) CISG). The seller had breached the contract by not delivering the machines within the time fixed by the contract (Art 33(b) CISG), thus giving the buyer the right to fix an additional period of time (Articles 49(1) (b) and 47(1) CISG). The buyer was therefore entitled to declare the contract avoided, even if the additional delivery period of two weeks was perhaps too short. According to the court, the period of seven weeks between announcement and actual declaration of avoidance was reasonable.

without result, the buyer declared the contract avoided. Consequently, when the car finally arrived seven weeks later, the buyer refused to pay. The seller then sued for the difference between the contract price and the price obtained from the sale of the car to another buyer.

The court dismissed the claim. It held that the buyer had correctly avoided the contract under art 49(1)(b). It stated that the clause reserving a change of the delivery date in the seller's standard conditions did not constitute a material alteration under art 19(2) and had therefore become part of the contract. However, since the clause did not determine a period of delivery, it had to be interpreted according to art 33(c) CISG, which provides for delivery to be made within a reasonable time after the conclusion of the contract. Even though the date specified in the buyer's offer was not binding on the seller, it could still serve as an indication of a reasonable time of delivery. When the seller did not deliver by that date, the buyer was entitled to fix an additional period of time under art 47(1) after which it could declare the contract avoided pursuant to art 49(1)(b). The court stressed that it did not consider the question of whether an additional period of one week was sufficient in the case at hand because the fixing of too short a period only triggers a reasonable period, which would also have lapsed by the time (the buyer) declared avoidance.[42] In any case, before the court or tribunal can hold that an additional period of time has been fixed for performance, the said period must be specific, clear and shown to be made in good faith. In the *Generator case (I)*[43] the court refused to presume that the buyer had fixed an additional period of time when it could not be gathered from the correspondences between the parties that a specific additional period of time to perform had been given.

Failure to deliver is very important in the lifespan of any contract of sale. It has been suggested that if the date of delivery is fixed or, from the circumstances surrounding the transaction, it can be said that the date of delivery has been made an important feature of the contract, then failure of the seller to deliver on the said fixed date or failure of the buyer to accept delivery on the date will amount to a fundamental breach of contract.[44] In other words, the remedy of avoidance can be invoked either under arts 49 or 64 of the CISG if it can be shown that it fundamentally strikes at the foundations of the contract. It can be inferred, therefore, that both the *Nachfrist* rule and the fundamental breach rule can work independently and in conjunction with each other.

There must be an additional period of time given upon which delivery can still be taken or performed, even though the parties to the contract of sale unequivocally agreed on a fixed date; the strict conditions of the *Nachfrist* rule must be apparently

42 This instant case is different from the situation of exemption since the seller cannot show that the delay in the delivery of the car is caused by an unforeseen impediment which the seller cannot cope with or is expected to overcome.

43 Landgericht Düsseldorf (District Court Düsseldorf) Germany, 11 October 1995 – 2 O 506/94, CISG-online 180 <https://cisg-online.org/search-for-cases?caseId=6156> accessed 28/9/2025.

44 Muller-Chen in Schlechtriem & Ingeborg *Schwenzer, Commentary on the UN Convention on the International Sale of Goods* (3rd edn, Oxford Publishers, 2010) para 5, 748.

adhered to, otherwise the non-delivery would be regarded as a mere irregularity evident in most commercial transactions.[45]

Additionally, it will be interesting to compare that the doctrine of exemption under art 79 of the CISG does not impose any obligation on either of the parties to cure or remedy the impediment that makes the contract of sale of goods impossible of performance, so the need to give additional time in order to remedy does not arise, especially when the performance of the contract has been rendered impossible by an unforeseeable and uncontrollable impediment without the fault of the parties.

What obtains, rather, is that the party who pleads exemption must diligently notify the other party of its existence and how it renders performance impossible. This duty to give notice is a major common feature in both the "avoidance" and "exemption" under the CISG.[46] While highlighting the importance of notice in avoidance of a contract, Henry Gabriel is of the view that "[w]hen there has been a fundamental non-performance, and when the non-performing party does not perform within the additional time for performance given by the aggrieved party, the party terminating the contract must give notice of the termination."[47]

For all these, it can be conveniently summarised that while the concept of avoidance under the CISG is fault-based, the doctrine of exemption is non-fault-based,[48] but where the fundamental breach of a party is the proximate cause of the impediment that brings the exempting event, then it can either be treated under arts 49(1)(a) or 64(1)(a), as a case where "avoidance" can serve as a remedy.

4.2 Avoidance (Termination) and *Force Majeure* under the UNIDROIT Principles

4.2.1 Background

Termination is provided under art 7.3.1 of the UNIDROIT Principles and it explains the situation which arises in a contract, especially a contract of sale of goods, when a party's (obligor) failure to perform an obligation accruing and due under the contract is of such a fundamental nature that it will legally trigger a reaction on the

45 More so, wrongful claim of right or justification for non-delivery may tilt towards a fundamental breach to justify avoidance if the party making the claim does so wilfully, knowing full well that they have no bona fide ground for their claims or defences in justification of non-delivery after failing to deliver within a given additional period of time. However, it will be useful to note that mere failure to deliver at a due date will not necessarily amount to a fundamental breach under Arts 25, 49 or 64 if delivery is still possible.

46 Arts 39, 79 (4), 47 (2) and 63 (2).

47 Gabriel (n 61) ch. 3, 177.

48 Asa Markel, "American, English and Japanese Warranty Law Compared: Should the US Reconsider Her Article 95 Declaration to the CISG" (2009) 21 *Pace Int'l L. Rev.* 163.

part of the other party (Obligee) who will be empowered under the law to treat the contract as finished, determined, or terminated.[49] Art 7.3.1 provides that:

(1) A party may terminate the contract where the failure of the other party to perform an obligation under the contract amounts to a fundamental non-performance.
(2) In determining whether a failure to perform an obligation amounts to a fundamental non-performance, regard shall be had, in particular, to whether
   (a) the non-performance substantially deprives the aggrieved party of what it was entitled to expect under the contract unless the other party did not foresee and could not reasonably have foreseen such result;
   (b) strict compliance with the obligation which has not been performed is of essence under the contract;
   (c) the non-performance is intentional or reckless;
   (d) the non-performance gives the aggrieved party reason to believe that it cannot rely on the other party's future performance;
   (e) the non-performing party will suffer disproportionate loss as a result of the preparation or performance if the contract is terminated.
(3) In the case of delay, the aggrieved party may also terminate the contract if the other party fails to perform before the time allowed it under Article 7.1.5 has expired.

The implication of termination is that it relieves the parties of the further legal duty to perform the obligations of the contract to its contracted conclusion. It does not extinguish other remedies available to an aggrieved party, and it does not stop further subcontracts or commitments like confidentiality obligations from running. The right to terminate a contract is sparingly exercised. Most commercial law enactments are very reluctant to make this remedy easily available. It is a last resort remedy because of risk and cost implication.[50] The above reasoning found support in the opinion of Peter Huber when he writes that:

> Termination of a contract will often result in a restitution of performances which have already been made; this may lead to considerable costs and risks which could be avoided if the contract was not terminated and if the

49 The above definition is in line with Arts 49 of the CISG and art 7.3.1 of the Unidroit principles, and art 9:301 of the Principles of European Contract Law (PECL). In all these legal instruments, fundamental breach, *Nachfrist* rule, and lack of cure (Art 8.104 of the PECL) are all manners through which further performance of a contract can be cancelled.

50 Peter Huber in Stefan Vogenauer & Jan Kleintheisterkamp (eds) (n 106) ch. 1, para 6, 819.
It can be added that the chief intentions of any international commercial law are to preserve business intentions, trust, and to build goodwill among buyers and sellers. Any remedy that can be invoked in order to defeat this end is rarely exercised, and in such occasions, it must be manifestly evident that the facts and circumstances of the contract, the manner and seriousness of the breach of obligation to perform, point at the deserving need to knock the bottom off the contract, and what remains is a decent end to it.

aggrieved party's interest in obtaining conforming goods was remedied by either repair or claim of damages.[51]

This view articulated by Huber explains why art 7.3.1(1)-(3) of the UNIDROIT Principles makes fundamental non–performance and the *Nachfrist* rule of additional time the main reasons why an aggrieved party can base his action to terminate the contract. These elements must be clearly proved, and adequate notice given, before they can be actualized.[52] This sub-chapter will go ahead to evaluate the relationship between the doctrine of *force majeure* and termination of contract under the UNIDROIT Principles. It is a matter of common knowledge that these two concepts often befuddle the minds of both academics and practitioners, but they do not mean the same thing. Their legal effect on commercial contracts is interwoven, but the principles or the underlying factors needed before each of the concepts can apply are not exactly the same.

4.2.2 Termination Differentiates from Avoidance under the UNIDROIT Principles

From the provisions of art 7.3.1, it can be analysed that termination and avoidance are not the same under the UNIDROIT Principles; avoidance gives a party the right to cancel the contract retroactively (*ab initio*) because there are circumstances that affect the validity of the contract,[53] while termination enables a party to cancel the further performance of a contract due to fundamental non-performance, absence of cure or delay in performance after an additional period of time given to perform. Under the UNIDROIT Principles, there are various grounds upon which a contract can be avoided; they range from mistake (art 3.2.1), fraud (art 3.2.5),[54] threat (art 3.2.6) and gross disparity (art 3.2.7) and all these grounds can determine the contract retroactively.[55] This means that the contract is regarded as never having existed, unfulfilled obligations fall away and performances made in fulfilment of

51 Ibid., para 6, 819.

52 John Duncan Jr, "Nachfrist Was Ist: Thinking Globally and Acting Locally: Considering Time Extension Principles of the UN Convention on Contracts for the International Sale of Goods in Revising the Uniform Commercial Code" (2000) *BYU L. Rev.* 1363.

53 Chapter 3 of the UNIDROIT Principles provides the ground upon which a contract can be avoided due to validity issues. In fact, art 3.1.4 makes provision relating to fraud, threat, gross disparity, and illegality of a mandatory character. It would be contrary to good faith for the parties to exclude or modify these provisions when concluding their contract. However, nothing prevents the party entitled to avoidance for fraud, threat, and gross disparity from waiving that right once that party learns of the true facts or is able to act freely.

54 Art 3.2.5 UNIDROIT Principles provides that:

> A party may avoid the contract when it has been led to conclude the contract by the other party's fraudulent representation, including language or practices, or fraudulent non-disclosure of circumstances which, according to reasonable commercial standards of fair dealing, the latter party should have disclosed.

55 Art 3.2.14 of the UNIDROIT provides that avoidance takes effect retroactively.

obligations have to be returned,[56] whereas termination is futuristic, and in accordance with art 7.3.5 releases both parties from their obligation to effect and to receive future performance. Art 7.3.5 provides that:

(1) Termination of the contract releases both parties from their obligation to effect and to receive future performance.
(2) Termination does not preclude a claim for damages for non-performance.
(3) Termination does not affect any provision in the contract for the settlement of disputes or any other term of the contract which is to operate even after termination.

Avoidance is also different from *force majeure,* because the latter does not affect the validity of the contract and will not retroactively determine the contract. A contract that falls foul of *force majeure* is not invalid but merely impossible of performance. The contract can still be performed if the impediment abates, unlike a contract that is affected by any of the grounds for avoidance; such a contract is simply invalid and of no effect. By and large, restitution of performances which have already been made can apply under avoidance in the UNIDROIT Principles just like termination and *force majeure*.[57] According to art 3.2.15(1) of the UNIDROIT Principles, either party may claim restitution of what the party has supplied under the contract or the part of it avoided.

Furthermore, the first part of the provision (art 7.3.1) for termination makes fundamental non-performance the focal point for action or inaction resulting in the termination of the contract.[58] It does not define what fundamental non-performance is, but the meaning and connotations as offered by art 25 (fundamental breach provisions) of the CISG, Section 3:502 of the DCFR and art 8:103 of the PECL can be used to interpret art 7.3.1(1) of the UNIDROIT Principles.[59]

56 Huber in Vogenauer & Kleintheisterkamp (eds) (n 106) ch. 1, para 6, 819

57 Art 3.2.15 of the UNIDROIT Principles provides thus:

(1) On avoidance either party may claim restitution of whatever it has supplied under the contract, or the part of it avoided, provided that the party concurrently makes restitution of whatever it has received under the contract, or the part of it avoided.
(2) If restitution in kind is not possible or appropriate, an allowance has to be made in money whenever reasonable.
(3) The recipient of the performance does not have to make an allowance in money if the impossibility to make restitution in kind is attributable to the other party.

Compensation may be claimed for expenses reasonably required to preserve or maintain the performance received.

58 The fundamental non-performance connotes the same meaning as fundamental breach under art 25 of the CISG and fundamental non-performance under art 8.103 of the principles of European Contract Law.

59 Section 3:502 of the Draft Common Frame of Reference (DCFR) can also be used to interpret the meaning of fundamental non-performance; it provides that:

The second part of this provision takes things to a clearer level; it makes a detailed enumeration of circumstances whose presence will be a pointer that obligee action or inaction has fallen into the fundamental non-performance requirement. Some factors provided under this part include substantial deprivation, non-compliance with the contract, suffering of disproportionate loss and recklessness on the part of the defaulting party.

The third part is a simple restatement of the general golden rule of international commercial law; it is known as the "*Nachfrist*" rule and simply means that when there is a non-performance which may be fundamental or non-fundamental, the aggrieved party gives the defaulting party an additional time period to tender performance, after which the failure to tender the demanded performance shall crystallise an action in termination or any other remedy available under the law.[60] While analysing the rule above, Vogenaur and Kleintheisterkamp write that:

---

(1) A creditor may terminate if the debtor's non-performance of a contractual obligation is fundamental.

(2) A non-performance of a contractual obligation is fundamental if:

(a) it substantially deprives the creditor of what the creditor was entitled to expect under the contract, as applied to the whole or relevant part of the performance, unless at the time of conclusion of the contract the debtor did not foresee and could not reasonably be expected to have foreseen that result; or

(b) It is intentional or reckless and gives the creditor reason to believe that the debtor's future performance cannot be relied on.

More so, art 8:103 of the Principles of European Contract Law (PECL) provides thus:

A non-performance of an obligation is fundamental to the contract if: (a) strict compliance with the obligation is of the essence of the contract; or (b) the non-performance substantially deprives the aggrieved party of what it was entitled to expect under the contract, unless the other party did not foresee and could not reasonably have foreseen that result; or (c) the non-performance is intentional and gives the aggrieved party reason to believe that it cannot rely on the other party's future performance.

60 The rule guiding the application of the *Nachfrist* is as provided under art 7.1.5 of the UNIDROIT Principles; the art provides that:

(1) In a case of non-performance, the aggrieved party may, by notice to the other party, allow an additional period of time for performance.

(2) During the additional period the aggrieved party may withhold performance of its own reciprocal obligations and may claim damages but may not resort to any other remedy. If it receives notice from the other party that the latter will not perform within that period, or if upon expiry of that period due performance has not been made, the aggrieved party may resort to any of the remedies that may be available under this Chapter.

(3) Where in a case of delay in performance which is not fundamental the aggrieved party has given notice allowing an additional period of time of reasonable length, it may terminate the contract at the end of that period. If the additional period allowed is not of reasonable length it shall be extended to a reasonable length. The aggrieved party may in its notice provide that if the other party fails to perform within the period allowed by the notice, the contract shall automatically terminate.

(4) Paragraph (3) does not apply where the obligation which has not been performed is only a minor part of the contractual obligation of the non-performing party.

> Article 7.1.5 enables the aggrieved obligee to adopt a proactive approach to non-performance … art 7.1.5 allows a clear and final time frame to be set within which the obligee will await performance. Moreover it allows the obligee to resort, after the period's lapse, to the full panoply of remedies, particularly to termination even if the delay in performance is not fundamental.[61]

This underlying foundation of *Nachfrist* has the tendency to aggravate a breach, thus making a minor non-serious non-performance be elevated to a notional, fundamental non-performance which can attract the remedy of termination. It is settled that *the Nachfrist* rule provision is absent in art 7.1.7 of the UNIDROIT Principles which provides for *force majeure*.[62] The reason for this is that the law does not favour parties to a frustrated (*force majeure*) contract to be bound willy-nilly by it. When a party to a contract invokes *force majeure*, the other party is not entitled to claim damages. This derives from the general rule of law that damages are in principle due in case of negligence, and *force majeure* implies the absence of any negligence of the party.[63] While it is paramount in the scenario of termination to save the contract by giving additional time to encourage performance, the overriding importance of *force majeure* is to excuse damages for non-performance under the CISG and the UNIDROIT Principles[64] or to automatically discharge the contract under English law.

61 Vogenauer & Kleintheisterkamp (eds) (n 106) ch. 1, para 1, 753.

62 Ndubuisi Nwafor and Chidi Lloyd. "Re-imagining the Doctrines of Hardship and Exemption/force Majeure under the CISG and UNIDROIT Principles of International Commercial Contracts" (2019) 8(1) *Global Journal of Comparative Law* 52.

63 Hubert Konarski, "Force Majeure and Hardship Clauses in International Contractual Practice" (2003) *Int'l Bus. LJ.* 405–428.

64 There are many other grey areas existing between termination and *force majeure*. Art 7.1.7 (4) of the UNIDROIT Principles provides that:

"Nothing in this art prevents a party from exercising a right to terminate the contract or to withhold performance or request interest on money due."

This important provision makes it clear that "termination" as a remedy can still be applicable in the situation of frustration; it doesn't matter that the end point of both concepts gears towards the severance of the contractual relationship existing between an obligor and obligee (at least under English law). It follows that in a situation of *force majeure*, termination can still be a remedy available to an aggrieved party both under the UNIDROIT principles and English law. This is not exactly the case with termination. In a situation of termination, frustration cannot be in contention either as a remedy or as a factor; both concepts are not interchangeable, but it seems that the facts that make up a frustrating event can be a ground for the termination of the contract, and most importantly, the elements that must be present and operative before either of them can be proved criss-crossed each other. This is because under UNIDROIT, the consequences of non-performance cannot be excused, but only liability in damages could.

A succinct example given of the above reasoning is demonstrated in the hypothetical case thus (UNIDROIT Principles 2004, 221) "Q , a company located in country K, buys oranges from H in country W. The Government of country K subsequently imposes an embargo upon the importation of agricultural products from country W. Although the impediment cannot be attributed to Q, H may terminate the contract." This presents a classic example where a frustrated contract, though outwith the fault of any of the parties, can nevertheless lead to termination/avoidance of the contract.

It has been briefly discussed earlier in this sub-chapter that under the UNIDROIT Principles, just like arts 81 and 82 of the CISG and art 3.2.15 (Restitution for avoidance of contract under the UNIDROIT Principles), restitution plays an important role after termination of the contract; either party may claim restitution of whatever it has supplied under the contract, provided that such party concurrently makes restitution of whatever it has received under the contract. This is provided for under art 7.3.6[65] of the UNIDROIT Principles (Restitution with respect to contracts to be performed at one time) and art 7.3.7[66] (Restitution with respect to contracts to be performed over a period of time). Restitution must normally be made in kind. There are, however, instances where instead of restitution in kind, an allowance in money has to be made. This is the case where restitution in kind is not possible. The allowance will normally amount to the value of the performance received.[67]

Art 3.3.2[68] of the UNIDROIT Principles also provides that where there has been performance under a contract infringing a mandatory rule, restitution may be granted if this would be reasonable in the circumstances. If restitution is granted under this article, it is governed by the rules set out in art 3.2.15 on restitution in the context of avoidance. These rules, however, need some adaptations in the sense that in paragraph (1) of art 3.2.15 the reference to avoidance is to be understood as a reference to the case where the contract becomes ineffective as a result of the infringement of a mandatory rule and the reference to avoidance of part of the

65 Art 7.3.6 provides thus:

(1) On termination of a contract to be performed at one time, either party may claim restitution of whatever it has supplied under the contract, provided that such party concurrently makes restitution of whatever it has received under the contract.
(2) If restitution in kind is not possible or appropriate, an allowance has to be made in money whenever reasonable.
(3) The recipient of the performance does not have to make an allowance in money if the impossibility to make restitution in kind is attributable to the other party.
(4) Compensation may be claimed for expenses reasonably required to preserve or maintain the performance received.

66 Art 7.3.7 provides thus:

(1) On termination of a contract to be performed over a period of time, restitution can only be claimed for the period after termination has taken effect, provided the contract is divisible.
(2) As far as restitution has to be made, the provisions of Art 7.3.6 apply.

67 Official Comment <http://www.unilex.info/dynasite.cfm?dssid=2377&dsmid=13637> accessed 2 September 2025.

68 Art 3.3.2 provides that:

(1) Where there has been performance under a contract infringing a mandatory rule under Art 3.3.1, restitution may be granted where this would be reasonable in the circumstances.
(2) In determining what is reasonable, regard is to be had, with the appropriate adaptations, to the criteria referred to in Art 3.3.1(3).
(3) If restitution is granted, the rules set out in Art 3.2.15 apply with appropriate adaptations.

contract as a reference to the case where only part of the contract becomes ineffective as a result of the infringement of a mandatory rule.[69]

4.2.3 Elements of Termination under the UNIDROIT Principles

4.2.3.1 Fundamental Non-Performance (Fundamental Breach)

According to UNILEX's *Official Comment on the UNIDROIT Principles*, fundamental non-performance means, "the non-performance which is material and not merely of minor importance."[70] This definition left much to be desired. It fails to shed light on the degree of importance that should be accorded to a breach before it can graduate from minor importance to fundamental importance. However, considering the more pliable art 25 CISG alongside the concept of fundamental non-performance under the UNIDROIT Principles might help in fathoming out any missing ingredient of what fundamental non-performance means.

The argument by Peter Huber that the concept of fundamental non-performance under "termination" is not based on fault is not totally true and cannot have been the intention of the draughtsmen under the UNIDROIT Principles. Huber argues that "[i]t is irrelevant whether there was any kind of fault on the part of the non-performing party as the provision of Art 7.3 of the PICC does not contain a fault requirement."[71]

Yet this argument does not justify the high level of reluctance in allowing termination shown by courts and tribunals; the most plausible explanation for this reluctance should be that non-fault breaches could hardly add up to fundamental non-performance. While some non-fault-based events can lead to termination, as seen under the doctrine of *force majeure*, the courts or tribunals will be less motivated to allow a party to terminate a contract based on a fault-free non-performance of an obligor.[72]

69 Official comment on art 3.3.2 <http://www.unilex.info/dynasite.cfm?dssid=2377&dsmid=13637&x = 1> accessed 26 August 2025; the provision of art 3.3.2 can be illustrated by this hypothetical case.

"Contractor A of country X enters into negotiations with D, the Minister of Economics and Development of country Y, with a view to concluding an agreement on a large infrastructure project ('the Contract'). D requests the payment of a 'commission' of 7.5% of the contract price in order to conclude the Contract. A pays the requested 'commission' and the Contract is concluded. After A has fulfilled all of its obligations under the Contract, a new Government comes to power in country Y and the new Minister of Economics and Development, invoking the payment of the 'commission,' refuses to pay the remaining contract price. A may be granted an allowance in money for the work done corresponding to the value of the infrastructure project."

70 Offcmt2 to art 7.3.1, 221.

71 Vogenauer & Kleintheisterkamp (eds) (n 106) ch. 1, para 10, 820.

72 Non-performance simply means the inability to tender or perform an obligation that accrues to a party under a contract. If termination of a contract can be effected irrespective of whether the non-performing party does so intentionally or recklessly, then the age- long commercial law policy of showing caution in the exercise of "termination" will be defeated. The proper practical interpretations arising from the provision of art 7.3.1 is to attribute some elements of fault to the action or inactions of an obligor which causes non-performance. This is basically what draws the line

While conceding the fact that termination can still be a remedy under the facts that give rise to art 7.1.7 situation, it must be noted that the degree of non-performance needed in a situation of termination is not the same that can easily lead to *force majeure*. A mere non-performance caused by an impediment that is unforeseeable and uncontrollable is enough to buttress a situation that leads to *force majeure* if it renders performance impossible[73] but under termination, a "fundamental non-performance" is needed among other elements. Thus, inasmuch as the same facts lead to both *force majeure* and termination of a contract, the degree or standard of non-performance must be separately proved. However, any non-performance which makes performance of a contract impossible must be probably fundamental.

The *Nachfrist* rule only applies where there is a possibility of performance, but where a non-performance has been clearly excused due to an impediment beyond the control of the parties, which they cannot possibly avoid or whose consequences they cannot overcome, then the obligee giving additional time to the obligor to perform will be an exercise in futility.[74] It can be summarised generally that where a fundamental non-performance is as a result of the non-performing party's failure in fulfilling his obligation, the aggrieved party can easily terminate the contract, but if the non-performance is a result of an event beyond the control of the non-performing party, then it can either result in *force majeure* and in accordance with art 7.1.7 the contract can be terminated after the *force majeure* conditions might have been met.

4.2.3.2 Substantial Deprivation

Art 7.3.1(2)(a) provides for substantial deprivation as one of the yardsticks in determining whether a failure to perform an obligation amounts to fundamental non-performance. Huber writes that:

> [T]he substantial deprivation factor in art 7.3.1(2) (a) is a slightly abridged version of the definition of 'fundamental breach', it focuses primarily on the adverse effects of the non-performance on the aggrieved party.[75]

---

between a fortuitous impediment, which can excuse performance, as is the case with the provision of art 7.1.7 (*force majeure*), and a reckless or intentional act of a party, which can lead to termination of the contract.

73 Peter Huber in Kleinheisterkamp and Vogenauer (n 106) ch. 1, para 12, 771, writes that "An impediment is simply the event which, according to the obligor, is the cause for its non-performance." remark does not suggest whether or not the non-performance under art 7.1. 7 needed to be fundamental.

74 Under a *force majeure* contract, an additional period of time to perform cannot cure an impossible performance; but it can elevate a non-performance to a fundamental non-performance in order for termination to apply. It will be important to add that the Nachfrist rule is only available in a situation where the other party has not tendered or executed performance. Performance inhibits the possibility to seek redress under the rule.

75 Ibid., 821, para 13.

What this "substantial deprivation" does is to enquire if the obligee has benefited from all there is to benefit from the contract; this idea of benefit should be juxtaposed with the concept of loss or detriment. If a party has suffered a reasonable scale of loss, then even if the offending party did not foresee the loss or its result, the aggrieved party can bring their cause of action under art 7.3.1(a).[76]

Substantial deprivation, therefore, means that the whole intentions or contractual expectations of the aggrieved party have been undermined. It must not always necessarily result in actual physical damage to goods; sometimes a broken promise, reckless mischief or incurably defective performance can be so fundamental as to deprive a party of the fruit of the contract substantially. There is a nexus between the concept of "impediment" as employed under art

7.1.7 (*force majeure*) of the UNIDROIT Principles and substantial deprivation. An impediment means an obstacle or event that stands in a party's way to the performance of their obligation in the contract. Substantial deprivation can be a direct consequence of an impediment, and this end result plays a vital role, together with other factors, in determining whether an impediment is sufficient to frustrate or terminate a contract.

A classic illustration showing substantial deprivation is presented thus: "on 1st May, A contracts to deliver standard software before 15 May to B, who has requested speedy delivery. If 'A' tender's delivery is on 15 June, 'B' may refuse delivery and terminate the contract."[77] The above scenario amounts to substantial deprivation because B specifically wants "time" to be of the essence in the contract by stipulating and insisting on speedy delivery of the standard software.

4.2.3.3 *Foreseeability*

If a party foresees the deprivation of non-performance to the victim party and does nothing to avert it or cure it, thereby allowing it to have a bad commercial effect, then the foreseeability rule provided under art 7.3.1(2)(a) will apply to make the former liable and thus empower the latter to terminate the contract.[78] The factors that constitute foreseeability depend on the peculiar facts of each case. It is true that the obligor's failure becomes non-performance under art 7.1.7 of the UNIDROIT Principles even if it is due to external events constituting *force majeure*. If the failure in fulfilment of an obligation which caused the aggrieved party substantial deprivation of interest is not foreseen, then it is not a proper case for the application of termination; any other remedy may therefore suffice in order to save the contract.[79]

76 Huber (n 106) ch. 1, para 28, 775.

77 UNIDROIT Principles of International Commercial Contracts (Rome 2004) 222.

78 NT Quynh, "Comparing Foreseeability in Contractual Damages under the CISG, Unidroit Principles and Principles of European Contract Law" (2024) 11(1) *Pázmány Law Review* 147.

79 Art 7.1.1 of the UNIDROIT Principles defines non-performance as "failure by a party to perform any of its obligations under the contract, including defective performance or late performance."

4.2.3.4 *Strict Compliance with Contractual Obligations/Intention and Recklessness*

Parties are always encouraged not to break the strict compliance with the obligation which is essential under the contract. Whenever any obligation is very important that the contract revolves around it, then non-performance of that obligation should be regarded as fundamental. Intention/recklessness is the mental element which needs to be examined before it can be said that a non-performance is fundamental. It has been held that:

> The policy justification for this rule is that the non-performing party merits less protection than the aggrieved party. It is therefore possible for a breach which does not meet the high standards set under art 7.3.1. (2)(a) and/or (b) to be regarded as fundamental if the non-performing party committed the breach recklessly or intentionally.[80]

Intention and recklessness should be present and operative in all situations of termination; it is indeed what differentiates termination from other concepts or doctrines like "*force majeure.*" It is important to understand that art 7.3.1 is not skewed towards non–fault policy, so the presence of intention and recklessness can aggravate a non-performance into a fundamental non-performance.

One of the situations where a non-fault event can be used to terminate a contract is where the event is an exempting impediment under art 7.1.7; termination can clearly apply under art 7.1.7(4) without being subject to art 7.3.1(2) (c). But a non-fault or unintentional event cannot be used where termination is used as a means of obtaining redress as well as to punish an obligor who has committed a fundamental non-performance.[81] In this situation, the obligee's intention and recklessness will be highly material.[82]

4.2.3.5 *Non-Reliance on Future Performance/Dis-Appropriate Loss*

According to art 7.3.1(2) (d) of the UNIDROIT Principles, whenever the non-performance gives the aggrieved party reason to believe that it cannot rely on the other party's future performance, then the aggrieved party can go ahead and terminate the contract.[83] If a party is to make its performance in instalments, and a defect found in one of the earlier performances will be repeated in all performances, the

80 Huber (n 106) ch. 1, para 43, 872.

81 Peng Guo, "Termination for a Compelling Reason Under the UNIDROIT Principles: The Status Quo and a Way Forward" (2018) 21 *Int'l Trade & Bus. L. Rev.* 1.

82 UNIDROIT Principles of International Commercial Contracts (2010). The Official Comment <http://www.unilex.info/dynasite.cfm?dssid=2377&dsmid=13637≥ accessed 3/9/2025 provides that "Paragraph (2)(c) deals with the situation where the non-performance is intentional or reckless. It may, however, be contrary to good faith (see Art 1.7) to terminate a contract if the non-performance, even though committed intentionally, is insignificant."

83 The case of *Andersen Consulting Business Unit Member Firms v Arthur Andersen Business Unit Member Firms and Andersen Worldwide Societe Cooperative* (2000, ICC International Court of

aggrieved party may terminate the contract even if the defects in the early instalment would not alone justify termination. Sometimes an intentional breach may show that a party cannot be trusted.[84]

On the other hand, art 7.3.1(2)(e) deals with circumstances in which a party that fails to perform has relied on the contract and has prepared or tendered performance. In this case, the extent to which that party suffers disproportionate loss if the non-performance is treated as fundamental should be evaluated.

Non-performance is less likely to be treated as fundamental if it occurs late, after the preparation of performance, than if it happens early, before such preparation. Whether a performance tendered or rendered can be of any benefit to the non-performing party if it is refused or has to be returned to that party is also of relevance.[85] The law seeks to minimise the loss parties will suffer if they have deployed resources and incurred costs in performing the contract. Damages can be awarded against a defaulting party, but outright termination of the contract is not advised.

Finally, under art 7.3.1(3), an aggrieved party may use the Nachfrist procedure to terminate a contract that may not otherwise be terminated due to delay. This must be interpreted in conjunction with art 7.1.5(3) of the UNIDROIT Principles, which provides that:

> Where in a case of delay in performance which is not fundamental the aggrieved party has given notice allowing an additional period of time of reasonable length, it may terminate the contract at the end of that period. If the additional period allowed is not of reasonable length it shall be extended to a reasonable length. The aggrieved party may in its notice provide that if the other party fails to perform within the period allowed by the notice the contract shall automatically terminate.

This is a signature use of the *Nachfrist* rule which will upgrade a non-performance that is not fundamental into a fundamental non-performance after the expiration of the additional period of time given so performance could be rendered by the defaulting party.

4.3 Avoidance (Termination) and Frustration under the Common Law and the Sale of Goods Act of 1979

4.3.1 Background

Under English law, especially the common law, "termination" of a contract is not a very popular term; rather, there is in place a powerful remedial system of doctrine

---

Arbitration, Geneva 9797) <http://www.unilex.info/case.cfm?id=668> accessed 2/9/2025 is very important in illustrating this view.

84 Official Comment <http://www.unilex.info/dynasite.cfm?dssid=2377&dsmid=13637> accessed 2/9/2025.

85 Ibid.

of discharge or determination of a contract.[86] In common law jurisdictions, there are a few statutory rules on termination and solutions to problems which are generally to be found in established precedents.[87]

Underscoring the low usage of the term "termination" in English law, it has been held that "the right to terminate a contract is, in practice, often the most important aspect of the law of contract, yet its significance is often concealed in the text books."[88] The above assertion is a result of what is known as the regime of procedure through which a contract can be discharged. In the English legal system, a contract can be discharged or determined by performance, by agreement, by frustration, and by breach. All these remedies are subsumed under the general term of "discharge of contract." The most important aspect of discharge is by breach and frustration;[89] however, these do not make other aspects less important. In fact, the most famous way of terminating a contract under English law is via a termination clause in a contract where the doctrine of party autonomy has it that parties to a contract are free to choose the clause and terms that suit them.[90]

Termination by performance means that full and complete performance[91] of the contract has been rendered and there are no outstanding obligations to be settled. This method of termination is different from termination for breach and termination for frustration. Termination itself literally means the practical severance of obligations, commitments and promises, caused by a serious breach of the obligor. It robs the contract of its efficacy and gives an injured party the platform upon which to treat the contract as finished, even though there may still remain some unspent obligations or other further interests not fulfilled. This definition is no doubt coming from the background of termination by breach of contract. This sub-chapter will discuss the relationship between frustration and termination under both the common law and the English statutes. It will also attempt a vigorous analysis of other concepts like rescission, which is closely associated with the concept of termination and frustration; the ties, differences and general connotations of all these doctrines and concepts will be highlighted.

86 This is not unconnected with the character of the common law, which is mostly grafted into the mainstream of the legal system by the decisions and pronouncements of the superior courts.

87 Filip De Ly, "Termination Clauses in International Contracts" (1997) 7 *I.B.L.J.* 801–836.

88 John Birds (eds), *Termination of Contract* (Wiley Chancery, 1995) 3.

89 Michelle White, "Contract Breach and Contract Discharge Due to Impossibility: A Unified Theory" (1988) 17(2) *The Journal of Legal Studies* 353.

90 When a clause agreed to by the parties provides for certain circumstances or procedures by which a termination of contract should be effected, then such a clause or terms must bind the parties unless by the operation of any law which strictly regulates termination in certain specialised contracts.

91 Tom Grace and Fenwick Elliott Grace, "The Termination of Contracts for Breach" (2010) <http://www.feg.com.au/documents/TerminationpaperTRG10.10.pdf> accessed 12 September 2025.

4.3.2 Fundamental Breach under the English Law

The development of the doctrine of "fundamental breach" is purely a judge-made law approach adopted in combating the draconian effect of some exemption clauses in the law of contract.[92] It has been the policy of English courts since the middle of the 1960's "to be reluctant in allowing a party to rely on such exemption clauses in respect of a breach that was particularly serious."[93] It was soon made popular by a plethora of cases that subsequently came up for judicial consideration; the success of this was mixed and mired with uncertainty. Just like other products of judicial precedents, its limits and extents were not conclusively streamlined until the statute law took over the burden of legislative control of the exemption clauses.

The most succinct definition of this doctrine was furnished by Lord Wilberforce when he held that:

> Next for consideration is the argument based on "fundamental breach" or, which is presumably the same thing, a breach going "to the root of the contract." These expressions are used in the cases to denote two quite different things, namely, (i) a performance totally different from that which the contract contemplates, (ii) a breach of contract more serious than one which would entitle the other party merely to damages and which (at least) would entitle him to refuse performance or further performance under the contract[94]

It will be politic to understand that the English legal system garnered the foundation for this doctrine through its age-long maritime practices.[95] The controversy of whether the doctrine of fundamental breach is a rule of law or a rule of construction is only restricted to its common law background and application. It will be instructive to point out that there is no such wrangling under the CISG or the UNIDROIT Principles. Under the common law, the implication of a fundamental breach being regarded as a rule of substantive law is that whenever there is a breach of serious nature, otherwise known as a repudiatory breach, then it should be regarded as a

92 The concept of fundamental breach under the English common law is steeped in controversy; it is no longer of any practical relevance and is now more suited for academic discussion than for courtroom briefs. It has been put to rest by statutes after creating a good deal of excitement among English court hierarchies.

Fundamental breach simply means a serious breach which goes to the root of the contract—it does not mean exactly what the doctrine means under the CISG or the UNIDROIT Principles.

93 Peel (n 72) ch. 2, 2003.

94 *Suisse Atlantique Societe d'Armament SA v NV Rotterdamsche Kolen Centrale* [1966] 1 Lloyd's Rep 558

95 *Hain Steamship Company Ltd. v Tate & Lyle Ltd.* [1936] 2 All ER 597; Lord Wright, while emphasising the seriousness of the breach of deviation in the charter-party contract, held that:

"I agree with the conclusion of the Lord Justice. An unjustified deviation is a fundamental breach of a contract of affreightment. Owing to the peculiar nature of a maritime adventure in which ship-owner and goods owner are jointly concerned, it is a fundamental condition that in the absence of express liberties, the ship shall proceed

by the ordinary and customary route: any deviation changes the adventure. It also has the serious consequences that it vitiates the goods owner's insurances."

rule of substantive law that no matter how the exemption term / clause is couched, it will not override the serious breach which goes to the root of the contract.

On the other hand, the proponents of fundamental breach being a rule of construction are of the opinion that whenever there is an abundance of evidence clearly showing that a fundamental breach should be excluded in any clause, then the court will see this as a rule of construction and give effect to the clear provision of the clause. In the *Suisse Atlantique Societe d'Armament SA v NV Rotterdamsche Kolen Centrale*[96] the tug of war between fundamental breach being a rule of substantive law or a rule of construction was reasonable as adjudicated upon by the House of Lords.

While rejecting the ship owners" contention that, as a matter of substantive law, the delay in loading and unloading the ship caused the charterer to have a lesser voyage as contemplated under the contract, the House of Lords did not endorse the owners' argument that the delays were so significant as to constitute a fundamental breach of the provision of the contract regarding time spent loading and unloading. Their Lordships held that the delays by the charterers were not a fundamental breach. Rather, as a matter of construction, the contract contemplated the possibility of delay and fixed damages (demurrage) to compensate the owners for that delay.

The most decisive blow that finally wrested the doctrine of fundamental breach from the clutches of substantive law was triggered by the complex case of *Photo Production Ltd. v Securicor Transport Ltd.*[97][98] Photo Productions Ltd. sued Securicor Transport Ltd. after Securicor's employee, Mr Musgrove, started a fire at Photo Production's factory to keep himself warm while at work and accidentally burnt it down, costing £615,000. Securicor argued that an exclusion clause in its contract meant they were not liable, as it said, "under no circumstances be responsible for any injurious act or default by any employee… unless such act or default could have been foreseen and avoided by the exercise of due diligence on the part of [Securicor]." Photo Productions argued that the clause could not apply under the doctrine of fundamental breach, that the breach of the contract went to the root of the contract and invalidated the whole agreement, and extinguished the exclusion clause.

Lord Denning at the Court of Appeal held that the doctrine of fundamental breach should be applied and that the defendant is guilty of such breach and liable; thus, Securicor Transport Ltd. cannot be allowed to be shielded under the cover of any exemption clause limiting their liability. Disassociating themselves from the position of the Court of Appeal and holding that the rule of construction should favour scrutinising the exemption clause in order to find out if it clearly limited

96 Suisse Atlantique Société d'Armement SA(n 94)

97 *Photo Production Ltd. v Securicor Transport* Ltd. [1980] 2 WLR 283; AC 827.

98 Saloni Khanderia, "Termination for Breach: The Prospects of the Unidroit Principles of International Commercial Contracts to Interpret and Supplement the Indian Law of Contract" (2022) 27(4) *Uniform Law Review* 512.

liability, Lord Wilberforce in the House of Lords found Securicor Transport Ltd. not liable and went on to write thus:

> My Lords, whatever the intrinsic merit of this doctrine, as to which I shall have something to say later, it is clear to me that so far from following this House's decision in the Suisse Atlantique it is directly opposed to it and that the whole purpose and tenor of the Suisse Atlantique was to repudiate it. The lengthy, and perhaps may I say sometimes indigestible speeches of their Lordships, are correctly summarised in the headnote – holding No. 3 [1967] 1 A.C. 361 , 362 – "That the question whether an exceptions clause was applicable where there was a fundamental breach of contract was one of the true constructions of the contract." That there was any rule of law by which exceptions clauses are eliminated, or deprived of effect, regardless of their terms, was clearly not the view of Viscount Dilhorne, Lord Hodson, or of myself.[99]

The statute laws have succeeded in manacling the development of the doctrine of fundamental breach under the English common law of contract. It is simply used now in a sense only to denote such a gravity of a breach which radically changes the character, expectations and obligations of a contract, thereby empowering the aggrieved party to terminate, rescind, claim damages, or any sundry remedies. Over the years, some key statutory enactments, such as the Carriage of Goods by Sea Act 1971 and the Unfair Contract Terms Act 1977, have been in operation to oversee the lacuna created by lack of proper positive enactment on the operation of the doctrine. These enactments have also brought certainty to bear on this area of law, leaving little room for hanging such an important aspect of the law of contract on the speculation about what the court would say or do. For instance, under the Unfair Contract Terms Act 1977[100] the Act in its Section 17 renders terms excluding or limiting liability ineffective or subject to reasonableness, depending on the nature of the obligation purported to be excluded and whether the party purporting to exclude or limit business liability is acting against a consumer.[101]

99 Ibid.

100 Section 17 of the Unfair Contract Act of 1977 provides that:

> (1) Any term of a contract which is a consumer contract or a standard form contract shall have no effect for the purpose of enabling a party to the contract—
> (a) who is in breach of a contractual obligation, to exclude or restrict any liability of his to the consumer or customer in respect of the breach;
> (b) In respect of a contractual obligation, to render no performance, or to render a performance substantially different from that which the consumer or customer reasonably expected from the contract; if it was not fair and reasonable to incorporate the term in the contract.
>
> (2) In this section "customer" means a party to a standard form contract who deals on the basis of written standard terms of business of the other party to the contract who themselves deal in the course of a business.

101 Norman Palmer and David Yates, "The Future of the Unfair Contract Terms Act 1977" (1981) 40(1) *The Cambridge Law Journal* 108.

This and other kindred provisions have relatively brought normalcy to bear on the application of the doctrine of fundamental breach of contract under English common law. Lord Denning may have lost the war as to whether this doctrine is a substantive rule of law or whether it is a rule of construction; nevertheless, the subsequent statutes that sprang up echoed the same view he aired in *U.G.S Finance, Ltd. v National Mortgage Bank of Greece*[102] where the law Lords held that "The doctrine of 'fundamental breach' is a recent introduction into our law. It has been developed to get over an injustice of 'standardised contracts.'"

The new rule of reasonableness, determination of bargaining power and consumer protection policies enunciated under the 1977 Act have set the modern trend for the application of the doctrine of fundamental breach of contract. It was held in *Hunter Engineering Co. v Syncrude Canada Ltd,*[103] that exclusion clauses do not automatically lose their validity in the event of a fundamental breach by virtue of some hard and fast rule of law. They should be given their natural and true construction so that the meaning and effect of the exclusion clause, which the parties agreed to at the time the contract was entered into, are fully understood and appreciated.

One of the final putsches on the traditional doctrine of fundamental breach under English law was articulated and executed by Mr Justice Flaux in 2011 in the case of *Astrazeneca UK Ltd. v Albermarle International Corp & Ors.*[104]The learned justice, reviewing and distinguishing the earlier strange decision in *Internet Broadcasting Corp Ltd. (trading as NETTV) v MAR LLC (trading as MARhedge)*[105] where the old substantive law argument of the doctrine of fundamental breach reared its head up once again, held that:

> Thus, in my judgment, the judgment in Marhedge is heterodox and regressive and does not properly represent the current state of English law. If necessary, I would decline to follow it. Even if the breach by Albemarle of its obligation to deliver [the product] had been a deliberate repudiatory breach as Astrazeneca contends, the question whether any liability of Albemarle for damages for that breach was limited by [the exclusion clause] would simply be one of construing the clause, albeit strictly, but without any presumption.

The above decision only served to unfetter the court or tribunal in following any precedent that will make the doctrine of fundamental breach a rule of law. It does not, however, stop the court or tribunal from considering the seriousness of any breach and its impact on the aggrieved party to the contract before deciding on

102 [1964] 1 Lloyd's Rep 446.
103 [1989] 57 D.L.R. (4th) 321 Supreme Court of Canada.
104 [2011] EWHC 1574 (Civ).
105 [2009] EWHC 844 (Ch) para 35.

whether the remedy of termination or other remedies will be appropriate in such instance.[106]

4.3.3 Discharge/ Termination/ Rescission / Frustration of a Contract under English Law

As has earlier been mentioned, the concept of discharge of contract is an omnibus ground through which a contract which has gone wrong, either because of mistake, misrepresentation, fraud, frustration and non-performance or other serious fundamental breaches, can be determined. It will be significant to note at this juncture that pulling a plug off a contract under English law is multi-dimensional; it can take the form of termination or rescission. These concepts are dissimilar, though connected, but achieve different ends; for instance, a right to rescind helps a buyer whose purchase is induced by misrepresentation, whether fraudulent, negligent or entirely innocent, to rescind the contract. Rescission of a contract negates the award of damages, but courts can, in deserving cases, award indemnity in order to alleviate the effect of rescission on the aggrieved party.[107] Hector MacQueen, while supporting this view, writes that in certain rescission cases:

> [A]ccrued rights under the contract remain valid and enforceable, and clauses in the contract designed to deal with the post-contractual situation and disputes, such as exclusion, liquidated damage and arbitration clauses, remain effective.[108]

It is also the opinion of the law that when a contract is rescinded for misrepresentation, it is wiped out from the start, the parties must be put back into the position they were in before the contract was made, and if that cannot be done, then the contract may not be rescinded;[109] this is called "*restitution in integrum*."

The above is clearly different from the situation of frustration, which does not entertain any misrepresentation. Frustrating events under common law must be solely fortuitous and independent of the parties' acts or omissions. Richard Stone is of the view that "frustrating event results following the formation of a valid contract, an event occurs which is not the fault of either party but which has a significant impact on the obligations contained in the contract."[110] Rescission differs from frustration because while rescission concerns events preceding the

106 All these arguments about the doctrine of fundamental breach do not affect the doctrine of frustration; this is because the doctrine of frustration is an exemption doctrine that deals with supervening impossibility rather than breach. When there is evidence of breach, whether fundamental or not, the frustration will not apply.

107 A.G. Guest, *Benjamin Sale of Goods* (7th edn, Sweet & Maxwell, 2006) 586, para 12–003.

108 Hector L. MacQueen "Remedies for Breach of Contract: The Future Development of Scots Law in its European and International Context" (1997) 1(2) *Edinburgh Law Review* 200–226.

109 J.C. Smith, *The Law of Contract* (4th edn, Sweet & Maxwell, 2002) 156.

110 *The Modern Law of Contract* (8th edn, Routledge-Cavendish, 2009), para 15.2, 530.

formation of the contract, frustration concerns events that occur after the contract comes into existence.[111]

Nonetheless, termination deals with a breach subsequent to or precedent to the valid contract; however, if the event preceding the contract involved misrepresentation or manipulation of facts, then the appropriate remedy should be rescission. It means that the contract never existed *ab initio*.[112] If it involves a breach subsequent to the contract that breaks the conditions of the contract, then termination will be appropriate, but if the breach subsequent is a result of an unforeseen event and non-fault of any of the parties, then the breach can be regarded as a frustrating event with the consequence that the parties are discharged from further obligations, and may be able to recover money or property transferred, and compensation for work done prior to the frustrating event.[113]

The right to terminate is jealously guarded; it is different from both rescission and frustration. It cannot be exercised as a matter of course. "The judiciary have shown their concern to ensure that the 'engines of industry' are slowed as little as possible by breach situations."[114] This is made very evident in the case of *Rice v Great Yarmouth Borough Council*[115] wherein the Council contracted with Rice to provide it with leisure management and grounds maintenance for a period of four years. It used a standard form of contract drafted by the Association of Metropolitan Authorities, and the clause dealing with termination stated, "If the contractor commits a breach of any of its obligations under the contract, the Council may, without prejudice to any accrued rights or remedies under the contract, terminate the contractor's employment by notice in writing having immediate effect." Despite the clear wording of the contract allowing the Council to terminate "if the contractor commits a breach of any of its obligations," the Court of Appeal held that a literal interpretation of that clause flew in the face of commercial common sense and that a common sense, commercial interpretation had to be applied. The court used the occasion of this case to accentuate the fact that what governs termination in a contract is not automatic but predicated on the degree of the severity of the breach, judging from the peculiar circumstances of each case.

Termination for breach takes effect from the moment of the avoidance. It is immaterial that the parties cannot be put back into the position in which they were before the contract was made, and rights and duties which accrued before the termination came into effect are not affected.[116] So it does not have the implication of retrospective rebutting of the contract from the very start, like rescission does.

The borderline between the right to terminate and the right to discharge the contract is worrisomely thin; it seems termination is a subset in the main set called "discharge." They seem to suggest the same facts, achieve the same end and give

111 Ibid., 531.
112 Upex and Bennett (n 100) ch. 2, 274.
113 Under the 1943 Frustrated Contract Act.
114 Linda Mulcahy, *Contract Law in Perspective* (Routledge Cavendish, 2008) 208.
115 [2000] *The Times*, 26th July.
116 J.C. Smith, *The Law of Contract* (Sweet & Maxwell, 2002) 156.

rise to the same legal implications. For instance, in analysing the right to discharge, it follows that "a party to a contract of sale who suffers serious breach through the actions or inactions of the other party can refuse to perform his own obligations or accept further obligations or performance from the other party."[117] In such a circumstance, it can be said that the aggrieved party has discharged the contract; it can also be gleaned that they have a right by reason of the other party's breach to terminate the contract, and then they can go for other damages like asking for price, damages, etc. The above painted a good picture of how the proliferation of terms has been the greatest burden in understanding when parties have the right to unbundle a contract and what term their actions will be known as.

Under the Sale of Goods Act of 1979, termination of a contract plays a prominent role with its kindred concept of rescission. Apart from trying to entrench the common law concept of conditions and warranties, Section 11(3) of the Sale of Goods Act of 1979 also provides for the circumstances by which a termination can be effected. The section provides that:

> Whether a stipulation in a contract of sale is a condition, the breach of which may give rise to a right to treat the contract as repudiated, or a warranty, the breach of which may give rise to a claim for damages but not to a right to reject the goods and treat the contract as repudiated, depends in each case on the construction of the contract; and a stipulation may be a condition, though called a warranty in the contract.

It can be argued from the above that it takes a serious breach to treat the contract as repudiated; it also appears that the term "repudiated" as used in Section 11(3) of the Sales of Goods Act of 1979 means the same thing as "terminated."[118] Then there is the intermediate term as propounded in the case of *Hong Fir Shipping Co v Kawasaki Kisen Kaisha Ltd,*[119] where Lord Diplock observed that there are so complex terms of the contract that neither condition, the breach which will give rise to termination nor warranty which gives rise to damages and other remedies but never termination. He went on to espouse that intermediate terms look not at the form or clauses of the contract but at the effect of the actual breach which occurred in order to know if the said breach substantially deprived the parties or any of them of the whole intention of the contract.

Furthermore, the categorisation of breaches into their degree of seriousness also casts a heavy reflection on the doctrine of frustration. It has been the settled view of the law that a mere, minor unforeseen event which has no grave implications on the contract cannot be allowed to frustrate the contract. It is only a total, impossible

117 A.G Guest (ed) (n 76) 596, para 12–018.

118 CB Jern and KL Fatt Kin, "Amendments to the Sale of Goods Act: A Critical Analysis" (1997) 18 *Sing. L. Rev.* 172.

119 [1962] 2 QB 26.

event which substantially altered the nature, performance, obligations and expectation of the contract that can be permitted to frustrate the contract.[120]

Also, the events and the legal implications of termination can be seen from the spectacle of whether or not the property has been passed. It has been held that:

> When the property has not passed to the buyer, the seller has the right to resell the goods if he chooses to terminate the contract upon the buyer's breach. If the seller following the buyer's repudiation or fundamental breach does terminate the contract, the seller is released from any further obligations under the contract.[121]

The other further implication of the above analysis/scenario is that the seller would have deemed to waive their right to the remedy of asking for the price, but they can still prevail on the remedy of damages.

However, when the property and possession have both passed to the buyer, then the seller will be much better off with other remedies other than termination of the contract; they cannot retake the goods, though they can ask for the price, damages or other remedies known within the purview of common law.[122] Where it is the seller who is guilty of a fundamental breach or repudiatory acts of his obligations under the contract, the buyer may hold the contract terminated; this is especially the case where the breach is that of condition or the repudiation touches at the root of the contract.[123] A buyer who exercises a *bona fide* right of rejection of the goods can treat the failure of the seller as a breach of condition; this is because such a failure to deliver, if it goes to the root of the contract, will be tantamount to a breach of condition.[124]

Finally, the Sale and Supply of Goods Act of 1994 has brought some regularity and equity to the doctrine of termination under the ambit of the sale of goods; it has finally unlocked it from the clutches of the common law. Section 35A of the 1994 Act is particularly important.[125] The main purpose of the above provision is to

120 Lord Loreburn explained in FA Tamplin v Anglo-Mexican Petroleum [1916] 2 AC 397, that the court: "Can infer from the nature of the contract and the surrounding circumstances that a condition which was not expressed was a foundation on which the parties contracted ... Where the altered conditions such that, had they thought of them, the parties would have taken their chance of them, or such that as sensible men they would have said 'if that happens of course, it is all over between us.'"

121 A.G Guest (ed) (n 97) ch. 1, para 17–095, 1110.

122 Ewan McKendrick, *Sale of Goods* (Informa Law from Routledge, 2020) 483–522.

123 Ibid.

124 Ibid.

125 Section 35a of the Sale and Supply of Goods Act of 1994 provides thus:

> (1) If the buyer –
> (a) has the right to reject the goods by reason of a breach on the part of the seller that affects some or all of them, but
> (b) Accepts some of the goods, including, where there are any goods unaffected by the breach, all such goods; he does not, by accepting them, lose his right to reject the rest.

provide the right of partial rejection so that where the buyer is entitled to reject the goods on account of a defect affecting some or all of them, but they accept some of them, he does not thereby lose the right to reject the remainder.[126] Another instructive provision of the aforementioned 1994 Act is seen in s15A[127] which makes a modification of remedies for breach of condition in non-consumer cases.

The whole idea of Section 15A is to treat as a warranty a breach of condition which is slight and has no dire consequences on the contract. The law will be prepared to look the other way in these circumstances when the buyer is a non-consumer. The rationale behind this provision is to not allow flimsy breaches which are not serious but, as a result of the pedagogic formulation of breaches into conditions and warranties, will operate to terminate a contract. However, Section 15A also provides for the rule of evidence by squarely putting the burden of proof on the seller (s 15A (1)(b)) to prove that the breach is such that it should be regarded as inconsequential or what is known as *de minimis* breach.

---

(2) In the case of a buyer having the right to reject an instalment of goods, subsection (1) above applies as if references to the goods were references to the goods comprised in the instalment.
(3) For the purposes of subsection (1) above, goods are affected by a breach if by reason of the breach they are not in conformity with the contract.
(4) This section applies unless a contrary intention appears in, or is to be implied from, the contract.

126 John Birds, *Termination of Contracts* (John Wiley & Sons, 1995) 54.
127 Section 15A of the Sale and Supply of Goods Act of 1994 provides thus:

(1) Where in the case of a contract of sale –
   (a) the buyer would, apart from this subsection, have the right to reject goods by reason of a breach on the part of the seller of a term implied by section 13, 14 or 15 above, but
   (b) The breach is so slight that it would be unreasonable for him to reject them; then, if the buyer does not deal as a consumer, the breach is not to be treated as a breach of condition but may be treated as a breach of warranty.
(2) This section applies unless a contrary intention appears in, or is to be implied from, the contract.
(3) It is for the seller to show that a breach fell within subsection (1)(b) above.
(4) This section does not apply to Scotland.
(2) In section 30 of that Act (delivery of shortfall or excess) after subsection (2) there is inserted –
   (2A) A buyer who does not deal as a consumer may not –
   (a) where the seller delivers a quantity of goods less than he contracted to sell, reject the goods under subsection
(1) above, or
   (b) where the seller delivers a quantity of goods larger than he contracted to sell, reject the whole under subsection (2) above,

If the shortfall or, as the case may be, excess is so slight that it would be unreasonable for him to do so, it is for the seller to show that a shortfall or excess fell within subsection (2A) above.
(2C) Subsections (2A) and (2B) above do not apply to Scotland.

4.3.4 Conclusion

The relationship between exemption, *force majeure* and frustration with other similar concepts like avoidance (termination), rescission and discharge is strong.[128] They all work as vitiating concepts, employed to disband a contract which has gone significantly contrary to the expectations of the parties. While conceding to the often-repeated principle that each case should be treated within its peculiar facts, there is a need to capture the legal basis of each of the concepts. *Force majeure* under the UNIDROIT principles arises when non-performance of a party is due to an unforeseeable and uncontrollable impediment. The parties can still terminate the contract, and the non-performance is not excused. Termination under the UNIDROIT Principles is a result of fundamental non-performance, the *Nachfrist* rule, or inability to cure non-performance.

Avoidance under the UNIDROIT Principles remains the means through which an invalid contract can be discharged; this peculiar meaning of avoidance under the UNIDROIT does not mean the same thing under arts 49 or 64 of the CISG. These arts (49, 64) are like the doctrine of termination (art 7.3.1) under the UNIDROIT Principles.[129] Generally, avoidance under the CISG, termination under both UNIDROIT Principles and English law, and exemption/*force majeure*/frustration all share the remedy of restitution as a way of putting the parties back to their original position before the breach or impediment that caused the non-performance.

Under the common law, termination is primarily as a result of a fundamental breach of contract, while frustration is all about the impossibility of the performance of a contract which is unforeseen and thus radically excusing the parties from continuing with the contract.[130] Under the CISG, avoidance of the contract through arts 49 and 64 brings about the consequences under arts 81 and 82 of the CISG, and all these are applicable to the doctrine of exemption under art 79.

It has been held that even if the party who is required to overcome an impediment under Art.79 CISG does so by furnishing a substitute performance, the other party could avoid the contract and thereby reject the substitute performance if that substitute performance was so deficient in comparison with the performance stipulated in the contract that it constituted a fundamental breach of contract.[131] This chapter will be summarised by stating the fact that while exemption, *force majeure* and frustration are as a result of the non-fault of the party, termination, avoidance and rescission are always fault-based.

128 Shiyuan Han, "Force Majeure, Change of Circumstances and Termination of Contract" (2016) 3(1) *Journal of Law, Society and Development* 31.

129 Avoidance of contract under the CISG, like the UNIDROIT Principles, involves fundamental breach; the *Nachfrist* rule of additional period to perform in the case of non-delivery and the rule of additional time to cure defective delivery can be inferred.

130 Andrey Chukreyev, "The Doctrine of Frustration in English Contract Law" (2017) *Law: J. Higher Sch. Econ.* 188.

131 Yasutoshi Ishida, "CISG Article 79: Exemption of Performance, and Adaptation of Contract Through Interpretation of Reasonableness-full of Sound and Fury, but Signifying Something" (2017) 30 *Pace Int'l L. Rev.* 331.

5 Hardship and Exemption/*Force Majeure*/Frustration

5.1 Relationship between Hardship and Exemption under the CISG

5.1.1 Background

Art 79 of the CISG provides for exemption; the *sumum bonum* of this provision is to excuse a party from liability if his failure to perform any of his obligations under the contract is due to an unforeseeable impediment that they would not reasonably be expected to take into account at the time of the conclusion of the contract and expected to avoid or overcome it or its consequences. The meaning of the word "impediment" as used under art 79 of the CISG has opened a vortex of academic and judicial speculation. The live issue under this chapter is whether hardship can be qualified as an impediment under art 79 of the CISG.[1] The answers to this question have further polarised the uniformity stance of the United Nations Convention on the International Contract of Sale of Goods 1980.

The CISG has been interpreted sometimes to the effect that the doctrine of "hardship" is not contemplated under the CISG.[2] The argument is that the CISG was drafted consciously avoiding the possibility of reading hardship into art 79 to eschew the same controversy that dogged art 74 of the ULIS (CISG's predecessor). The proponents of this view believe in the principle of interpretation that suggests that anything not listed is intended to be omitted (*expressio unius est exclusio alterius*), thus the deliberate omission of the doctrine of hardship under art 79 of the CISG is for all intents and purposes meant to remove it from the sphere of consideration during the application of art 79.[3] However, many other scholars and jurisdictions have stuck to their opinion in propounding the belief that the CISG is not robotic, and can be expanded in order to read the doctrine of hardship into its art 79 provision. They also believe that the international convention should be divorced from the technicalities that bedevilled national laws, and once a clear case is established in deserving circumstances, then there is no reason why the CISG

1 Konarski (n 63) ch. 4, 405–428; the author writes that "Theoretically, hardship is different from *force majeure*, because the performance of a contractual obligation, contrary to *force majeure*, need not be absolutely impossible."

2 Hector L. MacQueen, "Change of Circumstances: CISG, CESL and A Case from Scotland" (2012) 11(3) *JITLP* 300–305.

3 Uribe (n 44) ch. 1.

DOI: 10.4324/9781003667841-5

should not be given a human face and thus incorporate the doctrine of hardship under its art 79. Hardship itself has been defined as "[a] change of circumstances that could not reasonably be expected to have been taken into account, rendering performance excessively onerous."[4] This terse but complicated definition offered by the CISG Advisory body has opened a veritable starting point for inquiries by courts, practitioners, scholars and legal aficionados as to whether the impossibility clearly implied in the meaning of what makes up an "impediment" under the art 79 of the CISG can also accommodate onerous performance. Is it truly the intentions of the CISG to categorise a burdensome performance as an impediment? The answers to this question have left chasms and confusion in their wake.

5.1.2 Argument Against Hardship Being Part of Art 79 of the CISG

First, there is no provision of the CISG that mentions hardship.[5] This cannot be an oversight or a mistake, and thus it is a calibrated and calculated effort towards getting rid of the word "hardship" out of the international sale of goods law lexicon. Barry Nicholas holds the opinion that "exemption of liability on account of unexpected and excessive economic hardship was "out of place" in a sales law."[6] It has been argued that "as to the legislative history of art 79, there is ample support for the proposition that the Convention does not favour an easy exemption from non-performance and that the notion of "impediment" under art 79 points to an insurmountable obstacle that is unrelated to the more flexible notions of hardship, impracticability, frustration, or the like."[7]

Art 74 ULIS,[8] the predecessor of art 79 of the CISG, was more generous in the sense that it employed a more loose word, "circumstances," while providing for a

4 Alejandro M. Garro, Rapporteur: CISG-AC Opinion No. 7 "Exemption of Liability for Damages under Art 79 of the CISG": [12 October 2007] Columbia University School of Law, New York, NY, USA. Adopted by the CISG-AC at its 11th meeting in Wuhan, People's Republic of China <http://www.cisg.law.pace.edu/cisg/CISG-AC-op7.html> accessed 13/9/2025.

5 Catherine Kessedjian, "Competing Approaches to *Force Majeure* and Hardship" (2005) 25 *International Review of Law and Economics* 641–670.

6 Progress Report of the Working Group on the International Sale of Goods on the Work of its Fifth Session (A/CN.9/87, Annex III, reprinted in UNCITRAL Yearbook V: 1974 (1975) at 66.

7 CISG Advisory Council Opinion No. 7 "Exemption of Liability for Damages Under Art 79 of the CISG" [2007] <http://www.cisg.law.pace.edu/cisg/CISG-AC-op7.html> accessed 13/9/2025.

8 Art 74 ULIS of 1964 provides that:

1. Where one of the parties has not performed one of his obligations, he shall not be liable for such non-performance if he can prove that it was due to circumstances which, according to the intention of the parties at the time of the conclusion of the contract, he was not bound to take into account or to avoid or to overcome; in the absence of any expression of the intention of the parties, regard shall be had to what reasonable persons in the same situation would have intended.
2. Where the circumstances which gave rise to the non-performance of the obligation constituted only a temporary impediment to performance, the party in default shall nevertheless be permanently relieved of his obligation if, by reason of the delay, performance would be so radically changed as to amount to the performance of an obligation quite different from that contemplated by the contract.

possible event that can make a party who fails to perform any of his obligations under the contract of sale not liable. The use of "circumstances" in art 74 ULIS above can be interpreted to be a predisposition towards regarding hardship as part of the possible events contemplated under this convention. But a similar move has been shunned by the CISG through its total silence on the use of the doctrine of hardship under its present regime. It has been argued that:

> The legislative history of the CISG has revealed that the drafters did not want art 79 to cover the concept of hardship. In some of the cases in relation to art 79 the arbitral tribunals have tried to avoid the issue of hardship by either ruling that the economic hardship is not sudden, substantial or unforeseeable and in another case that the impediment could have been taken into account.[9]

Furthermore, it can be argued that international commercial law, more especially the contract of sale of goods, intends to only excuse a party's non-performance in the face of an impediment of impossible nature, which will otherwise make any manner of further physical performance a foregone impracticability. However, where the burden of performance has radically escalated, leaving the economic dynamics of the contract imbalanced and badly tilted, then it will not receive succour under art 79 of the CISG.[10] It is a matter within the parties' drafting expertise to incorporate such terms and clauses which will help in adjusting the contract in the event of hardship.

It has been suggested that the courts or tribunals will not inquire into the economic dynamics of the allocation of risks arising from bad bargains. This assertion was the foundation of the decision in the *Steel Bars case*, where the court, comparing Yugoslav law with art 79 of the CISG, held that:

> [T]he seller could be relieved of the obligation to deliver the goods at the contract price only if the contract contained a price adjustment clause, or in case of frustration of the contract, which was not the case here, since the increase in the market price was, in fact, neither sudden nor substantial nor unforeseeable.[11]

---

3. The relief provided by this art for one of the parties shall not exclude the avoidance of the contract under some other provision of the present Law or deprive the other party of any right which they have under the present Law to reduce the price, unless the circumstances which entitled the first party to relief were caused by the act of the other party or of some person for whose conduct they were responsible.

9 Tope Adebayo, "*Force majeure* And Hardship: To What Extent Does Art 79 of CISG Excuse Liability for Non Performance?" [10 July 2011] <http://topeadebayollp.wordpress.com/> Para 3.4, accessed 15/9/2025.

10 Harry M. Flechtner, "Issues Relating to Exemption ('*Force Majeure*') Under Art 79 of the United Nations Convention on Contracts for the International Sale of Goods ('CISG')" <http://ssrn.com/abstract=1118124> accessed 08/9/2025. He writes that "Hardship doctrine looks at the continuation of the contract while Art 79 seeks its termination."

11 ICC International Court of Arbitration, 26 August 1989 – 6281 (Final Award), CISG-online 8 [ICC Arbitration Case No. 6281 of 26 August 1989] "Steel Bars Case" <https://cisg-online.org/search-for-cases?caseId=5990> accessed 29/9/2025.

The case of *Nuova Fucinati v Fondmetall International*[12] will be succinct in driving home the opinion of the law on exclusion of hardship under art 79 of the CISG. The plaintiff, an Italian seller who failed to deliver the goods to the defendant, a Swedish buyer, claimed avoidance of the sales contract on the ground of hardship since the price of the goods had increased after conclusion of the contract and before delivery by almost 30%. The court held that the CISG does not apply in the instant case, but even if it does apply, the seller's cause of action based on avoidance by reason of hardship is not recognised under the CISG, since art 79 of the CISG does not provide for the doctrine of hardship. The blatant denial of the Italian court to accord or read hardship between the provisions of art 79 CISG was received with mixed reactions, while the proponents applauded it as the right step in the right direction; critics see it as over-reaching.[13]

Nevertheless, the Greek court in 2006 had the opportunity in the Sunflower seeds case[14] to answer the question of whether or not hardship can come under art 79 of the CISG. In this case, a Bulgarian seller who failed to supply sunflower seeds to a Greek seller despite repeated demands by the latter claimed impediment beyond his control thus:

(a) [t]hat prolonged dryness, which resulted in the destruction of a large quantity of the current harvest of sunflower seeds in Bulgaria and consequently reduction of production and availability of this product;
(b) the lowering of the level of the river Danube; thus the seller was unable to load the goods on a ship in a river port which was located in its premises and furthermore it was obliged to use a port located in the Black Sea; however, the necessity to load the goods in a sea port entailed increased transportation costs for the seller to that port, a fact that rendered the initially agreed price highly inexpedient for the seller.

The court rejecting to exonerate him from liability under art 79 held that:

> CISG art 79 does not entitle the promisor to be released from his contractual obligations due to change of the economic background on which the parties relied for the conclusion of the contract, since, in this case, the commencement

12 Tribunale di Monza (District Court Monza) Italy, 14 January 1993 – 4267/88, CISG-online 102 <https://cisg-online.org/search-for-cases?caseId=6082> accessed 15/9/2025.

13 It will be worthwhile to identify that the court declined jurisdiction to apply CISG to the dispute because at the time of the conclusion of the contract CISG was in force in Italy but not in Sweden (Art 1(1) (a) CISG), thus parties cannot be said to be contracting parties under the CISG. Also, based on the fact that the Convention should be excluded on the ground that the parties had chosen Italian law as the law governing their contract, holding that Art 1(1)(b) CISG operates only in the absence of a choice of law by the parties. Therefore, the court going ahead with a pronouncement on the merit of whether or not hardship is applicable under Art 79 or not was an afterthought, and thus unpersuasive.

14 Efetio Lamias (Court of Appeal Lamia) Greece, 2006 – 63/2006, CISG-online 5924 <https://cisg-online.org/search-for-cases?caseId=13838> accessed 21/9/2025.

> of transportation by ship could be performed at a sea port (instead by a river port), although this would entail higher costs for the seller.[15]

By and large, hardships are always associated with economic disequilibrium, and the courts are reluctant to aid parties who have failed to make provisions in their contracts to take care of such situations. The *Iron Molybdenum case*[16] established the doubtful attitude of the courts towards onerous economic situations that can befall a contract of sale. In this case, an English buyer, plaintiff, and a German seller, defendant, entered into a contract for the supply of iron-molybdenum from China, CIF Rotterdam, and delivery in October 1994. The goods were never delivered to the buyer, as the seller did not itself receive delivery of the goods from its own Chinese supplier. After the expiry of an additional period of time for delivery, the buyer concluded a substitute transaction with a third party and sued the seller for the difference between the price paid and the price under the contract. The court held that:

> The seller was not exempted from liability, neither under a *force majeure* clause of the contract, nor under art 79(1) of the Convention. The seller bears the risk of itself receiving delivery of the goods from its own supplier. Only if goods of an equal or similar quality were no longer available on the market would the seller be exempted from liability. Furthermore, the court held that it was incumbent upon the seller to bear the risk of increasing market prices at the time of the substitute transaction. Although the market price had raised to an amount triple the price that had been agreed at the time of the conclusion of the original contract, this did not amount to a sacrificial sale price, as the transaction was said to be highly speculative.[17]

Also, the court demurred further to find in favour of hardship in the case of *Vital Berry Marketing v Dira-Frost*[18] by holding that in a situation where the market price of purchased goods dropped after the conclusion of the contract, this is not enough to bring a cause of action under art 79 of the CISG. The court reasoned further that fluctuations of prices are foreseeable in the sphere of international trade, and the usual losses that occur cannot be said to be beyond the purview of the parties.

Recently, in the *Protective Masks Case*,[19] a German buyer contracted with a seller for the delivery of protective face masks during the height of the first COVID-19 wave. The seller failed to deliver. The seller made the argument that the pandemic

15 Ibid. (Commentary by Dionysios P. Flambouras).

16 Oberlandesgericht Hamburg (Court of Appeal Hamburg), [Germany, 28 February 1997, 1 U 167/95] CISG-online (Appellate Court Hamburg) 261 <https://cisg-online.org/search-for-cases?caseId=6235> accessed 19/9/2025.

17 Ibid.

18 District Court Hasselt Belgium, 2 May 1995 AR 1849/94, CISG-online 371 <https://cisg-online.org/search-for-cases?caseId=6343> accessed 20/9/2025.

19 Landgericht Bonn, judgment of 11 October 2021, Case No. 1 O 321/21.

and sudden export restrictions in the source country constituted an "impediment beyond control" under art 79. The German Court decided that the seller was not exempt from liability. The court held that because the masks were generic goods, the seller bore the "procurement risk." Unless the seller could prove that the entire global market had dried up, rather than just their specific supplier failing, the obligation to deliver remained. The seller was liable for damages, which shows the high threshold of art 79 even during a time of global crises.

However, there has been a mild scholarly approach towards finding a common ground as to whether a hardship situation can qualify as an impediment under art 79 of the CISG; it has been put forward that a hardship situation (economic hardship) can only be regarded as an impediment where it affects the physical performance of the contract, thus making performance impossible. John Honnold[20] argues that "art 79 also encompasses economic impediments; this entails that a party can be excused under the CISG on the basis of economic dislocations but only if it provides an impediment comparable to a non-economic impediment that excuses failure of performance." Nevertheless, not every scholar shares this view.[21]

Even further discrepancy between exemption and hardship can be seen in the definition offered by the International Chamber of Commerce (ICC) 2020 *Force Majeure* and Hardship Clauses.[22] And the provision for *force majeure* under the ICC has been held to resemble the provisions under art 79 of the CISG and art 7.1.7 of the UNIDROIT Principles.[23]

The definitions and aims of these two clauses are not the same, while the final destination as observed in paragraphs (4), (5), (6) of the ICC *force majeure* clause is to relieve liability even though other sundry remedies may apply; the hardship clause clearly does not excuse liability. Paragraph (1) of the ICC hardship clause is very instructive in this regard, and then paragraph 2(b) makes re-negotiation of the contract paramount in order to sort out alternative contractual terms suited best for the troubled contract. The tenor and applications of these two clauses are not alike.

20 John O. Honnold, *Uniform Law of International Sales under the 1980 United Nations Convention* (2nd edn, Kluwer Law and Taxation Publishers Deventer, Boston, MA, 1990) 543–544.

21 Carla Spivack, "Of Shrinking Sweatsuits and Poison Vine Wax: A Comparison of Basis for Excuse under
U.C.C. § 2–615 and CISG Art 79" (2006) 27 *Pennsylvania Journal of International Economic Law* 757–802. The author argues that "The language of Art 79, however, fails to support this inference -- an event which frustrates a contract's purpose does not necessarily prevent its performance. Moreover, the UNCITRAL debates during the drafting of the CISG show that the drafters adopted the term "impediment" because they opposed allowing economic hardship as an excuse for non-performance."

22 Published in February 2003 by ICC Publishing S.A., an affiliate of ICC: the world business organisation, 38 Cours Albert 1er, 75008 Paris, France.

23 Christopher Brunner, "*Force Majeure and Hardship under General Contract Principles: Exemption for Non-performance in International Arbitration (International Arbitration Law Library Series)*" (Kluwer Law International, 2008) 75. The author writes that ICC provision on *force majeure* is similar to Art 79 of CISG and Art 7.1.7 of the UNIDROIT Principles.

It will be enlightening to observe that, while the doctrine of hardship can be invoked at any time during the life-span of the contract (though mostly favoured after the conclusion of the contract) when the economic equilibrium[24] of the contract tilts heavily against any party, there may not necessarily be any breach. On the other hand, the doctrine of exemption can only be invoked under art 79 of the CISG when a breach of the contract by reason of non-performance has occurred, albeit to say the non-performance can even pre-exist the contract[25] (since CISG has no provision for mistake) provided the parties are totally unaware of it, and it is caused by an unforeseeable impediment that the parties cannot control or overcome.

Anja Carlsen also noted that the obvious difference in the end-point of both exemption and hardship portrays that the two doctrines are not meant to be used synonymously under art 79 of the CISG. While exemption does not affect the contract by way of overhauling it but merely excuses a party from liability for damages, the doctrine of hardship entails the contract should be re-negotiated, adapted or terminated upon failure to reach a new agreement.[26] All these are good pointers that will easily form a conclusion that the United Nations Convention on the International Contract of Sale of Goods deliberately left the burden of grappling with the doctrine of hardship where it has fallen with the ULIS of 1964.

5.1.3 Argument in Favour of Hardship Being Part of Art 79 of the CISG

The fundamental purpose of any international convention is to have the potential to keep up with the changing world views. CISG is not rigid, and it is constructively kinetic and thus can be interpreted in a manner to accommodate commercial justice. It has been argued that all situations of hardship must be evaluated on the basis of art 79 or be treated as a breach of contract. The CISG does not seem to have any provision that would allow a different solution than the ones mentioned above under art 79.[27] The most influential view in support of hardship being part of art 79 of the CISG can be seen in the CISG Advisory Council Opinion No 7.[28] This opinion provides inter alia in paragraphs 3.1 and 3.2 thus:

24 Werner Melis, "*Force Majeure* and Hardship Clauses in International Commercial Contracts in View of the Practice of the ICC Court of Arbitration" (1984) 1 *Journal of International Arbitration* 213.

25 Hans Stoll and Georg Gruber, "Art 79" in Peter Schlechtriem and Ingeborg Schwenzer (eds) *Commentary on the UN Convention on the International Sale of Goods* (Oxford University Press, 2nd English edn, 2005) para 10–24.

26 Anja Carlsen, "Can the Hardship Provisions in the UNIDROIT Principles Be Applied When the CISG is the Governing Law?" [1998] <http://www.cisg.law.pace.edu/cisg/biblio/carlsen.html> accessed 21/9/2025.

27 Lindström (n 41) ch. 2.

28 CISG Advisory Opinion <http://www.cisg.law.pace.edu/cisg/CISG-AC-op7.html> accessed 21/9/2025.

3.1 A change of circumstances that could not reasonably be expected to have been taken into account, rendering performance excessively onerous ("hardship"), may qualify as an "impediment" under Art 79(1). The language of Art 79 does not expressly equate the term "impediment" with an event that makes performance absolutely impossible. Therefore, a party that finds itself in a situation of hardship may invoke hardship as an exemption from liability under Art 79.

3.2 In a situation of hardship under Art 79, the court or arbitral tribunal may provide further relief consistent with the CISG and the general principles on which it is based.

The above opinions are a well-thought-out legal framework that will help the courts, tribunals, practitioners, merchants and academic writers in appreciating the meanings, applications and implications of art 79 of the CISG.[29] The legal think-tank that masterminded this opinion believed that hardship can be read within the ambit of art 79 of the CISG, thus the reason why they unequivocally held in paragraph 3.1 that hardship can be applied to art 79 of the CISG. It has been suggested that hardship has always been part and parcel of exemption (*force majeure*) events. The doctrine of *rebus sic stantibus*, which is still relevant in today's international commercial law, has always maintained that unforeseeable and extraordinary change of circumstances rendering a contractual obligation extremely burdensome though not absolutely impossible may entail the avoidance or even the revision or "adaptation" of the contract or one of its clauses.[30]

Hardship is absent from the CISG because of the tendency of using such loose words like "circumstances' in art 74 of the ULIS; many buyers and sellers may cash in on it, thereby twisting and looking for any available loophole to exploit and to excuse liability from a difficult or unfavourable contract. To discourage this negative surge towards non-liability, the CISG totally ignored the provision of hardship and drafted art 79 in a very strict manner by which the courts or tribunal should be prejudiced not to hold difficult contracts of sale as a ground to excuse liability. However, the court will progressively interpret art 79 in order to accommodate quagmire economic situations as an impediment under art 79 of the CISG. Thus, the forgoing predispositions of the draftsmen and the courts may be tempered with in deserving cases, like where the ultimate limit of sacrifice[31] has been disproportionately exceeded, or where the unexpected economic equation of a contract of sale has been badly distorted as to render the performance of the contract

29 While admitting that the CISG Advisory Council is a private initiative that features scholars who have in-depth knowledge and research interest in the CISG, their opinion offers a veritable tool through which international sales law has been developed. On 10 September 2012, the CISG Advisory Council was granted observer status by UNCITRAL. This will enable the CISG Advisory Council to attend future meetings of UNCITRAL and its working groups.

30 *Scafom International BV v Lorraine Tubes S.A.S* Belgian Supreme Court, [Belgium 19 June 2009 Court of Cassation] Belgium, 19 June 2009 – C.07.0289.N, CISG-online 1963 (Supreme Court) <https://cisg-online.org/search-for-cases?caseId=7880> accessed 29/9/2025.

31 Garro (n 4).

economically impossible (though notionally possible since there can still be room for physical performance).

The premise upon which hardship can be considered under art 79 is that performance is not impossible but is physically more difficult than the parties had imagined.[32] Honnold, while arguing on the possible inclusion of some hardship event under art 79 CISG, states that:

> Assuming that the supply of a material needed for performance of a contract unexpectedly becomes so reduced in quality and inflated in price that only a minority of producers that need this material can continue in production, this situation clearly constitutes an "impediment" barring performance by most producers whose contracts overlap the onset of the shortage.[33]

However, it has been articulated that a price fluctuation amounting to over 100% does not constitute grounds for exemption,[34] this clearly supports the fact that it takes an exceptional hardship of a significant magnitude to be categorised as a *force majeure* under art 79 of the CISG. It is equally persuasive that art 79 should cover ethical hardship which deals with a situation where the end use of the goods will fall into excessive depravity like the buying of chemical or nuclear matters for the purpose of manufacturing dirty prohibited bombs.[35]

Explaining the rationale for the application of the doctrine of hardship events under the CISG, Ingeborg Schwenzer opines that:

> The event in question must not fall in the sphere of risk of the aggrieved party; it must have been unforeseeable as well as unavoidable. Thus, hardship can be considered as a special group of cases under the general *force majeure* provisions. All that is added to the *force majeure* provisions on the level of prerequisites is a clarification of the term impediment in cases where performance in the strict sense is possible but just too onerous. This may justify dealing with hardship under the CISG.[36]

The above view received a tremendous boost in the recent case of *Scafom International BV v Lorraine Tubes S.A.S.*[37] In this case, the Belgian Supreme Court overturned the earlier decision of the Commercial Court Tongeren in dealing with economic hardship. The court, while considering the application of hardship under the CISG, held that:

32 James Gordley, "Impossibility and Changed and Unforeseen Circumstances" (Summer 2004) 52 *American Journal of Comparative Law* 513–530.

33 Honnold (n 39) ch. 1, para 432.2, 484–485.

34 Schletriem and Schwenzer (n 5) ch. 2, para 30, 1076.

35 Ibid., para 32, 1077.

36 "*Force majeure* and Hardship in International Sales Contract" (2008) 39 *VUWLR* also cited as <http://www.austlii.edu.au/nz/journals/VUWLawRw/2008/39.pdf> accessed 23/09/2025.

37 Belgian Supreme Court, [Belgium 19 June 2009 Court of Cassation] Belgium, 19 June 2009 – C.07.0289.N, CISG-online 1963 (Supreme Court) <https://cisg-online.org/search-for-cases?caseId=7880> accessed 29/09/2025.

> Under art 79(1) [CISG], a party is not liable for a failure to perform any of his obligations if he proves that the failure was due to an impediment beyond his control and that he could not reasonably be expected to have taken the impediment into account at the time of the conclusion of the contract or to have avoided or overcome it or its consequences. Changed circumstances that were not reasonably foreseeable at the time of the conclusion of the contract and that are unequivocally of a nature to increase the burden of performance of the contract in a disproportionate manner, can, under circumstances, form an impediment in the sense of this provision of the treaty.[38]

However, this judgement has been greeted with excitement and open arms, being viewed as a celebrated case. The question begging for answers remains "what is the parameter for measuring excessive onerousness that will bring hardship under art 79?" It has been held that it is questionable how the relevant threshold for giving rise to a hardship excuse is determined if no such special circumstances exist.[39]

In the absence of any parameter for gauging excessive onerousness, it seems that each case should be treated on its merits; there should be an incisive consideration towards the devastating nature of the hike or drop in price that causes the hardship, the duration of the hardship, the remote and proximate cause of the hardship, and the viability of other remedies beside the solution articulated under art 79. All these indices should be evaluated objectively before any decision can be reached.

Hardship and exemption are coterminous; they are akin in many respects, and hardship can comfortably don the toga or sobriquet as "adjustable or re-negotiable exemption." This is even more visible when it can be understood that:

> *Force majeure* as well as hardship can only exempt the aggrieved party from liability if the events causing the impediment could not reasonably be taken into account by the aggrieved party at the time of the conclusion of the contract. If they could have been taken into account by the aggrieved party, then it can be expected that this party would insist on incorporating a specific contract clause to deal with the problem. Thus, this party must be assumed to have taken the risk.[40]

Hardship and exemption also meet the mind of art 79(5) of the CISG. Both doctrines can be mitigated by other available remedies under the CISG except claiming damages.[41] It can equally be articulated that the carte-blanche tenor of the provision of art 79(5) implies that some mitigating measures like re-negotiation and adaptation

38 Ibid. (editorial commentary by Siegfried Eiselen).

39 Schwenzer (n 6) ch. 4.

40 Ibid.

41 Peter Schlechtriem, "Transcript of a Workshop on the Sales Convention: Leading CISG scholars discuss Contract Formation, Validity, Excuse for Hardship, Avoidance, Nachfrist, Contract Interpretation,

Parol Evidence, Analogical Application, and Much More" (1999) transcribed and edited by Flechtner, H.M., <http://cisgw3.law.pace.edu/cisg/biblio/workshop-79.html>. He writes thus:

of the periled contract can obviously be accommodated. This is because the provision specifically only excluded "damages" as a remedy under it. The rationale for this reasoning of implying re-negotiation and adaptation under the CISG draws support from art 77 of the CISG which provides that:

> A party who relies on a breach of contract must take such measures as are reasonable in the circumstances to mitigate the loss, including loss of profit, resulting from the breach. If he fails to take such measures, the party in breach may claim a reduction in the damages in the amount by which the loss should have been mitigated.

Then, there is the principle of temporary exemption; this is provided for in art 79(3) of the CISG. It simply means that the exemption provided under any *force majeure* event can only have effect for the period during which the impediment exists. This suggests that it is not every impediment that makes performance absolutely impossible; there are some impediments with a fluctuating effect, and the law can only excuse performance during the pendency of the impediment.

It can therefore be argued that many a hardship situation comfortably falls into this category, when performance has become excessively burdensome, then the exemption under art 79 can be extended to such situations until the gravity of the hardship has abated, or in a typical hardship situation until parties come back to the drawing board to re-negotiate or adapt the contract in order to suit all commercial intents and purposes.[42] These, with other provisions of the CISG like art 7(1), which provides for observance of good faith in international trade, will go a long way to suggest that the doctrine of hardship can be fashioned into art 79 of the CISG in order to do justice to deserving cases.[43]

In conclusion, there is no gainsaying the fact that any remarkable truce has been brokered between the warring factions who are for or against the marriage of hardship and frustration at the altar of art 79 of the CISG.[44] The issues really underscore

---

"It has also been argued that the remedy of a price reduction in Art. 50 is a reflection of a general principle of the CISG with regard to an adjustment or an adaptation to the contract in cases where there is a disturbed equilibrium between the counter-performances that can be used "as a springboard to develop a general rule of adjustment in hardship cases."

42 Henry D. Gabriel, "A Primer of the United Nations Convention on the International Sale of Goods: From the Perspective of the Uniform Commercial Code" (1997) 7 *Ind. Int'l & Comp. L. Rev.* 279, 307. The author argues that "The term 'impediment' may also cover the notion of an objective outside force that frustrates the purpose of the contract," therefore impediment short of total impossibility can be covered under Art 79.

43 Todd Weitzmann, "Validity and Excuse in the U.N. Sales Convention" (1997) 16 *Journal of Law and Commerce* 265–290. He writes that: "If courts were to apply a single standard for contractual excuse it would certainly help to achieve the Convention's goal of establishing uniformity in the field of international commercial sales law."

44 It will also be important to observe that recent international commercial law instruments like the PECL now provide separately for frustration and hardship in order to avoid the pitfall under Art 79 of the CISG. Art 6:111 of the PECL provides for "Hardship" as a separate doctrine to that of *force majeure* under its Art 8:108 provisions.

the socio-legal divide that always plays an important role in the interpretation of CISG among different legal systems. It is likely that a court or scholars coming from a civil law background where the doctrine of *force majeure* and hardship are not only well developed but advanced, will lump together the doctrine of hardship and frustration under art 79 of the CISG. Courts and scholars from a common law clime will surely tread this path with studied caution and will most likely lack the temerity to hold that an economic upheaval, no matter its degree of devastation, should be considered as an impediment in order to excuse a party who owes an obligation under a subsisting contractual relationship.

It will be more insightful to take solace from art 7(2) of the CISG which provides that:

> [Q]uestions concerning matters governed by this Convention which are not expressly settled in it are to be settled in conformity with the general principles on which it is based, or in the absence of such principles, in conformity with the law applicable by virtue of the rules of private international law.[45]

Catharine Kessedjian argues that art 79 alone does not provide the solution for a hardship occurrence, but that the mechanism provided in art 7(2) might be applied to help solve that problem.[46] By this, the door is wide open for the application of the doctrine of hardship under various domestic laws or arts 6.2.1, 6.2.2, 6.2.3 of the UNIDROIT principles.[47] This is because the UNIDROIT Principle is a model law of commercial contracts that incorporates general principles of international commercial law. It has no effect of binding positive law itself, but it can be used at the parties' consensus and court/tribunals' discretions in filling the gap or lacuna apparent under the CISG.[48] Whenever there is doubt as to whether the hardship doctrine can apply under the CISG, this can be decisively resolved, not by a wild

45 This could be interpreted to mean that the Principles may be used to supplement CISG only as long as they help in clarifying or supporting already existing general principles underlying the Convention. This opinion was shared by Anna Veneziano, "UNIDROIT Principles and CISG: Change of Circumstances and Duty to Renegotiate According to the Belgian Supreme Court" (2010) *Unif. L. Rev.* 137–151.

46 Kessedjian (n 5) 641–670.

47 Michael Joachim Bonell, "The UNIDROIT Principles of International Commercial Contracts and CISG—Alternatives or Complementary Instruments" (1996) 1(1) *Unif. L. Rev.* 26. The author writes:

"Yet besides clarifying unclear language, the UNIDROIT Principles may also be used to fill veritable gaps found in CISG. According to Art 7(2) CISG '[q]uestions, concerning matters governed by this Convention which are not expressly settled in it are to be settled in conformity with the general principles on which it is based.' He further argues that court's intervention in cases of hardship will only be applied to the extent that it does not run counter to the corresponding provisions of the applicable domestic law. This is because some national laws like English law hardly allow the court to amend or renegotiate a bad contract."

48 John Gotanda, "Using the UNIDROIT Principles to Fill Gaps in the CISG" in Djakhongir Saidov and Ralph Cunnington (eds) *Contract Damages: Domestic and International Perspectives* (Hart Publishing, May 2008) 107.

goose chase of legal arguments and justifications, but by applying the UNIDROIT Principles as general principles of law under which the CISG is based.

Niklas Lindström used the definition of hardship under the UNIDROIT Principle in deciphering its position under the CISG.[49] Liu Chengwei argues that the provisions for hardship under the PECL and the UNIDROIT Principles can be used to fill in the gap created by the absence of it under the CISG. He writes thus:

> Generally speaking, the two sets of Principles serve a gap-filling role for the interpretation of CISG contracts. The two Principles can be used to: (1) interpret the CISG; (2) answer unresolved questions that fall within the scope of the CISG; or (3) resolve issues that are not addressed in the CISG. The purpose of the two Principles' gap-filling role is to preclude an easy resort to the domestic law indicated by the conflict of law rule of the forum. Thus, when the CISG does not adequately resolve a given issue, a court may look to the two Principles (which are international in character) rather than resort to domestic law.[50]

More so, the Draft Model Frustration Clause presented in chapter eight of this book ultimately disassociated hardship from the doctrine of frustration; this, in the author's opinion, will help in upholding the traditional core of frustration against the intrusion of hardship.

5.2 Relationship between Hardship and *Force Majeure* under the UNIDROIT Principles

5.2.1 Background

Under the UNIDROIT Principles, it is a matter of common knowledge that the doctrine of hardship hardly means the same thing as the doctrine of *force majeure*.[51] The UNIDROIT Principles is a successful international model law that has taken bold strides toward fixing the frictional overlap between the two doctrines of hardship and frustration. It will be perceptive to mention again that hardship is provided

49 Niklas Lindström (n 41) ch. 2. The author writes further that: "Hardship is in this paper understood in accordance with the definition of hardship in the UNIDROIT Principles. Hence, there is hardship when an external event fundamentally alters the balance of the performances under the contract and an unreasonable burden is placed on one of the parties. The performance of the contract becomes excessively onerous due to changed circumstances for one of the parties who is thus faced with hardship."

50 Liu Chengwei, "Remedies for Non-performance – Perspectives from CISG, UNIDROIT Principles and PECL" (2003) <http://www.jus.uio.no/sisu/remedies_for_non_performance_perspectives_from_cisg_upicc_and_pecl.chengwei_liu/21.2.html> accessed 01/09/2025.

51 Daniele De Carolis, "Some Features of the Harmonisation of International Trade Law in the Third Millennium" (2010) 15(1) *Unif. L. Rev.* 37. The writer argues that: "Consequently, the UNIDROIT Principles' provision on hardship is innovative, because it provides courts and arbitrators with the greater flexibility required by international trade."

for under the chapter on performance in the UNIDROIT Principles.[52] The reason for this is that international commercial contract deems a burdensome contract, no matter the hue and cry it elicits, as still a subsisting contract worthy of performance, though under re-negotiated or adapted terms. It is therefore a cardinal precept of the UNIDROIT Principles that hardship cannot absolve a party who suffers excessively from performing his obligations in a contract; it can only provide a soft landing by way of mitigation of disparity that exists in the contractual performance and expectations.

On the other hand, a *force majeure* under the UNIDROIT Principles is provided for in the chapter that discusses non-performance. This stark difference in the two doctrines, as evident from the arrangement of the chapters of the provisions of UNIDROIT Principles, is a result of the age-old commercial law policy of not foisting performance in a situation where it is impossible to be achieved due to unforeseen impediments beyond the parties' control. By clearly locating these two doctrines within their contexts of application, the UNIDROIT Principles have laid to rest the intractable fallacy that befalls the CISG while trying to either keep mute about the existence of a situation of hardship in a contract of sale or allow the various jurisdictions to develop or sort out this anomaly; thereby defeating the uniformity posture of the CISG.

5.2.2 Hardship and Binding Nature of Contracts under the UNIDROIT Principles

Art 6.2.1 of the UNIDROIT Principles provides that:

> Where the performance of a contract becomes more onerous for one of the parties, that party is nevertheless bound to perform its obligations subject to the following provisions on hardship.

This provision restates the mantra of *pacta sunt servanda*, that a party having a contractual bad day cannot excuse him from the obligations they are bound to perform, but their situation can be made better by the provisions of hardship, thus making hardship an exception to the general rule of binding contractual obligations.[53] This provision fires the first salvo in drawing the line between hardship and *force majeure*. While hardship does not excuse performance, *force majeure* could

52 Michael Joachim Bonell, "The UNIDROIT Principles of International Commercial Contracts: Towards a New Lex Mercatoria" (1997) 2 *I.B.L.J.* 145–187.

53 Harry M. Flechtner, "The Exemption Provisions of the Sales Convention, Including Comments on "Hardship" Doctrine and the 19 June 2009 Decision of the Belgian Cassation Court" (2011) LIX(3) *Belgrade Law Review* 84–101. The author writes that:

> "In the Civil Law tradition, *force majeure* doctrine generally provides for release from liability for non-performance if post-contract-formation events rendered that performance impossible; hardship doctrine provides relief, even where a party's performance remains possible, if post-contract developments fundamentally change the expected equilibrium between that performance and what the party was to receive in exchange"

readily excuse specific performance when the performance of the contract has been rendered impossible.

Over the years, the courts, tribunals, arbitrators and other quasi-judicial bodies entrusted with the duty of interpretation of law have made consistent deference to the notion of binding effect of contractual obligations.[54] Some of this can be seen in an arbitration matter between a *Netherlands manufacturer and a Turkish buyer*. An arbitrator in Zurich, Switzerland held that a buyer, who due to financial constraint, paid only 3% of an advance payment instead of 5% agreed with the manufacturer and was unable to open a letter of credit within the agreed time limit, was held not to come under the purview of the provision of hardship and thus must perform as per the contract.[55]

The above case has shown that the court or tribunal will always be eager to protect the contract and enforce performance. The 1932 case of *Canadian Industrial Alcohol Co. v Dunbar Molasses Co*[56] will show the versatility and durability of this position. In this case, the plaintiff contracted with the defendant to purchase approximately 1,500,000 wine gallons of molasses. The defendant's supplier decided not to produce a sufficient amount of molasses and did not deliver to the plaintiff the full amount of molasses, which was provided for in the contract. The plaintiff brought this action to recover damages. The defendant contends that the duty to deliver was conditioned upon the production by the National Sugar Refinery of molasses sufficient in quantity to fulfil the plaintiff's order. The court held that where a seller brings contractual liability upon themselves to deliver a specified amount of goods on a specified date, they are bound to make good on that promise, notwithstanding any impossibility brought about by the seller's supplier reducing production, because the seller could have provided against that contingency.

5.2.3 Application of Hardship and the Doctrine of Good Faith under the UNIDROIT Principles

Again, the above analyses of cases merely introduce the general duty of performance. The doctrine of hardship has been entrenched in art 6.2.2 of the UNIDROIT

54 Kenneth Webster, "Contractual Obligations" (1965) 18 *Okla. L. Rev.* 385; Samir Manic, "Causa of Contractual Obligations as a Precondition for Valid Formation of a Mutually Binding Contract" (2022) 94 *Collection Papers Fac. L. Nis* 93; AI Sarhan, "Options That Impair the Binding Effect of Contract and Their Role in Protecting Contractual Consent: An Analysis of How Arab Civil Laws are Influenced by Islamic Jurisprudence" (2024) 1 *Manchester Journal of International Economic Law* 1.

55 Final award in case no. 8486 of 1996 <http://www.trans-lex.org/208486> accessed 1/9/2025. The sole arbitrator granted the claim for damages to the manufacturer, denied in part its claim for interest, and denied the counterclaim filed by the defendant, which sought to recover the advance payment made to the claimant. In particular, the sole arbitrator found that the circumstances for discharge from payment due to unforeseen circumstances were not met. The mandatory provisions of Dutch law on this matter were to be applied with restraint, and international contractual and arbitral practice, including the UNIDROIT Principles, were to be taken into consideration.

56 [1932] 80 A.L.R 1173.

Principles.[57] This provision, which with others defines the legal implications and applications of the doctrine of hardship, has been described by McKendrick[58] "as one of the more innovative aspects of the PICC."

The major key words are that there is a fundamental occurrence of an event which distorts the equilibrium of the contract, and that this fundamental event has not been assumed as a risk in the contract. It is a matter of concrete understanding that whenever there is an event which fundamentally alters the pattern of the contract, then it will not be regarded as a hardship if the event has been covered as a risk in the contract.[59] It has also been canvassed that the alteration in the equilibrium of the contract cannot mitigate for already performed obligations.[60]

The finer point of the doctrine of hardship is that it is futuristic and not retrospective; thus, it can only operate to aid unperformed future obligations which, unbeknownst to the parties, have had their cost of performance excessively increased or their value exceedingly diminished. If an event that brings hardship to a commercial contract occurred before the conclusion of the contract, then it is better treated under "mistake" instead of hardship.[61]

Again, it has been stated earlier that it should be a rule of thumb that whenever this is the case, the court or tribunal will choose an option that has the potential of saving the contract rather than an option that will end the contract. These being the case, the court will most likely choose the doctrine of hardship which can have

57 Art 6.2.2 UNIDROIT Principles provides that:

> There is hardship where the occurrence of events fundamentally alters the equilibrium of the contract either because the cost of a party's performance has increased or because the value of the performance a party receives has diminished, and
>
> a. the events occur or become known to the disadvantaged party after the conclusion of the contract;
> b. the events could not reasonably have been taken into account by the disadvantaged party at the time of the conclusion of the contract;
> c. the events are beyond the control of the disadvantaged party; and
> d. The risk of the events was not assumed by the disadvantaged party.

58 Vogenauer and Kleinheisterkamp (eds) (n 106) ch. 1, para 1, 711.

59 Frederick R. Fucci, 'Hardship and Changed Circumstances as Grounds for Adjustment or Non-Performance of Contracts: Practical Considerations in International Infrastructure Investment and Finance," American Bar Association Section of International Law Spring Meeting (2006) <http://cisgw3.law.pace.edu/cisg/biblio/fucci.html> accessed 28/09/2025. He opines thus: "[A] disadvantaged party cannot claim hardship if it has assumed the risk of an event."

60 Ibid.

61 In considering the time of the occurrence of a hardship event, it is paramount to inquire about when the aggrieved party gets to know of the event. If it is prior to the conclusion of the contract, then it falls within the grounds for mistake if the aggrieved party does not foresee the hardship event, but if they foresee the event, then there is a presumption that the event must have been within the bandwidth of risk contracted for by the disadvantaged party. But if the knowledge of the hardship event emerges only after the conclusion of the contract, then it will be a case for the application of Art 6.2.2(hardship). It is immaterial when the benefited party gets to know about the event that causes hardship in the contract; hitherto, this attribution of knowledge of the event of hardship should be guided by the doctrine of good faith.

the contract adapted or re-negotiated rather than *force majeure* which will excuse liability in damages under the contract.

Where a disadvantaged party ought to be aware of an onerous event that causes hardship to bear on a commercial contract/sale, and the alleged party complacently does nothing to uncover or abate the hardship, or fails to diligently put the other party on notice of the event or impending event, then the aggrieved party has no cause of action under art 6.2.2. This is because they acted in bad faith; the requirement to act in good faith is mandatory under the UNIDROIT Principles. Art 1.7 provides that:

(1) Each party must act in accordance with good faith and fair dealing in international trade.
(2) The parties may not exclude or limit this duty.

The more foreseeable the hardship events, the greater the expectation that the aggrieved party will have to take them into account in accordance with the spirit of good faith and fair trade.[62]

However, just like with a plethora of commercial law terms, the word fundamental as used in this provision is nebulous. It can be inferred that in order for a fundamental alteration in the equilibrium of a contract to be grounds for the application of hardship, it must be a severe and implacable state of disparity; a high degree of the distressed event will readily be viewed as a condition which can invoke hardship. It has been suggested that what is or is not fundamental is an issue for the court or tribunal and that "its meaning" will be established on the anvil of concrete cases.[63]

5.2.4 Some Events That Can Cause Hardship under the UNIDROIT Principles

In analysing events that can cause hardship, it is a common view that these types of events must have a strong economic undertone.[64] The foundations of hardship can be found in bad economic or financial interruptions. This is why it has been difficult to elevate hardship to the same status as *force majeure*. From time immemorial, business competition has been part of the lore and reality of business, as far as good faith is not wavering or absent; a party who suffers a business loss cannot be heard to complain that they have suffered hardship.[65]

Some of the common economic hardships can come in the form of inflation, scarcity of raw material, acts of terrorism, armed robbers and fraudsters. Others

62 Vogenauer and Kleinheisterkamp (eds) (n 106) ch. 1, para 13, 721.
63 Ibid., para 8, 719.
64 Peng Guo, "Effects of Hardship under the UNIDROIT Principles: Problems and Solutions" (2021) 25 *VJ* 1.
65 David Kuster and Carmilla Baasch Andersen, "Hardly Room for Hardship – A Functional Review of Article 79 of the CSIG" (2016) 35 *JL & Com.* 1.

can be an act of God, or government, as a proscribing degree of government can undermine a potential economic interest of a party.

In addition, an industrial action can only be categorised as a hardship if the aggrieved or disadvantaged party is in no position to control the event leading to the industrial action, but where it is their staff or workers that caused the industrial action, or where it is caused by independent contractors under his watch, then they cannot rely on them as a ground for hardship if the event causes a fundamental alteration of the equilibrium of the contract.[66] By and large, whenever a party has contracted to cover any given risk, or whenever it can be inferred that such a risk has fallen under the ambit of a party's contractual obligations, then the preservation of business efficacy shall be preferred to the doctrine of hardship.

5.2.5 Re-Negotiation/ Adaptation of Contract during Hardship under the UNIDROIT Principles

The above caption captures the whole essence of the doctrine of hardship. It is essential to have some remedial apparatus through which hardship can be fixed; the chief of these tools are renegotiation and adaptation of the contract.[67] Art 6.2.3 of the UNIDROIT Principles provides that:

(1) In case of hardship, the disadvantaged party is entitled to request renegotiations. The request shall be made without undue delay and shall indicate the grounds on which it is based.
(2) The request for renegotiation does not in itself entitle the disadvantaged party to withhold performance.
(3) Upon failure to reach agreement within a reasonable time, either party may resort to the court.
(4) If the court finds hardship, it may, if reasonable,
   (a) [t]erminate the contract at a date and on terms to be fixed; or
   (b)]a]dapt the contract with a view to restoring its equilibrium.[68]

This provision is very important in enumerating the effect of hardship and the solution thereto on a commercial contract.[69] It provides that the disadvantaged party who suffers hardship in a contract is entitled to call for renegotiation of the terms of

66 Ibid.

67 Under English law and French private law, there is no possibility to adapt or terminate a contract due to hardship, unless the parties themselves drafted an appropriate hardship clause. However, the hardship adaptation mechanism applies to French administrative law. See Zivkovic Velimir, "Hardship in French, English and German Law" (2012) <http://ssrn.com/abstract=2158583> accessed 09/09/2025.

68 UNIDROIT Principles art 6.2.3.

69 Ndubuisi Nwafor and Chidi Lloyd, "Re-imagining the Doctrines of Hardship and Exemption/Force Majeure under the CISG and UNIDROIT Principles of International Commercial Contracts" (2019) 8(1) *Global Journal of Comparative Law* 52.

the contract in order to meet up with the economic reality of the contract.[70] This call shall be done diligently as soon as the disadvantaged party is aware of the hardship situation, reason being that delay defeats good faith, and tardiness in calling for renegotiation might be a pointer to bad faith.[71] There is always juridical adaptation in order to restore the equilibrium of the contract.[72]

It is important to note that in proving hardship, the trite law of evidence that the party who alleges must prove is observed. Therefore, the disadvantaged party owes the obligation to supply particulars that will establish that a hardship has occurred and that they stand to lose exceedingly if the contract is not renegotiated or adapted. However, there can also be a case of *Rex Ipsa loquitur* if the event that causes the hardship is so notorious and well documented already. In such a situation, the burden may be lower on the disadvantaged party, and the advantaged party may have the burden shifted to him to prove that the alleged popular event does not have such a direct impact as to be a ground for the application of the doctrine of hardship in the present contract.

Another major inroad, in the application of the doctrine of hardship, is the role a court or tribunal has to play. The parties, unlike in the cases involving *force majeure* or avoidance, cannot terminate the contract *suo moto* (on their own will). It must be at the pleasure and discretion of a court. This view is rooted in the aims and objectives these doctrines set out to achieve. Termination of the contract under art 7.3.1 UNIDROIT principles presupposes that a party is guilty of failure to perform his obligations in the contract which amounts to fundamental non-performance, or where a party fails to perform after an additional period of time given to effect performance. Where these factors are met, a party can give notice to the other party and unilaterally terminate the contract.

On the other hand, under art 6.2.3(4), it is only a court or tribunal that can decree that the contract should be terminated or adapted after the failure of the

70 This is similar to German (Bürgerliches Gesetzbuch – BGB) under § 313. German law thus offers codified powers to the judge to adapt or terminate the contract which has become excessively difficult for parties to perform. See Basil Markesinis and others, *The German Law of Contract: A Comparative Treatise* (Hart Publishing, 2006) 324.

See also Velimir (n 67); the author argues that: "It should be mentioned that the German permissive attitude towards adaptation (but only, of course, in extreme circumstances of hardship) has been an inspiration for a number of national laws and harmonizing instruments. Often quoted in that regard, is the UNIDROIT Principles of International Commercial Contracts."

71 If performance is still possible albeit at high economic cost to the disadvantaged party, calling for renegotiation will not empower the party to withhold performance. The rationale behind this provision is that the doctrine of hardship does not contemplate that the contract is dead or impracticable, but only envisages a situation where parties to a contract will come around to tackle a fundamental alteration in the equilibrium of the contract which renders the contractual burden to be tilted on the disadvantaged party.

72 Hannes Rosler, "Hardship in German Codified Private Law: In Comparative Perspective to English, French and International Contract Law" (2007) 15 *European Review of Private Law (ERPL)* 483–513.

renegotiation by the parties.[73] This is because, though the hardship does not render performance impossible, it comes as a result of no fault of either of the parties and it will be unconscionable to allow any of the parties to bear the heavy economic burden. This is equally different from the provision of art 7.1.7 where an aggrieved party can terminate the contract if unforeseen events that they cannot control make the contract impossible to perform.[74] Thus the court will be willing to excuse liability in such a scenario.

The above analysis about the involvement of the court during the renegotiation or adaptation stage of a contract can be seen practically in the case of *Ministry of Defence of Iran v Cubic International Sales Corp.*[75] Two contracts for the sale and the installation of sophisticated military equipment were entered into in 1977 between a United States corporation (Cubic) and the Iranian Air Force (Iran). The contracts were duly performed until the advent of the Islamic Revolution in early 1979. The parties entered into a series of negotiations but were unable to reach an agreement as to how to proceed. Iran claimed reimbursement of payments made to Cubic in addition to damages, whereas Cubic, objecting that it was Iran which, by not paying the remainder of the price, had breached its contractual obligations, presented a counterclaim for damages.

The contracts contained a choice of law clause designating the law of Iran, but the parties eventually agreed to the complementary and supplementary application of general principles of international law. Thus, the tribunal made a finding that as a result of the chaotic events proceeding and following the Islamic Revolution in February 1979, each party was entitled to unilaterally request termination of the contracts or adaptation of their terms.

The arbitral tribunal expressly referred to art 6.2.3(4) of the UNIDROIT Principles, pointing out that from the covenant of good faith and fair dealing which is implied in each contract follows that in a case in which the circumstances of a contract undergo fundamental changes in an unforeseeable way, a party is precluded from invoking the binding effect of the contract.[76] Thus the court invoking art 6.2.3 of the UNIDROIT Principles held the contract terminated and awarded Iran $2.8 million to settle a dispute with Cubic Defense Systems, Inc.

73 Ibid. The author writes that "If the parties have been unable to find a solution within a reasonable period, the instruments provide for a termination of the contract at a date and on terms to be fixed by the court. Alternatively, the court can adapt the contract in order to restore its equilibrium. It is noteworthy that the rules show no preference for one or the other option (Art. 6:111 (3) PECL and Art. 6.2.3 (4) UNIDROIT Principles)."

74 Reinhard Zimmermann, "The Unwinding of Failed Contracts in the UNIDROIT Principles 2010" (2011) 16 *Unif. L. Rev*. 563.

75 ICC International Court of Arbitration, 05 May 1997 – 7365/FMS, CISG-online 6049 <https://cisg-online.org/search-for-cases?caseId=13963> accessed 4/9/2025.

76 Ibid.; the court held further that "In such restrictive and narrow form this concept of hardship or *clausula rebus sic stantibus* has been incorporated into so many legal systems that it is widely regarded as a general principle of law. As such, it would be applicable in the instant arbitration even if it did not form part of the Iranian law."

It can be concluded that parties to a contract still reserve the right subject to art 1.1 of the UNIDROIT Principles to freely enter into a contract and determine its content; this provision is also fine-tuned by art 1.5, which provides that the parties may exclude the application of these Principles or derogate from or vary the effect of any of their provisions, except as otherwise provided in the Principles. If this is the case, then it can only be logical that the doctrine of hardship can be modified in such a way to aid the business expediency of the parties. It is not a mandatory rule, and parties can put terms that will better serve their interest should an event that fundamentally alters the contract occurs.[77]

5.3 Relationship between Hardship and Frustration under Common Law/ Sale of Goods Act 1979

The English law does not recognise the doctrine of hardship; this is not unconnected with the ultimate end this doctrine is meant to serve, which is renegotiation and adaptation of an onerous contract. It has been suggested that "hardship and commercial impracticability" never developed in England because the English never developed a Canon law doctrine of changed circumstances; rather, the English courts used the doctrine of changed circumstances to explain the doctrine of impossibility."[78]

Common law economic background is built on capitalism, and the fundamental character of capitalism is based on economic freedom. The English judges see it as an aberration of spirit of capitalism if it is their duty to negotiate or adapt harsh contracts for parties. Put similarly, James Bremen argues that hardship is absent from English law because the doctrine goes against the principle of the sanctity of the parties' bargain on which the law of contract is based, where under English law, in the absence of an express term, a party can only terminate on the grounds of frustration or impossibility.[79] The doctrine of frustration under English law is very narrow and only inclined to consider cases of impossibility of performance; it has been canvassed, though, that where economic hardship has the potential to radically eclipse the whole intentions of the parties to the contract, or changes the contract itself, so that it is something unfamiliar to what the parties originally contracted for, then the doctrine of frustration shall cover this event as well as a case of frustration of purpose and no more.[80]

77 This is similar to the English law principle of freedom and sanctity of contract. See Chris Parker and Simon Chapman, "Escaping from a Bad Bargain: Suspending, Modifying or Terminating Performance of Long-term Energy Contracts" (2010) 7 *I.E.L.R.* 243–246.

78 Daniel Behn, "The Confusing Legal Development of Impossibility and Changed Circumstances: Towards a Better Understanding of Contractual Adaptation at Common Law" <Downloads/cepmlp_car13_77_282253210%20(1).pdf> accessed 01/9/2025.

79 "Economic Hardship Claims: Part 1" (2009) <http://www.constructionweekonline.com/art-7065-economic-hardship-claims-part-1/#.UML_8YM3Y2Y> accessed 5/9/2025.

80 Behn (n 78). The author argues that: "[T]he doctrine of frustration of purpose will excuse subsequent impossibility even when performance remains physically possible, but to perform the contract as agreed would be impossible."

However, English law has been cautious and refused to consider or soften the stringent rules of frustration of the contract in the face of whims and caprices of hardship events. In the *Amalgamated Investment & Property Co Ltd. v John Walker & Sons Ltd*[81] the plaintiff agreed to buy a property for redevelopment after an honest representation by the defendant that it was not a listed building and thus worth its value of £1,710,000, but just a day after the conclusion of the contract the Department of Environment declared their intentions to list the property anyway, and the value of the property nosedived to £210,000. The plaintiff sued the defendant and the court held that the contract was neither void for mistake nor frustrated. Lord Radcliffe added that "it is not a hardship or inconvenience or material loss itself which calls the principle of frustration into play."[82]

English law does not see judges as having the discretion to amend, adapt or re-negotiate a bad contract.[83] In *British Movietonews Ltd. v London and District Cinemas Ltd*[84] the issue for determination was whether or not parties should be released from a supplemental agreement since a subsequent 1943 Cinematograph Order had changed the basis and circumstances of the parties' initial contract. The House of Lords, while reversing the decision of Lord Denning at the Court of Appeal, held that:

> The suggestion that an un-contemplated turn of events is enough to enable a court to substitute its notion of what is just and reasonable for a contract as it stands, appears to be likely to lead to misunderstanding. The parties to an executor contract are often faced with a turn of events which they did not at all anticipate, a wholly abnormal rise or fall in prices, a sudden depreciation of currency and an unexpected obstacle to execution, or the like. Yet this does not in itself affect the bargain they have made.

The issue of hardship is categorised as cases of commercial impracticability under the US law,[85] but this falls short of being a standard hardship doctrine, where the doctrine of hardship has readily permitted contractual adaptation by the courts. The common law courts of the US are yet to fully develop cases where commercial impracticability has been found.[86] Daniel Behn argues that "while this doctrine falls short of the civilian concept of hardship, it has been used in a small number of cases to excuse performance where there is less than objective frustration of purpose."[87]

81 [1976] 3 All ER 509.
82 Ibid., 729.
83 Joseph M. Perillo, "Hardship and its Impact on Contractual Obligations: A Comparative Analysis" (1996)
M.J. Bonell Conferenze e seminari, Centro di studi e ricerche di diritto comparato e straniero, 5, 14.
84 [1952] AC 166.
85 Uniform Commercial Code § 2–615 (2006).
86 Behn (n 78).
87 Ibid.

As a general rule, under English common law, a party who suffers an impediment that makes performance impracticable cannot be excused from liability to perform the contract. It does not matter that hardship could be caused, as it has been settled in the case of *Davis.*

He writes that: "the common law has no developed doctrine of dissolving or adapting a contract because of hardship, but in the United States, at least, the Uniform Commercial Code has accepted and enacted into positive law the almost totally undeveloped doctrine of 'impracticability.'"

Contractors Ltd. v Fareham Urban DC[88] that the delays which caused an increase in a building project's cost are within the ordinary range of commercial probability and have not brought about a fundamental change of circumstances.

In conclusion, the only way hardship can excuse liability under English law is if the parties clearly contracted via unambiguous terms of the contract or *force majeure* clause that certain hardship events should be enough to excuse liability, but apart from that, other factors of impossibility can combine with the hardship events to bring frustration to bear on the contract. English law, otherwise, will always grant damages in deserving cases, but would be unlikely to hold a hardship-infested contract frustrated. This view is in line with the Draft Model Frustration Clause discussed in chapter eight of this book, which excludes the application of hardship in its paragraph 1(d).

5.4 Conclusion

There is no formal mention of hardship under the CISG,[89] and the UNIDROIT Principles have a provision for hardship under arts 6.2.1 and 6.2.3, while English law in principle could apply the doctrine of hardship as a special form of "frustration of purpose" without the contract adaptation, renegotiation and amendment mechanism.[90]

Comparatively, the doctrine of imprévision under the French law has the same meaning and connotation as the doctrine of hardship. A. H. Puelinckx defines imprévision as circumstances that destabilise the contract where economic conditions are such that fundamental and far-reaching changes occur,[91] but the doctrine of imprévision under the French law only applies under administrative law contracts, or where parties clearly stipulate that circumstances like unforeseen impediments can be regarded as a hardship (imprévision) in order for the court to adjudicate and adjust the contract.[92]

German law recognises that the contracted economic intentions of a contract can be fundamentally altered by a change of circumstances. Any contract has a

88 [1956] UKHL 3.

89 There have been vigorous arguments for or against the interpretation of hardship under Art 79 of the CISG in the earlier sections of this book.

90 Behn (n 78).

91 Puelinckx (n 22) ch. 1, 47–66.

92 Ibid.

basic aim and emanates from a basic intention of the parties, which cannot be achieved or realised in the absence of an existing environment, for example, the prevailing economic and social order, the value of the currency, and normal political conditions.[93]

It is therefore the duty of the judge to adjust and re-adapt a contract whose economic dynamics have changed in order to meet the parties' contracted aspiration. This is the essence of the doctrine of *Wegfall der Geschäftsgrundlage* under German law. Chengwei Liu summarised the application and relevance of this doctrine under German law thus:

> In German law, the theory of Wegfall der Geschäftsgrundlage (disappearance of the basis of the transaction) covers the effect of changed circumstances on the contract. It ensued from German court practice and "[U]nmöglichkeit," as embodied in section 275 of the German Civil Code (BGB), and provides relief for cases where the original economic basis of the contract has changed. When the circumstances have unforeseeably and substantially changed, the foundations of the transaction have been destroyed and the parties are no longer bound to their original contractual commitments.[94]

It will be a positive reform if the CISG introduces a provision to administer the application and interpretation of the doctrine of hardship. Also, the mechanism of negotiation and adaptation of onerous contracts is worth adopting following the UNIDROIT Principles and the German law examples. It has been suggested that England never faced the scale of inflation or other problems that plagued Germany after the World Wars. If it did, the doctrine of frustration would have succumbed to the widespread adaptation of contracts by courts, thereby creating a distinct doctrine of hardship.[95]

93 Ibid.

94 Chengwei Liu, "Changed Contract Circumstances" <http://www.cisg.law.pace.edu/cisg/biblio/liu5.html> accessed 30/09/2025.

95 Markesinis and others (n 70) 329.

6 Relationships between Mistake and Exemption/*Force Majeure*/ Frustration

6.1 Exemption and Mistake under the CISG

6.1.1 Background

Generally, the doctrine of exemption is considered different from the doctrine of mistake, but there are various links that are visibly similar when comparing the two doctrines. It has been put forward that one is excused under the exemption doctrine when an event unexpected at the time of contracting makes one's performance impossible, and one ought not to bear the loss from the occurrence of the event. While under mistake, one is excused under this doctrine provided that at the time of entering the contract, one or both parties entered the contract under a mistaken assumption. Where the assumption is a basic assumption of the contract, then one ought not to bear the loss resulting from the mistake.[1]

Facts are established that, while the events of exemption come after the conclusion of the contract and will be such as to render the performance impossible, the events of a mistake will precede the conclusion of the contract and invoke the validity question of the contract.[2] It is important to note that different facts are considered in reaching a conclusive definition of mistake or exemption, but sometimes the legal outcomes are always similar. It has also been argued that art 79 of the CISG does not make any difference like English law as to the time of the occurrence of impediments that will lead to frustration of the contract. The CISG does not differentiate between initial and subsequent impediments; even if performance of the contract is already impossible when concluding the contract, hitherto it has no effect on the validity of the contract as it would have under English Law.[3]

1 Richard Warner, "Impracticability Frustration Mistake" (2003) http://www.kentlaw.edu/faculty/rwarner/classes/contracts/impracticability_frustration_mis.html> accessed 21/9/2025.

2 Patrick C. Leyens "CISG and Mistake: Uniform Law vs. Domestic Law the Interpretative Challenge of Mistake and the Validity Loophole" (2003) http://www.cisg.law.pace.edu/cisg/biblio/leyens.html> accessed 9/09/2025. He writes that "[a] case of mistake is one of the challenges for the interpretation of CISG art 4(a). Under a number of domestic laws a case of mistake raises a question of validity. Does this indicate that we should apply CISG art 4(a) and open the way for domestic remedies? … The CISG is silent on the question of mistake but its art 4(a) excludes matters of the validity of the contract from its scope. Thus the interpretative challenge is to ascertain whether a case of mistake raises a question of validity that comes under CISG art 4(a)."

3 Atamer (n 41) ch. 1, para 48, 1073.

DOI: 10.4324/9781003667841-6

There is no definition or provision for mistake under the CISG. Art 4(a)[4] excluded issues relating to the validity of the contract from the jurisdiction of the CISG, and in accordance with art 7(2) of the CISG "[q]uestions concerning matters governed by this Convention which are not expressly settled in it are to be settled in conformity with the general principles on which it is based or, in the absence of such principles, in conformity with the law applicable by virtue of the rules of private international law."

It has been canvassed by Lookofsky that since the CISG is generally not concerned with validity, most problems which fall under this heading – like, e.g. fraud, duress, mistake or the reasonableness of contract terms – must be resolved in accordance with domestic rules of law.[5] However, owing to art 7(1) of the CISG which preaches interpretation of the CISG in order to project its international character and uniformity, thus relevant provisions of UNIDROIT Principles, PECL, and DCFR can be used to fill the gap created by the absence of mistake under the CISG.[6]

4 Art 4 of the CISG provides thus:

This Convention governs only the formation of the contract of sale and the rights and obligations of the seller and the buyer arising from such a contract. In particular, except as otherwise expressly provided in this Convention, it is not concerned with:

(a) the validity of the contract or of any of its provisions or of any usage;
(b) The effect that the contract may have on the property in the goods sold.

5 Joseph Lookofsky, In Dubio Pro Conventione "Some Thoughts About Opt-Outs, Computer Programs and Preemption Under the 1980 Vienna Sales Convention (CISG)" (2003) 13 *Duke Journal of Comparative & International Law* 263, at 280. Also at <http://www.law.duke.edu/> accessed 09/09/2025.

6 For instance, the provision of Section 7:201 Draft Common Frame of Reference (DCFR) provides thus:

(1) A party may avoid a contract for mistake of fact or law existing when the contract was concluded if:
  (a) the party, but for the mistake, would not have concluded the contract or would have done so only on fundamentally different terms and the other party knew or could reasonably be expected to have known this; and
  (b) the other party;
    (i) caused the mistake;
    (ii) caused the contract to be concluded in mistake by leaving the mistaken party in error, contrary to good faith and fair dealing, when the other party knew or could reasonably be expected to have known of the mistake;
    (iii) caused the contract to be concluded in mistake by failing to comply with a pre-contractual information duty or a duty to make available a means of correcting input errors; or
    (iv) Made the same mistake.
(2) However, a party may not avoid the contract for mistake if:
  (a) the mistake was inexcusable in the circumstances; or

The risk of the mistake was assumed, or in the circumstances should be borne, by that party.

The best definition that reflects international stance is the definition in the UNIDROIT Principles.[7] Art 3.2.1 of the UNIDROIT Principles defines mistake as "[a]n erroneous assumption relating to facts or to law existing when the contract was concluded." The art 3.2.1 of the UNIDROIT Principles definition suggests that a mistake can be as to facts of a contract of sale of goods or as to laws that govern the contract of sale of goods. The error must not be intentional as knowledge vitiates the doctrine of mistake (except unilateral mistake) and makes it to instead be "fraud" or misrepresentation. Therefore, when parties labour in mistake during the formation of a contract, the court or tribunal can apply this doctrine if there is absence of foreknowledge and bad faith. This lack of knowledge is the bridge that links some forms of the doctrine of mistake (for instance mutual and common mistake) and the doctrine of exemption.[8]

It has also been suggested that mistake has a strong relationship with the concept of risk. A party who owns the risk of a mistake in a contract cannot be relieved by the rule of mistake. It has been held in the case *of Associated Japanese Bank International Ltd. v Crédit du Nord S.A.*[9] that: "[l]ogically, before one can turn to the rules as to mistake ... one must first determine whether the contract itself provides who bears the risk of the relevant mistake. Only if the contract is silent on the point is there scope for invoking mistake."

6.1.2 Exclusion of Mistake under the CISG

Determining what falls under the validity perimeter in an international contract of sale of goods is not an easy task; there is no consensus on the items in this set. It depends on what a particular municipal law thinks can be categorised as touching on their own validity yardsticks. Jacob Ziegel appreciated the above problem when he writes that:

> Validity is not defined in Art 4 or elsewhere in CISG. Presumably it includes any defence that may vitiate the contract under the proper law or laws of the contract because, for example, of lack of capacity, misrepresentation, duress, mistake, unconscionability, and contracts contrary to public policy.[10]

However, the above-listed possible validity items are not conclusive; there are serious contentions on whether the issue of mistake should be regarded as falling under the validity items in the CISG. Many scholars are of the opinion that there is no conclusive exclusion of the doctrine of mistake under the CISG. Patrick Leyens

7 Leyens (n 2). The writer argues that "in cases in which both the CISG and the UNIDROIT Principles follow the same idea, where appropriate the UNIDROIT Principles can be referred to as an interpretative source under CISG art 7(2)."

8 Events under the doctrine of exemption, just like mutual and common mistake under the common law, must be without the knowledge of the parties.

9 [1988] 3 All ER 902.

10 Ziegel (n 57) ch. 1. "Report to the Uniform Law Conference of Canada on Convention on Contracts for the International Sale of Goods" (1981).

canvassed that the issue of exclusion should be approached from the different national laws perspective. He writes thus:

> If we look exclusively to domestic law for the answer of this question we will face a problem that perhaps is best illustrated by mistake in regard to the conformity of goods. For example, Austrian law would allow avoidance of the contract if such a mistake can be proven; whilst, under German law, a damage-based remedial scheme comparable to that of the CISG is applicable. Under Austrian law, we therefore could argue that a mistake in regard to the conformity of goods is a validity issue, whilst under German law we could not. The consequence would be that a mistaken party in one country, for example in Austria, could nullify the contract whilst in another country, for example Germany, the party would be restricted to the remedies provided under the CISG. With regard to the goal of the CISG to provide a uniform remedial scheme for all Contracting States, particularly in the field of breach of warranty, this result looks strange'.[11]

This analysis using Austria and German national laws brings to the fore the contention that mistake can be a validity issue excluded under art 4 of the CISG[12] if the legal end point of it leads to the contract being void, voidable, nullity, or avoided. Whereas if a CISG-like regime of remedies is the end point, then it is an issue that can come within the purview of other articles of the CISG.

There is also a strong case that the doctrine of mistake could be interpreted or adjudicated under art 35 of the CISG cited below.[13] Reflecting on the above

11 Leyens (n 2).

12 Ostensibly, the doctrine of mistake is among items excluded under the sphere of the CISG. It is a matter that falls within the domestic laws of validity. The CISG carefully shielded its applications from being tainted with the cumbersome and highly polarised validity issues in different national law jurisdictions. The inability of the CISG to categorically provide for the doctrine of mistake has created more problems than solving it; this research will suggest that the lack of provisions to tackle the issues of mistake is an area which must be revisited for possible amendment.

13 (1) The seller must deliver goods which are of the quantity, quality and description required by the contract and which are contained or packaged in the manner required by the contract.

(2) Except where the parties have agreed otherwise, the goods do not conform with the contract unless they:

(a) are fit for the purposes for which goods of the same description would ordinarily be used;

(b) are fit for any particular purpose expressly or impliedly made known to the seller at the time of the conclusion of the contract, except where the circumstances show that the buyer did not rely, or that it was unreasonable for him to rely on the seller's skill and judgement;

(c) possess the qualities of goods which the seller has held out to the buyer as a sample or model;

(d) Are [a]re contained or packaged in the manner usual for such goods or, where there is no such manner, in a manner adequate to preserve and protect the goods.

(3) The seller is not liable under subparagraphs (a) to (d) of the preceding paragraph for any lack of conformity of the goods if at the time of the conclusion of the contract the buyer knew or could not have been unaware of such lack of conformity.

provision (art 35 CISG), if the seller delivered goods which fell afoul of the requirement to conform to quantity, quality and description of the required contracted goods, then it doesn't matter if the cause of the non-conformity precedes the contract, it is a risk within the contractual domain of the seller and they must therefore be liable and thus subject to the provisions of art 35 CISG. This by necessary implication denotes that facts which can fit under the doctrine of mistake can be remedied under art 35 of the CISG. Art 35 though does not mention mistake but must be interpreted to accommodate situations where a seller fails to deliver goods that conform to the contract and more especially if the non-conformity existed erroneously before the conclusion of the contract.

Even though art 35(2) (b) provides that the goods do not conform with the contract unless they "are fit for any particular purpose expressly or impliedly made known to the seller at the time of the conclusion of the contract" this does not ultimately exclude non-conformities preceding the contract. The time of the existence of the non-conforming event will be immaterial if the buyer relies reasonably on the skills and judgement of the seller.

In addition, art 79 of the CISG is very important in determining the scope of mistake. There can be instances where the parties unknowingly proceed with a contract of sale of goods when the goods have perished. This can be called common mistake in the domestic common law parlance, but there is no doubt that this type of situation will render the contract impossible of performance if it goes to the root of the contract. In the absence of any provision for mistake under the CISG, it follows that art 79 will rise to the occasion and treat this fact as a case of exemption.[14]

6.2 *Force Majeure* and Mistake under the UNIDROIT Principles

6.2.1 Background

Under the UNIDROIT Principles, the relationships between the doctrine of mistake and *force majeure* are most noticeable. The first important fact is that the doctrine of mistake and the doctrine of *force majeure* are not considered to affect the "validity" of a contract under the UNIDROIT Principles. It has been argued that art 3.1.3 will apply "irrespective of how the relevant domestic law classifies its rule that initial impossibility leads to invalidity.".[15]

14 Leyens (n 2) was of the opinion that "According to a number of domestic laws, a case where the goods do not exist at the time of contract conclusion is classified as a validity issue. In contrast, under the CISG it is addressed as an issue of risk allocation or as an excuse for non-performance. Under CISG art 68, it is provided that if the goods are sold in transit the risk passes 'from the time of the conclusion of the contract'. Under CISG art 79(1), a party is excused from liability for non-performance "if he proves that the failure was due to an impediment beyond his control and that he could not reasonably be expected to have taken the impediment into account at the time of the conclusion of the contract.' Both rules can be interpreted as cross-references to domestic concepts that are labelled 'initial impossibility.'"

15 Peter Huber, "*Art 3.3*" in Vogenauer and Kleinheisterkamp (n 106) ch. 1, para 8, 410.

Art 3.1.3 of the UNIDROIT Principles provided below.[16] Paragraph (1) echoes the provision of art 7.1.7 which provides for *force majeure*. If the performance of a contract is impossible, then the contract will still be a valid contract even though it is a non-performable contract.[17] The doctrine of mistake talks about erroneous assumption of facts or law; it follows that if such an error of judgement is such that it is beyond the control and expectation of a party, then it will be a case for either mistake or *force majeure*. The only noticeable difference is the time of the existence of the impediment or error. While a mistaken error of facts or law will be existing before the conclusion of the contract, a *force majeure* impediment will mostly excuse the obligations of the parties if it occurs after the conclusion of the contract. This is illustrated in comment (1) to the Official Commentary UNIDROIT Principles which provides:

> A contract is valid even if the assets to which it relates have already perished at the time of contracting, with the consequence that initial impossibility of performance is equated with impossibility occurring after the conclusion of the contract. The rights and duties of the parties arising from one party's (or possibly even both parties') inability to perform are to be determined according to the rules on non- performance. Under these rules appropriate weight may be attached, for example, to the fact that the obligor (or the obligee) already knew of the impossibility of performance at the time of contracting[18]

Under the common law, the above hypothetical example falls within the doctrine of mistake, which underscores the validity of the contract. Moreover, under the CISG, the above scenario in the UNIDROIT commentary may be grouped with items clearly excluded from the CISG's jurisdiction in accordance with art 4. It is a validity issue that would be reserved for the national laws.[19] The UNIDROIT Principles, however, boldly state that such a situation does not affect validity and will be subject to its jurisdiction.

16 Art 3.1.3 UNIDROIT Principles provides thus:

(1) The mere fact that at the time of the conclusion of the contract the performance of the obligation assumed was impossible does not affect the validity of the contract.
(2) The mere fact that at the time of the conclusion of the contract a party was not entitled to dispose of the assets to which the contract relates does not affect the validity of the contract.

17 Nisreen Mahasneh, "Subject Matter and Consideration of the Contract: The Approaches of the 2010 UNIDROIT PICC, the 1980 CISG, and the 1976 Civil Code of Jordan" (2014) 19(3) *Unif. L. Rev.* 390.

18 UNIDROIT Principles of International Commercial Contracts (Rome 2004) Cite as <http://www.unidroit.org/english/principles/contracts/principles2004/integralversionprinciples2004-e.pdf> accessed 12/9/2025.

19 The above hypothetical case cannot apply under either the doctrine of exemption under Art 79 CISG, frustration under the common law or *force majeure* under the UNIDROIT Principles because one of the parties has knowledge of the impossibility of performance.

6.2.2 Definition of Mistake under the UNIDROIT Principles

Art 3.2.1 provides for the definition of mistake under the UNIDROIT Principles, which states that: "Mistake is an erroneous assumption relating to facts or to law existing when the contract was concluded." This definition is succinct in underlying the basic legal requirement for the application of the doctrine of mistake. There is an erroneous assumption when a party is in error by having a wrong or an incomplete understanding of the situation.[20] While commenting on the doctrine of mistake and its time element, the Official UNIDROIT commentary observes that:

> The purpose of fixing this time element is to distinguish cases where the rules on mistake with their particular remedies apply from those relating to non-performance. Indeed, a typical case of mistake may, depending on the point of view taken, often just as well be seen as one involving an obstacle which prevents or impedes the performance of the contract. If a party has entered into a contract under a misconception as to the factual or legal context and therefore misjudged its prospects under that contract, the rules on mistake will apply. If, on the other hand, a party has a correct understanding of the surrounding circumstances but makes an error of judgment as to its prospects under the contract, and later refuses to perform, then the case is one of non-performance rather than mistake.[21]

The UNIDROIT Principles, being a gap-filling model law, have provided a clue in the absence of the doctrine of mistake and/or other lacunae under the CISG.[22] Many courts and tribunals have aptly borrowed from this law in determining whether the doctrine of mistake is applicable to issues involving parties to a contract.[23] Though Franca Ferrari thinks this move is wrong and argues that the UNIDROIT Principles cannot be used to fill in the gap under the CISG but that:

> The principles can be useful, for instance, to corroborate a solution reached through the application of the CISG's rules, as evidenced not only by several arbitral awards, but also by one state court decision; on these occasions, the

20 Huber, "Art 3.4" in Stefan Vogenauer and Jan Kleinheisterkamp (eds) (n 106) ch. 1, para 3, 411.
Also, if the parties have acted in good faith but are in error as to the real position of their contractual positions, then it comes under the definition of mistake. It will be germane to note that an error in this context is equivalent to a fault. Then the time of the occurrence of the error, as mentioned before, is material in understanding the application of mistake and separating it from other non-performance doctrines like frustration, exemption, and *force majeure*.

21 Ibid.

22 ICC Court of Arbitration, arbitral award No. 8128 <http://www.unilex.info/case.cfm?pid=1&do=case&id=207&step=FullText&gt> accessed 25/09/2025.

23 [25.11.1994] [Zürich Chamber of Commerce] <http://www.unilex.info/case.cfm?id=642> accessed 14/9/2025.

> UNIDROIT Principles of International Commercial Contracts were used to find corroboration of the results reached by applying the rules of the CISG.[24]

Nevertheless, it is not every act of mistake that is relevant under the contract. There must be real and significant legal implications before a contract can be affected by the mistake of the parties in the contract. There is also a "reasonable person" test when determining the issue of whether or not there is a mistake under art 3.2.2.[25] This (art 3.2.2) detailed provision relating to the application of the doctrine of mistake is very apt in distinguishing the doctrine of mistake from that of *force majeure*. Under art 7.1.7 of the UNIDROIT Principles, there is no reasonable person's test, once the non-performance of a party can be proven to be beyond his control or expectations, and then the doctrine applies. However, under the doctrine of mistake, the question of whether or not a reasonable person would have acted differently if the true state of the mistake had been known is material in deciphering whether the error of fact or law can be said to be a mistake or not. It has been held that:

> [T]o be relevant, a mistake must be serious. Its weight and importance are to be assessed by reference to a combined objective/subjective standard, namely what "a reasonable person in the same situation as the party in error" would have done if it had known the true circumstances at the time of the conclusion of the contract. If it would not have contracted at all, or would have done so only on materially different terms, then, and only then, is the mistake considered to be serious[.][26]

There is no provision for temporary mistake under the UNIDROIT Principles just like art 7.1.7(2) of the UNIDROIT, which provides that when the impediment is

24 Franco Farrari, "Gap-filling and Interpretation of the CISG: Overview of International Case Law" (2003) 2 *I.B.L.J.* 221–239.

25 Art 3.2.2 UNIDROIT Principles provide thus:

> (1) A party may only avoid the contract for mistake if, when the contract was concluded, the mistake was of such importance that a reasonable person in the same situation as the party in error would only have concluded the contract on materially different terms or would not have concluded it at all if the true state of affairs had been known, and
> (a) the other party made the same mistake, or caused the mistake, or knew or ought to have known of the mistake and it was contrary to reasonable commercial standards of fair dealing to leave the mistaken party in error; or
> (b) The other party had not at the time of avoidance reasonably acted in reliance on the contract.
>
> (2) However, a party may not avoid the contract if
> (a) it was grossly negligent in committing the mistake; or
> (b) The mistake relates to a matter in regard to which the risk of mistake was assumed or, having regard to the circumstances, should be borne by the mistaken party.

26 UNIDROIT Principles of International Commercial Contracts, Cited as <http://www.unilex.info/instrument.cfm?pid=2&do=comment&pos=51≥ accessed 19/9/2025.

only transitory, the excuse shall have the effect for such period as is reasonable, having regard to the effect of the impediment on the performance of the contract.

Finally, both doctrines can result in termination and avoidance of the contract by the victim party respectively, and it is also possible that where parties have allocated risk in exercise of the principle of freedom of contract, then such risk will be assumed to have been duly covered if an error of fact or law, or an impediment beyond the control of the parties occurred. Such adversity should be borne by the party who owes the risk, though a contrary view has been argued by Sylvain Bollée, who writes that *force majeure* can discharge a party who owes the risk from liability.[27]

6.3 Frustration and Mistake under the English Law

6.3.1 Common Law Mistake

Ideally at common law, where a mistake was found to exist, the finding would be that the contract was void *ab initio*, and there would be total refusal to enforce the contract or clothe it with any form of legal rights.[28] On the other hand, it must be noted that courts are reluctant to set aside a contract merely because one or both parties made a mistake,[29] the court will always like to preserve a contract of the parties.

Mistake can therefore be defined as an erroneous state of facts or laws which are in existence before the conclusion of a contract and have the potency to have changed the contractual obligations undertaken in the contract had the parties been aware of the real situation.[30] It was equally held before at common law that no valid title passes to a party if the contract is void for mistake; even a *bona fide* third party purchaser without notice of the invalidity of the contract will be asked to return goods purchased whenever there was a finding for mistake. But these entire strict positions on mistake have softened over the years, and the courts are now willing

27 Sylvain Bollée, "The Theory of Risks in the 1980 Vienna Sale of Goods Convention" Pace Review of the Convention on Contracts for the International Sale of Goods, Kluwer (1999–2000) 245–290, the author writes that:

"The theory of risks must be clearly distinguished from the doctrine of *force majeure*, which is not concerned with the allocation of risk. The doctrine of *force majeure*, rather, exempts a defaulting party from liability in damages where failure to perform his obligation is due to an impediment beyond his control. For instance, if the goods are at the buyer's risk and perish or deteriorate, the buyer may be liable for damages for non-acceptance if the seller has suffered any (e.g., storage charges). In some legal systems, only *force majeure* can discharge the buyer from such liability. The rules as to risk are silent on this issue."

28 Richards (n 181) ch. 2. This is because of the presumption that something cannot be placed on nothing. Once the very foundation of a contract has been misconceived and the parties mistakenly concluded the contract based on that misconception, there will be an absence of real intention to create a legal agreement, resulting in the contract losing its legal binding efficacy.

29 Bruno Zeller, "Determining the Contractual Intent of Parties under the CISG and Common Law: A Comparative Analysis" (2002) 4(4) *European Journal of Law Reform (Kluwer)* 629–643.

30 Mark Pawlowski, "Common Mistake: Law v Equity" (2002) 152 *NLJ* 132; see also Georgia Smith, "Everybody Makes Mistakes" (2011) 22 *Cons. Law* 17.

in certain circumstances to accept the contract as voidable on the instance of the parties to the contract.

The difference between the doctrine of frustration and mistake under the common law is basically based on the time of the vitiating event. Just like the general principle that guides the application of mistake in both municipal and international commercial law, the events of mistake pre-date and exist prior to the formation of the contract, while the event of frustration will happen after the formation of the contract.[31]

There are some significant similarities[32] between the doctrine of frustration and mistake under the common law. It has been argued that "cases as to pre-existing facts and those as to subsequent facts are blurred because in some situations, it may not be wholly clear whether the relevant facts are indeed pre-existing or subsequent."[33] This goes a long way to buttress the point that sometimes, the same facts can give rise to either a cause of action in frustration or an action in mistake depending on the choice of the parties.

Drawing from Atiya's observations, it can be further articulated that in the coronation cases, it is possible the King had been nursing some illness and hoping to get well enough for the coronation, only for the fact to be announced after it is impossible for the King to make the coronation in good health and after the parties had concluded the contract. This species of cases can ripen to a cause of action in mistake since the parties are in mutual misapprehension about the facts of the King's health which pre-dates the conclusion of the contract, but due to want of proof or the nature of secrecy surrounding Royal private matters, parties readily fall back to an action in frustration instead.

The case of *Griffith v Brymer*[34] supports the argument above. At 11 am on 24 June 1902 the plaintiff had entered into an oral agreement for the hire of a room to view the coronation procession on 26 June. A decision to operate on the King, which rendered the procession impossible, was taken at 10 am on 24 June. Wright J held the contract void. The agreement was made on a mis-supposition of facts which went to the whole root of the matter, and the plaintiff was entitled to recover his £100. This case was able to be adjudicated under the doctrine of mistake due to the detailed proof as to the time of the decision to operate on the king; otherwise it would have been categorised under coronation frustrated cases.

Consequently, in *Amalgamated Investment & Property Co Ltd. v John Walker & Sons Ltd*[35] while presented with a very difficult situation, the court reached the conclusion that neither mistake nor frustration would apply. The facts of this case

31 Therefore, while parties to a mistaken contract can be said to be ignorant of the mistaken event, parties to a frustrated contract can be said to be unexpectant of the frustrating event.

32 This was canvassed in the Australian case of *Codelfa Construction v State Rail Authority of New South Wales*, [1982] 149 CLR 337 where it was held that "mistake and frustration can occur concurrently in certain cases."

33 Atiyah (n 186) ch. 2, 216.

34 [1903] 19 TLR 434.

35 [1976] 3 All ER 509.

are thus: John Walker's (JW) estate agents advertised some of their property for sale, describing it as 'for occupation or redevelopment.' In July 1973, Amalgamated Investment (AI) wrote to JW's estate agents and made an offer of £1,710,000 for the property; the offer was made subject to contract. Enquiries were made before contract in the ordinary way. A day after signing the contract, the Department of the Environment wrote a letter to JW notifying them that the property, the subject matter of the contract, had been selected for inclusion in the statutory list of buildings of special architectural or historic interest compiled by the Secretary of State.[36]

It was held that the mistake was not applicable because, at the relevant time of the conclusion of the contract, there was nothing to suggest that the building had been listed as being of "historic" interest. Then it cannot be a case of frustration because the risk of the building being listed was within the category of risks the plaintiff was bound to take, judging from the pre-contractual inquiries the plaintiff made.[37] Under English common law, mistake comes in different forms; there can be mutual mistake, common mistake, unilateral mistake, and mistake in equity.

6.3.2 Mutual Mistake

Mutual mistake is a fundamental mistake of offer and acceptance; it is a situation that arises when parties are in cross intentions and purposes with each other.[38] For instance, this can be a situation where a buyer offers to pay a price for goods and the seller mistakenly accepts to sell and deliver different goods thinking that that is what was offered.[39]

The case of *Raffles v Wichelhaus*[40] will be instructive in supporting the application of this form of mistake. In this case, Raffles (P) contracted to sell 125 bales of Surat cotton to Wichelhaus (D). The goods were to be shipped from Bombay to Liverpool, England, on the ship "Peerless." Neither party was aware that there were two ships named "Peerless" carrying cotton from Bombay to Liverpool, one arriving in October and the other in December. Wichelhaus thought he had purchased the cotton arriving on the October ship, but Raffles sent his cotton on the December ship. Wichelhaus refused to accept delivery of the cotton arriving on the December ship, and Raffles brought this lawsuit for breach of contract. It was held per *Mellish* that:

36 Ibid.

37 However, there has been a recommendation by T. Rose and K. Manley in "Effective Financial Incentive Mechanisms: an Australian Study" (Cape Town, South Africa: CIB World Building Congress, May 1418 2007) that "the construction risks could be shared equitably between the client and contractor, with flexibility being provided in the contract to handle unforeseen situations and relationship management in order to design a financial incentive mechanism strategy."

38 Francis Dawson, "Reflections on Contractual Mistakes" (2019) 3 *New Zealand Law Review* 291.

39 Nils Jansen and Reinhard Zimmermann, "Contract Formation and Mistake in European Contract Law: A Genetic Comparison of Transnational Model Rules" (2011) 31(4) *Oxford Journal of Legal Studies* 625.

40 [1864] EWHC, Exch, J19.

> A latent ambiguity appeared when the contract did not specify which 'Peerless' was intended. There is nothing on the face of the contract to show that any particular ship called Peerless was meant but the moment it appears that two ships called the Peerless were about to sail from Bombay, there is a latent ambiguity. Parole evidence will be admissible for determining the actual meaning that each party assigned to that ambiguity. From the evidence presented, each party attached a different meaning to that ambiguity. If different meanings were intended on a material term of a contract, there is no mutual assent and there is no contract.[41]

This case advanced the argument that a mutual mistake of fact in a contract will negate the consent of the parties to conclude a legal, enforceable contract. This type of mistake is not similar to the doctrine of frustration. This is because the contract was concluded on a mutual erroneous belief of an existing subject matter; the case of frustration involves a seemingly healthy contract which drastically goes wrong unexpectedly without fault of the parties.[42]

6.3.3 Common Mistake

In common mistake, the parties to a contract have the common assumption that certain states of affairs exist but which it is subsequently discovered do not exist.[43] The case of *Couturier v Hastie*[44] has been the classical signpost of the definition and application of the common mistake. The plaintiffs in that case (merchants) shipped a cargo of Indian corn and sent the bill of lading to their London agent, who employed the defendant to sell the cargo. On 15 May 1848, the defendant sold the cargo to Challender on credit. The vessel had sailed on 23 February but the cargo became so heated and fermented that it was unfit to be carried further and sold. On 23 May Challender gave the plaintiffs notice that he repudiated the contract on the ground that at the time of the sale to him the cargo did not exist. The plaintiffs brought an action against the defendant (who was a *del credere* agent, i.e., guaranteed the performance of the contract). It was held that the contract was void because the subject matter of the contract did not exist at the time the contract was made.

This form of mistake has a strong similarity with the doctrine of frustration of a contract because both involve the element of unforeseeability and non-fault of the

41 Ibid.

42 Melvin A. Eisenberg, "Impossibility, Impracticability, and Frustration" (2009) 1(1) *Journal of Legal Analysis* 207–261; he writes that " One of these practical differences concerns the role of fault, which in turn may impact the nature of judicial relief under the shared-assumption test."

43 The common mistake must be totally non-fault based. In *Associated Japanese Bank (International) Ltd. v Credit du Nord SA (1988) 138 N.L.J. Rep. 109 (QBD),* it was held that "A party could not be allowed to rely on a common mistake where a mistake was entertained by him without any reasonable grounds for such belief; that is, it was in part self-induced."

44 [1856] 5 HLC 673.

parties.[45] This is based on the fact that the parties are operating on the same tandem of ignorance of the real state of the subject matter or affairs of the contract.[46]

However, McKendrick is of the opinion that, "common mistake is often treated separately from frustration on the ground that the latter is concerned with the discharge of a contract, whereas mistake relates to the formation of a contract."[47] Thus while frustration discharges a valid, subsisting contract, mistake goes to the issue of validity and can render the contract void or voidable depending on the circumstances of each case. Nevertheless, it has been held that the major difference lies in the fact that "common" mistake scenarios involve events existing at the time of contracting, making it easier to allocate the ensuing risks to one or other party, as opposed to subsequent events which are inherently more difficult to anticipate, making the process of risk-allocation rather more conjectural.[48]

6.3.4 Unilateral Mistake

This form of mistake arises when one party is aware of a real state of affairs, but the other party erroneously has a different assumption towards the correct state of the affairs of the contract. It is a situation where one party is very well apprised of the facts and situation of the contract, while the other labours in ignorance of facts or law. This form of mistake vitiates consent on the instance of the ignorant party; the contract is not void but can be voidable if it goes to the root of the contractual obligations and purposes.[49]

In *Hartog v Colin & Shields*[50] the defendants mistakenly offered a large quantity of hare skins at a certain price per pound whereas they meant to offer them at that price per piece. This meant that the price was roughly one third of what it should have been. The claimant accepted the offer honestly believing a fair deal had been offered. The court held that the contract was void for mistake. Hare skins were generally sold per piece and given the price the claimant must have realised

45 Philip Norman and Pinsent Masons, "The Changing Nature of Risk" (2006) 17 *Cons. Law* 10.

46 A succinct explanation was given by John Cartwright in "*Solle v Butcher* and the Doctrine of Mistake in Contract" (1987) 103 *L.Q.R.* 594–623, he writes thus:

> "The idea of the common law intervening to relieve one or both parties to a contract, where the effect of their contract is fundamentally different from what had been expected, is not confined to mistake. There is a clear analogy with the doctrine of frustration, where an event subsequent to the formation of the contract may sometimes be relied on as discharging both parties from future performance. It should be noted that in Bell v. Lever Brothers Scrutton L.J. relied on frustration cases as an analogy with mistake."

47 *Contract Law* (Palgrave Macmillan, 7th edn, 2007) 295.

48 Adrian Chandler and others, "Common Mistake: Theoretical Justification and Remedial Inflexibility" (2004 Jan) *Journal of Business Law (J.B.L.)* 34–58.

49 It is often said that some unilateral mistakes, if fundamental and the other party is aware of them, render a contract void at common law. This view was canvassed by Terence Etherton, "The Role of Equity in Mistaken Transactions" (2013) 27(4) *Tru. L.I.* 159–171.

50 [1939] 3 All ER 566.

the mistake.[51] It is also important to show absence of bad faith or fraud in unilateral mistake; an excessive or diminished gain will be a pointer as to the gauge of good faith in such form of mistake. When a party wilfully induces the other by lie or misrepresentation into making a mistake about facts in a contract, then this is not a case of unilateral mistake but that of fraud.

6.3.5 Mistake in Equity

The common mistake case of *Bell v Lever Brothers*[52] served as the main catalyst that brought about the development of "mistake in equity." In this case, Lever Bros appointed Mr Bell and Mr Snelling (the two defendants) as chairman and vice-chairman to run a subsidiary company called Niger. Under the contract of employment, the appointments were to run for 5 years. However, due to the poor performance of the Niger Company, Lever Bros decided to merge Niger with another subsidiary and make the defendants redundant. Lever Bros drew up a contract providing for substantial payments to each if they agreed to terminate their employment. The defendants accepted the offer and received the payments. However, it later transpired that the two defendants had committed serious breaches of duty which would have entitled Lever Bros to end their employment without notice and without compensation. Lever Bros brought an action based on mistake in that they entered the agreement thinking they were under a legal obligation to pay compensation. The House of Lords held that this was only a mistake as to quality and did not render the contract essentially different from that which it was believed to be. The action therefore failed.[53]

This case drew the critical ire of some known jurists like Lord Denning, who was determined to clothe such common mistake cases with conscience and equity.[54] It has been argued that the borderline between mistake as to quality and mistake that touches the subject matter of a contract is blurred. It seems more apt to depose that whenever there is a mutual mistake which would have resulted in parties contracting differently if they had known of the existence of the mistake, then whether it is a mistake as to the subject matter of the contract or mistake as to quality will be immaterial, and the finding that there has been a mistake will be appropriate in the circumstance.[55]

51 Ibid.

52 [1932] AC 161 (House of Lords).

53 Ibid.

It has been argued that while justifying the decision that "It is perhaps not fanciful to suggest that in Bell v. Lever Bros. Ltd. a narrow doctrine of mistake corrected an injustice that would have flowed from the rule of law under which a relatively trivial breach, which caused the innocent party no loss, nevertheless gave that party a ground for rescinding the contract." This view was put forward by G.H. Treitel, "Mistake in Contract" (1988) 104 *L.Q.R.* 104, 501–507.

54 Ola Olatawura, "Appreciating and Reforming the Remedy of Equitable Rescission for Genuine Mistake in Contract Law" (2014) 40(1) *Commonwealth Law Bulletin* 49.

55 Isaac Ng, "An Inequitable Mistake? The UK's Abolishment of Mistake in Equity Contrasted with Singapore's Approach" (2021) *Sing. Comp. L. Rev.* 205.

Lord Denning finally got the opportunity to set the trend of equitable mistake in the case of *Solle v Butcher.*[56] In this case, Butcher let a flat to Solle for £250 per year. Both parties believed at the time of letting that the flat was not subject to the Rent Restriction Acts. If it had been subject to the Rent Restriction Acts, the appropriate rent would have been £140 per year. Butcher claimed that he relied on Solle's assurances that the flat was not subject to the Rent Restriction Acts. Later, Solle brought an action in the County Court claiming that the flat was subject to the Rent Restriction Acts and that, therefore, his rent should only be £140 per year. Butcher claimed that the lease was either void at common law for mistake or voidable in equity.[57] It was held by a majority decision that the lease should be set aside in equity upon terms deemed fit and proper in the circumstances by the court. Thus, the contract is not void under common law, but voidable in equity, and the court has the discretion to make further orders that will serve the justice of the instant case.

Unfortunately, this position didn't stand the test of time. It has been overturned in the case of *Great Peace Shipping Ltd. v Tsavliris Salvage (International) Ltd*[58] where Lord Phillips of Worth Matravers MR did not see the merit of employing equity where a common mistake was not such as to be said to be fundamental in order to void the contract, neither did he think that the contract is voidable simply because a higher number of hours will be put into performance of the contract. However, GPS refused to cancel the contract and brought an action for breach. The defendants sought to argue that the contract was void for mistake at common law, alternatively that it was voidable for mistake in equity.[59]

It was held that the mistake did not radically or fundamentally change the contractual obligations; nor did it change the subject matter of the contract. It was further held that equity cannot provide relief from mistake where there is no relief under the common law. The conclusion was that, just like the doctrine of frustration, the doctrine of common mistake will apply only if there is no provision in the contract covering the situation and its risks, and if the common apprehension significantly changed the contract. The law thus reverted to the earlier decision in Bell v Lever Brothers as the correct precedent to follow.[60]

6.4 Mistake and Frustration under the Sales of Goods Act of 1979

6.4.1 Background

Under the Sale of Goods Act of 1979, Section 6 provides for the doctrine of mistake. It is to the effect that: "[w]here there is a contract for the sale of specific goods, and

56 [1950]1 KB 671 (CA).

57 Ibid.

58 [2002] EWCA Civ 1407.

59 Ibid.

60 Stephen Waddams, "Equity in English Contract Law: The Impact of the Judicature Acts (1873–75)" (2012) 33(2) *The Journal of Legal History* 185.

the goods without the knowledge of the seller have perished at the time when the contract is made, the contract is void." This provision, following the tradition and tenor of the 1979 Act, is confined to peculiar circumstances involving a contract for the sale of specific goods, and perishing of the goods. The position of mistake is different from that of frustration under the 1979 Act because, while mistake contemplates an unknowing antecedent perishing of the goods after a completed contract of sale, frustration under Section 7 envisages subsequent perishing of the goods after an agreement to sell.

Frustration is only possible under the Act when the contract is still inchoate and undone. There will be no complete sale until risk and property are transferred to the buyer.[61] This situation casts doubt on the age-old belief that frustration is only permissible after the conclusion of a contract.[62] There is also a similar trend to presume that parties to both mistaken and frustrated contracts must not be at fault; the law is that fault will vitiate the application of these doctrines and will accord liability to the party at fault. However, it has been observed that the Sale of Goods Act is willing to treat issues arising from mistake as part of a broader offer-and-acceptance framework.[63] It is acceptable to subsume cases arising from mutual, common, unilateral and equitable mistakes under the sometimes erroneous relationship existing between contractual offer and acceptance. There are some obvious difficulties in the application and interpretation of Section 6 of the 1979 Act. In the case of *McRae v Commonwealth Disposals Commission,*[64] the Commonwealth Disposals Commission sold McRae a shipwreck of a tanker on the Journaund Reef, supposedly containing oil. No tanker ever existed. CDC (Defendant) argued that there was no liability for breach of contract because the contract was void because the subject matter did not exist. The risk of non-existence

61 Stephen Gold, Cartract (1987) 137, NLJ, 460; writes thus: "Sale in s. 21 did not include an agreement to sell, which by definition involved no transfer of property." In "an agreement to sell," there is no transfer of property to the buyer at the time of the contract. The conveyance of property takes place later so that the seller continues to be the owner until the agreement to sell becomes a sale either by the expiry of a certain time or the fulfilment of some condition.

62 While a mistake has been defined as an erroneous assumption of facts or laws in a contract before the conclusion of the contract, frustration has been provided under Section 7 as where there is an agreement to sell specific goods and subsequently the goods, without any fault on the part of the seller or buyer, perish before the risk passes to the buyer, the agreement is avoided. The basic ingredient of time which is at the centre of mistake seems to be overlapping in these two doctrines. Events that bring about a mistake must pre-exist the contract, and the event that brings about the frustration of a contract must be subsequent to the conclusion of the contract. Atiyah (n 186) ch. 2, 37. Also, the general common law rules, including laws merchant which are not inconsistent with the Act should apply under the Act. Therefore the common law position on the doctrine of mistake and frustration can be applied under the Sale of Good Act of 1979 if there are no reasons why they cannot be.

63 Atiyah (n 186) ch. 2, 37. Also, the general common law rules, including laws merchant which are not inconsistent with the Act should apply under the Act. Therefore the common law position on the doctrine of mistake and frustration can be applied under the Sale of Good Act of 1979 if there are no reasons why they cannot be.

64 [1951] 84 CLR 377

of the subject matter was thrown on one party; in this case, the defendant, who was held to have warranted the existence of the goods.

The *McRae* case should be contrasted with the case of *Barrow Lane & Ballard v Phillips*[65] where Wright J held that "[w]here a contract relates to specific goods which do not exist, the case is not to be treated as one in which the seller warrants the existence of those specific goods, but as one in which there has been failure of consideration and mistake." The difference between the two cases is that, in the Barrow Lane case, the parties had both assumed the goods existed. In contrast, in the *McRae* case, the Commonwealth Disposals Commission (CDC) had actually promised the tanker existed and therefore had taken the risk that it did not.

This book will argue that the latter case is the better of the two; there will be no room for an implied warranty when specific goods, without the seller's knowledge, have perished at the time the contract is made.

6.5 Conclusion

The relationship between frustration and mistake under the Sale of Goods Act 1979 is interesting to explore and determine in the light of Section 6 and Section 7 of the 1979 Act. There is a dearth of judicial or legal writers' opinions on the legal status of an event that happened after the agreement to sell but before the actual sale. Whether this kind of event can also be categorised as both mistake and frustration is still a moot point. All these, without doubt, contributed to making the Sale of Goods Act of 1979 *sui generis* and also due for simplified amendment. The Draft Model Frustration Clause (DMFC) discussed in Chapter eight of this book will apply to both antecedent (initial) and subsequent inhibitions, as art 79 of the CISG does.

The UNIDROIT principles provided copiously for the doctrine of mistake[66] and it is not considered a validity issue under this model law. There is a total omission of the doctrine of mistake under the CISG, and the English law view that an antecedent event will make a contract void or voidable for mistake is absent under the CISG. It does appear, therefore, that any impediment beyond the control of the parties which already existed at contract formation and unknown to the obligor can theoretically be good enough for exemption under art 79 of the CISG.[67]

65 [1929] 1 KB 574; Treitel has observed that the seller will not be held to have warranted the existence of the goods in English law any more than the buyer will be held to have bound himself to pay for them in any event. 'Neither party is bound and the contract can properly be called void." See Guenter Treitel, *Law of Contract* (Sweet & Maxwell, 11th edn, 2003) 296.

66 Morning-Glory Nwafor and Ndubuisi Nwafor, "Conceptualising the Relationship Between Doctrine of Mistake and Exemption (*Force Majeure*) under the CISG and the UPICC" (2019) 40 *Bus. L. Rev.* 111.

67 Atamer (n 41) ch. 1, para 48,1074.

7 Application of Shared Liability and Remedies under Exemption/*Force Majeure*/Frustration

7.1 Relationship between Exemption and the Remedy of Sharing of Liability under the CISG

7.1.1 Background

The doctrine of frustration under Art 79 CISG does not envisage any form of attributed liability on the part of either party.[1] It is applicable when parties are in a situation in which an unforeseen impediment renders performance of the contract impossible. Nevertheless, art 80 of the CISG provides that "[a] party may not rely on a failure of the other party to perform, to the extent that such failure was caused by the first party's act or omission." This is known as the sharing of liability, or what English tort law calls contributory negligence. A party that contributed to the failure of any of the obligations in a contract cannot rely on the other party's failure to perform the contract.[2] In other words, it can be said that "the promisor is exempted from his contractual obligations or punishment for impediments to performance caused by matters falling within the promisee's sphere."[3]

Art 80, therefore, serves the remedial function of barring a party from relying on a failure of the other party when there is a contributory fault from the former party. There is no counterpart to this provision in the Draft Model Frustration Clause (DMFC) attempted in chapter eight of this book; however, the general rule of good faith will apply to deny a party under the DMFC the benefit of their initial failure of obligation under the contract. Art 80 is not precisely the same as the doctrine of estoppel under English law; it can, however, like the English doctrine, serve as a shield, not a sword.[4] It can be used to shield a party from liability, but no claim or

1 Edgardo Munoz, "COVID-19 and Related Public and Private Measures as an Impediment to Perform Contracts Governed by the CISG" (2021) 57 *Tex. Int'l LJ* 61.

2 Schlechtriem argues that "Article 80 exempts all claims against the obligor; it gained importance when a proposal was rejected which would have extinguished the right to demand specific performance in a case where Article 79 exempts a party from liability for damages. If the buyer frustrated performance, such as by not providing drawings required for production or by not procuring an import permit, he can neither demand specific performance nor declare avoidance. He also may not reduce the price for defects caused by mistakes in the drawings he provided." See Schlechtriem (n45) ch.2. 105.

3 Schlechtriem & Schwenzer (n 5) ch. 2, para 1, 1088.

4 *Combe v Combe* [1951] 2 KB 215.

DOI: 10.4324/9781003667841-7

cause of action can be found upon it by either of the parties due to the contributory liability nature of the claim. The difference between art 79 and art 80 CISG is that, in contrast, art 79 excludes liability only for damages, thereby making other remedies available in the circumstances. Exemption under art 80, in contrast, apparently shields a party from all remedies for its failure to perform when the provision's requirements are satisfied.[5] The phrase "other side may not rely on the failure to perform" seems to apply to all remedies.[6]

While tracing the history of art 80 in the international sale law, Honnold held that the legislative history of art 80 links it closely to the rules on exemption in art 79. The idea expressed in art. 80 appeared as part of art. 74(3) of the ULIS 1964.[7] Delegates from Germany later made a strenuous case for the inclusion of former art 74(3) of the ULIS in the new convention. This proposal was given imprimatur when the Conference authorised the drafting committee to include this provision in the latest draft convention. This move was eventually capped as a success when the Plenary approved it.[8]

The above brief history of art 80 goes a long way toward suggesting that, though art 80 would not have been deemed a necessary provision under the CISG, the abundance of caution favoured the expediency of its enactment. This is because relegating this provision to the doctrine of good faith would unfairly burden art 7(1) CISG with excessive arbitrariness and discretion.[9] This is never the aim of any uniform international law, which thrives on bringing all hands on the same deck over the same matter.

Honnold made the rhetorical remark that art. 80 not only governs problems of exemption from liability but may have unwittingly modified all the remedial provisions of the CISG.[10] This assertion has set the pace for a vigorous analysis of what is the real or imaginary purpose of art 80. Thus it has created a field day for those who believe that art 80 is exclusively enacted to run errands within the meanings and connotations of exemptions and others who argued that art 80 is broader than the exemption and should be viewed as a provision touching on general obligations and similar to sundry provisions under Part III of the CISG.

5 *Inmed v Etablissements JR Maruani* Cour de cassation (Commercial Chamber), Appeal No. 18–10.969, 9 July 2019.

6 Harry M. Flechtner "The Exemption Provisions of the Sales Convention, Including Comments on "Hardship" Doctrine and the 19 June 2009 Decision of the Belgian Cassation Court" (2011) LIX(3) *Belgrade Law Review* 84–101.

7 Art 74(3) of the ULIS 1964 provides that:

> The relief provided by this Article for one of the parties shall not exclude the avoidance of the contract under some other provision of the present Law or deprive the other party of any right which he has under the present Law to reduce the price, unless the circumstances that entitled the first party to relief were caused by the act of the other party or of some person for whose conduct he was responsible.

8 Honnold (n 39) ch. 1, 496–500.

9 Dennis Tallon, "Article 80" Tallon in Bianca-Bonell Commentary on the International Sales Law (Giuffrè: Milan 1987) 596–600.

10 Honnold (n 39) ch. 1.

7.1.2 Art 80 CISG as a Rule of Exemption

Art 80 of the CISG is provided under Section IV (Exemptions), part of the Convention, just as art 79 of the CISG. It has been argued that art 80 functions as a self-evident statement,[11] Thus any party whose actions or omissions prevented the other party from performing the contract shall not be allowed to rely on the latter party's failure.[12] The underpinnings and applications of art 80 CISG are not a straightforward task. Slovenia (Oil Pump Case)[13] is very important in laying bare the attitude of the courts and tribunals when faced with art 80 CISG scenarios. In this case, the parties entered into a contract for the sale of water and oil pumps. Regarding payment, they agreed that the buyer (plaintiff) would open irrevocable letters of credit (L/Cs) to ensure payment for the pumps. After the buyer opened the L/Cs, the seller protested, stating that the L/Cs had not been completed correctly. The seller then refused to deliver the goods unless paid in advance. The buyer asked the seller to provide the text of the L/C conditions, but the seller failed to do so. The buyer then purchased equivalent goods elsewhere and brought a claim against the seller for payment of the difference between the substitute transaction price and the contract price. The court found that even if the letters of credit were considered not in conformity with the contract, the seller could not rely on this fact. Namely, under art 80 CISG, a party may not rely on the failure of the other party to perform when the failure was caused by the first party's act or omission. The seller should have sent the buyer the relevant information required to open new letters of credit if it felt that the letters of credit did not conform to the contract. Therefore, the court found that the seller was unable to rely on the buyer's failure to properly fulfil its obligations regarding the letters of credit because the seller had caused that failure.

More so, art 80 has been criticised as being vague and overreaching[14] consequently, it is not every breach (act or omission) that can be said to have caused the other party's failure to perform his obligations in the contract. Such a breach or act of the former party must be categorically linked to the failure to perform by the latter party and will leave no doubt that had it not been for the breach, the failure to

11 Ibid., 496.

12 This is regarded as a rule of exemption under the international contract on the sale of goods. It is a rule that tries to strike a balance between the breaches of the parties which resulted in a two-way cause of failure of obligations to perform a contract.

13 Slovenia 13 September 2011 Vrhovno sodišče Supreme Court <http://cisgw3.law.pace.edu/cases/110913sv.html> accessed 13 September 2025.

14 Flechtner opines that "The simple structure and straightforward language of Article 80, however, belies the power of the provision: as was noted above, the consequences of exemption under Article 80 are considerably more far-reaching than under Article 79. The lack of express limitations or exceptions on the principle expressed in Article 80, furthermore, creates the possibility of far-ranging applications that are, in my view, improper, and may even undermine important aspects of the Convention's system for regulating international sales." See Flechtner (n 55).

perform wouldn't have happened. This view was applied in the *Coal case*[15] where the arbitrators held that:

> [O]ur case cannot pass this test. The seller's failure was that it delivered coal of poor quality and the buyer could not in any way influence this failure committed by the seller. The seller could only have been influenced by this failure if, hypothetically, the buyer had chosen the coal in person and the choice was based on the colour or appearance of the coal – a situation that was very unlikely to have happened. The buyer's breach of the contractual obligation or any of its other acts did not affect the seller's breach. The seller's breach was caused by its own bad faith regardless of Article 7(1) of the Convention. That is why I disagree with the Court decision. Article 80 of the Convention is not applicable here.

Furthermore, it has been held that a delay by a buyer in sending a request for the procurement of some vital documents which would have aided completion of the contractual obligations is enough to bring art 80 of the CISG into play when apportioning damages from the breach that follows. This was the decision in the *Medicine's Case*.[16] All these cases discussed above have given instances where art 80 served the role of exempting parties from liabilities.

15 Ukrainian Coal Case 1, Arbitration Court at the Bulgarian Chamber of Commerce and Industry, [Bulgaria 24 April 1996] Arbitration Case 56/1995 56/ CISG-online 435 <http://cisgw3.law.pace.edu/cases/060215u5.html> accessed 13/9/2025.

16 Russia 26 January 2006 Arbitration proceeding 53/2005 Cite as: <http://cisgw3.law.pace.edu/cases/060126r1.html> accessed 14/9/2025.

In the above-mentioned case, a German (Seller) filed a claim against a Russian [Buyer] for damages for breach of contract pursuant to their obligations under a contract for the international sale of goods, which the parties executed on 2 September 2004. The [Seller] demanded termination of the contract and recovery of damages arising from the decline in price for the goods, the cost to store the goods, payment of interest for the delay in fulfilling the monetary obligations, as well as recovery of the arbitration fees for having to defend its interests through a legal representative. According to the [Seller]'s statement of claim, the [Buyer] did not fully fulfil its obligation to prepay for the goods ([Buyer] only transferred 10% of the contract price), which is why delivery was not implemented.

In its reply to the statement of claim, although not objecting to termination of the contract, the [Buyer] did not recognise the [Seller]'s demands for recovery of damages and for payment of other amounts. The [Buyer] alleges that the contract failed because of the [Seller]'s non-performance of the [Buyer]'s demands regarding the granting of documents necessary to clear import of the medicine into Russia according to current Russian legislation, which made executing the contract impossible.

The Arbitration Tribunal held while applying art 80 that the Claimant [Seller]'s failure to provide proper support to the Respondent [Buyer] resulting in the inability of the [Buyer] to receive permission to import the goods and, respectively, the breach of the contract, leads to the conclusion that the main reason for the breach of the contract was the [Seller]'s inaction. In addition, it is important to note that the [Buyer] sent the [Seller] a request to provide the necessary documents with a meaningful delay. Therefore, it is recognised that the resulting damages from the breach of the contract should be divided between the parties based on how much the action (inaction) of each of them would have affected the enforcement of their obligations.

7.1.3 Art 80 as the Restatement of General Principles of Law

Art 80 has also been linked with the part 111 chapter one (1) of the CISG. This part 111 of the CISG provides for rules that govern the general obligations of both the buyer and the seller simultaneously; they are provisions that are enacted based on the age-old established commercial practices. They are otherwise *lex mercatoria* rules which have stood the test of time. These rules occupy arts 25–29 of the CISG; they provide for the rules of fundamental breach, the rule of notice of avoidance of a contract, and the rule of privity of contract.

It seems that the role of art 80 is not restricted to exemption from contractual obligation. It cuts across all the contractual relationships between a seller and a buyer and it is a reflection of the doctrine of good faith.[17] It has been generally accepted that "art 80 requires that the debtor's failure to perform be caused by the creditor's act or omission. Whether there was fault on the creditors' behalf is irrelevant."[18] This assertion was made evident in the *Propane gas case*[19] which was decided under exemption and good faith. In this case the plaintiff, a German buyer, and the defendant, an Austrian seller, entered into an agreement for the FOB delivery of a certain quantity of propane gas.

The parties exchanged communications by facsimile and telephone on the terms of their agreement, including the method of payment (letter of credit). The buyer, however, did not obtain a letter of credit since an essential element was missing, i.e. the seller failed to name the port of origin. In addition, the seller made the delivery of the gas subject to the conditions that it was not to be resold in the Benelux countries. The court held that the seller has no remedy against the buyer because of his act or omission to nominate a port of origin which seriously contributed to the failure of the buyer's obligation to procure a letter of credit.[20] This decision is not only predicated on the rule of exemption, but it is also a bold statement on the generally held belief that no one shall be allowed to benefit from his fault.[21]

17 The CISG addresses the complex issue of contributory negligence also in art 80. This provision is not limited in its application to damages claims but extends to all kinds of breaches of contract. See Ulrich Magnus, "Remedies: Damages, Price Reduction, Avoidance, Mitigation and Preservation" in Larry A. Dimatteo (ed.), *International Sales Law, A Global Challenge* (Cambridge University Press, 2014) 279.

18 Ingeborg Schwenzer and Christiana Fountoulakis (eds), *International Sales Law* (Routledge-Cavendish, 2007) 577.

19 Austria 6 February 1996 Supreme Court CISG-online number 224 <https://cisg-online.org/search-for-cases?caseId=6198> accessed 17/9/2025.

20 Ibid.

21 Art 80 has been described as "the poor relative of art 79. It appears to be a straightforward statement of a simple and obvious general principle." Harry Flechtner further writes while comparing arts 79 and 80 that: "Whereas proving exemption under art 79 requires satisfying a long list of requirements that can be difficult to understand, challenging to distinguish, and daunting to apply, art 80 only requires proof that 1) there was an 'act or omission' by the other side, and 2) it caused the failure to perform by the party claiming exemption.

art 80 contains nothing beyond these two requirements that expressly limits, conditions, or adjusts its application.

That a party may not rely on a failure of the other party to perform, to the extent that such failure was caused by the first party's act or omission has been held to not only be restricted to a situation where the issue involves exemption from frustration, but to definitely have a link with arts 49 and 64 of the CISG (termination/avoidance provisions) and all the provisions of remedies under the CISG.[22] A good example of the interlocking relationship between art 80 and art 49 of the CISG can be seen in the *Key press case*,[23] in this case, a German seller and a Swiss buyer concluded a contract for the sale of industrial machinery manufactured by a third party who had previously concluded a distributorship agreement with the seller. The buyer paid the first instalment of the price before delivery. Thereafter, the manufacturer terminated its agreement with the seller. Nevertheless, the buyer and the manufacturer arranged, in the seller's presence, that the industrial machinery should be delivered to the buyer's place of business. The buyer then paid the rest of the price directly to the manufacturer and later declared the contract with the seller avoided. The seller commenced action against the buyer claiming payment. The court decided in favour of the seller. The buyer wittingly contributed to any perceived breach of the contract by accepting to get a delivery directly from the third party (distributor) in the presence of the seller. The buyer was not entitled to declare the contract avoided under art 49(1)(a) of the CISG. As a matter of fact, the buyer accepted delivery from the manufacturer when it was still bound by the contract concluded with the seller. This conduct certainly caused the seller to assume that it had fulfilled his own obligations towards the buyer. Therefore, failure to perform by the seller was caused by the buyer's own act (Art. 80 CISG).

This case goes to establish the fact that even in the event of a fundamental breach of contract, a party cannot exercise its rights under either art 49 or 64 of the CISG if that party's act or omission is to blame for the breach. This view no doubt locates art 80 at the centre of all the remedies and rights provided under the CISG.[24]

Art 79 includes special rules addressing a variety of specific sub-issues and procedural details, including exemption claims based on a third party's failure to perform (art 79(2)), treatment of temporary impediments (art 79(3)), and a party's obligation to notify the other side of a claim to exemption (art 79(4)). Art 80 includes no such detail. The fact that art 79 has five subsections, whereas art 80 is uncluttered by subdivisions, says much about the different approaches of the two provisions." See Flechtner (n 55) 84–101.

22 Art 80 CISG requires that the failure has been caused by the obligee's own act or omission. Whether the obligee was at fault is irrelevant. See Schwenzer and Fountoulakis (n 18) (2007) 577.

23 Landgericht Düsseldorf (District Court Düsseldorf) Germany, 09 July 1992 – 31 O 223/91, CISG-online 42 <https://cisg-online.org/search-for-cases?caseId=6022> accessed 17/9/2025.

24 ATT v Armco International Arbitration Court of the Belarusian Chamber of Commerce and Industry, 05 October 1995 [– 24/13–95] CISG-online 861 <https://cisg-online.org/search-for-cases?caseId=6787> accessed 27/9/2025; this case supports the general principles of law position of art 80. The Belarusian Chamber of Commerce and Industry International Court of Arbitration, in support of the general principle of law enunciated under art 80 of the CISG, has held that a party shall not be excused from performance of his obligations in a contract if the alleged breach of the latter party was caused by the former party's act or omission. The facts of the case where this decision was made are as follows:

Indeed, art 80 falls within chapter one (1) part three of the CISG. This means that it has relevance in the interpretation and application of the general provisions of the CISG. The loose and wide semantic and syntactic layout of art 80 is not an accident. This book reasons that it is so because the drafters did not wish to pinpoint art 80 or identify it with a particular function. It is drafted in such a way as to accommodate all situations where a party shouldn't be allowed to benefit from his earlier wrongdoing which causes the latter party failure of performance of obligation.

There is an argument that the doctrine of good faith as provided under art 7(2) CISG is enough to cover the sphere of importance of art 80 of the CISG, but sometimes it will be better not to allow justice at the mercy of discretion. What amounts to good faith and bad faith varies from climes and jurisdictions, but the clear, wide provision of art 80 is a very good starting point in determining what protection a party gets in the event his failure to fulfil his obligations is caused by the other party.[25]

A Belarusian seller and a Bulgarian buyer entered into a contract for the sale of refrigerators and deep freezers. After the buyer failed to pay for a portion of the goods received, the seller sued for the remaining purchase price. The buyer argued that its failure to pay was justified on the grounds that the seller had improperly suspended performance unilaterally and had delivered goods with latent defects. The Court first found that CISG was applicable on the basis of the Belarusian Civil Code, since the applicable law was to be that of the country in which the contract had been concluded, i.e. Belarus, a Contracting State (Art. 1(1)(b) CISG).

The Court rejected the buyer's argument that non-payment by the buyer was justified by the seller's incomplete delivery of the goods. Under art 80 CISG, a party to a contract cannot rely on the other party's lack of performance when lack of performance is due to its own acts or omissions. In the case at hand, the Court found that since the buyer had failed to pay for a significant amount of the goods already delivered, it could not rely on the seller's subsequent refusal to deliver additional goods as an excuse for non-performance.

25 Another case that illustrates the versatile application of art 80 is the *Equipment case* cited as Ukraine 21 June 2002 Tribunal of International Commercial Arbitration, Ukrainian Chamber of Commerce & Trade <http://cisgw3.law.pace.edu/cases/020621u5.html> accessed 29/9/2025.

Arpan Kumar Gupta gave the summary of this case thus:

"The seller agreed to deliver to the buyer equipment at the price of 2,500,000 Russian rubles. The buyer was required to pay a 50 per cent prepayment within two months from the moment of signing the contract; 25 per cent within five days from the day of manufacturing the equipment; and 25 per cent within five days from the signing of the certificate of acceptance. The buyer paid 1,000,000 Russian rubles as a prepayment and the seller shipped equipment worth 1,350,000 Russian rubles to the buyer. The goods were found to be defective and this was reported to the seller by the buyer. The goods were subsequently partially repaired. The buyer did not pay any further amounts.

The seller claimed a penalty for the buyer's delay in payment. The Arbitration Tribunal refused the claim under art 80 CISG. The Tribunal applied the CISG as it had been ratified by both parties' States. According to art 80 CISG 'a party may not rely on a failure of the other party to perform, to the extent that such failure was caused by the first party's act or omission.' The Tribunal found the shortage and malfunctions in the shipped goods were evidence of such omissions by the seller and thus no penalty for delay of the buyer's payment was awarded."

7.1.4 Shared of Liability and Mitigation under the CISG

Art 80 of the CISG highlights the issues of remedies, such as damages or restitution. This can be seen in its reading in conjunction with art 77 of the CISG. Art 77 provides that:

> A party who relies on a breach of contract must take such measures as are reasonable in the circumstances to mitigate the loss, including loss of profit, resulting from the breach. If he fails to take such measures, the party in breach may claim a reduction in the damages in the amount by which the loss should have been mitigated.

This provision is similar to art 80. It makes a case for the mitigation of damages by reason of shared liability. The difference between art 77 and art 80 is that while art 77 is predicated on the mitigation of loss and the consequences of the failure to do so, art 80 broadly tackles all other breaches, acts, or omissions (including the failure to mitigate) that may bring about the failure of the party to a contract of sale to perform his obligations. It also bars the first defaulting party from any remedy due to the non-performance that followed due to his (former party's) actions. Neumann further explores the relationship among arts 77, 79, and 80 of the CISG when he analysed that:

> [A]rticle 77 is placed under the heading 'damages' and concerns the calculation thereof. It primarily applies to post-breach situations, but it may already apply when a breach is threatened. Articles 79 and 80 are both placed under 'exemptions,' which presupposes that these two Articles apply only in post-breach situations. When a breach has been established and attributed to a party, Articles 79 and 80 provide for the possibility of being exempt from liability.[26]

The above analysis is important in tracing the comprehensive connection and vital role of these articles, which is to apportion risk and liabilities.[27] The major difference between arts 79 and 77 CISG lies in the fact that art 79 works to exempt liability in damages when the elements of the provision are proven; on the other hand,

---

The above discussions are geared towards establishing the fact that art 80 is more than a mere rule of exemption. It is a complete general principle of law with an independent application of its own.

26 Thomas Neumann, "Shared Responsibility under Article 80 CISG" (2/2009) *Nordic Journal of Commercial Law* 22.

27 It has been held that "Although a resale of goods or a substitute, purchase after contract avoidance are the most typical measures to mitigate the loss under Art. 77 CISG, other actions may be reasonable, as long as they are appropriate to reduce the damages expected to occur under the breach. It must further be considered that if more effective actions are subsequently found to have been available, the aggrieved party will be held responsible for not having undertaken these steps." See Jennifer Offermanns, "Damages Arising Out of a Cover Purchase within the Framework of Articles 74 to 77 CISG" (1/2006) 10 *Vindobona Journal of International Commercial Law & Arbitration* 1–14.

art 77 is in accordance with the generally accepted rule on contributory negligence. Even though the overwhelming doctrine takes the opposite view, the reduction in damages has to be equal to the amount by which the loss should have been mitigated. Thus, the amount owed by the liable party has to be established in order to determine the amount by which the loss that should have been mitigated has to be deducted.[28]

In the German case of *BMW 3 Series case*,[29] the relationship between damages and shared liability was brought to the fore. In this case, a German seller and an Italian buyer entered into a contract for the sale of eleven cars at a stated price. The cars were to be delivered by the end of October. About one month after the conclusion of the contract, the seller informed the buyer in a subsequent letter of the exact price for each car, option package included. In the same letter, it also informed the buyer that it would deliver the cars during "July, August, September [or] October." The buyer replied by sending back the seller's original letter and added in handwriting that it wanted to receive delivery of all cars that were on rush order by "July or August and at the latest by August 15." Some days after August 15, the seller informed the buyer that five of the ordered cars were ready for delivery and that the remaining six cars would be available by the beginning of October. By the end of October, the buyer notified the seller that it could not take delivery of the cars at that time due to substantial currency fluctuations and asked the seller to extend the delivery period until the currency situation returned to normal. The seller alleged damages for lost profits as a consequence of the buyer's breach of contract. The buyer commenced an action for restitution of the sum that the seller had obtained by executing a stand-by guarantee and asked for damages, alleging the seller's breach of contract for late delivery.[30] The court held with respect to the buyer's damages allegation that the non-delivery of the goods had been caused by the buyer's failure to take delivery. Therefore, it concluded that the buyer had lost its right to damages pursuant to art 80 CISG.[31]

Art 80 CISG, without doubt, laid the foundation for the application of art 77. They are of the same type and are enacted to oversee a situation where there is a two-way breach that causes failure of contractual obligations. The words of art 80 are loose and can be stretched to accommodate the fundamental principle of fairness and equity upon which the CISG is based. Art 80 of the CISG also canvasses for the apportionment of blame or remedy as the necessary instrument of maintaining commercial justice and equilibrium between the parties, though it is art 77 that categorically provides for mitigation and apportionment. Neumann[32] while rationalising on the relationship between arts 77 and 80, holds that:

28 Helmut Koziol, "Reduction in Damages According to Article 77 CISG" (2005–2006) 25 *Journal of Law and Commerce* 385–391.

29 Oberlandesgericht München (Court of Appeal Munich), Germany, 08 February 1995 – 7 U 1720/94, CISG-online 143 <https://cisg-online.org/search-for-cases?caseId=6121> accessed on 29/9/2025.

30 Ibid.

31 Ibid.

32 Neumann (686).

> Article 80 is seen as an all-or-nothing solution. Only cases where the failure to perform is caused solely by the other party can be subsumed under Article 80. Cases of shared responsibility are preferably solved by reference to Article 77 or to the underlying principle of Article 80. However, pro rata apportionment is nonetheless seen as the appropriate solution for shared responsibility, whatever the legal basis.

However, despite the doubt expressed by Neumann above, it can be deduced that both arts 77 and 80 apply to situations of shared liability and that an apportionment is appropriate in such cases. The concept of shared liability can similarly be seen in the arrangement of arts 39, 40 and 44 CISG. The starting point here is that a buyer will lose all available remedies if it does not give notice of non-conformity within a reasonable period of time; this thrusts responsibility to mitigate loss or damage by the victim party. However, the loss or remedies can be partial, depending on the circumstances. The concept of shared liability is also found in art 50, which has been used as the legal basis for a partial loss of price reduction.[33]

7.2 Shared Liability under the UNIDROIT Principles

7.2.1 Background

The doctrine of shared liability is by far more developed and eloquent under the UNIDROIT Principles than under the CISG. It is provided under the chapter 7 of the UNIDROIT Principles. Art 7.1.2 provides that "A party may not rely on the non-performance of the other party to the extent that such non-performance was caused by the first party's act or omission or by another event as to which the first party bears the risk."

This article, like art 80 of the CISG, is deeply rooted in good faith. It is a restatement of the doctrine of good faith as provided under art 1.7 of the UNIDROIT Principles. The only difference between art 80 of the CISG and art 7.1.2 of the UNIDROIT Principles is that while art 80 CISG bars a party from claiming remedy when his acts or omissions cause the other party to fail in his obligation to perform

33 Ibid. It can also be said that art 80 of the CISG is not only directly relevant in the interpretations of the outcome of what happens in a situation where a party is liable in the impediment that causes failure of obligation under art 79 of the CIS, it also provides its own independent rules of interpretations and applications of contractual obligations.

Furthermore, the phrase "to the extent" as employs under art 80 envisages a situation of the promisee's partial interference with the promisor's performance. This is, however, not unknown under art 79 of the CISG. In fact, art 79(3) provides that "The exemption provided by this article has effect for the period during which the impediment exists," which establishes the fact that temporary or partial exemption can be feasible under art 79 of the CISG till the impediment abates. It can be argued that as long as the impediment or breach or act/omissions of the first defaulting party under art 80 inure, then they cannot seek redress for the failure of the other party in fulfilling their obligations. This, in some cases, can be a temporary situation pending until the first party regularises their defaults; then they may be in a position to seek redress for the wrongdoing of the other party based on the atypical circumstances of the situation.

the contract of sale of goods, art 7.1.2, on the other hand, is in *pari materia* with art 80 but adds that events for which the claimant party bears its risk can be a bar to his claims for remedy if they cause failure of performance of the contract to the other party.[34] Thus, once it is established that the claimant party owes the risk of the event, they can be barred from turning around and seeking redress against the respondent party for their resultant failure of obligations.

The relationship between arts 7.1.2 and 7.1.7 (*force majeure* provision) is that both provisions are exempting provisions. If the elements that make up the provisions are present and operative, then they have the tendency to relieve a party of his liability in damages. Under art 7.1.7, liability will be relieved if the non–performing party falls short due to an unforeseen impediment that is beyond their control and that they could not reasonably be expected to have taken into account at the time of the conclusion of the contract or overcome it or its consequences. On the other hand, under art 7.1.2, liability will be relieved owing to the fact that the claimant is guilty of an act or omission which causes the respondent to fail in his obligations.

The official commentary on the UNIDROIT Principles elucidated further on art 7.1.2 thus:

> This article can be regarded as providing two excuses for non-performance. However conceptually, it goes further than this. When the article applies, the relevant conduct does not become excused non-performance but loses the quality of non-performance altogether. It follows, for instance, that the other party will not be able to terminate for non-performance.[35]

This comment draws a glaring difference between art 7.1.2 and art 7.1.7. While art 7.1.7 could be regarded as a case of excused non-performance due to non-defaulting and fortuitous elements impediment, art 7.1.2 deals with circumstances that make it loses the "quality of non-performance altogether." While art 7.1.2 operates, it forecloses any remedy available due to non-performance.[36] An example of the application of art 7.1.2 of the UNIDROIT Principles can be seen in the ICC case

34 Friederike Schäfer, "Commentary on Whether and the Extent to Which the UNIDROIT Principles May be Used to help Interpret Article 80 of the CISG" (2004) <http://www.cisg.law.pace.edu/cisg/principles/uni80.html> accessed 30/9/2025. The writer holds that: "The fact that such clarification does not appear in Article 80 CISG has no impact on the interpretation of this article. The understanding of Article 80 CISG as an expression of the general principle of the observance of good faith demands that a broad interpretation is adopted, i.e., the latter conclusion. This is because it is only appropriate to exempt a party from a non-performance the reason for which lies in the other party's sphere of risk. Virtually, this is the basic idea underlying Article 80 CISG as well as Article 7.1.2 UNIDROIT Principles."

35 UNIDROIT Principles Official Comment <http://www.unilex.info/dynasite.cfm?dssid=2377&dsmid=13637> accessed 1 September 2025.

36 Schäfer (n 34) argues that "[t]he effect of Article 7.1.2 UNIDROIT Principles is similar: The exemption provided by this article is extended to all remedies, but only to the extent the non-performance was due to the interference of the promisee. Article 7.1.2 UNIDROIT Principles is not applicable to cases of the interference acting only as a partial impediment to performance and concerning a non-performance of any other obligation independently from the promisee's act or omission."

involving the buying of an aircraft. In this case, the claimant, a European company and lessee of an aircraft, sold the aircraft, with the consent of the lessor, a financial institution, to the defendant, another European company. As the deregistration process in the claimant's country lasted longer than expected, the defendant decided to buy the aircraft under a second sale agreement from the lessor, which did not reserve the rights of the claimant. A dispute arose when claimant claimed damages from the defendant in the amount of its lost profit. The arbitration clause referred to Swiss law as the law applicable to the merits of the case. The arbitrator decided in favour of the claimant, awarding damages for violation by the defendant of the first sale agreement. According to the arbitrator, since the seller's impossibility to perform was due to the conduct of the buyer who acted in such a way that the conveyance of the title became impossible although it had not been impossible at the time of entering into the agreement, the first sale agreement was not nullified. Moreover, the arbitrator also pointed out that in the case at hand, the defendant could not rely on the non-performance of the claimant to the extent that such non-performance was caused by the defendant.[37]

Art 7.1.2 will also apply in a situation where it can be established that the claimant party bears a risk to an event that causes the respondent party to commit non-performance. Again, this second limb of art 7.1.2 provision underscores the no-fault posture of modern uniform commercial laws. Hence, once it can be established that a party bears the risk of the former event which causes the other party to fail to perform, then they cannot be heard to plead the event resulted in no fault of theirs. Thus, it is irrelevant for art 7.1.2 whether the obligee's failure to perform its duty to co-operate can be excused because of *force majeure* under art 7.1.7.[38] It can be summarised that where a *force majeure* impediment under art 7.1.7 of the UNIDROIT Principles occurs, and it shows that the risk or the impediment falls within the sphere of the claimant party, then it is a settled view of the law that the claimant party cannot have any remedy if that first impediment affected the failure of obligation to perform of the respondent party.[39]

37 ICC International Court of Arbitration [2006] <http://www.unilex.info/case.cfm?id=1177> accessed 4 September 2025.

38 Stefan Vogenauer and Jan Kleinheisterkamp (eds), *Commentary on the UNIDROIT Principles of International Commercial Contracts (PICC)* (Oxford University Press, 2009) para 4, 736

39 Official Comment on art 7.1.2. Illustration two (2) to the Official commentary goes a long way to state how this second part of art 7.1.2 involving risks works. It articulated thus:

A, a builder, concludes a construction contract to be performed on the premises of B who already has many buildings on those premises which are the subject of an insurance policy covering any damage to the buildings. If the parties agree that the risk of accidental damage is to fall on B as the person insured, there would normally be no reason to reject the parties' allocation of risk since risks of this kind are normally covered by insurance. Even therefore if a fire were to be caused by A's negligence, the risk may be allocated to B although it would clearly need more explicit language to carry this result than would be the case if the fire which destroyed the building were the fault of neither party.

7.2.2 Legal Consequences of Shared Liability under the UNIDROIT Principles

The first legal consequence of art 7.1.2 of the UNIDROIT principles is that it removes the stigma of non-performance from the failure of the respondent party to perform if it can be attributed to a prior act or omission or sphere of risk of the claimant party. This means that all the remedies that are available under the situation of non-performance will be clearly inapplicable. Secondly, art 7.4.7 is the equitable face of art 7.1.2; where the conduct of the aggrieved party contributes to the harm that it has suffered, the effect of art 7.4.7 is to reduce the damages to which the aggrieved party is entitled.[40] Art 7.4.7 provides that:

> Where the harm is due in part to an act or omission of the aggrieved party or to another event as to which that party bears the risk, the amount of damages shall be reduced to the extent that these factors have contributed to the harm, having regard to the conduct of the parties.

This provision apportions losses that result from mutual breaches of obligations of the parties that cause the failure of performance of the contract. The official commentary on the 2010 edition of the UNIDROIT Principles, which is still widely in use to date as a veritable guidance to the application of this provision, espouses that:

> The conduct of the aggrieved party or the external events as to which it bears the risk may have made it absolutely impossible for the non-performing party to perform. If the requirements of art 7.1.7 (*Force majeure*) are satisfied, the non- performing party is totally exonerated from liability. Otherwise, the exoneration will be partial, depending on the extent to which the aggrieved party contributed to the harm. The determination of each party's contribution to the harm may well prove to be difficult and will to a large degree depend upon the exercise of judicial discretion. In order to give some guidance to the court this article provides that the court shall have regard to the respective behaviour of the parties. The more serious a party's failing, the greater will be its contribution to the harm.[41]

40 The Official Comment to art 7.4.7 UNIDROIT Principles 2010 provides two illustrations of the applications of art 7.4.7 thus:

1. A, a franchisee bound by an "exclusivity" clause contained in the contract with B, acquires stock from C because B has required immediate payment despite the fact that the franchise agreement provides for payment at 90 days. B claims payment of the penalty stipulated for breach of the exclusivity clause. B will obtain only part of the sum due thereunder as it was B who provoked A's non-performance.
2. A, a passenger on a liner affecting a luxury cruise, is injured when a lift fails to stop at the floor requested. B, the shipowner, is held liable for the consequences of A's injury and seeks recourse against C, the company which had checked the lifts before the liner's departure. It is proved that the accident would have been avoided if the floor had been better lit. Since this was B's responsibility, B will not obtain full recovery from C.

41 The UNIDROIT Principles of International Commercial Contracts, Rome 2010.

This commentary sums up the attitude of the scholars and the drafters of the UNIDROIT Principles towards seeing to it that there must be a balance between sellers and buyers; more especially in a situation where it will be unconscionable to allow any party to benefit at the expense of the other party.[42] This view is supported by the World Intellectual Property Organization Arbitration and Mediation Centre[43] in a case between a French inventor and a German manufacturing company. In this case, the claimant, a French inventor, claimed damages from the defendant, a German manufacturing company, for an unjustified termination of the licensing and joint research agreement. The contract was governed by Swiss law.

The arbitral tribunal granted damages, but not to the extent claimed on account of the uncertainty surrounding the turnover the defendant could have made with the new product. In this regard, the arbitral tribunal referred to art 7.4.3 (2) of the UNIDROIT Principles of International Commercial Contracts, providing that the loss of a chance be compensated "in proportion to the probability of its occurrence." Furthermore, the Arbitral Tribunal, noting that the harm due to the termination of the contract was due in part to acts and omissions by the claimant, held that also for this reason the reduction of the damages claimed was justified and in this respect referred to art 7.4.7 according to which "where the harm is due in part to an act or omission of the aggrieved party … the amount of damages shall be reduced to the extent that these factors have contributed to the harm, having regard to the conduct of each of the parties."[44]

42 The view expressed is consistent with a dispute involving a Romanian manufacturer and an English defendant decided at the ICC International Court of Arbitration (2003) 12111 cited as <http://www.unilex.info/case.cfm?id=964> accessed 1 September 2025. In this case, the claimant, a Romanian manufacturer, entered into a contract with the defendant, an English company, for the sale of goods to be delivered to customers of the latter in a third country. Some of the customers complained that the goods delivered by the claimant were not in conformity with the agreed technical standards and refused payment. The defendant urged the claimant directly to contact the customers in order to find an amicable solution, but the claimant did not take any such step. On its part, the defendant refused to permit its bank to honour the letter of credit opened in favour of the claimant on the ground of minor discrepancies in the documents submitted by the claimant. The dispute arose when the claimant requested the defendant to pay the outstanding invoices for the goods delivered as well as the cost of the raw materials the claimant had bought to manufacture the goods ordered but subsequently rejected by the defendant, and the defendant refused to do so invoking the defects of the goods. The Arbitral Tribunal held that since both the claimant and the defendant refused to cooperate in order to find a mutually acceptable solution, the claimant was also prevented from claiming damages for the deliveries that were no longer performed, and in this respect, the Tribunal invoked Art. 7.4.7 of the UNIDROIT Principles according to which the amount of damages may be reduced when the loss results from an action or omission of the party claiming damages.

43 UNILEX [25/01/2007] <http://www.unilex.info/case.cfm?id=1179> accessed 1 September 2025

44 Arbitration Court of the Lausanne Chamber of Commerce and Industry [31/01/2003] <http://www.unilex.info/case.cfm?id=862> accessed 02/09/2025; in this case the court found it wise to apply art 7.4.7. A Turkish company and a company incorporated in Anguilla, West Indies, with an office in the Philippines, entered into an agreement concerning highly sophisticated equipment. The contract contained two provisions on the choice of law, which however appeared to contradict each other, since one was in favour of English law and the other in favour of Swiss law, the court opted for a neutral law (UNIDROIT Principles) that will best serve the interests of the par-

Finally, the extent to which a court or tribunal will apportion damages or remedies is subject to the peculiar facts of any given case, the discretion of the judge or arbitrator, and trade usage and customs that can be proved to be applicable in the instance. There is also a concomitant duty under art 7.4.8 for the aggrieved party to act in order to abate the damages caused by the defaulting party. This is in consonance with art 77 of the CISG. Art 7.4.8 of the UNIDROIT Principles provides that:

(1) The non-performing party is not liable for harm suffered by the aggrieved party to the extent that the harm could have been reduced by the latter party's taking reasonable steps.
(2) The aggrieved party is entitled to recover any expenses reasonably incurred in attempting to reduce the harm.

This provision is steeped in common sense and good faith; its relevance is most aptly captured by the official commentary to this provision thus: "[t]he purpose of this article is to avoid the aggrieved party passively sitting back and waiting to be compensated for harm which it could have avoided or reduced. Any harm which the aggrieved party could have avoided by taking reasonable steps will not be compensated.'[45]

7.3 Shared Liability under the English Law

7.3.1 Common Law and the 1979 Act

The doctrine of shared liability is predicated on the doctrine of good faith. Under the English common law, courts will not generally imply the duty of good faith, but will, however, give effect to it if it is manifestly present in a contract. The case of *Carter v Boehm*[46] established the position of good faith in the common law. Lord Mansfield stated that "[g]ood faith forbids either party by concealing what he privately knows, to draw the other into a bargain, from his ignorance of that fact

ties. The court, after having rendered on 17 May 2002 a Partial Award finding that one of the parties had not properly performed its obligations arising from the contract, the arbitral tribunal rendered a final award determining the amount of damages due by the non-performing party. In so doing, the arbitral tribunal referred to Arts. 7.4.2 and 7.4.7 of the UNIDROIT Principles in order to justify a reduction of the compensable harm in view of the fact that part of the harm was due to the conduct of the aggrieved party.

45 Evidently, a party who has already suffered the consequences of non-performance of the contract cannot be required in addition to take time-consuming and costly measures. On the other hand, it would be unreasonable from the economic standpoint to permit an increase in harm which could have been reduced by the taking of reasonable steps. The steps to be taken by the aggrieved party may be directed either to limiting the extent of the harm, above all when there is a risk of it lasting for a long time if such steps are not taken (often they will consist in a replacement transaction: see Art. 7.4.5), or to avoiding any increase in the initial harm.

46 (1766) 3 Burr 1905.

and his believing the contrary." Though the case was decided under the contract of insurance, the significance reaches out to other forms of commercial transactions.[47]

Broadly speaking, a party cannot be allowed to seek redress for a failure of performance of an obligation of the other party when the claimant party's acts or omissions cause the respondent party's failure of obligation. This general common law principle is encapsulated in the Latin maxim "*ex turpi causa non oritur* actio" this translates to "from a dishonourable cause an action does not arise," this is the closest principle in the common law that is similar to art 80 CISG and art 7.1.2 of the UNIDROIT Principles. This principle was applied in the case of *Holman v Johnson*[48] in this case, the claimant sold and delivered a quantity of tea to the defendant. The contract was made in Dunkirk. The defendant intended to smuggle the tea into England. The claimant was aware of the defendant's intention. The defendant failed to pay for the tea and the claimant brought an action for the price of the tea. Lord Mansfield held while developing this Latin maxim thus:

> The objection, that a contract is immoral or illegal as between plaintiff and defendant, sounds at all times very ill in the mouth of the defendant. It is not for his sake, however, that the objection is ever allowed; but it is founded in general principles of policy, which the defendant has the advantage of, contrary to the real justice, as between him and the plaintiff, by accident, if I may say so. The principle of public policy is this; *ex dolo malo non oritur actio*. No court will lend its aid to a man who founds his cause of action upon an immoral or an illegal act. If, from the plaintiff's own standing or otherwise, the cause of action appears to arise *ex turpi causa*, or the transgression of a positive law of this country, there the court says he has no right to be assisted. It is upon that ground the court goes; not for the sake of the defendant, but because they will not lend their aid to such a plaintiff. So if the plaintiff and defendant were to change sides, and the defendant was to bring his action against the plaintiff, the latter would then have the advantage of it; for where both were equally in fault, *potior est conditio defendentis*.[49]

This case established without doubt that public policy will not stand by and watch a party benefit from a failure of obligation of which they are unfortunately a part.[50] However, over the years, this Latin maxim has been identified more with the law of tort rather than with the law of contract.[51] The case of *Cross v Kirkby*[52] gives

47 Under English common law, it is recognised that parties to a contract shall exercise fair dealing during negotiations and performance of the obligations of the contract. This fair dealing is synonymous with the doctrine of good faith.

48 (1775) 1 Cowp 341.

49 Ibid.

50 Jonathan Mance, "Ex Turpi Causa–When Latin Avoids Liability" (2014) 18(2) *Edinburgh Law Review* 175; R. Gottschalk, "Illegality in Contract" (1967) 2 *Isr. L. Rev*. 589.

51 Ray Ryan, "Ex Turpi Causa: Negligence and Dangerous Drivers" (2005) 1 *Q. Rev. Tort L.*, 16; Liron Shmilovits, "When is Illegality a Defence to a Tort?" (2021) 41(4) *Legal Studies* 603.

52 [2000] EWCA Civ 426 Court of Appeal.

insight into how this Latin maxim works under English law of tort; in this case, the claimant was a hunt saboteur. He got into an altercation with the defendant, a landowner who allowed his land to be used by the hunt. The defendant had forcibly removed the claimant's girlfriend from the land. The claimant then attacked the defendant with a baseball bat. The defendant grabbed the bat and grappled to get it off the claimant. In the course of doing so, he struck the claimant on the head and fractured his skull. Consequently, the claimant suffered epileptic attacks. The claimant brought an action for damages for the injuries sustained. The defendant raised self-defence and *ex turpi causa*. The trial judge rejected both defences but reduced the damages under the Law Reform (Contributory Negligence) Act 1945. The defendant appealed. Allowing the appeal, Lord Beldam held that:

> I do not believe that there is any general principle that the claimant must either plead, give evidence of or rely on his own illegality for the principle to apply In my view the principle applies when the claimant's claim is so closely connected or inextricably bound up with his own criminal or illegal conduct that the court could not permit him to recover without appearing to condone that conduct.

The above case has established that whether under the law of tort or contract law, the English courts will always look at the moral side of any claim; more especially if such a claim is coming from a party who contributed to the fault.[53] The link between the principle of ex *turpi causa* and the doctrine of frustration under English law is evident. A party who is implicated in the event that destroys radically the performance of a contract cannot be heard to say the contract has been frustrated. And if such an event leads to the impossibility on the part of the other party to perform, the former party will still not be allowed to plead frustration.

The doctrine of frustration under English common law entails that due to unforeseen circumstances, the contract has become impossible of performance. This view is contrary to the principle of *ex turpi causa* where the blameworthiness must not only be present but must be directly linked to the actions or inactions of the parties. This will therefore constitute a bar to a claim.

In addition, the principle of shared liability under art 80 CISG resembles the doctrine of estoppel under English common law.[54] Estoppel has been described as "[a] rule of law that when person A, by act or words, gives person B reason to believe a certain set of facts upon which person B takes action, person A cannot later, to his (or her) benefit, deny those facts or say that his earlier act was improper."[55] It

53 Forsikringaktieselskapet Vesta v. Butcher [1989] A.C. 852; in this case, it was accepted that the plaintiffs were entitled to formulate the claim, which was based on § 4 of the Law Reform (Contributory Negligence) Act 1945, in either contract (breach of a contractual duty of care) or tort (tort of negligence).

54 Scaforn International BV & Orion Metal BVBA v. Exma CPI SA (2005) <http://cisgw3.law.pace.edu/cases/050125b1.html> accessed 28 September 2025.

55 In Combe v Combe a husband promised to make maintenance payments to his estranged wife but failed to do so. The wife brought an action to enforce the promise invoking promissory estoppel. Her

follows therefore that when two parties enter into a contractual obligation, and A (claimant-party) by his act or omission causes a breach which leads to a failure of obligation of the respondent-party, then the claimant-party shall be estopped from asserting any claim, redress or remedy based on the latter party's failure.

Under the Sale of Goods Act of 1979, a party cannot be allowed to make a claim when his prior fault constitutes the cause of the failure of obligation to the respondent party. This is a general principle of good faith provided under Section 60(3) of the Sale of Goods Act 1979. Section 60(3) provides that "A thing is deemed to be done in good faith within the meaning of the Act when it is in fact done honestly, whether it is done negligently or not." The above provision exerts the duty of good faith and fair dealing during contracts emanating from the sale of goods. Then even if a party has acted negligently, it is irrelevant once it can be established that they acted honestly.[56]

Finally, the case laws and principles of law applicable under the common law can also apply under the Sale of Goods Act 1979 in so far as they are not inconsistent with the provisions of the Act. In fact, Section 62(2) provides that:

> The rules of common law, including the law merchant, except in so far as they are inconsistent with the provisions of this Act , in particular the rules relating to the law of principal and agent and the effect of fraud, misrepresentation, duress or coercion, mistake, or other invalidating cause, apply to contracts for sale of goods.

By the above provision, all the discussions and case laws cited under the common law will also be applicable when determining a similar scenario under the Sale of Goods Act of 1979. Application of Section 7 of the Sale of Goods Act is strongly backed by the doctrine of good faith. The contract of sale of goods is not avoided where a seller is in breach of good faith and the goods perished before the risk has passed to the buyer.

---

action failed. There was no pre-existing agreement which was later modified by a promise. The wife sought to use promissory estoppel as a sword and not a shield. Lord Denning held that :

"where one party has, by his words or conduct, made to the other a promise or assurance which was intended to affect the legal relations between them and to be acted on accordingly, then, once the other party has taken him at his word and acted on it, the one who gave the promise or assurance cannot afterwards be allowed to revert to the previous legal relations as if no such promise or assurance had been made by him. He must accept their legal relations subject to the qualification which he himself has so introduced, even though it is not supported in point of law by any consideration but only by his word."

56 The doctrine of shared responsibility can only be used as a shield and not a sword; thus, if a party, while acting honestly but negligently, causes a situation that leads to the failure of an obligation to perform by the other party, the first party will still be barred from seeking redress based on the failure of the obligation of the latter party. The former party's honest but negligent act or omission can only be considered during the apportionment of damages or remedies, but gives him no right to a cause of action.

In conclusion, arts 80, 79, and 77 of the CISG are organically linked. They are regarded as post-breach provisions.[57] This means that they are set in motion after a breach or impediment has occurred to cause failure of parties' performance of obligations in a contract of sale of goods.[58] The differences among these three provisions are that art 77 is fashioned to oversee a situation where shared liability is a result of failure of a party to mitigate the loss caused by the defaulting party. The first party has nothing to do with the causation of the breach, but sound commercial practice, which is rooted in good faith, demands that a party cannot stand by and watch the deterioration of a subject matter of a contract simply because it is not their deed. However, art 79 is in contradistinction to art 77; this is because art 77 concerns failure to mitigate by the injured party. Though it does not eliminate liability in damages, it will reduce the amount of damages recovered.[59] Then art 79 governs a situation when an unforeseen impediment, which is beyond the control of a party, occurs and inhibits the performance of the obligations of the contract of sale. In such a situation, the party will not be held liable in damages. Finally, art 80 applies to a situation where a party who wishes to make a claim or rely on any available remedy has contributed to the causation of the breach that causes the failure of obligation.[60] Such a party will not be allowed to exploit such a situation at the expense of the second defaulting party. However, the latter party cannot use art 80 as a sword if they are in breach of any obligations in the contract of sale. Thus, this makes art 80 not only a general restatement of law but a veritable rule of equity.

The UNIDROIT principles do well in laying down the rules that guide the conduct of the parties when they are confronted with a cross-fire of breaches situation. The combined effects of arts 7.1.2, 7.4.7, 7.4.5, and 7.4.8 are to develop a well-articulated rule that will checkmate the winners-take-all attitude during a commercial contract relationship. These, however, resemble the doctrine of estoppel, good faith and contributory negligence under English law, which operate to diffuse inequality of bargaining power between parties and to prevent a party from reaping from his wrongdoing.

57 A.W. Katz, "Remedies for Breach of Contract under the CISG" (2005) 25(3) *International Review of Law and Economics* 378–396.

58 Ibid.

59 Jeffrey S. Sutton, "Measuring Damages Under the United Nations Convention on the International Sale of Goods" (1989) 50 *Ohio State Law Journal* 737–752; it has also been suggested that "The party taking reasonable measures under Article 77 to mitigate the threatened loss will likely expend money to this aim. The expended sum of money is considered as a loss suffered as a consequence of the breach of contract. Therefore, the party expending the money has the right to claim compensation for it even if the actions to mitigate the loss were in vain, provided that they were reasonable under the circumstances." See Knapp (n 11) ch. 4, 559–567.

60 Michael Müller, "Rezension zu Neumann, The Duty to Cooperate in International Sales. The Scope and Role of Article 80 CISG" (2012) 9(5) *Zeitschrift für Gemeinschaftsprivatrecht* 251–252.

7.4 Exemption and Remedies under the CISG

7.4.1 Background

The doctrine of exemption under the CISG is not exclusive of other known rights and remedies that can accrue to a disgruntled party in a contract.[61] This has been explained earlier in this work to be paradoxical. The uniqueness of the doctrine of exemption lies in the non-liability of a party in damages when there is a failure due to a non-fault, unforeseen impediment. But the gateway remedies provision of art 79(5) of the CISG has hugely reduced this important doctrine of contract law into a farce. Art 79(5) provides that nothing in this art prevents either party from exercising any right other than to claim damages under this Convention.

The implications of this concluding part of art 79 are that all remedies like avoidance, specific performance, sellers'/'buyers' right to substitute performance, reduction of price, sellers'/'buyers' right to compel, and other incidental remedies are still applicable under an exempted contract of sale of goods in the 1980 Convention. The only specifically mentioned exception to this carte blanche application of remedies is that no party can claim damages.

7.4.2 Specific Performance and Exemption under the CISG

The remedy of specific performance seems antithetical to the very foundation, meanings and applications of the doctrine of exemption, though it seems this remedy is permitted under art 79(5) CISG.[62] It is a trite Latin maxim that *lex nil frustra facit* (the law does nothing in vain).[63] This fundamental maxim underlies the reluctance of the court or any legal instrument to provide a remedy that will be unattainable in law or equity. The CISG therefore will need an amendment to reflect the inapplicability of the remedy of specific performance just like art 8:101(2) of the

61 Yasutochi Ishida, "CISG Article 79: Exemption of Performance, and Adaptation of Contract Through Interpretation of Reasonableness—Full of Sound and Fury, but Signifying Something" (2017) 30 *Pace Int'l L. Rev* 331.

62 Jussi Koskinen, "CISG, Specific Performance and Finnish Law" (1999) Faculty of Law of the University of Turku, Private Law Publication Series B, 47. The author writes that "Art 79 does not seem to be ambiguous as it expressly provides that an aggrieved party can always claim for performance even in the case of impossibility."

63 Reinhard Zimmermann, "Remedies for Non-performance: The Revised German Law of Obligations, Viewed against the Background of the Principles of European Contract Law" (2002) 6(3) *Edin. L.R.* 271–314; the author writes that:

"Under German law § 275 I BGB: a claim for specific performance is excluded, as far as such performance is impossible. This rule has a very long tradition; it ultimately derives from the Roman principle of *impossibilium nulla est obligation.*"

Principles of European Contract Law (PECL).[64] Arts 46(1)[65] and art 62[66] of the CISG provide for the remedy of specific performance for both the buyer and the seller respectively. It follows therefore that this remedy can be applicable under art 79(5) of the CISG since it is ostensibly not excluded. However, what remains to be seen is how far this remedy (specific performance) can go in being legally potent in the face of the nature of the doctrine of exemption which thrives on the notion of impossibility of performance.[67] Schwartz argues that whenever there is a disproportion between the changed costs of performance and the interest of the buyer in receiving performance in kind, the seller ought to have the right to refuse a performance claim. The law should not encourage economically irrational behaviour.[68]

Analysing these provisions, it will be important to start with the fact that arts 46 and 62 are not absolute under the CISG and have been qualified by art 28 of the CISG which provides that:

> If in accordance with the provisions of this Convention, one party is entitled to require performance of any obligation by the other party, a court is not bound to enter a judgement for specific performance unless the court would do so under its own law in respect of similar contracts of sale not governed by this Convention.

It follows that whenever the remedy of specific performance is against the provisions of a national law whose court is adjudicating a CISG-related matter, then the court is not bound to defer to the remedy of specific performance as provided under arts

64 Art 8:101(2) provides thus:

> (2) Where a party's non-performance is excused under Art 8:108, the aggrieved party 416 may resort to any of the remedies set out in Chapter 9 except claiming performance and damages.

65 Art 46 provides thus:

> (1) The buyer may require performance by the seller of his obligations unless the buyer has resorted to a remedy which is inconsistent with this requirement.
> (2) If the goods do not conform to the contract, the buyer may require delivery of substitute goods only if the lack of conformity constitutes a fundamental breach of contract and a request for substitute goods is made either in conjunction with notice given under art 39 or within a reasonable time thereafter.
> (3) If the goods do not conform to the contract, the buyer may require the seller to remedy the lack of conformity by repair, unless this is unreasonable having regard to all the circumstances. A request for repair must be made either in conjunction with notice given under art 39 or within a reasonable time thereafter.

66 Art 62 provides that:

> The seller may require the buyer to pay the price, take delivery or perform their other obligations, unless the seller has resorted to a remedy which is inconsistent with this requirement.

67 Richard Backhaus "The Limits of the Duty to Perform in the Principles of European Contract Law" (2004) 8(1) *Electronic Journal of Comparative Law* <http://www.ejcl.org/> accessed 17/09/2025. The writer argues against the application of specific performance, citing German law thus: "A comparison with the German concept of impossibility only is less fruitful as the effect of an impossible performance under German law is entirely different. It only excludes the general claim for specific performance notwithstanding fault and foreseeability on the part of the debtor."

68 A Schwartz, "The Case for Specific Performance" (1979) 89 *Yale L.J.* 271.

46(1) and 62 of the CISG unless the court can do so under its own internal jurisdiction in respect of contracts of sale governed by its national law.[69] The reason behind the soft-landing approach adopted under art 28 of the CISG in respect of the remedy of specific performance has been offered by Honnold when he writes:

> [T]his concession to the procedures of the forum was granted by ULIS (1964) in response to the objection that common-law systems compelled ("specific") performance only when alternative remedies e.g., (damages) were not adequate. Comparative research also revealed that some civil law systems would not always compel performance by the coercive measures, such as imprisonment for contempt, which may be available in "common law" systems; as a consequence flexibility based on art 28 is not confined to common law jurisdictions.[70]

It is also essential to add that the remedy of specific performance is not available to a party who has resorted to a remedy which is inconsistent with specific performance. For example, a party who has exercised his right to avoid the contract or sought damages (though not applicable under art 79) will not be heard to seek the remedy of specific performance. Also, when a party in accordance with art 80 of the CISG caused the first party's act or omission that resulted in the failure of obligation in the contract, then that party too will not bring a claim under arts 46(1) or 62 of the CISG.[71]

69 Shael Herman, "Specific Performance: A Comparative Analysis: Part 1" (2003) 7(1) *Edin. L.R.* 75–26 writes that "If the phrasing of art 28 is taken literally, then the CISG's approach to specific performance should be appraised in light of the domestic legal systems of the signatory states."

70 Honnold (n 20) ch. 1, 304–312. Furthermore, the connection between art 46(1), 62 and 28 was made evident in Magellan Int'l Corporation v Salzgitter Handel GmbH, US District Court for the Northern District of Illinois, USA, 07 December 1999 – 99 C 5153, CISG-online 439 <https://cisg-online.org/search-for-cases?caseId=6409> accessed 25/9/2025. In this case, a United States distributor entered into negotiations with a German trader with a view to reaching an agreement for the purchase of steel bars from a Ukrainian manufacturer. During the negotiations, the parties agreed on several matters (seller acting as middleman between the US buyer and the Ukrainian manufacturer, quantity of the goods, amount and method of payment, instructions for manufacturing). Nevertheless, a dispute arose when the seller, in view of the buyer's refusal to modify the letter of credit issued for payment, threatened not to perform its contractual obligations and to sell the goods elsewhere. The buyer brought an action for anticipatory breach of contract claiming damages and specific performance of the seller's obligations.

Many issues were raised and answered by the court, but in dealing with the issue of specific performance, the court held inter alia that:

"Under (Art 46 (1) CISG and with the exception that a Court is not bound to enter judgment for specific performance unless it would do so under its own law of contracts. After having recalled that, according to modern judicial interpretation of Par. 2–716 (1) UCC, specific performance may be granted when the buyer proves the difficulty of obtaining similar goods on the market, the Court upheld the buyer's claim."

71 Steven Walt, "For Specific Performance Under the United Nations Sales Convention" (1991) 26 *Tex. Int'l L. J.* 211–251.

There can be a situation envisaged under art 79(3) of the CISG where the impediment that causes the frustration is temporary, and then it seems right and proper for a party who is being owed an obligation in the contract to demand specifically from the other party to perform his obligation when it is due and not impossible to perform. There can be possible confusion on when and the most appropriate time to demand specific performance in such a scenario, again, if the parties are aware that though the impediment renders immediate performance impossible, it is such that will abate within a certain or reasonable period of time, then the victim-party's right to specific performance will not accrue until the abatement of the supervening impediment and when it is clear that the performance of the contract is no longer impossible.

It is clear that under art 46 of the CISG, paragraphs (2) and (3) are not applicable to an exempted contract; they only apply to a scenario where the "goods do not conform to the contract" and this suggests that the contract is performable only if the goods may not have been in compliance with the agreement in the contract.

In conclusion, it has been argued that specific performance can apply under art 79 of the CISG in a situation where late or defective performance constitutes the impediment that frustrated the contract.[72]

7.4.3 Remedy of Cure and Exemption under the CISG

The remedy of cure is directly opposite to the doctrine of exemption.[73] There cannot be a possible cure for an exempted contract. Art 48[74] of the CISG provides

72 Kroll and others (n 41) ch. 1, para 16, 1061.

73 The provision for cure under Art 37 CISG is not applicable since it entails the seller has delivered the goods before the date set for delivery and the seller has delivered goods before the date for delivery; they may, up to that date, deliver any missing part or make up any deficiency in the quantity of the goods delivered, or deliver goods in replacement of any non-conforming goods delivered or remedy any lack of conformity in the goods delivered, provided that the exercise of this right does not cause the buyer unreasonable inconvenience or unreasonable expense. However, the buyer retains any right to claim damages as provided for in this Convention. Thus, this is contradictory to exemption since performance is still possible.

74 Art 48 CISG provides that:

(1) Subject to art 49, the seller may, even after the date for delivery, remedy at his own expense any failure to perform his obligations, if he can do so without unreasonable delay and without causing the buyer unreasonable inconvenience or uncertainty of reimbursement by the seller of expenses advanced by the buyer. However, the buyer retains any right to claim damages as provided for in this Convention.

(2) If the seller requests the buyer to make known whether he will accept performance and the buyer does not comply with the request within a reasonable time, the seller may perform within the time indicated in his request. The buyer may not, during that period of time, resort to any remedy which is inconsistent with performance by the seller.

(3) A notice by the seller that he will perform within a specified period of time is assumed to include a request, under the preceding paragraph, that the buyer make known his decision.

(4) A request or notice by the seller under paragraph (2) or (3) of this art is not effective unless received by the buyer.

for the cure of any obligations owed to a buyer by a seller in the contract of sale. Jacob Ziegel has noticed that "art 48 reaches the same results as the common law where the breach is non-essential or the buyer elects not to avoid the contract.[75] The article attaches conditions to the seller's entitlement to offer cure, but this could be implied at common law."[76] This suggests that art 48 applies to a situation where either the breach/failure of obligations are non-fundamental or the contract is not exempted.

It will be easy to conclude that the remedy of cure is neither here nor there in the face of an exempted contract, but there can be cure in art 79(3) situations where the cause of the impediment that frustrated the contract is of impermanent nature[77] (There is no partial frustration under English law, unlike what is obtainable under the CISG and the UNIDROIT Principles) then parties can cure whatever lack of impediment there is and go ahead with the performance of the contract when the impediment that frustrated the contract ceases.[78]

7.4.4 Remedy of Reduction of Price and Exemption under the CISG

This remedy provides for a situation where the buyer has already received delivery of non-conforming goods.[79] It is hardly a remedy that any of the parties under an exempted contract can practically have recourse to except under art 79(3) where the impediment is not of permanent nature. The buyer, in such instance, can make a case for reduction in price if the value they would have got from the contract had diminished due to the temporary impediment. Art 50 of the CISG provides reduction of price. Art 50 and the remedy it provides for are not within the context of art 79 of the CISG.[80] The grounds for the application of art 79 will make it

75 Olga Gonzalez, "Remedies under the U.N. Convention for the International Sale of Goods" (1984) 2 *Int'l Tax & Bus Law* 79. The author writes that: "Art 37 CISG like Art 48 cannot apply when the remedy of avoidance has been exercised."

76 Ziegel (n 57) ch. 1.

77 Philip Davis and Graham Ludlam, "Wynn or Lose?" (2007) 157 *NLJ* 535; the authors write that: "Frustration is an all or nothing event; English law does not recognise the concept of partial frustration."

78 Peter Huber and Markus Altenkirch, "Buyer's Right to Cure" (2008) 4(4) *European Review of Contract Law* 540–545; the writers argue that: "according to Art 48 CISG the seller has to take the initiative and offer cure within a reasonable period of time in order to prevent a claim for damages. If he fails to do so without undue delay, the buyer is entitled to repair the goods himself and to demand the costs of repair from the seller."

79 John Honnold, *Uniform Law for International Sales under the 1980 United Nations Convention* (Wolters Kluwer, 2009) 444, para 309.

80 Peter A. Piliounis, "The Remedies of Specific Performance, Price Reduction and Additional Time (Nachfrist) under the CISG: Are These Worthwhile Changes or Additions to English Sales Law" (2000) 12 *Pace International Law Review* 1–46, the author writes that:

> "...price reduction can be seen as a self-help remedy that can be implemented by the buyer without any requirement to have the determination upheld by a court, expert or other tribunal. In practice, however, this difference is largely illusory. Any price reduction by the buyer must certainly be reasonable; otherwise it would be disputed by the seller and subject to review by a court."

difficult for price reduction to apply. The UNITRAL in a published comment on art 50 articulated that:

> Art 50 applies when goods that have been delivered do not conform to the contract. Non-conformity is to be understood in the sense of art 35, i.e., defects as to quantity, quality, description (aliud) and packaging. In addition, defects in documents relating to the goods can be treated as a case of non-conformity. The remedy of price reduction is, however, not available if the breach of contract is based upon late delivery or the violation of any obligation of the seller other than the obligation to deliver conforming goods.[81] The comment above makes a detailed analysis of the situations upon which art 50 can best be applied, and unfortunately the doctrine of exemption as envisaged under art 79 of the CISG does not feature.[82]

7.4.5 Damages and Exemption under the CISG

The CISG provides for strict liability for non-performance,[83] but art 79(5) unequivocally removes the remedy of damages from applying under exempted contracts governed by the CISG.[84] It will be instructive to understand that this is a heavy blow to the common law jurisdiction where damages remain the chief remedy though for a breach of contract and frustration entails under common law that there is no breach.[85]

Art 74 of the CISG provides for damages; it reads thus:

> Damages for breach of contract by one party consist of a sum equal to the loss, including loss of profit, suffered by the other party as a consequence of the breach. Such damages may not exceed the loss which the party in breach foresaw or ought to have foreseen at the time of the conclusion of the

81 Digest of Art 50 case law [2008] http://www.cisg.law.pace.edu/cisg/text/digest-art-50.html accessed 17/09/2025.

82 But price reduction can still apply under Art 79 since it is not ostensibly excluded. Parties can exercise any remedy applicable within the context of the exempted contract of sale except claiming damages.

83 Karl Riesenhuber, "Damages for Non-Performance and the Fault Principle" (2008) 4(2) *European Review of Contract Law* 119–153.

84 Patanjali (n 59) ch. 1. The author writes that:

"Under CISG arts 45(1)(b)23 and 61(1)(b)24 a party has a right to claim damages for any non-performance of the other party without the necessity of providing fault or a lack of good faith or the breach of an express promise on his part, as is required by some legal systems. However, under CISG art.79 the non-performing party is exempt from liability."

85 It can be argued that this remedy (damages) could be appropriate in a situation where, though the contract has been frustrated by an unforeseen impediment, a party had already benefited from the contract at the expense of the victim party. In such instances, specific performance may not be very apt; but paying damages for an expended cost can be very reasonable and fair. However, the provisions for restitution under Art 81 and 82 CISG are better suited to deal with the above scenario after either of the parties might have avoided the contract.

> contract, in the light of the facts and matters of which he then knew or ought to have known, as a possible consequence of the breach of contract.

The foundation of damages is predicated upon breach according to art 74. A party in a contract can suffer losses by the non-performance of the other party even though there is no breach by the other party, as can be seen in an exempted contract situation. It will, however, be worthwhile to state that the remedy of damages can still be applicable under art 79(4) of the CISG. This provision provides:

> The party who fails to perform must give notice to the other party of the impediment and its effect on his ability to perform. If the notice is not received by the other party within a reasonable time after the party who fails to perform knew or ought to have known of the impediment, he is liable for damages resulting from such non- receipt.

The implication of this provision is to introduce the use of damages in the compensation of a party who was not given reasonable notice of the impediment that causes failure to perform any obligations of the contract by the party who owes the obligation and fails to perform it.[86] However, the parameter for measuring damages coming by way of non-receipt of notice of exemption and damages for non-performance is not provided under the convention.

7.5 Remedies and *Force Majeure* under the UNIDROIT Principles

7.5.1 Background

The UNIDROIT Principles are by far more articulated and fashioned in dealing with the fallout of remedies in a frustrated contract situation. Art 7.1.7(3) (4)[87] of the UNIDROIT Principles is apt in defining the applications of remedies under the doctrine of frustration in the UNIDROIT Principles. Subsection (3) of art 7.1.7 details the remedies available against a party who fails to give notice of an impediment within a reasonable time and subsection (4) provides for the right to terminate the contract or to withhold performance or request interest on money due. The legal effect of sub-sections (3) and (4) is to remove the rigidity that is associated with the doctrine of *force majeure*. The aftermath is no longer absolute discharge and

86 Atamer (n 41) ch. 1, para 95, 1095; see also Ingeborg Schwenzer and others (n 43) ch. 1, para 45.75, 666.

87 art 7.1.7(3)(4)

> (3) The party who fails to perform must give notice to the other party of the impediment and its effect on its ability to perform. If the notice is not received by the other party within a reasonable time after the party who fails to perform knew or ought to have known of the impediment, it is liable for damages resulting from such non-receipt.
>
> (4) Nothing in this art prevents a party from exercising a right to terminate the contract or to withhold performance or request interest on money due.

parties can have recourse to a remedy that will best cushion off their losses and the application of restitution will bring about interest on money due.

For example, in the *Governments and International Organizations with Claims Arising out of Iraqi Invasion of Kuwait*,[88] it was held following art 7.1.7(4) that termination of a contract for *force majeure* does not release the aggrieved party from its obligation to return the monetary deposit made by the other party. The above case arose following the creation of the United Nations Compensation Commission (the "Commission") by the United Nations Security Council to deal with claims arising out of Iraq's invasion of Kuwait. Thus the Commission made a finding that monetary deposits should be returnable to the aggrieved parties who made them despite the event of frustration/*force majeure*. This established the fact that there can be remedies even in the face of a frustrated contract under the UNIDROIT Principles.

7.5.2 Damages and Force Majeure *under the UNIDROIT Principles*

Art 7.4.1 of the UNIDROIT Principles, which provides to the effect that:

> Any non-performance gives the aggrieved party a right to damages either exclusively or in conjunction with any other remedies except where the non-performance is excused under these Principles.

The general commentary on art 7.1.7, however, supported the provision of art 7.4.1 of the UNIDROIT Principles[89] and to the effect that damages are not available against a party whose liability has been excused under any provisions of the UNIDROIT Principles.[90] The commentary reads thus:

> The Article does not restrict the rights of the party who has not received performance to terminate if the non-performance is fundamental. What it does do, where it applies, is to excuse the non-performing party from liability in damages.[91]

88 Panel of the Commissioners, Panel F1 (1997) <http://www.unilex.info/case.cfm?id=639> accessed 19/09/2025.

89 Karl Riesenhuber, "Damages for Non-Performance and the Fault Principle" (2008) 4(2) *European Review of Contract Law* 119–153.

90 Zimmermann (n 74) ch. 5, 563, the author writes that:

> (The question of the recipient's liability to pay the value of the performance only arises if the deterioration or destruction occurs before avoidance or termination of the contract. If what has been performed deteriorates or is destroyed after avoidance or termination of the contract, the recipient of the performance is under a duty to return what he has received. Any non-performance of that duty gives the other party a right to claim damages according to Art 7.4.1 PICC, unless the non-performance is excused under Art 7.1.7. In other words: from the moment of termination the normal rules on non-performance apply).

91 http://www.unidroit.org/english/principles/contracts/principles2004/integralversionprinciples2004-e.pdf accessed 14/9/2025.

However, sub-section 7.1.7 (3), just like art 79(4) of the CISG, clearly approves the integration of the remedy of damages into *force majeure* contracts under the model law, especially when there is a failure to notify the victim party of the *force majeure* event.

The case of *Centro de Arbitraje de México (CAM)*[92] will be very useful in driving home the judicial interpretation of art 7.1.7(3). In this case, the defendant, a Mexican grower, and the claimant, a US distributor, entered into a one-year exclusive agreement according to which the defendant undertook to produce specific quantities of squash and cucumbers and to provide them to the claimant on an exclusive basis, while the claimant had to distribute the goods on the Californian market against a commission.

The contract, which was concluded in September 2004, contained an arbitration clause in which the parties expressly referred to the UNIDROIT Principles of International Commercial Contracts as the law governing the substance of any potential disputes. The claimant brought an action before the Centro de Arbitraje de México against the defendant, arguing that the defendant had breached the contract by not providing the goods referred to in the contract and by violating the exclusivity clause. The claimant asked for termination of the contract as well as damages for the harm suffered as a result of the defendant's failure to provide the goods. They also asked for payment of the penalty stipulated in the contract in case of violation of the exclusivity clause. The defendant objected that its failure to deliver the goods was due to the destruction of the crops by a series of extraordinarily heavy rainstorms and flooding caused by the meteorological phenomenon known as "El Niño." According to the defendant, these events amounted to a case of *force majeure* and/or hardship and therefore any liability on its part was excluded. The defendant argued further that the contract entered into with the claimant was null and void since it had not been formalised or registered before the Mexican authorities.

It was held concerning the defendant's argument that the rainstorms and flooding which destroyed the crops did not amount to a case of *force majeure*, that the meteorological events in question did not meet all the criteria set out in art 7.1.7 (1) of the UNIDROIT Principles defining *force majeure*. Indeed, while the rainstorms and flooding were undoubtedly beyond the defendant's control, their occurrence could not be considered unforeseeable by the defendant who in the course of their long-standing activity in the agricultural sector had already several times experienced similar events.[93]

Moreover, according to the arbitral tribunal, an additional reason for confirming the liability of the defendant for its non-performance was that the defendant failed

92 30.11.2006 <http://www.unilex.info/case.cfm?id=1149> accessed 15 September 2025.

93 Alison Mayfield, "Force of Nature" (2011) 161 *NLJ* 773; the author writes that :

> "The party that seeks to rely on the *force majeure* clause bears the burden of proving that it has been wholly or partially prevented or hindered from performing the contract as a result of the *force majeure* situation. In addition, the affected party may be required to take reasonable steps to avoid or mitigate the consequences of the *force majeure* situation."

to give notice to the claimant of the events in question and of their effect on its ability to perform as required by art 7.1.7(3) of the UNIDROIT Principles.[94]

It follows logically that even if liability for non-performance has been excused, the non-performing party owes the legal obligation to go ahead and notify the victim party of his non-performance, the impediment and its effect on his performance.[95] Failure to do so will not affect his general contractual non-liability if other factors that ground an action for *force majeure* are present and operative. Thus, the non-performing party will be liable not for damages resulting from the impediment but for not giving the notice of the impediment.[96]

7.5.3 Remedy of Cure and **Force Majeure** *under the UNIDROIT Principles*

The remedy of cure is central in international commercial law, more especially in the contract of sale of goods. It has been a rewarding commercial practice for parties to do everything possible in order to preserve a commercial contract. It is not always feasible to cure in a frustrated contract situation. This is because the situation entails a total breakdown of the will and means to perform the contract due to an impediment that is beyond the control of the parties, and which the parties could not reasonably be expected to have taken into account or to have avoided or overcome at the time of the conclusion of the contract. In this traditional frustration situation, the remedy of cure would be a toothless bulldog in applying to this situation.

On the other hand, there can be a situation where the remedy of cure can apply in a *force majeure* contract. Just like under the CISG, when an impediment is only temporary (Art7.1.7 (2)), the non-performing party can cure the impediment when

94 Supra.

95 Marel Katsivela, "Contracts: *Force Majeure* Concept or *Force Majeure* Clauses" (2007) 12(1) *Unif. L. Rev.* 101.

96 Damages in the above scenario will normally be measured or calculated from the time and event that happen at the period the former party fails to put the victim party on notice about the impediment that caused non-performance. Art 7.4.2 of the UNIDROIT has provided insight into what such calculable damages could comprise; it provides that:

(1) The aggrieved party is entitled to full compensation for harm sustained as a result of the non-performance. Such harm includes both any loss which it suffered and any gain of which it was deprived, taking into account any gain to the aggrieved party resulting from its avoidance of cost or harm.

(2) Such harm may be non-pecuniary and includes, for instance, physical suffering or emotional distress.

It therefore adds up to argue that damages in the face of frustration may normally accrue under Art 7.4.2(2) heading, and that since *force majeure* involves a non-fault, beyond control and unforeseeable happening, it seems right that the appropriate damages should be for non-pecuniary losses suffered as a result of failure to put the victim party on notice about the impediment.

it is practicable to do so and go on with fulfilling the obligations he owes in the contract.[97] Art 7.1.4[98] of the UNIDROIT provides for the remedy of cure.

From the art 7.1.4 provision, it can be espoused that whenever the remedy of cure is attainable under *force majeure* contract, the non-performing party owes the obligation to give notice of the manner and time of the cure to the victim party. It is also reasonable to add that whenever the remedy of cure is set into motion in a *force majeure* contract situation, all other remedies are put in abeyance until the time set out for the cure has elapsed.[99]

7.5.4 Specific Performance and **Force Majeure** *under the UNIDROIT Principles*

Just like under the CISG and the common law, this remedy is very difficult to attain under *force majeure* contracts. But there can be specific performance under art 7.1.7(2) when the impediment is of a temporary nature; a victim party can seek that the non-performing party should go ahead and perform obligations owed in the contract. A party can also withhold performance or request interest on money due. The UNIDROIT Principles provide separately for specific performance of monetary obligations and specific performance of non-monetary obligations. Art 7.2.1 provides that: "Where a party who is obliged to pay money does not do so, the other party may require payment."

The above provision is only possible if performance is not impossible, but where the contract has been affected by *force majeure*, it will be a farce to rely on this remedy.[100]

97 Perillo (n 35) ch. 1, writes thus: "Temporary impossibility gives rise to prospective inability to perform. Although the obligor may be excused by temporary impossibility, the prospective inability will normally give the promisee a power to suspend performance and demand assurance of due performance."

98 Art 7.1.4 UNIDROIT Principles provides thus:

(1) The non-performing party may, at its own expense, cure any non-performance, provided that
  (a) without undue delay, it gives notice indicating the proposed manner and timing of the cure;
  (b) cure is appropriate in the circumstances;
  (c) the aggrieved party has no legitimate interest in refusing cure; and
  (d) Cure is effected promptly.
(2) The right to cure is not precluded by notice of termination.
(3) Upon effective notice of cure, rights of the aggrieved party that are inconsistent with the non-performing party's performance are suspended until the time for cure has expired.
(4) The aggrieved party may withhold performance pending cure.
(5) Notwithstanding cure, the aggrieved party retains the right to claim damages for delay as well as for any harm caused or not prevented by the cure.

99 This will be in line with the commercial policy of affecting the possible performance of the contract rather than discharge of it.

100 UNIDROIT Principles 2010, (The commentary on this Art by the UNIDROIT throws light on the application and interpretation of this art thus:

Art 7.2.2[101] on the other hand, provides for the non-monetary specific performance. The provision re-echoes the fundamental position that specific performance can only be achievable when it is not impossible in law or fact. It can be concluded, therefore, that the doctrine of *force majeure* does not foreclose justifiable remedies from applying to mitigate the impediment caused in the circumstances. The doctrine of termination/avoidance, which has been given pride of place in the earlier chapter, can also apply if the impediment that causes non-performance is of fundamental degree.[102]

7.6 Frustration and Remedies under Common Law/ Sale of Goods Act of 1979

7.6.1 Background

Under common law, the legal consequences of frustration are not a function of what the parties think or make of their situation. The common law has maintained the approach of either denying the possibility of relief or restricting the ambit of relief as far as possible.[103] It is now accepted under common law not to accede that a contract has been frustrated lightly.[104]

In the case of *Jan Gryf-Lowczowski v Hinchinbrook Healthcare NHS Trust*,[105] it was held that the Trust was disentitled from relying on the doctrine of frustration of contract of employment with the claimant when the frustrating event was as a result

---

This art reflects the generally accepted principle that payment of money which is due under a contractual obligation can always be demanded and, if the demand is not met, enforced by legal action before a court. The term "requires" is used in this art to cover both the demand addressed to the other party and the enforcement, whenever necessary, of such a demand by a court.

101 Art 7.2.2 provides that:

Where a party who owes an obligation other than one to pay money does not perform, the other party may require performance, unless

(a) performance is impossible in law or in fact;
(b) performance or, where relevant, enforcement is unreasonably burdensome or expensive;
(c) the party entitled to performance may reasonably obtain performance from another source;
(d) performance is of an exclusively personal character; or
(e) The party entitled to performance does not require performance within a reasonable time after it has, or ought to have, become aware of the non-performance.

102 Furthermore, the remedies can be in the form of withholding performance or request interest on money due, the right to require repair, replacement, or other cure of defective performance. When a contract is frustrated, remedies cease to be a matter of course, but are subject to the practical and justiciable exigencies of each particular case with its peculiar circumstances.

103 Audrey Diamond in Ewan McKendrick (ed.), *Force Majeure & Frustration* (Lloyd's of London Press Ltd, 1991) 262.

104 *DVB Bank SE v Shere Shipping Company Limited and others* [2013] EWHC 2321;

Also in *Melli Bank plc v Holbud Limited* [2013] EWHC 1506. In this case, the court rejected an argument that a contract was frustrated because its performance had become illegal. The reason was that the defendant's failure to use the contract was not related to the imposition of sanctions.

105 [2005] EWHC 2407.

of their fault. It has been held that though frustration cannot be implied lightly, it can have an end point which will make the opinion of the parties neither totally determinative nor irrelevant.[106]

Frustration operates spontaneously and discharges the contract,[107] it can be invoked by either of the parties to the contract[108] and it is not based on breach or default. Under the general common law, frustration according to Treitel discharges the parties only from duties of future performance. In other words, rights that have been invested and accrued before the frustrating event will remain enforceable, but those which would have been accrued if not for the frustrating event will not become due and enforceable.[109] However, this common law rule has been ameliorated by the Frustrated Contract Act of 1943.

There are some remedies that will apply under the common law and the Sale of Goods Act of 1979. Damages are very important in the common law jurisdictions and will apply in certain cases where other remedies could not, but it could hardly apply under a frustrated contract due to the fact that the concept of damages is based on fault whereas the doctrine of frustration is based on fortuitous non-blameworthy happening.[110] Thus, the CISG, the UNIDROIT Principles and English law are in tandem about treating the concept of damages with suspicion when it concerns a frustrated contract.

Money had and received under a frustrated contract can be specifically ordered to be paid back or any other restitution remedy can be specifically ordered by the court, but on the other hand, the performance of the contract cannot be ordered; discharge by frustration does not depend on the choice or election of the parties or court because it is automatic.[111] Then, there is the Frustrated Contract Act of 1943 which was enacted in order to streamline the reliefs available to parties in a frustrated contract when the contract has not been frustrated by the perishing of the goods and when the contract does not fall under Section 7 of the Sale of Goods Act of 1979.[112]

106 The Wenjiang (No.2) [1983] 1 Lloyd's Rep.

107 Stephen Hackett and Clare Arthurs, "A Frustrating Experience" (2011) 161 *NLJ* 95; Ioanna Magklasi and Eleni Magklasi, "No Oral Modification Clauses to the Test: How Relevant are they in the COVID-19 Shock and beyond?" (2020) 12 *EJCCL* 56.

108 Trietel (n 46) ch. 1, para 15–005 549 "Frustration is different from recession because recession emanates on the election of the victim party."

109 Peel (n 72) ch. 1, 909.

110 In Minnevitch v. Cafe De Paris (Londres) Ltd. [1936] 1 All ER 884; it was held that a claim for damages succeeded in a case of temporarily excused non-performance and not a proper frustration scenario. This case, however, does not suggest that the court has the power to adapt or modify the contract or award damages.

111 Denny Molt & Dickson v James B Fraser [1944] A.C 265 at 274.

112 Under Section 7 of the Sale of Goods Act 1979, both parties are discharged from contractual obligation where the price, or part thereof, has been paid – it can be recovered on a total failure of consideration. Consequently, on a total failure of consideration, the seller cannot deduct anything for expenses incurred before the frustrating event occurred.

Also payments made under a contract under Section 7 cannot be recovered if there is only a partial failure of consideration. Finally, if the price has not been paid but the seller has delivered

7.6.2 Application of Frustrated Contract Act of 1943

The premises upon which the Frustrated Contract Act was made necessary can be traced in a cocktail of common law cases with uncomfortable outcomes. Cases of *Appleby v Myers* and *Chandler v Webster* applied the principle that rights accrued or which failed to accrue before the supervening impediment should either be enforceable or unenforceable as the case may be. In *Appleby v Myers*[113] plaintiff undertook to erect machinery upon the defendant's premises, the work to be paid for upon completion. When the work was almost completed both the premises and the machinery already erected were destroyed by fire. It was decided that the contract was frustrated; however, the plaintiff could recover nothing for the work done since the obligation to pay didn't arise until completion. Also, in *Chandler v Webster*[114] the above common law remedial rule was applied to make the hirer (Chandler) pay the remaining £41, 15s which had accrued and was due before the illness of the King frustrated the procession view-room contract. Chandler was also barred from getting back his initial deposit payment of £100 from Webster.

These two cases follow the guideline laid down in the principle that the loss should lie where it has fallen due. However, these two cases are no longer the face of the remedial application of the consequences of frustration under the common law and the sale of goods. *The Fibrosa case*[115] brought a new lease of life and also its own controversy to the application of frustration remedies. In this case, it was held that a Polish company could recover back an advance contract payment sum of £1000, which it paid to the English company before the German occupation of Gdynia frustrated the contract. The House of Lords based their action on the total failure of consideration to further fulfil the contract, which became impossible to be performed.

The fallout of the *Fibrosa* case, along with the oppressive decision in the case of *Whincup v Hughes*,[116] where a watchmaker died after performing one year of his contractual obligations. None of the £25 paid could be recovered, despite just a small portion of the contractual obligations being fulfilled, were the stimulating factors that heralded the enactment of the Law Reform (Frustrated Contracts) Act 1943. Recent case law illustrates that while the Act exists to remedy these injustices arising from frustration, modern courts apply a rigorous standard before allowing parties to access the Act's relief. In *Canary Wharf (BP4) T1 Ltd. v European Medicines Agency*,[117] the European Medicines Agency (EMA) sought to escape a 25-year lease (worth approx. £500 million) for its headquarters in London. The EMA argued that Brexit constituted a frustrating event that rendered the lease

---

some goods, he cannot sue for the price because of the common law rule of partial failure of obligation.

113 [1867] LR 2 CP 651.

114 [1904] 1 KB 493.

115 [1942] 2 All ER 122.

116 [1871] LR 6 CP 78.

117 [2019] EWHC 335 (Ch).

illegal or impossible to perform, as the agency was legally required to be headquartered in an EU member state. The High Court held that the lease was not frustrated. Because the court found that the contract remained valid, the remedial provisions of the Frustrated Contracts Act 1943 (which would have allowed the court to apportion losses) were not triggered. The court emphasised that frustration is not a tool to escape a bad bargain or political shifts, even if they are momentous. The EMA remained liable for the rent, preventing the "unjust enrichment" of the tenant at the expense of the landlord, but via strict contract enforcement rather than statutory relief. Generally, the court will not apply this Act to a contract forbidden by legislation.[118]

The Law Reform (Frustrated Contracts) Act 1943 is an Act of the Parliament of the United Kingdom; it applies only where the contract is governed by English law.[119] It is a remedial provision of positive law which establishes the rights and liabilities of parties involved in frustrated contracts.[120] It amended previous common law rules on the complete or partial return of pre-payments, where a contract is deemed to be frustrated, as well as introducing a concept that valuable benefits may also be returned.[121]

However, it is a restricted piece of legislation,[122] which falls short of covering situations where specific goods have perished. This makes the statute look non-inclusive and restricted when faced with the kind of frustration articulated under Section 7 of the Sale of Goods Act 1979 and other forms of contract like charter-party, except a time charterparty or a charterparty by way of demise or contract for the carriage of goods by sea and insurance contract. The parties to a contract can also choose to oust the jurisdiction of the Act and thus render it inapplicable.[123]

118 Nicholas J. McBride, "Restitution for Services Performed Under an Illegal Contract" (1998) 57 *The Cambridge Law Journal* 449–451.

119 James Fawcett and others, *International Sale of Goods in the Conflict of Laws* (Oxford University Press, 2005) para 19.43, 1163.

120 Goff J. held in *BP v Hunt* [1979] 1 W.L.R. 783 at 799 that the aim of the Act is to " prevent the unjust enrichment of either party to the contract at each other's expense."

121 Andrew Burrows, "The Relationship between Common Law and Statute in the Law of Obligations" (2012) 128 *L.Q.R.* 232–259. He writes thus:

"The scope of the Act--and hence the area in which the common law has been replaced--is governed by s.2(5) of the Act which lays down that the Act does not apply, for example, to contracts for the carriage of goods by sea or contracts of insurance. The common law on restitution of an unjust enrichment continues to apply to the frustration of those types of contract."

122 Ewan McKendrick and Matthew Parker, "Drafting *Force Majeure* Clauses: Some Practical Considerations" (2000) 11(4) *ICCLR* 132–138.

123 Stephen Hackett and Clare Arthurs, "A Frustrating Experience" (2011) 161 *NLJ* 95, the writers argue that: (the Law Reform (Frustrated Contracts) Act 1943 applies to many commercial contracts, unless it has been expressly excluded or alternative provisions have been agreed. By contracting out of the Act, a party may protect its position in respect of moneys and expenses paid or due before the frustrating event occurred, as well as ruling out a claim for a "just sum" where a valuable benefit has been conferred).

While it delimits the jurisdiction of the Act,[124] Section 2(5) provides for the limitation in the application of Section 7 of the sales of Goods Act; however, it has been argued that it is hard to see why the sale of specific goods should be distinguished from sales of unascertained goods, or why the result should differ according to the nature of the frustrating event.[125]

Section 1 of the above Act provides for the adjustment of the rights and liabilities of the parties to a frustrated contract.[126] The provision is very instructive in

124 Section 2(5) 1943 Act provides thus:

This Act shall not apply –

(a) to any charterparty, except a time charterparty or a charterparty by way of demise, or to any contract (other than a charterparty) for the carriage of goods by sea; or
(b) to any contract of insurance, save as is provided by subsection (5) of the foregoing section; or
(c) to any contract to which [section 7 of the Sale of Goods Act 1979] (which avoids contracts for the sale of specific goods which perish before the risk has passed to the buyer) applies, or to any other contract for the sale, or for the sale and delivery, of specific goods, where the contract is frustrated by reason of the fact that the goods have perished.

125 P. S. Atiyah (n 75) 357.

126 Section 1 of the 1943 Act provides thus:

1(1) Where a contract governed by English law has become impossible of performance or been otherwise frustrated, and the parties thereto have for that reason been discharged from the further performance of the contract, the following provisions of this section shall, subject to the provisions of section two of this Act, have effect in relation thereto.
(2) All sums paid or payable to any party in pursuance of the contract before the time when the parties were so discharged (in this Act referred to as "the time of discharge") shall, in the case of sums so paid, be recoverable from him as money received by him for the use of the party by whom the sums were paid, and, in the case of sums so payable, cease to be so payable:

Provided that, if the party to whom the sums were so paid or payable incurred expenses before the time of discharge in, or for the purpose of, the performance of the contract, the court may, if it considers it just to do so having regard to all the circumstances of the case, allow him to retain or, as the case may be, recover the whole or any part of the sums so paid or payable, not being an amount in excess of the expenses so incurred.

(3) Where any party to the contract has, by reason of anything done by any other party thereto in, or for the purpose of, the performance of the contract, obtained a valuable benefit (other than a payment of money to which the last foregoing subsection applies) before the time of discharge, there shall be recoverable from him by the said other party such sum (if any), not exceeding the value of the said benefit to the party obtaining it, as the court considers just, having regard to all the circumstances of the case and, in particular,—
    (a) the amount of any expenses incurred before the time of discharge by the benefited party in, or for the purpose of, the performance of the contract, including any sums paid or payable by him to any other party in pursuance of the contract and retained or recoverable by that party under the last foregoing subsection, and
    (b) The effect, in relation to the said benefit of the circumstances giving rise to the frustration of the contract.
(4) In estimating, for the purposes of the foregoing provisions of this section, the amount of any expenses incurred by any party to the contract, the court may, without prejudice to the generality of the said provisions, include such sum as appears to be reasonable in respect of overhead expenses and in respect of any work or services performed personally by the said party.

lending a helping hand to the common law rule of remedy in the face of a frustrated contract. Section 1(2) has overturned the common law stance that there is no remedial recovery of payments made under a contract where the failure of consideration has been partial. Section 1(2) is being complemented by Section 2(4) of the Act.[127] The implication of this Section 2(4) is to sever the executed from the frustrated part of the contract, and then the partial failure of consideration in respect of the whole contract would be turned to a total failure of consideration in respect of the frustrated part of the contract. This is solely for the purposes of enabling the payer to recover his payment.[128]

It is also one of the major contributions of the Act to allow a party whom the sums were paid or payable, to keep part or the entire sum if they can show that they have incurred reasonable expenses in furtherance of the performance of the contract before the contract became frustrated. This succour was provided in the second limb of Section 1(2) of the Act. But there is also a proviso that what the party will recover or retain will not be in excess of the expenses incurred. Section 1(2) abolishes the common law rule limiting the right of recovery to cases of total failure of consideration.

The effect of Section 1(2) is to rescue the payer from a possible oppressive bargain because the prepayment is recoverable irrespective of the consideration which they would have received had the contract been performed.[129] It does not apply in a case where a customer merely deposited money with a bank. It only applies to sums paid or payable in pursuance of the contract,[130] the sum must have been paid before the time of discharge and in some cases the payee may be entitled to set off

---

(5) In considering whether any sum ought to be recovered or retained under the foregoing provisions of this section by any party to the contract, the court shall not take into account any sums which have, by reason of the circumstances giving rise to the frustration of the contract, become payable to that party under any contract of insurance unless there was an obligation to insure imposed by an express term of the frustrated contract or by or under any enactment.

(6) Where any person has assumed obligations under the contract in consideration of the conferring of a benefit by any other party to the contract upon any other person, whether a party to the contract or not, the court may, if in all the circumstances of the case it considers it just to do so, treat for the purposes of subsection (3) of this section any benefit so conferred as a benefit obtained by the person who has assumed the obligations as aforesaid.

127 Section 2(4) 1943 Act provides thus:
Where it appears to the court that a part of any contract to which this Act applies can properly be severed from the remainder of the contract, being a part wholly performed before the time of discharge, or so performed except for the payment in respect of that part of the contract of sums which are or can be ascertained under the contract, the court shall treat that part of the contract as if it were a separate contract and had not been frustrated and shall treat the foregoing section of this Act as only applicable to the remainder of that contract.

128 Atiya (n 75) ch. 2.

129 McKendrick (n 71) ch. 2, 229.

130 Libyan Arab Foreign Bank v Banker's Trust Co [1989] O.B. 728, 772.

against a claim, by the payer's amount of any expenses incurred, before the time of discharge in furtherance of performance of the contract.[131]

Section 1(3) enables a party to recover the benefit other than payment of money his performance of any part of the contract conferred on the other party. This section does not define "benefit" unlike its kindred improved legislation of British Columbia District of Canada where Section 5(1) defines benefit.[132] Benefit according to the case of *BP v Hunt*[133] can either be the end-point of the services or, in some cases, the services themselves; Section 1(3) is chiefly concerned with non-monetary benefit. This section has been described as the restitutionary right for benefits rendered. In *BP Exploration Co (Libya) Ltd. v Hunt (No 2)*[134] the Judge, while applying Section 1(3), held that a just sum which will prevent the unjust enrichment of the defendant at the claimant's expense should be awarded to BP for the benefit their pre-performance of the contract gave to Mr Hunt. Thus, under Section 1(3), a party who has failed to perform an obligation other than one to pay money can be liable for the consequences of his non-performance of that obligation and they will be unable to offset any liability in respect of the non-performance as Section 1(3) only deals with benefit obtained before the time of discharge.[135]

One of the major shortcomings of Section 1(3) is that the determination of "just sum" is left entirely to the discretion of the court, and in the absence of any judicial precedent, this can be a recipe for confusion. But fortunately, in accordance with Section 2(3)[136] parties can contract out of this Act or modify the provisions of this Act according to their agreed terms. In addition, there will be no restitution for services performed under an illegal contract. Also, it has been held that breaches

131 This principle of law is predicated upon the defence of change of position where it will be inequitable to require a person whose position has changed to make restitution in full. See *Likin Gorman v Karonale Ltd.* [1991] 2 A.C. 548.

Also pre-contract expenditure, except those (expenditure) incurred in the reasonable belief that a contract will be concluded, according to Ewan Mckendrick, is unlikely to be included as an expense under Section 1(2) because at the time of the expenditure, there was no contract for the expenses to be incurred in the performance of the contract.

132 Frustrated Contract Act [RSBC 1996] Chapter 166:

Section 5(1) "In this section, 'benefit' means something done in the fulfillment of contractual obligations, whether or not the person for whose benefit it was done received the benefit."

133 [1983] 2 A.C 352.

134 Supra

135 McKendrick (n 71) ch. 2, 239.

136 Section 2(3) of the Law Reform (Frustrated Contracts) Act 1943 provides thus:

Where any contract to which this Act applies contains any provision which, upon the true construction of the contract, is intended to have effect in the event of circumstances arising which operate, or would but for the said provision operate, to frustrate the contract, or is intended to have effect whether such circumstances arise or not, the court shall give effect to the said provision and shall only give effect to the foregoing section of this Act to such extent, if any, as appears to the court to be consistent with the said provision.

prior to discharge remain actionable, and services performed, benefits conferred and payments made after the frustrating event are outside the scope of the Act.[137]

7.7 Conclusion

This chapter captured the relevance of remedies in the application of exemption/frustration/*force majeure*. It commenced with the examination of art 80 of the CISG, art 7.1.2 of the UNIDROIT Principles, other relevant provisions and the good faith related doctrines of estoppel and contributory negligence under English law. The purpose of the in-depth analysis offered in this chapter is to elucidate the remedial policy that a party cannot exploit a wrong/failure they contributed to. This is relevant under the impossibility doctrine, where fault vitiates the application of the doctrines (exemption frustration/*force majeure*).

Besides, some remedies, such as price reduction, which can apply under the CISG and the UNIDROIT Principles, cannot apply under the English law doctrine of frustration because of the latter's automatic discharge posture. Under the CISG, the buyer may request a price reduction even if the delivery of defective goods was not attributable to the seller under art 79.[138]

Even though common law, due to its strict rules, produced a litany of irreconcilable principles via some celebrated cases, as analysed above, these didn't help in bringing real justice to bear on what remedies are suitable after frustration occurred. Even the enactment of the Frustrated Contract Act of 1943 has not resolved the problems of balancing risk, frustration, and justice under a frustrated contract.[139]

It has been canvassed that the primary purpose of the 1943 Act is to provide a flexible machinery for the adjustment of loss,[140] still, the restrictive sphere of the applications of the Act and the needless isolation brought by the distinctions between specific goods/unascertained goods *vis-à-vis* frustration by perishing of goods/other kinds of frustration depict a pursuit of rhetoric and academics other than justice and fair play.[141] Moreover, Section 1(2) can be abused in certain situations involving only a bad bargain. It is not palatable that a payer can get a shield under Section 1(2) of the 1943 Act to escape the consequences of a bad bargain. This, without doubt, runs counter to the traditional common law principle that there is hardly any succour for a bad bargain made by a party to a contract. This is always the case if the circumstance is onerous and discharges the contract.

This book will recommend a more inclusive and simpler regime of remedies, in which all modes of frustration should be brought together without the need for

137 Bugden and Lamont-Black (n 83) ch. 2, para 25–032, 652. See also *Mohamed v. Alaga & Co.* [1998] 2 All E.R. 720.

138 Atamer (n 41) ch. 1, para 41, 1070.

139 Catharine Macmillan, "Covid-19 and the Problem of Frustrated Contracts" (2021) 32(1) *King's Law Journal* 60.

140 Haycroft Waksman, "Restitution and Frustration" (1984) *J.B.L.* 207, 225.

141 Sagi Peari and Zamir Golestani, "A Theory of Frustration and Its Effect" (2022) 43(2) *Liverpool Law Review* 263.

the technical distinctions that currently hold sway. Section 2(5), especially 2(5)(c), has been criticised. Goff and Jones[142] are of the opinion that the aforementioned provision should be repealed. In fact, the South Australia Frustrated Contract Act of 1988, which is a better and revamped version of the 1943 Act, applies to contracts that generally wouldn't be covered under the 1943 Act, as categorised under Section 7 of the Sale of Goods Act of 1979. The Draft Model Frustration Clause discussed in Chapter eight makes things easier by holding, in 5(c), that parties to a frustrated/exempted/*force majeure* contract may have recourse to any other remedies that are not inconsistent with the legal implications of the exempted contract under this heading. The purpose of this provision is to accommodate any justiciable remedy that will be appropriate in a given circumstance.

142 Lord Goff of Chieveley and Gareth Jones *The law of Restitution* (7th edn, Sweet & Maxwell Ltd, 2009) 450.

8 Conclusion

8.1 Difficulties Arising from the Lack of a Clear Definition

It can be recapped that this work is a fundamental step towards understanding the legal standpoints of the CISG, the UNIDROIT Principles, and English law regarding the discharge of contract by frustration, or an excuse from damages in cases of exemption and *force majeure*. These three legal instruments should be complementary and help ensure uniform interpretation of the doctrine of frustration/*force majeure*/exemption.[1]

Under traditional *force majeure* provision, exemption provision or under the doctrine of frustration, the legal basis of these doctrines remains to excuse liability for non-performance of an obligation in a contract when the performance has become impossible due to unforeseen inhibition.[2] This book is geared towards the restoration of impossibility as a significant factor in the consideration of exemption, *force majeure*, or frustration.[3] This book has also presented a common front by arguing in chapter one that, though there may be different historical and consequential angles within the doctrines of exemption, f*orce majeure*, and frustration as used under the CISG, the UNIDROIT Principles, and English law, they all work as impossibility doctrines. They derive their character as an exception to the rule of *pacta sunt servanda*.

It has been argued in Chapter One that exemption under art 79 of the CISG does not mean the same thing as *force majeure* or frustration; however, the term exemption, as used to denote the doctrine espoused under art 79, is more apt to be categorised under the *force majeure* and frustration umbrella. This is because

1 There can be instances where the UNIDROIT Principles can be deployed to interpret or supplement applicable national law; also, the UNIDROIT Principles may furthermore be used to interpret and supplement uniform international law like the CISG. See Maud Piers and Johan Erauw, "Application of the UNIDROIT Principles of International Commercial Contracts in Arbitration" (2012) 8(3) *J. Priv. Int. L.* 441–472.

2 Alison Mayfield, "Force of Nature, Procedure & Practice" (2011) 161 *NLJ* 773.

3 There can be performance impossibility, logical or natural impossibility, juristic impossibility and practical impossibility. All these forms of impossibilities lead to the inference that "performance by no means can be accomplished at the time and in the manner required." See Tom Southerington, "Impossibility of Performance and Other Excuses in International Trade" (2011) <http://www.cisg.law.pace.edu/cisg/biblio/southerington.html> accessed 9 September 2025.

DOI: 10.4324/9781003667841-8

other exempting doctrines, such as mistake, breach, misrepresentation, fraud, and duress, have the effect of exempting a party from performing an obligation under a contract.

Also, *a force majeure clause is different from an* exemption/frustration or *force majeure* under the UNIDROIT Principles. According to Bugden and Lamont-Black, a *force majeure* clause is a contractual term under which a party is entitled to be excused from performance of the whole or some part of their obligations under the contract.[4] This is further complicated by art 80 of the CISG, which serves the role of not exempting a party who contributed to the failure of any of the obligations in a contract from relying on the other party's failure to perform the contract.[5]

It has also been argued that generalisations about the relative scope of the doctrines of frustration, exemption, and *force majeure* cannot be easily substantiated; cases abound in which the doctrines lead to similar results.[6] In the case of *Smyth (Ross T.) & Co. (Liverpool) Ltd v W. N. Lindsay Ltd*,[7] it has been held that under the English law of frustration, a seller of goods is not excused by requisition if there was the slightest chance of his delivery before the requisition took effect. This is similar to the position under *force majeure*,[8] and very similar to the doctrine of exemption under art 79 CISG. The contribution to knowledge this book offers is by way of fashioning a draft model clause that can strike a balance among these legal instruments and improve them uniformly.

8.2 Background to the Draft Model Frustration Clause

The doctrine of frustration/exemption/*force majeure*, as mentioned earlier, is not absolute; it is subject to who owes the risk of performance of a contract, and this has been thoroughly discussed in Chapter Three of this book. This doctrine *(frustration/force majeure*/exemption) aligns with the doctrine of freedom of contract. Notwithstanding the CISG, the UNIDROIT Principles, or English law, the court

4 Bugden and Lamont-Black (n 83) ch.1 para 25–025, 646. It can be summarised that frustration and *force majeure* are used interchangeably in this book due to the fact that similar elements can ground an action for both, but they are different from the *force majeure* clause. While the *force majeure* clause connotes a provision in a contract that lists the possible fortuitous events or impediments that can excuse the performance of an obligation in a contract, frustration, on the other hand, implies the catch-all written or unwritten impediments or events whose occurrence can radically change the contract and render it impossible to perform. Thus, in accordance with the decision in the case of Peter Dixon and Sons Ltd v Henderson, Craig and Co Ltd [1919] 2.*K.B* 788 at 779, it was held that "*[f]orce majeure* clause can clearly apply even though the obstacle to performance which has arisen is not insurmountable."

5 Art 80 of the CISG is not only directly relevant in the interpretations of the outcome of what happens in a situation where a party is liable in the impediment that causes failure of obligation under art 79 of the CISG, it also provides its own independent rules of interpretation and application of contractual obligations.

6 Trietel (n 46) ch. 1, 434.

7 [1953] 1 WLR 1280.

8 Planiol and Ripert, *Traité pratique de droit civil français* (2nd edn) Vol vii, nr 838.

cannot shift the risk burden that a party willingly contracted to bear under a contract. This is why the provision of art 6 of the CISG which provides that "the parties may exclude the application of this Convention or, subject to art 12, derogate from or vary the effect of any of its provisions" is very important not only in the determination of the doctrine of frustration/exemption/*force majeure* under the CISG but also in the determination of other non-mandatory provisions of this Convention. Schlechtriem summarises the opinion of both the court and academic writers on the freedom of contract *vis-à-vis* the doctrine of frustration when he writes that:

> [T]he terms of the contract will often describe the extent to which the obligor is expected to prevent impediments to performance which lie outside his own area of control. Guarantees can increase the scope of his liability; disclaimers and limitation can diminish it.[9]

Against this background, the Draft Model Frustration Clause proposed in this book is not a mandatory rule; just like its predecessors, it can be contracted out of by the parties involved, and in accordance with their commercial exigencies.

Besides, it will be enlightening to advocate a change in the loose and pliable words employed by art 79 of the CISG and art 7.1.7 of the UNIDROIT Principles while defining exemption and *force majeure*.[10] Some phrases like "impediment beyond his control," "could not reasonably be expected to have taken the impediment into account," "to have avoided or overcome it or its consequences" do not decisively lay down the threshold or degree of the circumstances that can conclusively result in a situation of *force majeure* or exemption of the contract.[11] A detailed glossary or interpretation provisions that explain or provide examples of situations that can result in the phrases mentioned above will be welcomed under the CISG and the UNIDROIT Principles.

The importance of such a glossary will be to fulfil the spirit of the provision of art 7 of the CISG, which provides that "[i]n the interpretation of this Convention, regard is to be had to its international character and to the need to promote uniformity in its application and the observance of good faith in international trade." Thus, the Draft Model Frustration Clause proposed in this book will be more effective when accompanied by a well-thought-out glossary or interpretation section that at least gives a working definition of the concepts used in the provision. The use of detailed interpretation provisions will provide a unified view and interpretation of the provisions of both arts 79 and 7.1.7 of the CISG and the UNIDROIT Principles,

9 Uniform Sales Law – The UN Convention on Contracts for the International Sale of Goods (1986) <http://www.cisg.law.pace.edu/cisg/biblio/schlechtriem.html> accessed 13/12/2014. It has been argued that "ultimately, it is all a question of whether the risk assumed under the contract as compared to actual events rendered the performance radically different from that contracted for by the contract." See Bugden and Lamont-Black (n 83) ch. 1, para 25–037, 651.

10 Nicholas (n 261) ch. 3.

11 It will be important to note that "impediment beyond the control" as used under art 79 CISG is familiar with kindred provisions under French civil code *force majeure*, English common law frustration, and even the German concept of Geschäftsgrundlage. See Kroll et al para 20, p 1063.

respectively. The significant disadvantages of these present "phrases" are that they can elicit different interpretations, which will bear strong allegiance to the original national laws' interpretations of the impossibility doctrine.[12]

8.3 Draft Model Frustration Clause (DMFC)

The proposed Draft Model Frustration Clause (DMFC) intends to: entrench the impossibility perspective in the interpretation of frustration/exemption/*force majeure*, review the positions of self-induced frustration, avoidance/termination, exclude hardship from the Draft Model Frustration Clause, reaffirm the position of mistake *vis-à-vis exemption/frustration/force majeure* and re-balance the issue of remedies. DMFC provides thus:

(1) A party is exempted from damages and specific performance from failure to perform any of their obligations in a contract if they prove that the failure was due to an inhibition beyond their control at the time of the conclusion of the contract and that:[13]
   (a) [s]uch inhibition falls within events which they are reasonably not expected to foresee, avoid or overcome its consequences, thereby leaving the performance of the contract unconditionally impossible.
   (b) [w]hen there is any doubt about the party's reasonableness in foreseeing, avoiding and or overcoming an inhibition or its consequences, then the

12 Dennis Tallon argues that:

"The notion of 'impediment beyond his control' is not easy to explain, owing partly to the difference that exists for instance between the English and French versions. By using the expression indépendant de sa volonté (literally, independent of his will), the French text appears to adopt a more subjective approach. In a sense, it is contrary to the drafters' intention and the English version is more in keeping with the proposed objective. If the impediment is not extraneous to the activity of the defaulting party, i.e., if it is under his control, it produces no exempting effect" See Tallon, in Bianca-Bonell *Commentary on the International Sales Law* (Giuffrè: Milan, 1987) 572–595.

13 This provision is closely moulded to reflect the new trend of the law enacted under the CISG, UNIDROIT Principles, the PECL, the DCFR and the CESL (Common European Sales Law). It follows also from the traditional position under the *force majeure* and the doctrine of frustration that exclude damages under the circumstances of unforeseeable and uncontrollable inhibitive events. But unlike the doctrine of frustration under the common law and section 7 of the Sale of Goods Act 1979, future performance of the contract is not discharged under the Draft Model Frustration Clause (DMFC). It has been argued that if an excuse is available under art 79 of the CISG, it is deemed a breach and wouldn't stop the remedies normally available to a victim party except that the non-performing party is excluded from liability in damages. This is unlike the position of the common law and Uniform Commercial Code Section 2–615 where such excuse is not regarded as a breach and in the case of common law, the 1943 Act applies to apportion liabilities and reward. See Eldon Reiley, *International Sales Contracts: The UN Convention and Related Transnational Law* (Carolina Academic Press, 2008) 140.

doubt will be resolved against the party who owes the responsibility to perform an obligation in the contract.[14]

(c) [t]he inhibitions that can excuse performance under paragraph one above are as listed but not limited to those provided in Article … of this Convention/Principle/Act (Interpretation section).

(d) [a]n inhibition arising out of commercial hardship, bad bargain, inequality of bargaining power, expected act of government and uncommon but predictable financial disruption cannot be regarded as an inhibition under paragraph (1) above.[15]

(e) [i]nhibition that results in hardship which requires renegotiation and adaptation of the contract should not be adjudicated under this law.

(2) If the party's failure is due to the failure by a third person whom they have engaged to perform the whole or a part of the contract, that party is exempted from liability only if:

(a) They are exempt under the preceding paragraph; and

(b) The person whom they have so engaged would be so exempted if the provisions of that paragraph were applied to them.

(3) The exemption provided by this article has effect for the period during which the inhibition exists.[16]

(4) The party that fails to perform must give notice to the other party of the inhibition and its effect on its ability to perform. If the notice is not received by the other party within a reasonable time after the party who fails to perform knew

14 This provision is articulated from the legal assumption that the party who alleges must prove. Though this is not a criminal case that should be proved beyond reasonable doubt, the hallmark of exemption, *force majeure*/frustration is impossibility of performance. Whenever there is a doubt whether performance is possible or not, the non-performing party will be bound by the doctrine of *pacta sunt servanda*. Moreover, it has been held in the *Milling Equipment case,* Germany 2 February 2004 Appellate Court Zweibrücken <http://cisgw3.law.pace.edu/cases/040202g1.html> accessed 13/9/2025, confirmed that "the [Seller] bears the burden of proof for the impediment it is alleging; otherwise, he cannot invoke that the failure to perform his contractual obligations was due to an impediment for which relief can be accorded pursuant to Article 79 CISG."

15 The purpose of this provision is to keep apart the muddling up of the application of the doctrine of frustration/exemption/*force majeure* and the doctrine of hardship. This is the major shortfall of the CISG. Thus, this provision will not support the CISG Advisory opinion no 7 which canvasses the application of the doctrine of hardship under art 79 CISG. See CISG-AC Opinion No. 7, Exemption of Liability for Damages under art 79 of the CISG, Rapporteur: Professor Alejandro M. Garro, Columbia University School of Law, New York, N.Y., USA. Adopted by the CISG-AC at its 11th meeting, in Wuhan, People's Republic of China, on 12 October 2007.

16 This provision is very important because an inhibition may be impossible to overcome during a reasonable life span of a contract, but it mustn't be permanently necessary. Arts 79 and 7.1.7 of the CISG and the UNIDROIT Principles respectively provide for the situation of temporal exemption/*force majeure*; however, this is unknown under the common law and the Sale of Goods Act of 1979. It has been held by Matthew Parker and Ewan McKendrick that "There is lack of any relief at common law in the event of partial frustration or where an event requires the affected party to choose between performing one contract or another." See Parker and McKendrick (n 122) ch. 7.

or ought to have known of the inhibition, the party is liable for damages resulting from such non-receipt.

(5) Parties to the contract under this heading shall:

(a) [a]void the contract and make claims for restitution if it can be proved that the other party has benefited from the inhibition that causes non-performance and the claimant party suffers some material losses which it will be unconscionable to leave unrequited.[17]

(b) [p]ursuant to paragraph (1), parties shall refrain from pursuing a remedy in specific performance unless the inhibition to the performance of the contract is of a temporal nature as in paragraph (3) above and the party who owes the obligation fails to perform when the inhibition has abated and it is still possible to tender performance.[18]

(c) [h]ave recourse to any other remedies that are not inconsistent with the legal implications of exempted contract under this heading.

The major changes are evident in paragraphs one and five of this draft model provision. Paragraph one is drafted in such a way that the interpretation section should help guide the proper interpretations to be given to "inhibition" and other sundry phrases used in the provision to address the issues arising from inelegant use of loose words and phrases under the CISG and UNIDROIT Principles.[19] Art 74 of the Uniform Law of International Sales 1964 provided for "circumstances," a very loose term that can encompass various onerous (hardship) situations that disrupt the sale of goods. Art 79 of the CISG uses "impediment" in such a way that only objective circumstances that prevent performance will be excused, but the use of the word "inhibition" under the DMFC is to fine-tune the definitive and objective nature of an event that can be permitted to frustrate a contract or exempt a party from liability in damages.

17 A party who has performed his or her obligation in the contract without receiving his contracted returns due to an inhibition beyond the control and foresight of the other party will be entitled to treat the contract as a breach and avoid the contract. Equity will deem it that the victim party will be entitled to the restitution of whatever they have supplied or paid under the contract. John Honnold argued that "Without the right of avoidance, temporary impediment would be unmanageable." See John O. Honnold, *Uniform Law for International Sales under the 1980 United Nations Convention* (Kluwer Law International, 3rd edn, 1999) 472–495.

18 This provision strictly narrows the application of specific performance to a situation where a remedy other than damages is needed in special circumstances. An instance is the case of temporal frustration. See John Honnold, *Uniform Law for International Sales under the 1980 United Nations Convention*, Harry Flechtner (ed.) (Kluwer Law International, 4th edn, 2009) para 435.5, p 642.

19 Barry Nicholas, while analysing art 79 of the CISG, holds that the attempt in paragraph (1) to define the circumstances in which the exemption will apply has yielded a formula that is so vague that there are bound to be differences of interpretation in different jurisdictions, and the prime purpose of any uniform law will, in consequence, be defeated. See Barry Nicholas, in Galston & Smit, ed., *International Sales: The United Nations Convention on Contracts for the International Sale of Goods* (Matthew Bender, 1984) ch. 5, pages 5-1–5-24.

It must be an event that affords and passes the practical impossibility test. It should be added that the law should be given the benefit of reality; thus, if the expected purpose of a contract has been practically made impossible by an unforeseen and uncontrollable inhibitive event, then the provision of the DMFC can still apply despite the stringent impossibility undertone of section 1(a) of the DMFC. Some inhibitive events that may be provided for in the interpretation sections or glossary can range from provisions covering natural disasters such as hurricanes, floods, earthquakes, and weather disturbances sometimes referred to as "acts of God." Other events may include war, terrorism or credible threats of terrorism, civil disorder, labour strikes or disruptions that strike permanently at the root of the contract, fire, disease or medical epidemics or outbreaks that last for a duration, making the contract impossible to perform even after the outbreaks have ceased.

The interpretation section will be construed *ejusdem generis* (of the same kind); the test for whether the event constitutes inhibition is whether it has radically changed the performance of the contract and renders it impossible. Another issue that requires clarification under the three instruments examined in this book is the thresholds for parties' responsibility. It has been suggested under the Draft Model Frustration Clause 1(a) that the degree of reasonableness required in the phrases ("they are reasonably not expected to foresee, avoid or overcome its consequence") shall be high; any doubt will be resolved against the non-performing party.[20] The reason for raising this threshold of responsibility is to discourage a party that owes an obligation in a contract from easily being excused under the doctrine of frustration/exemption or *force majeure*.[21] The paragraph 1(b) provision will reasonably cure the loose interpretations that similar phrases have been subjected to under the CISG and the UNIDROIT Principles to maintain the high degree of good faith, ensuring that a contract cannot be discharged lightly.[22]

There is also a need to present a more consistent and proactive set of remedial provisions to effectively manage the fallout from exemption/*force majeure*, or frustration. Because of the difficulties arising from art 79(5) of the CISG in terms of vagueness in the determination of remedial applications, this book is of the opinion that there is a need for a complete overhaul of the provision. The issue of the application of the remedy of specific performance has been resolved under Draft Model Frustration Clause by excluding this remedy as of right and relegating it to

20 This does not mean beyond any iota of doubt, but requires a very high degree of certainty.

21 Traditionally, to invoke a defence of *force majeure*, the debtor must show that performance has been made impossible, and not merely onerous. In this respect, *force majeure* resembles English law frustration and art 79 exemption. See McKendrick (ed.) (n 67) ch. 1, 6; The model frustration clause will therefore take into special account physical and legal impossibility and will leave impracticability and onerousness at the realm of hardship.

22 The aim of paragraph 1 (b) is to exert the highest degree of good faith in ensuring that a contract cannot be discharged lightly.

only the situation where the inhibition that causes non-performance has abated, and performance is not impossible afterwards.[23]

In relation to the common law, the Draft Model Frustration Clause will be invaluable for codification or enactment of positive law in the area of frustration. The common law views on frustration need to be codified or enacted into positive law to curtail the constant paradigm-shift decisions that have been the bane of this doctrine under common law.[24] It is a well-established fact that what the English courts will have to say about the doctrine of frustration will ultimately depend on the facts of a particular case and on the sentiment or worldview of the presiding judge. This insecure stance regarding the application of the doctrine of frustration is not conducive to the continuity and progress of the law in this area. The Draft Model Frustration Clause will also be beneficial under the Sale of Goods Act 1979 provisions and interpretations of the doctrine of frustration, as well as in all contract and commercial law situations, without the need for the limitations provided under Section 7 of The Sale of Goods Act and the ever-changing perspectives being churned out by common law judges.

The reason for the above recommendation is that the statutory provision for the doctrine of frustration under Section 7 of the Sale of Goods Act 1979 is notoriously inadequate, and a law reform extending the scope of this provision will be needed. It will be expedient to observe that the Sale of Goods Act of 1979 is merely an amendment of its parent, the Sale of Goods Act of 1893, which was enacted during the era of legal technicalities. Lord Chalmers, in propagating the 1893 Act, was not attempting to codify the general principles of the law of contract, and Section 7 only reflects peculiar cases.[25] As a matter of fact, by the 1890s, the rule relating to the doctrine of frustration was still evolving, and Section 7 of the 1979 Act does not take care of varieties of contracts because "finite limits had to be drawn to sever rules peculiar to the contract of sale."[26] This is why the distinction made in the Act not applying to unascertained goods, or when the goods must not have been destroyed other than by perishing or when there is actual sale

23 This provision goes against the extreme views that specific performance cannot apply under a frustrated contract. For instance, Ingeborg Schwenzer and others held that "impossibility removes the claim for specific performance; the obligee cannot require the obligor to perform an act that is impossible." See Ingeborg Schwenzer and others (n 43) ch. 1, para 41.12, 536.

24 The doctrine of frustration has seen many transformations. This doctrine under English law automatically discharges the contract; this is in contrast with *force majeure* clauses, such clauses provide for the consequences of a *force majeure* event as agreed by the contracting parties. A frustration provision that will be wider than section 7 of the Sale of Goods Act will be welcomed. Another issue can be seen in the pre-1893 case of Howell v Coupland (1876) 1 Q.B.D. 258, which allowed partial frustration of unspecific goods. It has been suggested that this precedent was rejected during the codification because "Frustration is directed towards the contract as a whole and not to the particular obligation which has been affected by the unforeseen event" see Ewan McKendrick (n 67) ch. 1, 46). Thus, a consistent and positive codification of the legal implications of the doctrine of frustration, coupled with a succinct definition of the doctrine, will be welcomed.

25 McKendrick (n 71) ch. 2, 257.

26 Ibid., 258.

vis-à-vis an agreement to sell, needed to be revamped and amended. The doctrine of frustration/exemption/*force majeure* should be able to apply irrespective of the fact that the goods are ascertained or unascertained,[27] and where it can be proved that the goods have been destroyed without the fault of the parties, then the question of whether the destruction is by the act of perishing of the goods or not will be an exercise in technicality, provided the risk of performance has not been passed to the buyer or the seller does not own the risk.[28] However, the position of the 1979 Act regarding frustration of specific goods and unascertained goods is not entirely without substance. It can be added that some forms of contract, like C.I.F. contracts, are, by their nature, not easily frustrated; for instance, a C.I.F. contract for the sale of unascertained generic goods cannot be frustrated even if the goods are destroyed before shipment.[29]

8.4 Reviewing Self-Induced Frustration and Avoidance/ Termination

It has also been examined in this book that self-induced frustration cannot suffice to crystallise a cause of action under the doctrine of frustration/exemption/*force majeure*, which is why, to eliminate the ambiguity, the Draft Model Frustration Clause retains the basic unforeseeability and non-fault elements of the doctrine of frustration/exemption/*force majeure*. Consequently, despite the differences in the application of the doctrine of frustration under the CISG, the UNIDROIT Principles and English law, it seems there is a consensus that a party will not be allowed to be excused from their liabilities under the doctrine of frustration if their act or omission can be blamed for the impediment which makes performance of the contract impossible. This rule, as harped on earlier in this book, is deeply rooted in the doctrine of good faith and fair play. A line has also been drawn between the doctrine of frustration/exemption/*force majeure* and other similar doctrines of discharge discussed in this book. While the doctrine of frustration can occur without fault of the parties, it is a self-evident truth that the doctrine of avoidance or termination of a contract is the direct opposite.[30]

27 Crabtree and others (n 60) ch. 3; the authors write that " However, even in contracts for the sale of unascertained goods, a frustrating event may occur, such as the passing of legislation dealing with the goods in question; that is, a prohibition on export from a country which is the only source of the goods or an outbreak of war."

28 Once the risk has passed, the party who owes the risk will not be shielded under the doctrine of frustration/exemption/*force majeure*.

29 AG Guest, *Benjamin's Sale of Good* (n 97) ch. 1, para 19–25, 1557; it is instructive to note that even a C.I.F contract may be frustrated if it provides for a method of performance which becomes impossible, or where the contemplated method of performance is impossible.

30 Alison E. Williams "Forecasting the Potential Impact of the Vienna Sales Convention on International Sales Law in the United Kingdom" Pace Review of the Convention on Contracts for the International Sale of Goods (CISG), Kluwer Law International (2000–2001) 9–57; the author writes that:

"Only for a breach of serious nature does the right to avoid the contract or the right to demand substitute goods in respect of the non-conformity of the goods arise, unless art 49(1)(b) applies.

Under the CISG, a contract may be avoided for a fundamental breach by any party.[31] This fundamental breach will render the further performance of the contract fruitless and radically disagreeable. Nevertheless, this book, under the Draft Model Frustration Clause paragraph (1)(a), argues that the doctrine of frustration/exemption/*force majeure* will not need a fundamental breach to be invoked, but a fundamental occurrence of inhibition that is unconnected with the blame of the parties.

Likewise, under the UNIDROIT Principles, a contract can only be avoided by fundamental non-performance by either party. This requirement is similar to the provisions of the CISG and even to the now defunct common-law doctrine of fundamental breach of contract. This book reviews the working relationship between the doctrine of frustration/exemption/*force majeure* and avoidance/termination. While avoidance (termination) of the contract is one of the remedies available to parties under a frustrated contract, the reverse is not the case under the doctrine of contract termination.[32] All the more, restitution, which is a legal consequence of avoidance/termination, helps in making exemption/*force majeure*/frustration manageable when any of the parties to such a contract exercises that right (restitution).

8.5 Excluding Hardship from the Draft Model Frustration Clause

Hardship is ostensibly excluded from the Draft Model Frustration Clause, even though this book has shown the strong ties between the doctrines of hardship and frustration/exemption/*force majeure*. While it is debatable whether or not hardship should be read along with the provision of art 79 of the CISG, the same cannot be said about the UNIDROIT Principles, which categorically put these two doctrines in their proper partitions.[33] It has been agreed that since the CISG does not

---

Therefore, under the CISG, every term becomes an innominate term under which breach of an obligation may only result in the right to avoid the contract if the breach is fundamental."

31 Bruno Zeller writes that "As has been observed it is important to note that, in contrast to its treatment in Common Law states, fundamental breach under the CISG is not restricted to the interpretation of exception clauses. It goes to the heart of the contract and, therefore, a fundamental breach is the essential precondition for avoiding a contract. In other words, it decides whether a contract lives or dies." See Bruno Zeller, "The Remedy of Fundamental Breach and the United Nations Convention on the International Sale of Goods (CISG) – A Principle Lacking Certainty?" (2/2007) 11 *Vindobona Journal of International Commercial Law & Arbitration* 219–236.

32 It will be important to point out that avoidance under the CISG, UNIDROIT principles and English law are now exactly the same. Moreover, it has been held that one of the striking differences between avoidance under the CISG and English law is the introduction of "A completely new concept to common law jurisdictions is the buyer's right to fix an additional period for performance, the Nachfrist notice. There is no real common law counterpart to this legal phenomenon." See Tobias Plate, "The Buyer's Remedy of Avoidance under the CISG: Acceptable from a Common Law Perspective?" (2002) 6 *Vindobona Journal of International Commercial Law and Arbitration* 57–82.

33 In a situation under the UNIDROIT Principles where both the requirements of *force majeure* and hardship are satisfied, the party struck by the impediment can choose which action to pursue. The choice will likely depend on the party's wish to either be excused of their non-performance (art 7.1.7) or to renegotiate the terms and thereby opting for continuation of the contract (art 6.2.3). See

apparently provide for the doctrine of hardship, this omission has been viewed as a green light that an unexpected economic turn, which radically affects the intentions of the parties in a contract, should be interpreted to have fallen within the range of art 79 of the CISG. However, other views hold that since the CISG, after the long debates before its enactment, decided to consciously omit the doctrine of hardship as part of its provisions, then this gap can be filled by importing from the provision of hardship under the UNIDROIT Principles and shouldn't be muddled up under art 79 of the CISG.[34]

The major difference between the doctrine of hardship and the doctrine of frustration/exemption/*force majeure* is that there is hardship when the occurrence of events fundamentally alters the equilibrium of the contract, either because the cost of a party's performance has increased or because the value of the performance a party receives has diminished. This event can give rise to renegotiation and adaptation of the contract.[35] On the other hand, since the obligor generally guarantees his financial ability to procure and produce the promised goods, increased procurement and production costs do not constitute an exempt impediment. Admittedly, many writers have thrown their support behind the interpretation of the doctrine of hardship under art 79 of the CISG. Ingeborg Schwenzer and Pascal Hachem are of the view that:

> CISG itself, however, is even better suited for a practical solution of the problem of change of circumstances. Although taken at face value, art 79 CISG deals primarily with exemption in cases of *force majeure*, a change of circumstances can also amount to an impediment in the sense of this provision[.][36]

Indeed, the impossibility and uncertainty envisaged under the doctrine of exemption/*force majeure* and/or frustration have been proven not to be absolute impossibilities; a *force majeure* clause can help determine which events parties could regard as an impediment under hardship or under the impossibility doctrines.[37] A contract, which, though it can still be hypothetically performed, will surely be in sharp contrast to the aims and objectives of the parties to the contract, cannot be

Mads Bryde Andersen & Joseph Lookofsky, Lærebog i Obligationsret I, vol. 3. Udgave (2010) 195; cited by Rolf Kofod, "Hardship in International Sales CISG and the UNIDROIT Principles" Book, University of Copenhagen-Faculty of Law (2011).

34 Anukarshan Chandrasenan, "UNIDROIT Principles to Interpret and Supplement the CISG: An Analysis of the Gap-filling Role of the UNIDROIT Principles" (2007) 11 *Vindobona Journal of International Commercial Law and Arbitration* 65–80.

35 Scott D. Slater, "Overcome by Hardship: The Inapplicability of the UNIDROIT Principles' Hardship Provisions to CISG" (Summer 1998) 12 *Florida Journal of International Law* 231–262.

36 Ingeborg Schwenzer and Pascal Hachem, "The CISG - Successes and Pitfalls" (Spring2009) 57 *American Journal of Comparative Law* 457–478.

37 Uncertainty is therefore inherent in the doctrine of frustration. This uncertainty can, however, be eliminated to a large extent by the incorporation into a contract of a suitably drafted *force majeure* clause; the clause can specify its sphere of operations, and the role of the court will simply be to interpret the clause.

held to be still the original contract entered into by the parties. Under the eyes of the law, it can be regarded as something different and can be discharged by way of frustration of purpose.[38] This analysis provides the basis for the application of the doctrine of frustration in a seemingly hardship situation under the CISG and the English common law. The high point of the Draft Model Frustration Clause is that it closes the door on the application of hardship and exacts the strictest measures of impossibility before frustration/exemption/*force majeure* can apply. The combined effects of paragraph 1(b)(c)(d) are to exclude the application of hardship in frustrated/exempted/*force majeure* contract situations.

In fact, paragraph 1(a) provides that the contract must be unconditionally impossible of performance before frustration can apply; paragraph 1(b) provides for a higher degree of responsibility to perform the contract before any inhibition can excuse performance; and paragraph 1(d) specifically excludes the application of commercial hardship as an inhibition under a frustrated contract. The Draft Model Frustration Clause may not go down well, given that many jurisdictions, including common law and CISG, are prepared, in deserving circumstances, to treat a purely hardship situation as similar to frustration. Thus, the Draft Model Frustration Clause will only operate in a situation in which there is a separate provision for a hardship scenario.[39] The principles of hardship and frustration are not the same. While the legal implications of hardship are to strike a balance in apportioning commercial losses, the legal consequences of frustration are to excuse liability in damages and discourage the tender of impossible performance. It will therefore be discerning to separate these two doctrines and keep them apart.[40]

8.6 Reaffirming the Position of Mistake vis-à-vis Exemption / Frustration / *Force Majeure*

The Draft Model Frustration Clause does not address the doctrine of mistake, as it is not the primary focus of this book; however, as expected, the book also makes comparisons between the doctrine of frustration/exemption/*force majeure* and the doctrine of mistake. These two doctrines are not overtly similar because the mistake can only apply if the facts that crystallised the mistaken assumption happened before the conclusion of the contract. But the legal outcome of mistake and

38 As mentioned in chapter five, frustration of purpose is referred to as "impracticability" under the Uniform Commercial Code of the USA.

39 This is because many jurisdictions still have not accepted this legal doctrine as an appropriate contractual remedy. It has been held that "in the context of impediments, it can be important that parties provide solutions in their contract. The statement is arguably truer for situations of hardship given the relatively fewer jurisdictions which recognize it as part of the default system." See Ingeborg Schwenzer and other (n 43) ch. 1, para 45.79, 666.

40 Even under the doctrine of frustration of purpose and impracticability, which are the nearest things to hardship under English law, the mere fact that the transaction has become less profitable is insufficient to establish frustration of purpose; it thus only permits discharge when a party's principal purpose is substantially frustrated, whereas the doctrine of hardship is more focused on the severity of economic equilibrium. See Sarah Howard Jenkins (n 100) ch. 1, 2015–2030.

frustration always tends to exculpate a party from any liability that has ripened because of this unknowing change in circumstances.

The doctrine of mistake is excluded from the application of the CISG under art 4 provision which removes validity matters from the jurisdiction of the CISG. However, it has been proposed in this book that some species of mistake, like common mistake, can still be applicable under art 79 if the subject matter of the contract has been destroyed and it is not clear if this happened after or before the conclusion of the contract.[41]

The court, faced with the above type of hypothetical issue, may dispense with the strict time requirement for the applications of these two doctrines (frustration/mistake) and may allow the similar endpoint of both doctrines, which is to excuse liability in damages for such common, innocent, fault-free non-performance of the contract. The doctrine of mistake is not a validity factor under the UNIDROIT Principles. It is basically grouped under non-performance with the doctrine of *force majeure*, and this defies the age-long views of many national laws, like the common law, that the issue of mistake goes to the validity of the contract. The official commentary to art 3.1.3 of the UNIDROIT Principles lends credence to the view that mistake is not a matter of validity.[42]

The above view has softened the major distinction between the doctrines of mistake and frustration/exemption/*force majeure*. Under exceptional circumstances, the doctrine of mistake can be applied under art 79 of the CISG without the need to play the validity card, which has set apart these two doctrines from having a confluence point.[43] In addition, it has been observed in the earlier chapters that art 79 will apply to situations of prior impossibility under the CISG, UNIDROIT Principles and the Draft Model Frustration Clause. This is the parting point with English law, where the doctrine of frustration is chiefly tied to supervening impossibility, and prior impossibility implies the doctrine of common mistake at best.

8.7 Re-Balancing the Issue of Remedies

However, the relationships among various remedies and the doctrine of frustration/exemption/*force majeure* under the CISG, the UNIDROIT Principles, and English law constitute a significant flashpoint in this book. The most inimical are

41 It has been argued that the international sale laws (CISG, UNIDROIT Principles) deal with all situations of inhibitions, initial or subsequent. This is unlike the common law, where the time at which the inhibition preventing performance occurs is relevant as it may in effect remove the situation from one of exemption (frustration) to one of validity (mistake). See Schwenzer and others (n 43) ch. 1, para 45.34, 657.

42 Art 3.1.3 UNIDROIT Principles official Comment provides that:

> "Contrary to a number of legal systems which consider a contract of sale void if the specific goods sold have already perished at the time of conclusion of the contract, paragraph (1) of this Article, in conformity with the most modern trends, states in general terms that the mere fact that at the time of the conclusion of the contract the performance of the obligation assumed was impossible does not affect the validity of the contract."

43 Ibid.

the remedies of specific performance and damages.[44] It has been argued in this book that the remedy of specific performance will be ill-disposed to be applied under a frustrated/exempted/*force majeure* contract.[45]

Even in milder cases of frustration involving hardship, it is not viable to employ specific performance as a remedy when renegotiation or re-adaptation of the contract is most appropriate.[46] When a contract has been rendered impossible of performance, seeking specific performance of the same contract will be an exercise in futility.[47] The remedy of damages is central to this book; it has been denied a place in the CISG, the UNIDROIT Principles, and English law whenever the issue of frustration/exemption/*force majeure* arises for determination. Nevertheless, this book will suggest that this remedy is still involved in the doctrine of frustration. The combined effects of art 79(4) of the CISG and art 7.1.7(3) of the UNIDROIT Principles and paragraph 4 of the Draft Model Frustration Clause are to allow the application of remedy of damages in these laws albeit with a limit that it only applies where a party who because of an impediment beyond their control could not perform a contract fails to notify the victim party of the existence and particulars of the impediment at a reasonable time.

There may be a temptation to hold that damages as provided under these laws cannot be equated with the same meanings and connotations of damages under the English common law or under art 7.4.2 of the UNIDROIT Principles and art 74 of the CISG. This argument cannot stand, as there is nothing in these laws to support it. Art 74 of the CISG provides for damages, similar to art 7.4.2 of the UNIDROIT Principles. It goes without saying that the concept of damages is precisely the same when it applies under the circumstances of failure to give the notice of inhibition. The only difference is that while exemption/frustration/*force majeure* excludes damages as a legal consequence of non-performance of an obligation in a contract, damages can, however, apply in a restricted manner as a direct consequence of the fault in failing to notify the victim party of the operation of an inhibiting event.[48]

44 See Schwenzer and others (n 43) ch. 1, para 45.58, p 662, the authors argue that "the primary exemptions typically given due to an impediment are exemptions from specific performance. This exemption is logical as the very nature of an impediment is that it renders performance impossible."

45 Para 5(b) of the DMFC categorically provides for parties to refrain from the remedy of specific performance unless in a situation of temporal frustration when the contract can still be performed after the inhibiting event has ceased.

46 Schwenzer and others (n 43) Ch.1 para 45.111, p 672 "A duty to negotiate in the face of hardship appears on its face to be the most practical solution, it keeps the control of the adaptation of the contract in the hands of the parties, and also it keeps the contract alive."

47 Ibid., para 45.59, p 663; "Wherever the right to claim performance would undermine the obligor's exemption, performance cannot be demanded."

48 However, it can be confusing that the CISG, UNIDROIT Principles exclude damages as a consequence of non-performance and later introduce the same as a remedy for failure to give notice. The basis for this contention is that there is no procedure that is in place to decipher the meanings of "damages" as provided under arts 79(4) CISG and 7.1.7(3) of the UNIDROIT Principles on one hand and arts 79(4) CISG and 7.4.1 of the UNIDROIT Principles on the other hand. National laws can capitalise on this inelegant draft and come up with some absurd interpretations, thus making a mockery of the uniform posture of the CISG.

Under English law, the 1943 Frustrated Contract Act reflects common-law cases that have, in a significant way, helped harmonise the regime of remedies set out in common-law judges' decisions. This Act, however, needs to be amended in order to open up its frontiers and accommodate all types of frustrated contracts without the unnecessary technical restrictions barring it from applying in situations where the goods have perished, carriage of goods by sea and charterparty contracts.

8.8 General Summary

In the final analysis, the doctrine of frustration/*force majeure*/exemption is very significant in the law of contract. It is a method of discharging a contract and has been applied avidly in both national and international commercial contracts. This book tilts more towards the contract for the sale of goods. Still, numerous other forms of contract were discussed to highlight the doctrine's overwhelming importance.[49] The Draft Model Frustration Clause articulated in this book is moulded in such a way that it can serve as a workable doctrine of frustration under the CISG, the UNIDROIT Principles, and English law. Notwithstanding, paragraphs 2(a), (b) and 3, 4 of the Draft Model Frustration Clause resemble the third-party provision, temporal exemption provision, and giving of notice provision under the CISG and the UNIDROIT Principles, respectively. This book, therefore, is an improvement on existing laws, achieved by highlighting areas of deficiency and proposing improvements.

The doctrine of frustration/exemption/*force majeure* is also very much in touch with all the major laws of contract doctrines.[50] The comprehensive exposition and analysis of the working relationships between the doctrine of frustration/exemption/*force majeure* and other similar laws of contract doctrines offered by

49 There are mentions of various forms of contract like shipping, land, employment, and construction contracts in order to highlight how all these impact the doctrine of frustration, exemption, and *force majeure*. For instance, in the admiralty case of Chrysalis [1983] 1 Lloyd's Rep. 505, it was held that a contract of charter-party has been frustrated by war when the war started on 22 September and the charterer terminated the contract on 14 November due to the impediment of the war making the performance of the contract impossible. In the case of *The Evia* (No 2) [1983]1A.C 736(HL) it was held that an impediment which parties had foreseen cannot frustrate a contract. These examples transverse all modes of contract. The aim of the research is to show how the impossibility doctrine impacts these contracts.

50 The relationships between the doctrine of exemption/*force majeure* and frustration with other legal principles and doctrines like mistake, hardship, risk, and avoidance were vividly discussed. It is also worth mentioning that it has been suggested the doctrine of estoppel has a strong link with the impossibility doctrine. It was held in the case of *Black Clawson Intl Ltd v Paprierwerke Waldhof-Aschaffenburg* [1975] AC 591 that frustration may be excluded on the ground that the party relying on it had affirmed the contract. But this reasoning was rejected in *BP Exploration Co Ltd v Hunt*, where Lord Goff held that "Where estoppel might prevent a party from relying on a legal right, they could not prevent a party from relying on frustration because frustration is not a legal right but a legal doctrine."

this book will provide a new dimension towards a more valuable appreciation, application and interpretation of (frustration/exemption/*force majeure*), especially when parties who are not at fault are faced with a situation where unforeseen inhibitions, which they cannot control or whose consequences they cannot overcome, happen to render performance of the contract impossible.

Bibliography

Ahmed B.A. and Hussein H.M., "Avoidance of Contract as a Remedy under CISG and SGA: Comparative Analysis" (2017) 61 *JL Pol'y & Globalization* 126.

Ajayi O. Lp, *Disruptions and the Law* (LexisNexis, 2022) 93.

Aquinas T., Summa theologiae I-II q. 13 a. 5 ad 1.

Atiya P.S., *Introduction to the Law of Contract* (5th edn, Oxford Claredon Press, 1996).

Atiya P.S., et al., The Sale of Goods (11th edn, Pearson Educational Ltd, 2005).

Backhaus R., "The Limits of the Duty to Perform in the Principles of European Contract Law" (2004) 8(1) *Electronic Journal of Comparative Law.*

Bianca C.M. and Bonnell MJ., "Commentary on the International Sales Law – The 1980 Vienna Sales Convention" (Giuffrè: Milan 1987) <https://digitalcommons.law.uga.edu/cgi/viewcontent.cgi?referer=&httpsredir=1&article=1697&context=gjicl>.

Birds J. and others (eds), *Termination of Contract* (Wiley Chancery, 1995).

Bonell M.J., *A New Approach to International Commercial Contracts* (Kluwer Law International, 1999).

Bonell M.J., "The UNIDROIT Principles of International Commercial Contracts and CISG — Alternatives or Complementary Instruments?" (1996) *Unif. L. Rev* <https://doi.org/10.1093/ulr/1.1.26>.

Bonell M.J., "The UNIDROIT Principles of International Commercial Contracts: Towards a New lex mercatoria" (1997) *I.B.L.J.* 145–187.

Bonell M.J., "Unification of Law by Non-Legislative Means: The UNIDROIT Draft Principles for International Commercial Contracts" (1992) 40 *Am. J. Comp. L.* 617, 618–619 <https://scispace.com/papers/unification-of-law-by-non-legislative-means-the-unidroit-3mob4l018x>.

Bridge M., *Benjamin's on Sale of Goods* (Sweet & Maxwell, 5th edn, 2010)

Bridge M., *The International Sale of Goods* (Oxford, 3rd edn, 2013).

Brunner C., *Force Majeure and Hardship under General Contract Principles: Exemption for Non-Performance in International Arbitration* (Wolters Kluwer, 2009).

Bugden P.M. and Lamont-Black S., *Goods in Transit* (Sweet & Maxwell, 2013).

Bund J.M., "Force majeure Clauses: Drafting Advice for the CISG Practitioner" (1998) 17 *Journal of Law and Commerce* 381–413.

Burnett R. and Bath V., *Law of International Business in Australasia* (The Federation Press, 2009).

Burrows A., "The Relationship Between Common Law and Statute in the Law of Obligations" (2012) 128 *L.Q.R.* 232–259.

Campbell D., ed., *Structuring International Contracts* (Kluwer Law International, 1996).

Chandler A. and others, "Common Mistake: Theoretical Justification and Remedial Inflexibility" (2004) *Journal of Business Law (J.B.L.)* 34–58.

Chandrasenan A., "UNIDROIT Principles to Interpret and Supplement the CISG: An Analysis of the Gap-filling Role of the UNIDROIT Principles" (2007) 11 *Vindobona Journal of International Commercial Law and Arbitration.*

Chen-Wishart M., *Contract Law* (Oxford University Press, 3rd edn, 2010).
Crabtree J. and others, *International Sale of Goods* (Croner Publications Ltd, 1991).
Choudhary M., "Transfer of Risk and Liability of Carrier in International Sales: A Comparative Analysis" (2023) 5 Issue 1 *Indian JL & Legal Rsch.* 1.
Chukreyev A., "The Doctrine of Frustration in English Contract Law" (2017) *Law: J. Higher Sch. Econ.* 188.
Dalhuisen J., *Dalhuisen on International Commercial, Financial and Trade Law* (Oxford and Portland, OR, 2nd edn, 2004).
Dawson F., "Reflections on Contractual Mistakes" (2019) 3 *New Zealand Law Review* 291.
Davis P. and Ludlam G., "Wynn or Lose?" (2007) 157 *NLJ* 535.
De Carolis D., "Some Features of the Harmonisation of International Trade Law in the Third Millennium" (2010) *Unif. L. Rev.*
Dennis J.M., "Modernizing and Harmonizing International Contract Law: The CISG and the UNIDROIT Principles Continue to Provide the Best Way Forward" (2014) 19(1) *Unif. L. Rev.*
Dietrich M., "Hardship and Force Majeure" (1992) *Am. J. Comp. L.*
Dikovska I., "War, Sanctions and Exemption from Liability under Contracts Falling within the Scope of the CISG" (2024) 105 Studia Iuridica 7.
DiMatteo L.A. and others, "The Interpretive Turn in International Sales Law: An Analysis of Fifteen Years of CISG Jurisprudence" (Winter 2004) 34 *North-western Journal of International Law and Business.*
Djakhongir S. and Cunnington R. (eds), *Contract Damages: Domestic and International Perspectives* (Hart Publishing, May 2008).
Dimatteo L., Dhooge L., Greene S. and Pagnattaro M., *International Sales Law: A Critical Analysis of CISG Jurisprudence* (Cambridge University Press, 2005).
Duncan Jr J., "Nachfrist Was Ist: Thinking Globally and Acting Locally: Considering Time Extension Principles of the UN Convention on Contracts for the International Sale of Goods in Revising the Uniform Commercial Code" (2000) *BYU L. Rev.* 1363.
Dutton K., "Risky Business: The Impact of the CISG on the International Sale of Goods-A Guide for Merchants to Limit Liability and Increase Certainty Inside and Outside of the CISG" (2005) 7 *Eur. JL Reform* 239.
Eisenberg M.A., "Impossibility, Impracticability, and Frustration" (2009) 1(1) *Journal of Legal Analysis* 207–261.
Enderlein F. & Maskow D., *International Sales Law* (Oceana, 1992).
Erauw J., "CISG Articles 66–70: the Risk of Loss and Passing It" (2005) 25 *JL & Com.* 203.
Farrari F., "Gap-filling and Interpretation of the CISG: Overview of International Case Law" (2003) 2 *I.B.L.J.*
Felemegas J. (ed.), *An International Approach to the Interpretation of the United Nations Convention on Contracts for the International Sale of Goods (1980) as Uniform Sales Law* (Cambridge University Press, 2007)
Feltham J.D., "The U.N. Convention on Contracts for the International Sale of Goods" [1981] *J. Bus. L.* 346, 359.
Ferrari F. (ed.), *The CISG and its Impact on National Legal Systems* (European Law Publishers, 2008).
Flambouras D.P., "The Doctrines of Impossibility of Performance and clausula rebus sic stantibus in the 1980 Vienna Convention on Contracts for the International Sale of Goods and the Principles of European Contract Law: A Comparative Analysis" (2001) 13 *Pace International Law Review.*
Flechtner H., "Article 79 of the United Nations Convention on Contracts for the International Sale of Goods (CISG) as Rorschach Test: The Homeward Trend and Exemption for Delivering Non-Conforming Goods" [2007] 19 *Pace International Law Review* 29–51.
Flechtner H.M., "The Exemption Provisions of the Sales Convention, Including Comments on 'Hardship' Doctrine and the 19 June 2009 Decision of the Belgian Cassation Court" (2011) LIX(3) *Belgrade Law Review* 84–101.

Fucci F.R., "Hardship and Changed Circumstances as Grounds for Adjustment or Non-Performance of Contracts Practical Considerations in International Infrastructure Investment and Finance" (2006) American Bar Association Section of International Law Spring Meeting.

Gabriel H.D., "A Primer of the United Nations Convention on the International Sale of Goods: From the Perspective of the Uniform Commercial Code" (1997) 7 *Ind. Int'l & Comp. L. Rev.*

Gabriel H.D., *Contracts for the Sale of Goods: A Comparison of US and International Law* (Oxford University Press, 2nd edn, 2009).

Galston & Smit (eds) *International Sales: The United Nations Convention on Contracts for the International Sale of Goods* (Matthew Bender 1984).

Garro A.M., Columbia University School of Law, New York, N.Y., USA. Adopted by the CISG-AC at its 11th meeting, in Wuhan, People's Republic of China, on 12 October 2007.

Garro A.M. and Zimmermann R., "Remedies for Non-performance: The Revised German Law of Obligations, Viewed against the Background of the Principles of European Contract Law" (2002) 6(3) *Edin. L.R.*

Givati Y., Kaplan Y. and Listokin Y., "Excuse 2.0" (2024) 109 *Cornell L. Rev.* 629, 630.

Gold S., "Cartract" (1987) 137 *NLJ.*

Gonzalez O., "Remedies under the U.N. Convention for the International Sale of Goods" (1984) 2 *Int'l Tax & Bus Law*.

Gordley J., "Impossibility and Changed and Unforeseen Circumstances" (2004) 52 *American Journal of Comparative Law* 513–530.

Gottschalk R., "Illegality in Contract" (1967) 2 *Isr. L. Rev.* 589.

Graffi L., "Case Law on the Concept of 'Ffundamental Breach' in the Vienna Sales Convention" (2003) *I.B.L.J.*

Griffin B., *The Law of International Trade* (3rd edn, Butterworth's Lexis Nexis, London, 2003).

Guest A.G. and others, *Benjamin Sale of Goods* (Sweet and Maxwell, London, 2006).

Guo P., "Termination for a Compelling Reason under the UNIDROIT Principles: The Status quo and a Way Forward" (2018) 21 *Int'l Trade & Bus. L. Rev.* 1.

Hackett S. and Arthurs C., "A Frustrating Experience" (2011) 161 *NLJ.*

Han S., "Force Majeure, Change of Circumstances and Termination of Contract" (2016) 3(1) *Journal of Law, Society and Development* 31.

Harry F. and others (eds), *Drafting Contracts Under CISG* (Oxford University Press 2008).

Herman S., "Specific Performance: A Comparative Analysis: Part 1" (2003) *Edin. L.R.*

Hoffmann B., *International Sale of Goods: Dubrovnic Lectures* (P. Sarcevic and P. Volken eds, Oceana, 1986).

Hoffmann D.A. and Hwang C., "The Social Cost of Contract" (2021) 121 *COLUM. L. REV.* 979.

Honnold J. (ed.), *Uniform Law for International Sale Uniform Law for International Sales under the 1980 United Nations Conventions* (Wolters Kluwer Law and Business 2009).

Honnold J., "Uniform Law of International Sales under the 1980 United Nations Convention" (2nd edn, Kluwer Law and Taxation Publishers, Deventer, Boston, 1990).

Houtte H., *Law of International Trade* (Sweet & Maxwell, 1995).

Huber P. and Altenkirch M., "Buyer's Right to Cure" (2008) 4(4) *European Review of Contract Law*.

Indira C. and Goldby M., *International Trade Law Statutes and Conventions 2011–2013* (Routledge 2012).

International Chamber of Commerce (Incoterms 2000 published in September 1999 by ICC Publishing S.A., International Chamber of Commerce).

Ishida Y., "CISG Article 79: Exemption of Performance, and Adaptation of Contract Through Interpretation of Reasonableness-full of Sound and Fury, but Signifying Something" (2017) 30 *Pace Int'l L. Rev.* 331.

James F. and others, *International Sales of Goods in the Conflict of Laws* (Oxford University Press, 2005).

Jansen N. and Reinhard Zimmermann, "Contract Formation and Mistake in European Contract Law: A Genetic Comparison of Transnational Model Rules" (2011) 31(4) *Oxford Journal of Legal Studies* 625.

Jelena V., "Provisions Common to the Obligations of the Seller and the Buyer" in Petar Sarcevic & Paul Volken eds., *International Sale of Goods: Dubrovnik Lectures* (Oceana, 1986).

Jenkins S.H., "Exemption for Non-performance: UCC, CISG, UNIDROIT Principles – A Comparative Assessment" (1998) 72 *Tulane Law Review* 2015–2030.

Jern C.B. and Kin K.L., "Amendments to the Sale of Goods Act: A Critical Analysis" (1997) 18 *Sing. L. Rev.* 172.

Johnston J.S., "An Economic Perspective on Contractual Excuse Lessons from COVID_19" (2025) 30(1) *Standford Journal of Law, Economics & Business* 72–132.

Katsivela M., "Contracts: Force Majeure Concept or Force Majeure Clauses" (2007) 12(1) *Unif. L. Rev.*

Kaur N., "Impediment: A Concept under CISG, UNIDROIT and Indian Contract Law-A Comparative Analysis" (2011) 15 *VJ* 91.

Kelley J., "So What's Your Excuse - An Analysis of Force majeure Claims" (2007) 2 *Tex. J. Oil Gas & Energy L.* 91.

Kessedjian C., "Competing Approaches to Force Majeure and Hardship" (2005) 25 *International Review of Law and Economics* 641–670.

Khanderia S., "Termination for Breach: The Prospects of the Unidroit Principles of International Commercial Contracts to Interpret and Supplement the Indian Law of Contract" (2022) 27(4) *Uniform Law Review* 512.

Kofod F., *Hardship in International Sales CISG and the UNIDROIT Principles*, University of Copenhagen-Faculty of Law, Copenhagen (2011).

Konarski H., "Force majeure and Hardship Clauses in International Contractual Practice" (2003) *Int'l Bus. LJ.* 405–428.

Koskinen J., "CISG, Specific Performance and Finnish Law" (1999) Faculty of Law of the University of Turku, Private Law Publication Series B, 47.

Kritzer A., *Guide to Practical Applications of the United Nations Convention on Contracts for the International Sale of Goods* (Kluwer Law and Taxation Publishers 1989)

Kritzer A., Vanto J. and Eiselen S. (eds), *International Contract Manual* (Sweet & Maxwell A Thomson Reuters Business, Vol. 5, 2009).

Kröll S. and others (eds), *UN Convention on Contracts for the International Sale of Goods (CISG)* (Hart Publishing 2011).

Kull A., "Mistake, Frustration, and the Windfall Principle of Contract Remedies" (1991) 43 *Hastings L.J.*

Kuster D. and Andersen C.B., "Hardly Room for Hardship - A Functional Review of Article 79 of the CSIG" (2016) 35 *JL & Com.* 1.

Lindström N., 'Changed Circumstances and Hardship in the International Sale of Goods" (2006/1) *Nordic Journal of Commercial Law.*

Liu C., "Effects of Avoidance: Perspectives from the CISG, UNIDROIT Principles and PECL and Case Law" (2005) *NJCL* 1.

Liu F., "The Doctrine of Frustration: An Overview of English Law" (1988) 19 *J. Mar. L. & Com.* 261.

Lookofsky J., "Article 79 Liability Exemptions for Failure to Perform in 'The 1980 United Nations Convention on Contracts for the International Sale of Goods'" Published in J. Herbots and R. Blanpain (eds.), *International Encyclopaedia of Laws – Contracts*, Suppl. 29 (December 2000).

Lookofsky J., In Dubio Pro Conventione "Some Thoughts about Opt-Outs, Computer Programs and Premption under the 1980 Vienna Sales Convention (CISG)" (2003) 13 *Duke Journal of Comparative & International Law* 263.

Lookofsky J., *Understanding the CISG* (Kluwer Law International, 3rd edn, 2008).
Lord Goff of Chieveley and Gareth Jones, *The Law of Restitution* (Sweet & Maxwell, 7th edn, 2009).
Ly D.F., "Termination Clauses in International Contracts" (1997) 7 *I.B.L.J.* 801–836.
MacQueen H.L., "Change of Circumstances: CISG, CESL and a Case from Scotland" (2012) *JITLP.*
MacQueen H.L., "Remedies for Breach of Contract: The Future Development of Scots Law in its European and International Context" (1997) 1(2) *Edinburgh Law Review* 200–226.
Mads B.A. & Lookofsky J., *Lærebog i Obligationsret I*, vol. 3. Udgave (2010) 195.
Mahasneh N., "Subject Matter and Consideration of the Contract: The Approaches of the 2010 UNIDROIT PICC, the 1980 CISG, and the 1976 Civil Code of Jordan" (2014) *Unif. L. Rev.*
Mance J., "Ex Turpi Causa–When Latin Avoids Liability" (2014) 18(2) *Edinburgh Law Review* 175.
Markel A., "American, English and Japanese Warranty Law Compared: Should the US Reconsider Her Article 95 Declaration to the CISG" (2009) 21 *Pace Int'l L. Rev.* 163.
Markesinis B. and others, *The German Law of Contract: A Comparative Treatise* (Hart Publishing 2006).
Mascareño A. and Mereminskaya E., "The Making of World Society through Private Commercial Law: The Case of the UNIDROIT Principles" (2013) 18(4) *Unif. L. Rev.* 447.
Maskow D. "Hardship and Force Majeure" (1992) 40 *Am. J. Comp. L.* 657, 659.
Maud P. and Erauw J., "Application of the Unidroit Principles of International Commercial Contracts in Arbitration" (2012) 8(3) *J. Priv. Int. L.*
Maureira B.N. and others (ed.), *Review of the Convention on Contracts for the International Sale of Goods (CISG)* (Kluwer Law International, 2002).
Mayfield A., "Force of Nature" (2011) 161 *NLJ* 773.
Mazzacano P., "The Treatment of CISG art 79 in German Courts: Halting the Homeward Trend" (2013) Comparative Research in Law & Political Economy, Research Paper No. 7.
MCkendrick E., *Contract Law* (Palgrave Macmillan, 7th edn, 2007).
MCkendrick E. (ed.), *Force Majeure and Frustration of Contract* (Lloyd's of London Press Ltd., 1995).
Melis W., "Force Majeure and Hardship Clauses in International Commercial Contracts in View of the Practice of the ICC Court of Arbitration" (1984) 1 *Journal of International Arbitration* 213.
Mulcahy L., *Contract Law in Perspective* (Routledge Cavendish 2008).
Müller M., "Rezension zu Neumann, The Duty to Cooperate in International Sales. The Scope and Role of Article 80 CISG" (2012) 9(5) *Zeitschrift für Gemeinschaftsprivatrecht* 251–252.
Munoz E., "COVID-19 and Related Public and Private Measures as an Impediment to Perform Contracts Governed by the CISG" (2021) 57 *Tex. Int'l LJ* 61.
Nagy B., "Unreliable Excuses: How do Differing Persuasive Interpretations of CISG Article 79 Affect its Goal of Harmony?" (March 2013) 26(2) *New York International Law Review*.
Neumann T., "Shared Responsibility under Article 80 CISG" (2/2009) *Nordic Journal of Commercial Law* 22.
Ng I., "An Inequitable Mistake? The UK's Abolishment of Mistake in Equity Contrasted with Singapore's Approach" (2021) *Sing. Comp. L. Rev.* 205.
Nicholas B., *International Sales: The United Nations Convention on Contracts for the International Sale of Goods* (Matthew Bender, 1984).
Norman P. and Masons P., The Changing Nature of Risk (2006) 17(7) *Cons. Law* 10.
Nwafor N. and Lloyd C., "Re-imagining the Doctrines of Hardship and Exemption/force majeure under the CISG and UNIDROIT Principles of International Commercial Contracts" (2019) 8(1) *Global Journal of Comparative Law* 52.

Nwafor N and Nwafor N., "Conceptualizing the Relationship Between Doctrine of Mistake and Exemption (Force Majeure) under the CISG and the UPICC" (2019) 40 *Bus. L. Rev.* 111.

Offermanns J., "Damages Arising Out of a Cover Purchase within the Framework of Articles 74 to 77 CISG" (1/2006) 10 *Vindobona Journal of International Commercial Law & Arbitration* 1–14.

Okany M.C., *Nigerian Commercial Law* (Africana First Publishers 2009).

Olazábal A.M. and others, "Global Sales Law: An Analysis of Recent CISG Precedents in US Courts 2004-2012" (2011) 67 *Bus. Law.* 1351.

Palmer G.E., *The Law of Restitution* (Boston, 1978).

Palmer N. and David Ye, "The Future of the Unfair Contract Terms Act 1977" (1981) 40(1) *The Cambridge Law Journal* 108.

Parker C. and Chapman S., "Escaping from a Bad Bargain: Suspending, Modifying or Terminating Performance of Long-term Energy Contracts" (2010) 7 *I.E.L.R.* 243–246

Parker M. and McKendrick E., "Drafting Force Majeure Clause" [2000] 11(4) *ICCLR*.

Patanjali A., "A Comparative Study and Analysis of the Doctrine of Frustration under the CISG, UNIDROIT Principles and UCC" (2012) 23(5) *I.C.C.L.R* 174.

Patterson E., "The Apportionment of Business Risks Through Legal Devices" (1924) 24 *Colum. L. Rev.* 335.

Pawlowski M., "Common Mistake: Law v Equity" (2002) 152 *NLJ* 132.

Peel E., *The Law of Contract* (Sweet & Maxwell, 12th edn, 2007).

Perillo J., "Force Majeure and Hardship under the UNIDROIT Principles of International Commercial Contract" (Universidad Nacional Autónoma de México – Universidad Pan Americana, 1998).

Perillo J.M., "Hardship and its Impact on Contractual Obligations: A Comparative Analysis" (1996) M.J. Bonell Conferenze e seminari, Centro di studi e ricerche di diritto comparato e straniero.

Piliounis P. A., "The Remedies of Specific Performance, Price Reduction and Additional Time (Nachfrist) under the CISG: Are these worthwhile changes or additions to English Sales Law" (2000) 12 *Pace International Law Review.*

Plate T., "The Buyer's Remedy of Avoidance under the CISG: Acceptable from a Common Law Perspective?" (2002) 6 *Vindobona Journal of International Commercial Law and Arbitration.*

Posner R.A. & Rosenfield A. M., "Impossibility and Related Doctrines in Contract Law: An Economic Analysis" (1977) 6 *The Journal of Legal Studies.*

Progress Report of the Working Group on the International Sale of Goods on the Work of its Fifth Session (A/CN.9/87), Annex III, reprinted in UNCITRAL YEARBOOK V: 1974 (1975).

Puelinckx A.H., "Frustration, Hardship, Force Majeure, Imprévision, Wegfall der Geschäftsgrundlage, Unmöglichkeit, Changed Circumstances: A Comparative study in English, French, German and Japanese Law" (1986) 3(2) *J.Int'l Arb.*

Puri K., "Copyright and Employment in Australia" (1996) 27(1) *IIC* 53.

Quynh N.T., "Comparing Foreseeability in Contractual Damages under the CISG, Unidroit Principles and Principles of European Contract Law" (2024) 11(1) *Pázmány Law Review* 147.

Rapsomanikas M. G., "Frustration of Contract in International Trade Law and Comparative Law" (1979–1980) 18 *Duquesne Law Review.*

Reiley E.H., *The UN Convention and Related Transnational Law* (Carolina Academic Press, 2008).

Review of the Convention on Contracts for the International Sale of Goods, 2000-2001 (Edited by Pace International Law Review, Kluwer Law Intl 2002).

Richards P., *Law of Contract* (Longman, 2002).

Riesenhuber K., "Damages for Non-Performance and the Fault Principle" (2008) 4(2) *European Review of Contract Law*.

Rimke J., "Force majeure and Hardship: Application in International Trade Practice with Specific Regard to the CISG and the UNIDROIT Principles of International Commercial Contracts" (1999–2000) Pace Review of the Convention on Contracts for the International Sale of Goods, Kluwer.

Romein A., "The Passing of Risk: A Comparison between the Passing of Risk under the CISG and German Law," Heidelberg book: English translation (1999) or (2000) 4 *Vindobona Journal*.

Rosler H., "Hardship in German Codified Private Law: In Comparative Perspective to English, French and International Contract Law" (2007) 15 *European Review of Private Law (ERPL)* 483–513.

Ryan R., "Ex Turpi Causa: Negligence and Dangerous Drivers" (2005) 1 *Q. Rev. Tort L.* 16.

Sarcevic P. and Volken P. (eds.), *International Sale of Goods: Dubrovnik Lectures* (Oceana, 1986).

Schlechtriem P., "Basic Structures and General Concepts of the CISG as Models for a Harmonisation of the Law of Obligations" (2005) 10 *Juridica International* 27.

Schlechtriem P., *Uniform Sales Law* (Manz Vienna, 1986).

Schlechtriem P. and Bulter P., *UN Law on International Sales* (Springer, 2009).

Schlechtriem P. and Schwenzer I. (eds.), *Commentary on the U.N Convention on the International Sale of Goods* (Oxford University Press, 2nd edn, 2005).

Schurr F., European Journal of Contract Law (3/2009).

Schwenzer I. and Fountoulakis C., International Sales Law (Routledge – Cavendish, 2007) 567.

Schwenzer I. and others, *Global Sales and Contract Law* (Oxford University Press, 2012).

Schwartz A.A., "Contracts and COVID-19" (2020) 73 *Stan. L. Rev. Online* 48.

Schwartz A.A., "Frustration, the MAC Clause, and COVID-19" (2021) 55 *UC Davis L. Rev.* 1771.

Schwenzer I. and Fountoulakis C. (eds.), *International Sales Law* (Routledge-Cavendish 2007).

Schwenzer I. and Hachem P., "The CISG – Successes and Pitfalls" (2009) 57 *American Journal of Comparative Law*.

Schwenzer I. and others, *International Sales Law* (Hart Publishing, 2nd edn, 2012).

Shmilovits L., "When is Illegality a Defence to a Tort?" (2021) 41(4) *Legal Studies* 603.

Slater S.D., "Overcome by Hardship: The Inapplicability of the UNIDROIT Principles' Hardship Provisions to CISG" (1998) 12 *Florida Journal of International Law* 231–262.

Smit H., "Frustration of Contract: A Comparative Attempt at Consolidation" (1958) 58 *COLUM. L. REV* 287.

Smith G., "Everybody Makes Mistakes" (2011) 22(2) *Cons. Law* 17.

Smith J.C., *The Law of Contract* (Sweet & Maxwell, 4th edn, 2002).

Southerington T., "Impossibility of Performance and Other Excuses in International Trade" (2001) Publication of the Faculty of Law of the University of Turku, Private Law Publication Series B:55.

Sutton J.S., "Measuring Damages Under the United Nations Convention on the International Sale of Goods" (1989) 50 *Ohio State Law Journal* 737–752.

Stone R., *The Modern Law of Contract* (Routledge-Cavendish, 8th edn, 2009).

Treitel G., *Frustration and Force Majeure* (Sweet & Maxwell, 1994).

Treitel G., "Mistake in Contract" (1988) *L.Q.R.*

Ubaldis de B., Commentaria Corpus iuris civilis to Dig. (1597) 12.4.8.

Ulrich M., "The Remedy of Avoidance of Contract Under CISG General Remarks and Special Cases" (2005) 25 *Journal of Law and Commerce*.

UNDROIT Principles of the International Commercial Contracts (Rome 2004 Published by International Institute for the Unification of Private Law).

Upex R. and Bennett G., *Davies on Contract* (Sweet & Maxwell, 9th edn, 2004).

Uribe R., "Change of Circumstances in International Instruments of Contract Law: The Approach of the CISG, the PICC, the PECL, and the DCFR" (2011) 15(2) *VJ.*

Uribe R., "The Effect of a Changed Circumstances on the Binding Force of a Contracts; Comparative Perspectives" (Intersentia, 2011).

Van Houtte H., "Changed Circumstances and Pacta Sunt Servanda" in: Gaillard (ed.), "Transnational Rules in International Commercial Arbitration" (1993) *ICC Publ. Nr.* 480,4.

Veneziano A., "UNIDROIT Principles and CISG: Change of Circumstances and Duty to Renegotiate according to the Belgian Supreme Court" (2010) *Unif. L. Rev.*

Vogenauer S. and Kleintheisterkamp J. (eds.), *Commentary on the UNIDROIT Principles of International Commercial Contracts* (1st edn Oxford University press).

Waddams S., "Equity in English Contract Law: The Impact of the Judicature Acts (1873–75)" (2012) 33(2) *The Journal of Legal History* 185.

Waksman H., "Restitution and Frustration" (1984) *J.B.L.*

Walt S., "For Specific Performance Under the United Nations Sales Convention" (1991) 26 *Tex. Int'l L. J.* 211–251.

Wanki W. L., "Exemptions of Liability Under the 1980 United Nations Convention" (1990) 8 *Dickinson J. Int'l Law*.

Webb C., "Performance and Compensation: An Analysis of Contract Damages and Contractual Obligation" (2006) 26(1) *Oxford Journal of Legal Studies* 41–71.

Weitzmann T., "Validity and Excuse in the U.N. Sales Convention" (1997) 16 *Journal of Law and Commerce* 265.

Werner M., "Force Majeure and Hardship Clauses in International Commercial Contracts inView of the Practice of the ICC Court of Arbitration" (1984) 1 *Journal of International Arbitration.*

White F., "Sale of Goods Law Reform: an Irish Perspective Sale of Goods Law Reform" (2013) 42(2) 10 *CLWR* 17.

White M., "Contract Breach and Contract Discharge Due to Impossibility: A Unified Theory" (1988) 17(2) *The Journal of Legal Studies* 353.

Zeller B., *CISG and the Unification of International Trade Law* (Routledge-Cavendish, 2007).

Zeller B., "Determining the Contractual Intent of Parties under the CISG and Common Law: A Comparative Analysis" (2002) 4(4) *European Journal of Law Reform (Kluwer)* 629–643.

Zeller B., "The Remedy of Fundamental Breach and the United Nations Convention on the International Sale of Goods (CISG) – A Principle Lacking Certainty?" (2/2007) 11 *Vindobona Journal of International Commercial Law & Arbitration.*

Zhang H., "Buyer's Remedies and Cure by Seller-A Study of the Harmonization of European Sales Law from the Perspective of Comparative Private Law" (2014) 11 *US-China L. Rev.* 1428.

Zimmermann R., "TheUnwinding of Failed Contracts in the UNIDROIT Principles 2010" (2011) 16 *Unif. L. Rev.* 563.

Online Sources

Anja C., "Can the Hardship Provisions in the UNIDROIT Principles Be Applied When the CISG is the Governing Law?" (1998) <http://www.cisg.law.pace.edu/cisg/biblio/carlsen.html>.

Bremen J., "Economic Hardship Claims: (Part 1, 2009)" <http://www.constructionweekonline.com/article-7065-economic-hardship-claims-part-1/#.UML_8YM3Y2Y>.

Carlsen A., "Can the Rules of Hardship Be Applied as a Validity Defence?" <http://www.jus.uio.no/pace/can_upicc_hardship_provisions_be_applied_when_cisg_is_governing_law.anja_carlsen/_4.en.html>.

Chengwei L., "Remedies for Non-performance – Perspectives from CISG, UNIDROIT Principles PECL" (200) <http://www.sisudoc.org/sisu/remedies_for_non_performance_perspectives_from_cisg_upicc_ and_pecl.chengwei_liu/19.5.html>.

CISG Advisory Opinion, "Exemption of Liability for Damages Under Article 79 of the CISG" (2007) <http://www.cisg.law.pace.edu/cisg/CISG-AC-op7.html>.

Ferrari F., "Burden of Proof under the CISG" (2000–2001) <http://cisgw3.law.pace.edu/cisg/biblio/ferrari5.html>.

Flechtner H., "Article 79 of the United Nations Convention on Contracts for the International Sale of Goods (CISG) as Rorschach Test: The Homeward Trend and Exemption for Delivering Non-Conforming Goods" (2007) <http://cisgw3.law.pace.edu/cisg/biblio/flechtner7.html>.

Garro A.M., "Comparison between Provisions of the CISG Regarding Exemption of Liability for Damages (Art. 79) and the Counterpart Provisions of the UNIDROIT Principles (Art. 7.1.7)" (2005) <http://cisgw3.law.pace.edu/cisg/principles/uni79.htm>.

Grace T. and Fenwick E., Grace F.E., "The Termination of Contracts for Breach" (October 2010) <http://www.feg.com.au/documents/TerminationpaperTRG10.10.pdf>.

Houtte H.V., "Changed Circumstance and pacta sunt servanda" (1993) <http://www.trans-lex.org/117300#Footnote-c3e12ef0152ec6edd322306cb5d88078.

Honnold J.O., "Article 46 'Buyer's Right to Compel Performance'" (1999) <http://www.cisg.law.pace.edu/cisg/biblio/ho46.html>.

Honnold J.O., "Article 79 Impediments Excusing Party from Damages ('Force Majeure')" (1999) <http://www.cisg.law.pace.edu/cisg/biblio/ho79.html>.

Honnold J.O., "Article 80 Failure of Performance Caused by Other Party" (1999) <http://www.cisg.law.pace.edu/cisg/biblio/ho80.html>.

Honnold J.O., "Risk of Loss" (1984) <http://www.cisg.law.pace.edu/cisg/biblio/honnold5.html>.

Jenkins S.H., "Exemption for Non-performance: UCC, CISG, UNIDROIT Principles – A Comparative Assessment" (1998) <http://www.cisg.law.pace.edu/cisg/biblio/jenkins.html>.

Knapp V., "Article 64" (1987) <http://www.cisg.law.pace.edu/cisg/biblio/knapp-bb64.html>.

Leyens P., "CISG and Mistake: Uniform Law vs. Domestic Law The Interpretative Challenge of Mistake and the Validity Loophole" (2003) <http://www.cisg.law.pace.edu/cisg/biblio/leyens.html>.

Lookofsky J., "Article 49 Buyer's Right to Avoid for Seller's Breach" (2000) <http://cisgw3.law.pace.edu/cisg/biblio/loo49.html>.

Lookofsky J., "Article 66: Loss or Damage after Risk Has Passed to Buyer" (2000) <http://cisgw3.law.pace.edu/cisg/biblio/ho66.html>.

Lookofsky J., "Article 66 Passing of Risk" (2000) <http://cisgw3.law.pace.edu/cisg/biblio/loo66.html>.

Lookofsky J., "Article 68 Goods Sold in Transit" (2000) <http://www.cisg.law.pace.edu/cisg/biblio/loo68.html>.

Lookofsky J., "Article 69" (2000) <http://cisgw3.law.pace.edu/cisg/biblio/loo69.html>.

Lookofsky J., "Article 70" (2000) <http://www.cisg.law.pace.edu/cisg/biblio/loo70.html>.

Loofosky J., "Article 79 Liability Exemptions for Failure to Perform" (2000) <http://cisgw3.law.pace.edu/cisg/biblio/loo79.html>.

Neumann T., "Shared Responsibility under Article 80 CISG' Nordic Journal of Commercial Law (2/2009)" <http://www.cisg.law.pace.edu/cisg/biblio/neumann1.html>.

Nguyen H.T., Nguyen A.N.C. and Tran L.N.T., "Extension for Contract Performance under the CISG 1980 and Implications for Vietnamese Businesses" (2022) 6(2) *Journal of Economics, Law and Management* 2689.

Nicholas B., "Article 66" (1987) <http://www.cisg.law.pace.edu/cisg/biblio/nicholas-bb66.html>.

Nicholas B., "Article 67" (1987) <http://cisgw3.law.pace.edu/cisg/biblio/nicholas-bb67.html>.

Nicholas B., "Article 68" (1987) <http://www.cisg.law.pace.edu/cisg/biblio/nicholas- bb68.html>.

Nicholas B., "Article 69" (1987) <http://cisgw3.law.pace.edu/cisg/biblio/nicholas-bb69.html>.

Nicholas B., "Article 70" (1987) <http://www.cisg.law.pace.edu/cisg/biblio/nicholas-bb70.html>.

Nicholas B., "Impracticability and Impossibility in the U.N. Convention on Contracts for the International Sale of Goods" (1984) <http://cisgw3.law.pace.edu/cisg/biblio/nicholas1.html>.

Osadare B., "Force Majeure and the Performance Excuse: A Review of the English Doctrine of Frustration and Art 2–615 of the Uniform Commercial Code" <https://iiste.org/Journals/index.php/JLPG/article/download/35571/36598>.

Perillo J.M., "Force Majeure and Hardship under the UNIDROIT Principles of International Commercial Contracts" (1998) <http://www.cisg.law.pace.edu/cisg/biblio/perillo3.html>.

Rimke J., "Force majeure and Hardship: Application in International Trade Practice with Specific Regard to the CISG and the UNIDROIT Principles of International Commercial Contracts" (1999–2000) <http://www.cisg.law.pace.edu/cisg/biblio/rimke.html>.

Schlechtriem P., "Article 69" [1986] <http://cisgw3.law.pace.edu/cisg/biblio/schlechtriem-69.html>.

Schlechtriem P., "Basic Structures and General Concepts of the CISG as Models for a Harmonisation of the Law of Obligations" [2005] <http://www.cisg.law.pace.edu/cisg/biblio/schlechtriem12.html>.

Schlechtriem P., "Uniform Sales Law – The UN-Convention on Contracts for the International Sale of Goods" (1986) <http://cisgw3.law.pace.edu/cisg/biblio/schlechtriem-67.html>.

Schlechtriem P., "Uniform Sales Law – The UN-Convention on Contracts for the International Sale of Goods" (1986) <http://www.cisg.law.pace.edu/cisg/biblio/schlechtriem-79.html>.

Schwenzer I., "Force Majeure and Hardship in International Sales Contract" (2008) <http://www.austlii.edu.au/nz/journals/VUWLawRw/2008/39.pdf>.

Spurin C.H, "The Law of International Trade and Carriage of Goods" (2004) <http://www.nadr.co.uk/articles/published/shipping/002CHAPTERTWOTRADE3.pdf>.

Tallon B., "Article 79" (1987) <http://cisgw3.law.pace.edu/cisg/biblio/tallon-bb79.html>.

Tallon D., "Article 80" (1987) <http://www.cisg.law.pace.edu/cisg/biblio/tallon-bb80.html>.

Warren Khoo, "Article 2" <http://www.cisg.law.pace.edu/cisg/biblio/khoo-bb2.html>.

Will M., "Article 25" (1987) <http://cisgw3.law.pace.edu/cisg/biblio/will-bb25.html>.

Williston P., "The Law of Contract" <http://chestofbooks.com/business/law/Law-Of-Contracts-3/Sec-1563-Inferior-Quality-Of-The-Goods.html>.

Ziegel J.S., "Report to the Uniform Law Conference of Canada on Convention on Contracts for the International Sale of Goods" (1981) <http://www.cisg.law.pace.edu/cisg/text/ziegel79.html>.

Ziegel J.S., "Report to the Uniform Law Conference of Canada on Convention on Contracts for the International Sale of Goods" (1981) <http://cisgw3.law.pace.edu/cisg/text/ziegel25.html>.

Index

Note: Page numbers followed by "n" and a number indicate notes.